I0829294

THE FEAST OF LAPITHÆ.—[SEE PAGE 20.]

BRED IN THE BONE;

OR,

LIKE FATHER, LIKE SON.

A Novel.

BY THE AUTHOR OF

"A BEGGAR ON HORSEBACK," "GWENDOLINE'S HARVEST,"
"CARLYON'S YEAR," "ONE OF THE FAMILY,"
"WON—NOT WOOED," &c.

WITH ILLUSTRATIONS.

NEW YORK:
HARPER & BROTHERS, PUBLISHERS,
FRANKLIN SQUARE.
1872.

James Payn's Novels.

A WOMAN'S VENGEANCE. (*In Press.*)

A BEGGAR ON HORSEBACK; or, A County Family. 8vo, Paper, 35 cents.

BRED IN THE BONE; or, Like Father, Like Son. Illustrated. 8vo, Paper, 50 cents.

CARLYON'S YEAR. 8vo, Paper, 25 cents.

CECIL'S TRYST. 8vo, Paper, 50 cents.

FOUND DEAD. 8vo, Paper, 50 cents.

GWENDOLINE'S HARVEST. 8vo, Paper, 25 cents.

ONE OF THE FAMILY. 8vo, Paper, 25 cents.

WON—NOT WOOED. 8vo, Paper, 50 cents.

BRED IN THE BONE.

CHAPTER I.

CAREW OF CROMPTON.

HAD you lived in Breakneckshire twenty years ago, or even any where in the Midlands, it would be superfluous to tell you of Carew of Crompton. Every body thereabout was acquainted with him either personally or by hearsay. You must almost certainly have known somebody who had had an adventure with that eccentric personage—one who had been ridden down by him, for that mighty hunter never turned to the right hand nor to the left for any man, nor paid attention to any rule of road; or one who, more fortunate, had been "cleared" by him on his famous black horse *Trebizond*, an animal only second to his master in the popular esteem. There are as many highly colored pictures of his performance of this flying feat in existence as there are of "Dick Turpin clearing the Turnpike-gate." Sometimes it is a small tradesman cowering down in his cart among the calves, while the gallant Squire hurtles over him with a "Stoop your head, butcher." Sometimes it is a wagoner, reminding one of Commodore Trunnion's involuntary deed of "derring-do," who, between two high banks, perceives with marked astonishment this portent flying over himself and convoy. But, at all events, the thing was done; perhaps on more than one occasion, and was allowed on all hands not only as a fact, but as characteristic of their sporting idol. It was "Carew all over," or "Just like Carew."

This phrase was also applied to many other heroic actions. The idea of "keel-hauling," for instance, adapted from the nautical code, was said to be practically enforced in the case of duns, attorneys, and other objectionable persons, in the lake at Crompton; while the administration of pommelings to poachers and agriculturists generally, by the athletic Squire, was the theme of every tongue. These punishments, though severe, were much sought after by a certain class, the same to which the purchased free and independent voter belongs, for the clenched fist invariably became an open hand after it had done its work—a golden ointment, that is, was always applied after these inflictions, such as healed all wounds.

Carew of Crompton might at one time have been member for the county, if he had pleased; but he desired no seat except in the saddle, or on the driving-box. He showed such skill in riding, and with "the ribbons," that some persons supposed that his talents must be very considerable in other matters, and affected to regret their misuse; there were reports that he knew Latin better than his own chaplain; and was, or had been, so diligent a student of Holy Writ, that he could give you chapter and verse for every thing. But it must be allowed that others were not wanting to whisper that these traits of scholarship were greatly exaggerated, and that all the wonder lay in the fact that the Squire knew any thing of such matters at all; nay, a few even ventured to express their opinion that, but for his recklessness and his money, there was nothing more remarkable in Carew than in other spendthrifts; but this idea was never mooted within twenty miles of Crompton. The real truth is, that the time was unsuitable to the display of the Squire's particular traits. He would have been an eminent personage had he been a Norman, and lived in the reign of King John. Even now, if he could have removed his establishment to Poland, and assumed the character of a Russian proprietor, he would doubtless have been a great prince. There was a savage magnificence about him, and also certain degrading traits, which suggested the Hetman Platoff. Unfortunately, he was a Squire in the Midlands. The contrast, however, of his splendid vagaries with the quiet time and industrious locality in which he lived, while it diminished his influence, did, on the other hand, no doubt enhance his reputation. He was looked upon (as Waterford and Mytton used to be) as a *lusus naturæ*, an eccentric, an altogether exceptional personage, to whom license was permitted; and the charitable divided the human race, for his sake, into Men, Women, and Carew.

The same philosophic few, however, who denied him talent, averred that he was half mad; and indeed Fortune had so lavishly showered her favors on him from his birth, that it might well be that they had turned his head. His father had died while Carew was but an infant, so that the surplus income from his vast estates had accumulated to an enormous sum when he attained his majority. In the mean time, his doting mother had supplied him with funds out of all proportion to his tender years. At ten years old, he had a pack of harriers of his own, and hunted the county regularly twice a week. At the public school, where he was with difficulty persuaded to remain for a short period, he had an allowance the amount of which would have sufficed for the needs of a professional man with a wife and family, and yet it is recorded of him that he had the audacity—"the boy is father to the man," and it was "so like Carew," they said—to complain to his guardian, a great lawyer, that his means were insufficient. He also demanded a lump sum down, on the ground that (being at the ripe age of fourteen) he contemplated marriage. The reply of the legal dignitary is preserved, as well as the young gentleman's application: "If you can't live upon your allowance, you may starve, Sir; and if you marry, you shall not have your allowance."

You had only—having authority to do so—to advise Carew, and he was positively certain to go counter to your opinion; and did you attempt to oppose him in any purpose, you would infallibly insure its accomplishment. He did not marry at fourteen, indeed, but he did so clandestinely in less than three years afterward, and had issue; but at the age of five-and-thirty, when our stage opens, he had neither wife nor child, but lived as a bachelor at Crompton, which was sometimes called "the open house," by reason of its profuse hospitalities; and sometimes "Liberty Hall," on account of its license; otherwise it was never called any thing but Crompton; never Crompton Hall, or Crompton Park—but simply Crompton, just like Stowe or Blenheim. And yet the park at Crompton was as splendid an appanage of glebe and avenue, of copse and dell, as could be desired. It was all laid out upon a certain plan—somewhere in the old house was the very parchment on which the chase was ordered like a garden; a dozen drives here radiated from one another like the spokes of a wheel, and here four mighty avenues made a St. Andrew's cross in the very centre—but the area was so immense, and the stature of the trees so great, that nothing of this formality could be observed in the park itself. Not only were the oaks and beeches of large, and often of giant proportions, but the very ferns grew so tall that whole herds of fallow deer were hidden in it, and could only be traced by their pounds. There were red deer also, almost as numerous, with branching antlers, curiously mossed, as though they had acquired that vegetation by rubbing, as they often did, against the high wooden pale—itself made picturesque by age—which hedged them in their sylvan prison for miles. Moreover, there were wild-cattle, as at Chartley (though not of the same breed), the repute of whose fierceness kept the few public paths that intersected this wild domain very unfrequented. These animals, imported half a century ago, were of no use nor of particular beauty, and would have dwindled away, from the unfitness of the locality for their support, but that they were recruited periodically, and at a vast expense. It was enough to cause their present owner to strain every nerve to retain them, because they were so universally objected to. They had gored one man to death, and occasionally maimed others, but, as Carew, to do him justice, was by no means afraid of them himself, and ran the same risk, and far oftener than other people, he held he had a right to retain them. Nobody was obliged to come into his park unless they liked, he said, and if they did, they must "chance a tossing." The same detractors, whose opinion we have already quoted, affirmed that the Squire kept these cattle for the very reason that was urged against their existence; the fear of these horned police kept the park free from strangers, and thereby saved him half a dozen keepers.

That his determination in the matter was pigheaded and brutal, there is no doubt; but the Squire's nature was far from exclusive, and the idea of saving in any thing, it is certain, never entered into his head. The time, indeed, was slowly but surely coming when the park should know no more not only its wild-cattle, but many a rich copse and shadowy glade. Not a stately oak nor far-spreading beech but was doomed, sooner or later, to be cut down, to prop for a moment the falling fortunes of their spendthrift owner; but at the time of which we speak there was no visible sign of the coming ruin. It is recorded of a brother prodigal, that after enormous losses and expenses, his steward informed him that if he would but consent to live upon seven thousand a year for the next ten years, the estate would recover itself. "Sir," returned he in anger, "I would rather die than live on seven thousand a year." Our Carew would have given the same reply had twice that income been suggested to him, and been applauded for the gallant answer. The hint of any necessity for curtailment would probably have caused him to double his expenditure forthwith, though, indeed, that would have been difficult to effect. He had already two packs of hounds, with which he hunted on alternate days, and he had even endeavored to do so on the Sunday; but the obsequious "county" had declined to go with him to that extent, and this anomaly of the nineteenth century had been compelled to confine himself on the seventh day to cock-fighting in the library. He kept a bear to bait (as well as a chaplain to bully), and ferrets ran loose about Crompton as mice do in other houses. He had a hunter for every week in the year, yet he often rode his horses to death. He had a stud of racers, and it was this, or rather his belief in their powers, which eventually drained his vast resources. Not one of them ever won a great race. This was not their fault, nor that of their trainer, but his own; he interfered in their management, and would have things his own way; he would command every thing, except success, which was beyond his power, and in missing that he lost all. Otherwise, he was lucky as a mere gambler. His audacity, and the funds he always had at his disposal, carried him triumphantly, where many a more prudent but less wealthy player withdrew from the contest. Games of skill had no attraction for him, but at an earlier date in his career he had been a terror to the club-keepers in St. James's, where his luck and obstinacy had broken a dozen banks. It was said—and very likely with truth—that he had once cut double or quits for ten thousand pounds.

His moral character, as respected the softer sex, was such as you might expect from these traits. No modest woman had been seen at Crompton for many a year; although not a few such—if at least good birth and high position include modesty—had, since his majority, striven to give a lawful mistress to the place. His eccentricities had not alarmed them, and his shamelessness had not abashed them. Though his constitution was said to be breaking up through unparalleled excesses, his heart, it was currently reported in domestic circles, was sound: and what a noble feat would it be to reclaim him! It was also reckoned impossible that any amount of extravagance could have seriously embarrassed such a property as he had inherited, indeed long since, but of which he had had the sole control only a few years. At the time of which we speak

Carew was but thirty-five, though he looked much older. His muscles were still firm, his limbs yet active, and his hand and eye as steady with the gun or bridle as ever. But his bronzed face showed signs of habitual intemperance; his head was growing prematurely bald; and once or twice, though the fact was known to himself only, his iron nerve had of late failed him. The secret consciousness of this last fact made him more venturesome and reckless than ever. "Time," he swore, "should never play *him* tricks. He was as good a man as ever he was. There was a quarter of a million, more or less, to be got through yet, and, by Jove, he would see it out!" Of course he did not swear by Jove; for, as we have said, he kept a chaplain, and was therefore no heathen.

One of the arguments that the mothers of those young ladies who sought his hand were wont to make use of, to their great comfort, was that Mr. Carew was a churchman. There was a private chapel at Crompton, the existence of which, of course, explained why his presence did not grace the parish church. Then his genealogy was of the most satisfactory description. Carews had dwelt at Crompton in direct succession for many a century. Charles I., it is almost unnecessary to state, had slept there—that most locomotive of monarchs seems to have honored all old English mansions with a night's visit—and had hunted in the chase next morning. Queen Elizabeth had also been most graciously pleased to visit her subject, John Carew, on which occasion a wooden tower had been erected for her in the park, from which to see "ten buckes, all having fayre lawe, pulled down with greyhoundes;" she shot deer, too, with her own virgin hands, for which purpose "a cross-bowe was delivered to her by a nymph with a sweet song." These things, however, were in no way commemorated. Carew was all in all: his devouring egotism swallowed up historical association. His favorite female bull-dog, with her pups, slept in the royal martyr's apartment. The places in Crompton Chase held remarkable were those where its present owner had made an unprecedentedly long shot, or had beaten off one of the wild cattle without a weapon, or had run down a stag on foot. There was no relic of ancient times preserved whatever, except that at midsummer, as in Lyme, that very curious custom was kept of driving the red deer round the park, and then swimming them through the lake before the house—a very difficult feat, by-the-by, to any save those who have been accustomed to "drive deer." One peculiar virtue of Carew—he was addressed, by-the-way, by all his inferiors, and some of his equals, as "Squire" only—was, we had almost forgotten to say, his regard for truth, which may truly be said to have been "passionate," if we consider the effect produced in him when he discovered that any one had told him a falsehood. He would fall upon them tooth and nail, if they were menials; and if guests, he would forbid them his house. This was surely one excellent trait. Yet it was maintained by those carpers already alluded to, that to tell truth was comparatively easy in one who was as careless of all opinion as he was independent in means; moreover, that a love of truth is sometimes found to exist in very bad company, as in the case of the Spartan boy who stole the fox, and if the veracious Squire did not steal foxes (which he did, by-the-by, indirectly, for a bagged one was his delight), he was guilty of much worse things. However, this is certain, that Carew of Crompton never told a lie.

CHAPTER II.

WAITING FOR AN INTRODUCTION.

We have said that Carew was not exclusive; so long as he had his own way in every thing he was good-tempered, and so very good-natured that he permitted not only his friends but his dependents to do pretty much as they would. He was a tyrant only by fits and starts, and in the mean time there was anarchy at Crompton. Every soul in the place, from the young lords, its master's guests, down to the earth-stopper's assistant, who came for his quantum of ale to the back-door, did pretty much as seemed right in his own eyes. There were times when every thing had to be done in a moment under the master's eye, no matter at what loss, or even risk to limb or life; but usually there was no particular time for any thing—except dinner. The guests arose in the morning, or lay in bed all day, exactly as they pleased, and had their meals in public or in their own rooms; but when the great dinner-gong sounded for the second time it was expected that every man should be ready for the feast, and wearing (with the single exception of the chaplain) a red coat. The dinner-parties at Crompton—and there was a party of the most heterogeneous description daily—were literally, therefore, very gay affairs; the banquet was sumptuous, and the great cellars were laid under heavy contribution. Only, if a guest did happen to be unpunctual, from whatever cause, even if it were illness, the host would send for his bear, or his half-dozen bull-dogs, and proceed to the sick man's room, with the avowed intention (and he always kept his word) of "drawing the badger." In spite of his four-legged auxiliaries, this was not always an easy task. His recklessness, though not often, did sometimes meet with its match in that of the badger; and in one chamber door at Crompton we have ourselves seen a couple of bullet-holes, which showed that assault on one side had met with battery upon the other. With such rough manners as Carew had, it may seem strange that he was never called to account for them at twelve paces; but, in the first place, it was thoroughly understood that he would have "gone out" (a fact which has doubtless given pause to many a challenge), and would have shot as straight as though he were partridge-shooting; and secondly, as we have said, he had a special license for practical jokes; the subjects of them, too, were not men of delicate susceptibilities, for none such, by any accident, could have been his guests. In consideration of good fare, good wine, a good mount in the hunting-field, excellent shooting, and of a loan from the host whenever they were without funds, men even of good position were found to "put up" very good-naturedly with the eccentricities of the master of Crompton, and he had his house full half the year. It is not to be wondered at, therefore, that his servants were found willing to compound for some occasional ill usage, in return for general laxity of rule, and many unconsidered trifles in the way of perquisites. His huntsmen and whips got now and then a severe beating; his grooms found it very inconvenient when "Squire" took it into his mad head to sally forth on horseback across country by moonlight; and still worse, when he would have the whole stud out, and set every servant in his employ, not excepting his fat French cook, in the saddle, to see how they would comport themselves under the unaccustomed excitement of a steeple-chase. But upon the whole, the retainers at Crompton had an easy berth of it, and seldom voluntarily took their discharge.

Perhaps the best situations, as being less liable to the *per contras* in the shape of the master's passionate outbursts, were those of the park-keepers, of whom old Walter Grange was one. He was a bachelor, as almost all of them were. It was not good for any one with wife or daughter (if these were young, at least) to take service with Carew at all; and living in a pleasant cottage, far too large for him, in the very heart of the chase, Grange thought it no harm to take a lodger. The same old woman who cooked his victuals and kept his rooms tidy would do the same office for another who was not very particular in his food, and could rough it a little in other respects; and such a one had Walter lately found in the person of a young landscape-painter, Richard Yorke. This gentleman was a stranger to Crompton and its neighborhood; but having (as he said) happened to see a certain guarded advertisement in the *Times* headed, "To Artists and Others," that lodgings in the midst of forest scenery could be procured for what seemed next to nothing, he had come down from London in the autumn on the chance, and found them suitable.

To poet or painter's eye, indeed, the lodge was charming; it was small, of course, but very picturesquely built, and afforded the new tenant a bow-windowed sitting-room, with an outlook such as few dwellings in England, and probably none elsewhere, could offer. In the fore-ground was an open lawn, on which scores of fine-plumaged pheasants strutted briskly, and myriads of rabbits came forth at eve to play and nibble—bordered by crops of fern, above which moved statelily the antlered deer. A sentry oak or two of mighty girth guarded this open space; but on both sides vast glades shut in the prospect with a wall of checkered light and shadow that deepened into sylvan gloom. But right in front the expanding view seemed without limit, and exhibited all varieties of forest scenery; coppices with "Autumn's fiery finger" on their tender leaves; still, shining pools, where water-fowl bred and dwelt; broad pathways, across which the fallow deer could bound at leisure; or one would leap in haste, and half a hundred follow in groundless panic. The wealth of animal life in that green solitude, where the voice of man was hardly ever heard, was prodigious; the rarest birds were common there; even those who had their habitations by the sea were sometimes lured to this as silent spot, and skimmed above its undulating dells as o'er the billow. The eagle and the osprey had been caught there; and, indeed, a specimen of each was caged in a sort of aviary, which Grange had had constructed at the back of the lodge; while Yorke's sitting-room was literally stuffed full of these strange feathered visitants, which had fallen victims to the keeper's gun. The horse-hair sofa had a noble cover of deer-skin; the foot-stool and the fire-rug were made of furs, or skins that would have fetched their price elsewhere, and been held rare, although once worn by British beast or "varmint." The walls were stuck with antlers, and the very handle of the bell-rope was the fore-foot of a stag. Each of these had its story; and nothing pleased the old man better than to have a listener to his long-winded tales of how and where and when the thing was slain. All persons whose lives are passed in the open air, and in comparative solitude, seem in this respect to be descendants of Dame Quickly; their wearisome digressions and unnecessary preciseness as to date and place try the patience of all other kinds of men, and this was the chief cross which Grange's lodger had to bear as an offset to the excellence of his quarters. It must be confessed that he did not bear it meekly. To stop old Walter in mid-talk—without an open quarrel—was an absolute impossibility; but his young companion would turn the stream of his discourse, without much ceremony, from the records of slaughter into another channel (almost as natural to it)—the characteristics and peculiarities of his master Carew. Of this subject, notwithstanding that that other made him fret and fume so, Yorke never seemed to tire.

"I should like to know your master," he had said, half musingly, after listening to one of these strange recitals, soon after his arrival; to which Grange had answered, laughing: "Well, Squire's a very easy one to know. He picks up friends by every road-side, without much troubling himself as to who they are, I promise you."

The young man's face grew dark with anger; but the idea of self-respect, far less of pride, was necessarily strange to a servant of Carew's. So Grange went on, unconscious of offense: "Now, if you were a young woman," he chuckled, "and as good-looking as you are as a lad, there would be none more welcome than yourself up at the big house. Pretty gals, bless ye, need no introduction yonder; and yet one would have thought that Squire would know better than to meddle with the mischievous hussies—he took his lesson early enough, at all events. Why, he married before he was your age, and not half so much of a man to look at, neither. You have heard talk of that, I dare say, however, in London?"

Richard Yorke, as the keeper had hinted, was a very handsome lad—brown-cheeked, blue-eyed, and with rich clustering hair as black as a sloe; but at this moment he did not look prepossessing. He frowned and flashed a furious glance upon the speaker; but old Grange, who had an eye like a hawk, for the objects that a hawk desires, was as blind as a mole to any evidence of human emotion short of a punch on the head, and went on unheeding:

"Well, I thought you must ha' heard o' that too. We folk down here heard o' nothing else for all that year. She got hold o' Squire, this ere woman did, though he was but a school-boy, and she old enough to be his mother, bless ye, and was married to him. And they kep' it secret for six months; and that's what bangs me most about it all. For Carew, he can keep nothing secret—nothing: he blurts all out; and that's why he seems so much worse than he is to some people. Oh, she must have been a deep one, she must!"

"You never saw her, then?" asked Yorke, carelessly shading his eyes, as though from the westering sun, which Midas-like, was turning every thing it touched in that broad landscape into gold.

"Oh yes, I see her; she was here with Squire near half a year. Mrs. Carew—the old lady, I mean—was at Crompton then; and the young one—though she was no chicken neither—she tried to get her turned out; but she wasn't clever enough, clever as she was, for that job. Carew loved his mother, as indeed he ought, for she had never denied him any thing since he was born; and so, in that pitched battle between the women, he took his mother's side. And in the end the old lady took his, and with a vengeance. I do think that if it had not been for her, young madam would have held on— Why, what's the matter, young gentleman? That was an oath fit for the mouth of Squire hisself."

"It's this cursed toothache," exclaimed Yorke, passionately. "It has worried me so ever since you began to speak that I should have gone mad if I had not let out at it a bit. Never mind me; I'm better now."

"Well, that's like the Squire again," returned the keeper, admiringly. "He seems allus to find hisself better for letting out at things, and at people too, for the matter of that. To hear him sometimes, one would almost think the ground must open; not that he means any harm, but it's a way he's got; but it does frighten them as is not used to him, surely. I mind that day when he first took the fox-hounds out, and Mr. Howard the sheriff as was that year—he's dead and gone long since, and his grandson is sheriff now again, which is cur'ous—well, he happened to ride a bit too forward with the dogs, and our young master— Oh dear, dear," and the old man began to chuckle like a hen that has laid two eggs at a time, "how he did swear at the old man!"

"You were talking about Mrs. Carew the elder," observed the artist, coolly.

"Was I? True, so I was. Well, she and the young Squire was for all the world like a deer with her fawn—all tenderness and timidity, so long as he was let alone; but when this 'ere woman came, as she considered his enemy, she was as bold as a red stag—nay, as one of our wild-cattle. It was through her, I say, that the bride got the sack at last; and when that was done the old lady seemed to have done her work, and was content enough when her son portioned her off, and persuaded her to live at the dower-house at Morden; and indeed she could hardly have staid at Crompton, with such goings on as there are now—feastings and fightings and flirtings—"

"Just so," interrupted the young painter; "she got her way, I know. But with respect to the younger lady, Mrs. Charles Carew, what was *she* like, and what did people say of her?"

"Well, not much good, I reckon. What could they say of a school-mistress who marries her pupil?"

"A school-mistress, was she?" said Yorke, in a strange husky voice. "We never heard that in London."

"Well, she was summat of that sort, Sir, though I don't know exactly what. Young as he was, Carew was not quite child enough to be at a dame's school, that's true. But she was not a mere servant-girl, as some said, any way, for she could play and sing—ay, songs that pleased him too—and she had book-learning, I've heard, such as would have astonished you; so that some folks said she was a witch, and had the devil's help to catch Carew. But a woman don't want magic, bless you, to come over a lad of seventeen —not she. What nonsense people talk! If any pretty girl about Crompton was to take a fancy to *you* now, as is like enough, do you suppose—"

"But I thought you said that Mrs. Charles Carew was not a girl?"

"Nor more she was: she was five-and-thirty if she was a day; and yet—*there* was the wonder of it—she did not look much over twenty! I've heard our gentlemen, when out shooting, liken her to some fine Frenchwoman as never grew old, and was fell in love with unbeknown by her grandson. Now, what was her name? I got it written down somewhere in my old pocket-book; it was summut like Longclothes."

"*Ninon de l'Enclos?*" suggested Yorke, without a smile.

"Ay, that's the name. Well, Mrs. Charles Carew, as you call her, was just like her, and a regular everlasting! She was not what you would call pretty, but very "taking" looking, and with a bloom and freshness on her as would have deceived any man. Her voice was like music itself, and she moved like a stag o' ten; and the Squire being always manly looking and swarthy, like yourself, there was really little difference between them to look at. I dare say she's gone all to pieces now, as women will do, while the Squire looks much the same as he did then."

"I have never even seen him," said the landscape-painter, moodily.

"Well, don't you stare at him, young master, when you do get that chance, that's all. Some comes down here merely to look at him, as if he was a show, and that puts him in a pretty rage, I promise you; though to get to know him, as I say, is easy enough, if you go the right way about it. If you were a good rider, for instance, and could lead the field one day when the hunting begins, he'd ask you to dinner to a certainty; or if you could drive stags—why, he would have given you a hundred pounds last midsummer, when we couldn't get the beasts to swim the lake. There's a pretty mess come o' that, by-the-by; for, out of the talk there was among the gentlemen about that difficulty, the Squire laid a bet as *he* would drive stags; not as *we* do, mind you, but in harness, like carriage-horses; and, cuss me, if he hasn't had the break out half a dozen times with four red deer in it, and you may see him tearing through the park, with mounted grooms and keepers on the right and left of him, all galloping their hardest, and the Squire with the ribbons, a-holloaing like mad! For my part, I don't like such pranks, and would much sooner not be there to see 'em. There will be mischief some day with it yet, for all that old Lord Orford, down at Newmarket some fifty years ago, used to do the same thing, they say. It ain't in nature that stags should be druv four-in-hand, even by Carew. However, the Squire won his wager; and we haven't seen none o' *that* wild work o' late weeks, though we may see it again any day."

"I have heard of that strange exploit," observed Yorke; "but as driving deer, even in the ordinary way, is not my calling, and as I am no great rider, even if I had a horse, I don't see how I am to introduce myself to your mad Squire, and yet I have a great fancy for his acquaintance. Do you think he'd buy any of these drawings, taken in his own park, from his own timber?" The young man touched a port-folio, already well stocked with studies of oak and beech. "Here is a sketch of the Decoy Pond, for instance, with the oldest tree in the chase beside it; would not that interest him, think you? You think not?"

"Well, young gentleman," said the keeper, frankly, "if I say no, it ain't that I mean any slight to your drawing. It's like the tree enough, for certain, with the very hoop of iron as I put round it with my own hands twenty years ago—and, by the same token, it will want another before this winter's out; but I don't think the Squire cares much for such matters. He might, maybe, just give a look at it, or he might bid you go to the devil for a paper-staining son of a—well—what you will. He does not care a farthing, bless 'ee, for all the great pictures in his own gallery, though they cost his grandfather a mint of money, and are certainly a fine sight—so far as the frames go. And, on the other hand, if he happens to be cross-grained that day, he might tear it up before you could say 'Hold,' and kick you down the Hall steps into the bargain, as he has done to many a one. That's where it is, you see, the Squire is so chancy."

"I don't think he would kick *me* down his Hall steps," said Yorke, grimly.

The keeper grinned. "Well, you see, nobody can tell that till it's tried. The Squire is a regular bruiser, I promise you, though I grant you are a strapping young fellow, and you have told me that you know how to use your fists. That's a great thing, mind you, for a man to ha' learnt; a deal better than Latin or such-like, in my opinion. Folks talk of life-preservers and pistols, but there's nothing like a good pair of well-handled fists when one has to tackle a poacher. I've been at Crompton, man and boy, these fifty years, and had a good many rough-and-tumbles with that sort, and I have never had the worst of it yet. It prevents bloodshed on both sides; for if you haven't no shooting-iron, there's few Englishmen, poachers or not, who will draw trigger on you; and as for a bludgeon, it's as likely to be in my hand as another's after the first half minute."

"Is there much poaching now at Crompton?" inquired Yorke, mechanically. It would have been plain to any less obtuse observer than his companion that he no longer gave him his attention.

"Well, no; nothing to be called serious has happened lately; though I dare say we shall have some scrimmages as the winter comes on; there's allus a good deal of what I calls hanky-panky work in the fawn season. Women and children—especially children—will come into the park, under pretense o' picking up sticks; and they'll put away a new dropped fawn in their bundles, if they get the chance; and then they take it home, to be reared until it grows up, and can be sold for venison."

"I should have thought there would have been no market for such a commodity—that is, in the case of people such as you describe," observed Yorke, yawning.

"Market!" echoed the keeper, contemptuously; "there'd be a market to-morrow morning for the whole herd o' our wild-cattle, if they were stolen to-night; there'd be a market for a rhinoceros or a halligator, if we happened to keep 'em, bless 'ee, as easy as for a sucking pig! But I don't call that poaching—I mean the fawn-stealing. It's the professionals from the Midland towns as come by tens and twenties at a time as is our trouble. We generally gets wind of 'em beforehand, and then out we all goes, and Squire with us—for he dearly loves a fight—and then there's broken crowns and bloody noses; but, thank God, there's been no murder done, at least, not in my time, at Crompton. And that reminds me, Sir, that it's time for me to start on my evening rounds."

"Well, when you next have any news of such an incursion, Grange, I hope you will let me make one of your party," said Yorke, good-humoredly. "I can hit out straight from the shoulder; and perhaps I might get to know the Squire *that* way."

"And as likely a road to lead you into his good graces, Sir," said the keeper, rising, "as any I know. Are you for a walk round the park this fine evening, Sir?"

"No; not to-night, thank you, Grange. I have got to fill in this sketch a bit that I took this morning."

"Then, good-night, Sir, for I sha'n't return before daylight."

But it was not till long after the keeper had taken his departure that Richard Yorke turned hand or eye to his unfinished drawing. He sat staring straight before him with steadfast eyes and thoughtful face, for hours, murmuring to himself disjointed sentences; and ever and anon he started up and paced the little room with rapid strides. "He shall see me, and know me, too," muttered he, at last, between his clenched teeth, "though it should cost one of us our lives. She shall not say I came down to this wilderness, like some hunted beast to covert, for nothing."

CHAPTER III.

THE NIGHT-WATCH.

It was an easy thing enough, as Walter Grange had said, to make acquaintance with Carew of Crompton, and possible even to become his bosom friend at a short notice, for his friendships, all made in wine, at play, or in the hunting-field, were soon cemented; but then, if the introduction was effected in an unpropitious time or manner, it was like enough to end in affront or downright insult. A gulf might be fixed just where you wanted a causeway, and of this—though he had feigned to inquire about it so innocently of the honest park-keeper—Richard Yorke was well aware. He had, as has been hinted, come down to Crompton with the express view of throwing himself in the way of its eccentric master, and to do so opportunely, and he was content to bide his time. Thus, though the autumn had far advanced, and the time had come for men of his craft to hasten from the dropping, dripping woods, no longer fair, to hive at home their sweet memorials of the summer time, Richard remained at Crompton, not willingly, indeed, nor even patiently, but with that sort of dogged resolve which is engendered, even in a restless spirit, by long watching. He had stopped so long that he would not now give up his watch; the fortress, indeed, showed no more sign of breach than when he first sat down before it; but still he would not raise the siege. This persistency excited no surprise in his house companion; Walter Grange was no gossip, nor curious about other men's affairs; it was easy, even for him, to see that his tenant had a proud stomach, and he had set down his talk about desiring an introduction to Carew as merely another phrase for wishing for a good chance of disposing of his wares to best advantage in that market to which so many of such various callings thronged. He did not think, as he had honestly confessed, that there was much chance of the Squire becoming a patron of the fine arts, but he wished the young fellow luck, and was glad, for more than one reason, that he staid on.

It was at least three months after his young lodger's arrival that Walter burst into his sitting-room one afternoon, without his usual knock at the door, with the great news that he had just had word, by a safe hand, that a gang of poachers would be in the Home Park that very night, and that all the staff of keepers would be out in waiting for them.

"You know," said he, quite indignant that the young man did not show his enthusiasm, "you told me I was to be sure and let you know, Mr. Yorke; but, of course, you needn't make one of us unless you like."

"Oh yes, I'll come," laughed the young fellow—"that is, provided it is fine. I can't fight in the rain, even for the game laws."

"It'll be a lovely night, Sir, with just enough of moonlight to know friends from foes," went on the keeper, rubbing his hands, and unconsciously moistening them in his excitement. "I knew you'd come. I said to myself: 'Mr. Yorke 'll never turn tail;' and we shall be really glad of your help, for the fact is we are short-handed. Napes is down with the rheumatics, and two of our men are away from home, and there ain't time to send to the out-beaters. So we shall be only nine—including yourself—in all. Let's see," continued the old man, counting on his fingers: "there'll be Bill Nokes, and Robert Sloane, and—"

"Spare me the roll-call, Grange," interrupted the painter; "and tell me where I am to be, and when, and I'll be there."

"Very good, Sir," said the keeper, musing. "I'll put you at the Squire's oak—the one as you drawed so nicely—that 'll be at the Decoy down yonder, and close to home. You have only to use this whistle, and you'll get help enough if you chance to be set upon; there will be a fight, no doubt. They must be a daring lot to poach the near park, within sound of the house: they ain't a done that these ten year; for the last time they brought Squire and his bull-dogs out, which was a lesson to one or two of 'em. However, he's for town, they say, to-day."

"All right, Grange; we must do without him, then," returned the young man, cheerfully. "What time am I to be on guard?"

"You should be there at ten at latest, Sir. There'll be plenty of us within whistle-call, you understand. But nobody will come aneist you as has any business there; so whoever you see you must go in at."

Yorke nodded, smiling, and doubling his white fists, hit out scientifically with his right.

"You're one after the Squire's own heart," exclaimed the keeper, admiringly; "and I do wish you could foregather with him. What a reach of arm you've got, and what a play of muscle! The fist is the weapon for a poacher—that is, I mean *agin* him—if you only know how to use it. I can depend on the Decoy being guarded by ten, Sir, can I? for I must be off to the head-keeper's with the rest."

"Yes, you can."

"Then, good-by, Sir, for the present."

"Now what a poor fool is that!" soliloquized the young painter, contemptuously, as the door closed upon his late companion. "To think that I should risk my life against a poacher's on even terms! Of course, if they suffice, I shall only treat him to my knuckles; but if not—if he be a giant, or there be more than one of them—then here is a better ally than mere bone and sinew." Yorke took out of a drawer a life-preserver, made of lead and whalebone, struck with it once, to test its weight and elasticity, then slipped it into his shooting-jacket pocket. "That will enlarge their organs of locality," said he, grimly; "they will not forget the Decoy Pond in a hurry whose heads knock against this."

He made a better supper than was usual with him that night; filled his pocket-flask with brandy, and his pouch with tobacco; and then making sure that the whistle Grange had given him, and which he had hung round his neck, was within easy reach of his fingers, sallied out, well wrapped up as to his throat, and with his hands in his pockets. If Richard Yorke was doomed not to have life made easy for him, he made it as easy as he could. He never omitted a precaution, unless it gave him trouble to take it out of proportion to the advantage it conferred; he was never imprudent, unless the passion of the moment was too strong for him; but sometimes, unfortunately, his mere whims were in their intensity passions, and his passions, while they lasted, fits of madness. He was a landscape-painter, partly because he had some taste that way, but chiefly because he hated regular work of any sort. He had no real love for his art, and not the least touch of poetic feeling. He knew an oak from a beech-tree, and the sort of touch that should be used in delineating the foliage of each; a yellow primrose was to him a yellow primrose, and he could mix the colors deftly enough which made up its hue. His education had been by no means neglected, but it had been of a strange sort; every thing he had learned was, as it were, for immediate use, and of a superficial but attractive character. The advocates of a classical curriculum would have shaken their heads at what Richard Yorke did know, almost as severely as at his lack of knowledge. He had read a good deal of all kinds of literature, including much garbage; he could play a little on the piano, and speak French with an excellent accent. In a word, he had learned every thing that had pleased him, as well as a little Latin and some mathematics, which had not. He knew English history far better than most young Englishmen; but the sight of tomb or ruin had never made his heart pulse faster with an evoked idea by a single beat. Historical associations had no charm for him. This mighty oak, for example, under the shadow of which he now stands sentry, and which he had transferred so deftly to his port-folio, has no longer any interest for him. He has "done it," and its use and pleasure are therefore departed in his eyes. He knows quite well that though it is called the Squire's, in token, probably, of some wholesale slaughter of wild-ducks effected by Carew from its convenient cover, that this tree is hundreds of years old — the oldest in all the chase. He has read the "Talking Oak," for indeed he can quote Tennyson by the yard, and in dulcet voice; and it would have been natural enough, one would think, in such a time and place, that some thoughts of what this venerable monarch of the forest must have witnessed would perforce come into his mind. The same moonlight that now shines down between its knotted naked branches must have doubtless lit on many a pair of lovers, for it was ever a favorite place for tryst in bygone years. The young monk, perhaps, may here (when Crompton was an abbey) have given double absolution, to himself and to the girl who confessed to him her love. Roundhead maiden and Cavalier gallant must many a time have forgotten their political differences beneath this oak, as yet a tree not sacred to royalty; nay, perhaps even those of York and Lancaster may here have been compounded for, in one red rose of a blush. Bluff Harry had haply hunted beneath its once wide-spreading arms, and certainly the martyr king had done so, with a score of generations of men of all sorts, dead and gone, God alone knows whither. Though no more the bugle sounded, nor the twanging bow was heard, there was surely an echo of their far-away music in the young painter's ear! No, there was none.

> Heard melodies are sweet, but those unheard
> Are sweeter,

was a line Richard Yorke had read, perhaps, but certainly had not understood. He heard the bare branch creak and sway above his head as the wind slowly took it; he heard the night-jar croak, as it flew by on silent wing; and now and then he heard, or thought he heard, the sound of the voices of his fellow-watchers a great way off, which was his only touch of fancy. They were all silent, and in close hiding.

It is not to be supposed, however, that his mind was fixed upon the matter in which he was engaged, so that other subjects were thereby excluded from it. The repression of night-poaching was not a matter that interested him either in principle or practice. He would just as soon that the keeper had not reminded him of his offer to share his watch—the whim that had once seized him to do so had died away; but having once promised his company, he was not one to break his word. So here he was.

The young man's thoughts were busy, then, neither with the past nor the present, but with the future—that is, *his own* future. The path of life did not lie straight before Richard Yorke, as it does before most men of his age, and in fact it came, so to speak, abruptly to a termination exactly where he stood.

In such a case, the choice of the wayfarer becomes boundless, and is only limited by the horizon and circumstances. As matters were, he had scarcely enough to live on—not nearly enough to do so as his tastes and habits suggested; and yet, by one bold stroke, with luck to back it, he might, not "one day" (*that* would have had small charm for him), but at once, and for his life-long, be rich and prosperous. He could not be said to have expectations, but his position was not without certain contingencies, the extreme brilliancy of which might almost atone for their vagueness. It was from a dream of future greatness, or what seemed to him as such, wherein he saw himself wealthy and powerful, surrounded with luxury and with the ministers of every pleasure, that he was suddenly and sharply awakened by a trifling incident—the snapping of a dead twig in the copse hard by. In an instant the glittering gossamer of thought was swept aside, and the young fellow was all ear and eye. The wind had dropped for some time, and the silence was intense; that solemn hush seemed to pervade the forest which some poet has attributed to the cessation of spiritual life, as though the haunters of the glade were *waiting* for the resumption of their occupations until the interloping mortal should pass by. Nothing stirred, or, if so, it was motion without sound, as when the full-feathered owl slid softly through the midnight air above him. Not a dead leaf fell; and where the leaves had fallen there they lay. How was it, then, that a twig broke? The deer were couched; the pheasants sat at roost, their heads beneath that splendid coverlet, their wing; and though there were creeping things which even midnight did not woo to rest in that vast wilderness, Yorke had imbibed enough of forest lore to know that the noise which he had heard was produced by none of these. A rat in the water-rushes, or a stoat pushing through the undergrowth, would have announced itself in a different fashion. Again the sound was heard, and this time it was no longer the crackling of a twig, but the breaking of a branch; then cautious footsteps fell upon the frosty leaves, and, with a light leap on the bank that fringed the copse, the poacher stood in the open.

That such he was, Yorke had no doubt whatever; the moonlight streamed full upon him, and showed him to be none of the Crompton keepers, unless, indeed, he was disguised. For an instant, it passed across his mind that this might be Walter Grange himself — he was about the same height and build—come to play a trick upon him to test his courage, for the man's face was blackened like a burglar's; but this idea was dismissed as soon as entertained. The keeper, he reflected, thought far too seriously of the night's doings to make jest of them, and besides, he could never have sprung upon the bank as yonder fellow did, his limbs, though sturdy, being stiff with age and occasional rheumatism. The intruder seemed quite alone, and it was probable, while his confederates paid attention to the pheasants in the Home Park, that he was bent upon making a private raid upon the sleeping water-fowl. He had no gun, however, nor, as far as Yorke could make out, any other weapon; and as soon as he had got near enough to the pond to admit of it the watcher sprang out from be-

"THE MAN TURNED AT ONCE, AND SPRANG AT HIM LIKE A TIGER."

neath the shadow of the oak, and placed himself between the stranger and the copse from which he had emerged. Yorke was the taller by full six inches, and believing himself to be more than a match for his antagonist, had not so much as laid finger on his concealed weapon; but if he had now any thought of doing so, it was too late; for, with a cry of eager rage, the man turned at once, and sprang at him like a tiger. It needed all his skill and coolness to parry the fierce blows which fell upon him like hail, and which he had scarcely time to return. Yorke was an adept at boxing, and in the chance encounters into which a somewhat dissipated and reckless youth had led him, he had been an easy victor; but it now took all he knew to "keep himself." An instant's carelessness, or the absence of a hand in search of that which he would now have gladly seized, and his guard would have been broken through, and himself placed at his foe's mercy. Nothing but his long reach preserved him from those sledge-hammer blows, which seemed as though each must break the arm they fell upon. As for using his whistle, the opportunity, of course, was not afforded him; and, moreover, he had no breath to spare for such a purpose. Breath, however, was also a desideratum with the poacher, and the more so inasmuch as he accompanied every blow—as Brian de Bois-Guilbert was wont to hammer home his mace-strokes with "Ha! Beauseant, Beauseant!"—with some amazing oath. It is recorded of an American gentleman, much given to blasphemy, that he could entertain "an intelligent companion" for half a day with the mere force and ingenuity of his expletives; and this singular talent seemed to be shared by Richard Yorke's antagonist. That one of the most accomplished roughs of the Midlands had fallen to the young painter's lot in that night's *mêlée*, he could not for a moment doubt; but this reflection did not go far to soothe him. He did not care for fighting for its own sake, while his pride revolted against thus being kept at bay by a brutal clown. If he could but get the chance, he made up his mind to end this matter once for all, and at last the opportunity seemed to be afforded. The poacher suddenly stepped back to the very margin of the pond, a long oval piece of water, and not very deep, and quick as thought, Yorke drew his deadly weapon. But at the same moment there was a sound of racing feet, and down the drive there came two men at headlong speed. Yorke did not doubt that they were poachers; but his blood was up, and he was armed—he felt like an iron-clad against whom three wooden ships were about to pit themselves. "Where I hit now I make a hole," he muttered, savagely, and stood firm; nor did he even put his lips to the whistle that hung round his neck.

But as the men came nearer, in the foremost he recognized Walter Grange, and at the same moment saw his late antagonist plunge wildly into the ice-cold pond, and begin to wade and swim across it.

"Cuss him! I durst not do it," gasped Walter, just too late, and mindful, even in his passionate disappointment, of rheumatic pains. "Dash after him, Bob, while Mr. Yorke and I run round."

But Bob had had the rheumatism too, or had seen the unpleasant effects of it in others, and shook his shaggy head.

A mocking laugh burst from the poacher, already nearing the opposite bank.

"Dang him! If I'd got a gun, I'd shoot him. Run, man!" cried Walter, excitedly—"run, man, run! He can never get along in his wet clothes." And off the two men started in hot pursuit.

Yorke watched them toiling round the pond, while the poacher landed, shook himself like any water-dog, and leisurely trotted off.

"It was lucky for him," murmured he, as he replaced his weapon in his pocket, "that the help came on *my* side;" then lit his pipe, and leisurely walked home.

Three hours later returned the keeper (for whose arrival he had been sitting up), with twinkling eye and a look of triumph.

"Well, you caught the beggar, did you, Grange?"

"Oh yes, we caught him fast enough," responded the other, grinning; "we caught the whole lot of them. And who d'ye think they were? Why, it was the whole party from the house, as had come out to play at poachers! Who ever heard of such a game? Some on 'em got it hot, I reckon, in the new spinney yonder. But *that* was no matter. We've all had our skins full of rum punch, and a sov. apiece, because Squire says we proved ourselves good watch-dogs. And here," continued the old man, exultingly, "are a couple of sovs. for yourself. 'Give them to that tall young fellow,' says Squire, 'as you posted by the Decoy Pond, for he knows how to use his fists.' Why, that 'ere chap as you had the tussle with was Carew hisself!"

A deadly paleness overspread the young man's cheeks.

"Was that Carew?" he said.

"Yes, indeed, it was; though none of us know'd it. You needn't look so skeared. He ain't annoyed with you; he's pleased, bless 'ee, and here's the proof of it."

"You may keep the guineas, Grange," said Yorke, gravely; "only keep my secret too. If he thinks I was a night-watcher, let him continue in that belief."

"Why, it's the best introduction to Carew as you could have!" insisted the astonished keeper. "You have only to go up to the great house to-morrow, and say: 'Here's the man as proved your match last night,' and—"

"You must allow me to be the best judge of my own affairs," interrupted the young fellow, haughtily; "so you will be so good as to say nothing more about the matter."

"Just as you please, Sir; and I am sure you are very kind," answered the keeper, slipping the coins into his pocket. "Squire hisself could not be more liberal, that's certain. You are tired, I see; and I wish you good-night, Sir, or rather good-morning."

"Good-night, Grange."

"Now, that's what I call pride," said Walter, grimly, as he closed the door upon his lodger; "and I am sure I hope, for his sake, it may never have a fall."

When Richard Yorke was thus left to himself he did a curious thing; he took out the life-preserver from its receptacle, and having made up the fire, placed it in the centre of the burning mass, so that in the morning there was nothing left of it save a dull lump of lead.

CHAPTER IV.

ACROSS THE THRESHOLD.

A DAY or two passed by, and nothing more was heard of Carew's combat with the young watcher; some other mad frolic had doubtless entered into the Squire's head and driven that one out. The hot punch imbibed after his swim in the Decoy Pond seemed to have averted all evil consequences, or perhaps he was case-hardened to such things. It was not uncommon with him to spend whole winter nights on a neighboring "broad," in pursuit of the mere-fowl that haunted it, in water or ice or swamp. He treated his body as an enemy, and strove to subdue it—though not for the good reasons of the Apostle—by every sort of harshness and imprudence; or rather he behaved toward it as a wayward father toward his child—at one time with cruel severity, at another with the utmost luxury and indulgence. No rich man, probably, ever gave his heir so many chances of inheritance, or excited in him so many false hopes, as did the Squire of Crompton, who had no heir.

The hunting season had begun with him after its usual fashion; he seldom troubled himself to find a fox, but turned one out of a bag to insure sport, or ran a drag over the most difficult and dangerous country that could be selected.

Yorke had almost made up his mind to take the keeper's advice, and distinguish himself by putting his neck to the same risks as Carew, on horseback, in order to recommend himself to his notice, when an event occurred by which he attained his end in another way.

Tired of the park, wherein he had dwelled so long, and which every day the approach of winter made more bare and desolate, he had taken a solitary walk along the highway which led to the market-town. He was returning, and had reached the top of the long hill where the park fence began, and a high solid gate—so that no dogs could enter—gave access to that wild domain, when a confused murmur in the keen blue air caused him to look back. For a mile or more the road was straight, and the leafless trees and hedges left the prospect open to him in all directions; at the extremity of the road was some huge moving object, which, advancing at great speed, disclosed the Squire's mail phaeton, drawn by four antlered stags, and followed at some distance by three or four mounted grooms, apparently unable to keep up with him. Carew himself was standing up like some charioteer of old, and, although he already outstripped the very wind, was laying about him frantically with his whip, as up the hill the frightened creatures tore as if the ground were level. The reason of this headlong speed was at the same time made evident by the appearance of a pack of hounds, which, followed by a numerous field in scarlet, was coming across the grass-land in full cry. The spectacle, though weird and strange, was by no means without a certain grandeur—like some barbarous pageant. Yorke understood the situation at a glance. He had heard the keeper say that, not content with his wild progresses through the park, the Squire had sworn to drive his stags one day into the market-town, and this he had doubtless actually accomplished; but, on his return, he had had the misfortune to be caught sight of by one of his own packs of hounds, which were now in full pursuit of him, like another Actæon. The terrified stags, with that deep-mouthed menace of their natural enemies ringing in their ears, at once threw off all control, and had left their grooms behind them in half a dozen bounds. If only the harness held, they would be at the lodge gate in a very few minutes; but, on the other hand, the hounds were nearer to that point, which they were approaching diagonally. They were running, of course, by sight, like greyhounds, and with greyhounds' speed. Above their eager mellow notes, and the mad shouting of the excited sportsmen, and the ceaseless winding of the disregarded horn, above the thunder of his own wheels, and of the hoofs of his strange steeds upon the wintry road, rang out Carew's hoarse tones: "The gate, the gate!" If only that wooden wall could be interposed between his stags and their pursuers, all might yet be well. But, though the lodge-keeper had been drawn by the tumult to his door, he stood there like one amazed and fascinated by the spectacle before him, and paralyzed with the catastrophe that seemed impending.

"Gate, gate, you gaping idiot!" roared the Squire, with a frightful curse; but the poor shaking wretch had not the power to stir; it was Yorke himself who dashed at the latch, and threw the long gate wide to let the madman pass, and then slammed it back upon the very jaws of the hounds. They rushed against the solid wood like a living battering-ram, and howled with baffled rage; and some leaped up and got their fore-paws over it, and would have got in yet, but that Richard beat them back with his bare hands.

In the mean time Carew and his stags swept up the park like a whirlwind, and presently, coming to a coppice, the frightened creatures dashed into it, doubtless for covert, where wheel and rein and antler, tangling with trunk and branch, soon brought them to a full stop.

"Good lad!" exclaimed Carew, as Yorke hurried up to help him; "you are a good plucked one, you are; you shall keep the lodge, if you will, instead of that lily-livered scoundrel who was too frightened to move. Oh, I ask pardon; you are a gentleman, are you?"

"Sir, I hope so," answered the young man, stiffly, his anger only half subdued by the necessity for conciliation.

"Then, come up to the house and dine, whoever you are; I'll lend you a red coat. Curse those grooms! what keeps them? One can't sit upon a stag's head to quiet him as though he were a horse." (Two of the stags were down, and butting at one another with their horns.) "What a pace we came up White Hill! I tried to time them, but I could not get my watch out. You moved yourself like a flash of lightning, else I thought we must have pinned you against the gate. It was well done, my lad, well done; and I'm your debtor."

The Squire held out his hand, for the first time, for Yorke to shake.

"Why, what's this?" said he, peering into the other's eyes. "I have seen your face before, my friend."

"Yes, Sir; a week or two ago I played the part of night-watcher in your preserves—it was a mad prank; but"—and here the young fellow smiled roguishly—"it was better than poaching, you must admit."

"What!" cried the Squire, delighted, "are you the fellow that had that bout with me in the Decoy Pond? Why, I thought you were one of my own men, and sent you something; but, of course, my scoundrels drank it. I'm glad to see you, Sir, by daylight. It was the uncertain moonshine that hampered me, else, by Jove, I'd have given you 'one, two!' We must have it out another day, for a drawn battle is just the thing I hate. What's your name, young gentleman, and where do you live?"

"I live close by, Sir; I am in lodgings for the present."

"Ay, ay, for the hunting, I suppose," said the impetuous Squire. "Hark to those devils of dogs; they are howling yet; they would have had my stags by this time but for you. Well, well; send for your portmanteau, and take up your quarters at Crompton; you shall have a hearty welcome; only don't be late for dinner—seven, Sir, sharp. Here are my knavish grooms at last."

And, under cover of the fire of imprecations which the Squire poured upon his approaching retainers, the young landscape-painter withdrew. He had obtained his end at last, and he wished to retire before Carew should put that question to him for a second time—what is your name? —which, at such a moment, it would, for certain reasons, have been embarrassing to answer.

He betook himself at once to the keeper's lodge, and packing up his wardrobe, which, though of modest dimensions, comprised all that was requisite for a gentleman's costume, dispatched it to the great house. He followed it himself shortly afterward, only waiting to dash off a note by the afternoon's post for town. It was literally a "hurried line," and would have better suited these later telegraphic days, when thoughts, though wire-drawn, are compressed, and brevity is the soul of cheapness, as of wit. "*I have got my foot in, and however it may be pinched, will keep the door open. Direct to me at Crompton.*"

It was not a nice trait in the young man, if it was a characteristic one, that he did not take the trouble even to leave so much word as that for the old keeper, who was engaged in his outdoor duties, but simply inclosed the few shillings in which he was indebted to him inside an envelope, addressed to Walter Grange. The old man liked him, as he well knew, and would have prized a few words of farewell; but Yorke was in a hurry to change his quarters for the better; he had climbed from low to high, and gave no further thought to the ladder which had so far served him. But yet he had some prudence too. Though he had dwelled so long in the Carew domains, so careful had he been not to intrude his presence inopportunely on its master, that he had never so much as seen, except at a distance, the mansion to which he was now an invited guest. How grand it showed, as his elastic step drew near it, with tower and turret standing up against the gloomy November sky, and all its broad-winged front alive with light! How good it would be to call so fine a place his home! How excellent to be made heir to the childless man who ruled it, and who could leave it to whomsoever his whim might choose!

It was unusual for a guest to approach Crompton for the first time on foot. The Squire's jovial friends used for the most part strange conveyances, such as tandems and randems, and the great flower-beds in the lawn in front gave sign that some such equipage had been lately driven up not altogether with dexterity. It is difficult at all times to drive "unicorn," and more so if the horses are not used to that method of progression, and still more so if the charioteer is somewhat inebriated; and all these conditions had been fulfilled a few minutes previously in the case of Mr. Frederick Chandos, a young gentleman of twenty-one years of age, but of varied experience, who had just arrived that day on his first visit. But when Yorke appeared at the front-door, there was no less attention paid to him than if he had driven up with four-in-hand. Obsequious footmen assisted him to take off his wrappers in the great hall, whose vastness dwarfed the billiard-table in its centre to bagatelle proportions. A profusion of wax-lights—and no others were permitted at Crompton, save in the servants' offices—showed eight shining pillars of rare marble, and a grand staircase broad enough for a coach-and-four, and up which, indeed, Carew *had* ridden horses for a wager; while all the walls were hung with huge-figured tapestry—"The Tent of Darius" and "The Entry of Alexander into Babylon," both miracles of patient art. The grandeur of the stately place was marred, however, by signs of revel and rough usage. The Persian monarch, spared by his Grecian conqueror, had been deprived, by some more modern barbarian, of his eyes; while the face of his royal consort had been cut out of the threaded picture, to judge by the ragged end of the canvas, by a penknife. The very pillars were notched in places, as though some mad revelers had striven to climb to the pictured ceiling, from which gods and men looked down upon them with amaze; the thick-piled carpet of the stairs was cut and torn, doubtless by horses' hoofs; and here and there a gap in the gilt balusters showed where they had been torn away in brutal frolic. A groom of the chambers preceded the new guest up stairs, and introduced him to a bachelor's apartment, small, but well furnished in the modern style, whither his portmanteau had been already taken. "Squire has given orders, Sir," said he, respectfully, "that he should be informed as soon as you arrived. What name shall I say, Sir? But here he is himself."

As the groom withdrew, Carew made his appearance at the open door. He was smoking a cigar, although it was within an hour of dinner-time; and at his heels slouched a huge bull-dog, who immediately began to growl and sniff at the new guest. "Quiet, you brute!" exclaimed the Squire, with his customary garnish of strong expletive. "Welcome to Crompton, Mr.— I forget your name; or rather you forgot, I think, to favor me with it."

"My name is Richard Yorke, Sir."

"Yorke, Yorke—that sounds easterly. You are of the Cambridgeshire stock, I reckon, are you not?"

"No, Sir," returned the other, with a slight tremor in his voice, which he could not control; "I come from nearer home. Your wife's first husband was called Yorke, if you remember, and I bear his name, although I am her lawful son, by you, Sir."

CHAPTER V.

AT CROMPTON.

After the bold avowal made at the conclusion of the last chapter, Richard Yorke and his father (for such indeed he was) stood confronting one another, for near a minute, without a word. A tempest of evil passions swept over Carew's swarthy face, and his eyes flashed with a fire that seemed to threaten personal violence. The bull-dog, too, as though perceiving his master's irritation with the stranger, began to growl again; and this, perhaps, was fortunate for the young man, as affording a channel for the Squire's pent-up wrath. With a great oath, leveled alike at man and brute, he raised his foot, and kicked the latter to the other side of the room.

"Impudent bastard!" cried he; "how dare you show your face beneath my roof?"

"How *dare* I?" responded the young man, excitedly, and with his handsome face aglow. "Because there was naught to fear; and if there were, I should not have feared it."

"Tut, tut! so bold a game could never have entered into your young head. Your mother must have set you on to do it—come, Sir, the truth, the truth."

"She did not set me on, father," insisted the other, earnestly. "I came here of my own will. I have been dwelling within a stone's-throw of your house these six months, in hopes to see you face to face. She told me *not* to come—I swear she did."

"So much the better for her," ejaculated the Squire, grimly. "If I thought that she had any hand in this, not another shilling of my money should she ever touch. It was agreed between us," he continued, passionately—"and I, for my part, am a man who keeps his word—that she and hers should never meddle more with me and mine; and now she has broken faith."

"Nay, Sir, but she has not," returned the young man, firmly. "I tell you it was against her will that I came hither."

"The devil it was!" exclaimed the Squire, suddenly bursting into a wild laugh. "If you get your way with *her*, when she says 'no,' you must be a rare one. You are my son for certain, however, or you would never dare to stand here. It was a rash step, young Sir, and might have ended in the horse-pond. I had half a mind to set my bull-dog at you. Since you *are* here, however, you can stay. But let us understand one another. I am your father, in a sense, as I am father, for aught I know, to half the parish; but as to being lawfully so, the law has happened to have decided otherwise. I know what you would say about 'the rights of it;' but that's beside the question; the law, I say, for once, is on my side, and I stand by it. Egad, I have good reason to do so; and if your mother had been *your* wife, as she was mine, you would be with me so far. Now, look you," and here again the speaker's manner changed with his shifting mood, "if ever again you venture to address me as your father, or to boast of me as such, I will have you turned out neck and crop; but as Mr. Richard Yorke, my guest, you will be welcome at Crompton, so long as we two suit each other; only beware, young Sir, that you tell me no lies. I shall soon get rid of you on these terms," continued the Squire, with a chuckle; "for to speak truth must be as difficult to you, considering the stock you come of, as dancing on the tight-rope. Your mother, indeed, was a first-rate rope-dancer in that way, and I rarely caught her tripping; but you—"

"Sir," interrupted the young man, passionately, "is this your hospitality?"

"True, lad, true," answered the Squire, good-humoredly; "I had intended to have forgotten Madam Yorke's existence. Well, Sir, what *are* you?—what do you do, I mean, for a livelihood—beside 'night-watching?'"

"I am a landscape-painter, Sir."

"Umph!" grunted Carew, contemptuously; "you don't get fat on that pasture, I reckon. Have you never done any thing else?"

For a single instant the young man hesitated to reply; then answered, "Never."

"You are quite sure of that?" inquired the other, suspiciously.

"Quite sure."

"Good! Here, come with me."

His host led the way along an ample corridor, hung with tall pictures of their common ancestors, and opened the door of another bedroom. It was of a vast size; and even when the Squire had lit the candles upon the mantle-piece, and those which clustered on either side of the great pier-glass, the darkness did but give place to a sort of shining gloom: the cause of this strange effect was the peculiarity of the furniture; the walls were of bog-oak, relieved, like those of a ball-room, by silver sconces; the chairs were of the same material. The curiosity of the room was, however, the bedstead; this was of an immense size, and adorned above with ostrich feathers, which gave it the appearance of a funeral car; the pillars were of solid ebony, as were also the carved head and foot boards; it was hung with crimson damask curtains, trimmed with gold braid; and upon its coverlet of purple silk lay a quilt of Brussels point lace of exquisite design.

"I will have your traps brought in here," said Carew, throwing away the end of his cigar, and drawing from his pocket a heap of filberts; "it will be more convenient. You will find a room through yonder door, where you can sit and paint to your heart's content."

"You lodge me so splendidly, Sir, that I shall feel like Christopher Sly," observed the young fellow, gratefully.

"Ay, sly enough, I'll warrant," returned the Squire, who had just cracked a nut and found it a bad one. "That's Bred in the Bone with you, I reckon. Look yonder!" As he spoke, a porcelain vase clock upon the chimney-piece struck the half hour, and a gilt serpent sprang from the pedestal, showing its fang, which was set in brilliants. "That's my serpent clock, which always reminds me of Madam, your mother, and the more so, because it goes for a twelvemonth, which was just the time she and I went in double harness. But here are your clothes, and you must be quick in getting into them, for we dine sharp at Crompton.—Watson, go to my man, and bid him fetch a red coat for this gentleman.—You'll hear the gong, Mr. Yorke, five minutes before dinner is served." And with a careless nod to his guest, and a whistle to his four-footed companion, Carew sauntered off.

The young man would have given much to

have had half an hour at his disposal to think over the events of the last few minutes, and to reflect upon his present position; but there was no time to lose, if he would avoid giving umbrage to his host by being late. He therefore dressed in haste, and before the first note of the gong was heard was fully equipped. If the Squire, in introducing him to this splendid lodging, had had it in his mind to overcome him by a mere exhibition of magnificence, the design had failed; it was only Yorke's artistic sense that had been impressed; the fact was that the young fellow was of that character on whom superiority of any sort has small effect; while in the present case the signs of wealth about him gave him self-confidence, rather than any feeling of inferiority; insomuch as he considered himself "by rights," as the Squire had said, the heir of all he saw, and by no means despaired of becoming so, not only *de jure*, but *de facto*. Certainly, as he now regarded himself in the pier-glass in his scarlet coat, it was not to be wondered at that he reflected complacently that, so far as personal appearance went, he was not likely to find a superior in any of the company he was about to meet. A handsomer young fellow had indeed never answered the importunate summons of the Crompton gong.

He had no difficulty about finding his way to the drawing-room, for a stream of red-coated guests was already setting thither from their respective chambers, and he entered it with them unannounced. This was the only apartment in the house which did not bear traces of mischievous damage, because, as on the present occasion, it was used for exactly five minutes every evening, and at no other time whatever. After dinner the Squire's guests invariably adjourned to the billiard-table or the library, and the yellow drawing-room was left alone in its magnificence. This neglected apartment had probably excited more envy in the female mind than any at Crompton, although there were drawing-rooms galore there, as well as one or two such exquisite boudoirs as might have tempted a nun from her convent. It was a burning shame, said the matrons of Breakneckshire, that the finest room in the county should not have a lawful mistress to grace it; and it was not their fault (as has been hinted) that that deficiency had not been supplied. It was really a splendid room, not divided in any way, as is usual with rooms of such vast extent, but comprehending every description of architectural vagary—bay-windows, in each of which half a dozen persons might sit and move, and recesses where as many could ensconce themselves, without their presence being dreamed of by the occupants of the central space.

At present, however, the flood of light that poured from chandelier and bracket, and flashed upon the gorgeous furniture and on the red coats of the guests, seemed to forbid concealment, and certainly afforded a splendid spectacle—a diplomatic reception, or a fancy-ball, could for brilliancy scarcely have exceeded it, though the parallel went no farther; for, with all this pomp and circumstance, there was not the slightest trace of ceremony. New guests, like Yorke himself, flocked in, and stood and stared, or paraded the room; while the less recent arrivals laughed and chatted together noisily, with their backs to the fires—of which there were no less than three alight—or lolled at full length upon the damask sofas. These persons were not, upon the whole, of an aristocratic type; many of them, indeed, were of good birth, and all had taken the usual pains with their costume, but a life of dissipation had set its vulgarizing mark on them: on the seniors the pallid and exhausted look of the *roué* was indeed rarely seen—country air and rough exercise had forbidden that—but drink and hard living had written their autographs upon them in another and worse handwriting. Blotches and pimples had indeed so erased their original likeness to gentlemen that it was even whispered by the scandalous that it was to prevent the confusion with his menials, that must needs have otherwise arisen, that the Squire of Crompton compelled his guests to wear red coats. The *habitués* of the place, who were the contemporaries of the Squire, had, as it were, gone to seed. But there was a sprinkling of a better class, or, at all events, of a class that had not as yet sunk so low as they in the mire of debauchery: a young lord or two in their minority, whom their parents or guardians could not coerce into keeping better company; and other young gentlemen of fashion, in whose eyes Carew was "A devilish good fellow at bottom;" "Quite a character, by Jove!" and "A sort of man to know." Among these last was Mr. Frederick Chandos, who had so lately got among the chrysanthemums with his gig-wheels, and Mr. Theodore Fane, his bosom friend, who always sat beside him on his driving-seat, and, in return for sharing his perils, was reported to have the whip-hand of him. Nor was old age itself without its representative in the person of Mr. Byam Ryll, once a master of fox-hounds, now a pauperized gourmand, who, in consideration of his coarse wit and "gentlemen's stories," was permitted to have the run of his teeth at Crompton. This Falstaff to the Squire's Prince Hal was a rotund and portly man, like his great prototype, but singularly handsome. His smile was winning yet, and, in spite of his load of years and fat, he still considered himself agreeable to the fair sex.

For this information and much more, respecting the character of his fellow-guests, Yorke was indebted to a very singular personage, who had introduced himself to him as "Parson Whymper," and whom he now knew to be the Squire's chaplain. The reverend divine was as proud of that office (and infinitely more comfortable in it) as though he had been chaplain to an archbishop. He was the only man present who wore a black coat, and he had a grave voice and insinuating manner, which really did smack something of the pulpit.

"Mr. Yorke," said he, blandly, "I make no apology for introducing myself to you; Carew and I have been just having a talk about you, and he has no secrets from his ghostly adviser. I take your hand with pleasure. I seem to feel it is the flesh and blood of my best friend. Sooner or later, mark me, he will own as much, and, be sure, no effort of mine shall be wanting to insure so desirable a consummation."

Yorke flushed with pleasure, not at the honeyed terms, nor the good-will they evidenced, but at the news itself—the fact of his father having revealed their relationship to him seemed so full of promise—and yet he resented the man's professions, the audacity of which seemed certainly to imply that he was taken for a fool.

"I am sure, Mr. Whymper," said he, stiffly, "I ought to be greatly obliged to you."

"Hush! Not Mr. Whymper, if you please, for that's a fine here. Every body at Crompton calls me 'Parson.' Obliged, Sir! Not at all. It is only natural that, being what I am, I should wish you well. The law, it is true, has decided against your legitimacy, but the Church is bound to think otherwise. In my eyes you are the Squire's only son"—here he made a whispering-trumpet of his brawny hands, and added with great significance—"and heir."

"I see," said Yorke, smiling in spite of himself.

"Of course you do; did you think I was trifling with your intelligence? I tell you that it is quite on the cards that you may recover your lost position, and regain what is morally your own again. Carew is delighted with you, not so much because you saved his stags as because you fought such a good battle with him by the Decoy Pond. He has been consulting me professionally as to whether it would be contrary to the tables of affinity to have another set-to with you. I am sorry my reply was in the negative, for, now I look at you, I do believe you would have thrashed him; but I was so afraid of his getting the better of you, which might have ruined your fortunes."

Richard could only repeat his thanks for the good clergyman's kindness. "You know nobody here, I suppose," observed the latter, "and, with a few exceptions, which I will name to you, that is not of much consequence. It is a shifting lot: they are here to-day and gone to-morrow, as says the Scripture, and I wish they were all going to-morrow except Byam Ryll. That's old Byam yonder, with the paunch and his hands behind him; he has nowhere else to put them, poor fellow." And here Parson Whymper launched into biography as aforesaid.

The clock on the chimney-piece, on which the two were leaning, broke in upon the divine's scarcely less dulcet accents with its silver quarter.

"This is the first time," said Whymper, "that I have ever known your father late; and to you belongs the honor of having caused him to transgress his own immutable rule."

While he was yet speaking a hunting-horn was blown in the hall beneath, and the whole company turned *en masse*, like a field of poppies before a sudden wind, to the door where Carew was standing.

CHAPTER VI.

THE FEAST OF LAPITHÆ.

The host himself led the way down stairs; while the rear of the party was brought up by Mr. Whymper, to whom Yorke attached himself.

When they reached the dining-room, and before they took their seats at the ample table, the chaplain, with sonorous voice, gave a view holloa! which was the Crompton grace.

"It is very distressing to me to have to act in this way," whispered he to his young friend, whose countenance betrayed considerable astonishment; "but it is the custom of the house; and, after all, there is no great harm in it. *De minimis non curat lex*, you know."

"That does not hold good with respect to the law of affiliation, parson," observed Mr. Byam Ryll, who sat on the other side of him, "if, at least, I have not forgotten my *Burns*."

"I always understood that Burns had very loose views upon such matters," returned the chaplain, demurely.

"My dear parson, your remark is like that excellent condiment which I wish I could see at this otherwise well-provided table—caviare to the multitude. Why is it not furnished? You have only to say the word." Here he addressed himself to Yorke: "This worthy divine who sits at the bottom of the table, young gentleman, and who has neglected his duty in not having introduced us, is all-powerful here; and we all endeavor to make friends of him; nor is that circumstance, it is whispered, the only respect in which he resembles the mammon of unrighteousness."

A shadow of annoyance crossed the parson's smiling face.

"Mr. Richard Yorke," said he, "this is Mr. Byam Ryll, our unlicensed jester."

"The parson, on the contrary," retorted the other, with twinkling eyes, "is our Vice, and gives himself every license. What is the matter with Carew to-night? He looks glum. I dare say he has been eating greens and bacon at some farm-house, and is now regretting the circumstance. He has no moral courage, poor fellow, and knows not how to deny his appetite."

"You never did such a wasteful thing in your life, Byam, I'll warrant," said the parson, smiling; "and yet some say that you have been a profligate."

"I know it," replied the gourmand, shaking his head; "and I forgive them. They call me a slave to my stomach; if it be so, I at least serve a master of some capacity, which is not the case with every body."

"You are saying something about *me*, you big fat man," cried Carew, from the other end of the table, and his voice had a very unpleasant grasp in it. "Come, out with it!"

"If our venerable friend does not stoop to deception," whispered the parson into Yorke's ear, "he will now find himself in an ugly hole."

"I was observing that you did not eat your lamperns, Squire," said the stout gentleman, "and remarked that you were in no want of a feeder."

"What's a feeder?" returned the host, ill-temperedly. "If it's a bib, you'll soon want one yourself, for, egad, you're getting near your second childhood!"

"It must have been my plumpness and innocence which suggested that idea," responded the other, smiling. "But if you have never known a feeder, you have missed a great advantage, Squire. When you dine with my Lord Mayor the question is always asked, Will you have a feeder, or will you not? If you say 'Yes,' you pay your half-guinea, and get him. He is generally a grave old gentleman like myself, and much resembles a beneficed clergyman. He stands behind your chair throughout the feast, and delicately suggests what it is best for you to eat, to drink, and to avoid. 'No; *no* salmon,' he murmurs, if you have had turbot already; and, '*Now*, a glass of Burgundy, *if* you please, Sir;' or, '*Now*, a glass of sherry.' If an indigestible or ill-compounded *entrée* is handed, he will whisper: 'No, Sir: neither now nor never,' with quite an outburst of honest indignation; nor will he suffer you to take Gruyere cheese, nor port with your Stilton. The consequence is, that the next morning you feel as lively as though you had not feasted on the previous evening, and convinced that you made a good investment of your half-guinea in securing his services. If there was a feeder at Crompton," concluded the old gourmand, sighing, and with a hypocritical look, "it would be a boon to some of you young fellows, and might produce a healthy and devout old age."

"That's a good one!" "Well done, Byam!" "You won't beat that!" resounded from all sides, for such were the terms in which the gallery at Crompton expressed their approbation, whether of man or beast; but Mr. Frederick Chandos and a few others, inclusive of Mr. Theodore Fane, kept a dignified silence, as over a joke that was beyond their capacities—they reserved their high approval for "gentlemen's stories" only. As for the grim Squire, for whom alone the narrative had been served and garnished, at so very short a notice, he observed upon it, that "when he had used up old Byam's brains he should now have the less scruple in turning him out-of-doors, inasmuch as it seemed there was a profession in town that was just suited to him."

How wondrous is the power of naked wealth—of the mere money! Simply because he had a large rent-roll, this mad Carew could find not only companions of his own calibre—reckless good-for-naughts, or dull debauchees—but could command graybeard experience, wit, the art of pleasing, in one man; and in another (what he was not less destitute of, and needed more), politic management and common-sense. We do not say, as the Squire himself sometimes did, when in a good-humor with his two satellites, that Parson Whymper and Byam Ryll had more brains in their little fingers than all his other friends had in their whole bodies, but it was certain that, even when drunk, they were wiser than the others when sober; the one had astuteness enough for a great statesman (or what has passed for such in England) to hold the most discordant elements together, and to make what is rotten seem almost sound; and, indeed, without his chaplain's dextrous skidding, Carew would long ago have irretrievably lost social caste, and dissipated his vast means to the last shilling. On the other hand, Byam Ryll was gifted with even rarer qualities; he was essentially a man of mark and character, and might have made his fortune in any pursuit by his own wits; but his fortune had been ready-made when he came of age, and he had occupied himself very agreeably instead in getting through it, in which he had quite succeeded. Parson Whymper, who had never known what it was to have a ten-pound note to call his own, was now no worse off than he. They would both have frankly owned, had they been asked, that they detested work of any kind. Yet the chaplain had almost as much business on his hands as the bursar of a great college, in the administration of Carew's affairs, besides filling an office which was by no means a sinecure, in that of his master of the ceremonies. Many a rudeness in that house would have been bitterly avenged, and many a quarrel would have had a serious termination, but for the good offices of Parson Whymper. Nor would Mr. Byam Ryll have been considered by every body to earn an easy livelihood in making jests out of every occasion, to tickle the fancy of a dull-witted audience and of a patron, as often as not, morose; yet the flesh-pots of Egypt had attracted both these men to the Squire's service, their poverty as well as their will consenting; and in exchange for meat and drink, and lodging of the best, they had sold themselves into slavery. Upon the whole, they were well disposed to one another; the bond of intelligence united them against the rich "roughs" with whom they had to deal; they tilted together, side by side, against the *canaille;* yet each, from the bitter consciousness of his own degradation, took pleasure in the humiliation or discomfiture of the other, at the rude hands of their common master.

"Profession," said Chandos, in reply to Carew's last remark; "gad, your ancient friend is lucky to have found one in these days. They tell me that no young gentleman can now get his living without answering questions, writing down things, drawing maps, and passing— What the deuce do they call them?"

"Hanged if *I* know," said the Squire. "Ask Byam; he knows every thing."

"I say, Mr. Byam," drawled the young man, somewhat insolently, but without being aware that he was addressing a stranger by his Christian name, "Carew says you know every thing. What is it that a gentleman is now obliged to go through before he can get any of these snug things one used to get for the asking? What is the confounded thing one has to pass?"

"Muster," answered Ryll, derisively, as though it was a riddle.

Carew laughed aloud. The nearer a retort approached to a practical joke, provided it was not at his own expense, the better he liked it.

"What did the old beggar say?" inquired Mr. Frederick Chandos, his fair face crimson with anger.

"He asked for the mustard; he didn't hear you," answered the Squire, mischievously; "he never does hear a fellow who lisps."

"I asked you, Mr. Byam," repeated the young man with tipsy gravity, "what is the name of those examinations?"

"The name of the gentleman on my left, Mr. Chandos, is Ryll, and not Byam—except to his intimate friends," interposed the chaplain; "and the name you are in want of is competitive."

"That's it," said the young man, slapping the table, and forgetting both his mistake and his anger in the unaccustomed acquisition of an idea. "Competitive examination is what they call it. Well, you know, there was my young brother—confound him!—looking to me to pay his bills; and, in fact, having nothing to live upon, poor devil, except what I gave him. So, of course, I was anxious to get him off my hands."

"Very natural," assented Carew. "For my part, I could never see what younger brothers were born for."

"You'd see it less if you had one to keep," continued Chandos. "In old times, now, I could have got Jack something warm and snug under government, or in the colonies; and so I should now, but for one thing—that he had to pass one of these cursed examinations first. However, as it had to be done, and as Jack, according to his own account, was as much out of form for one as another of them, I recommended him to try his luck for something in India; for as long as you can keep a fellow on the other side of the world he can't dun you—not to hurt; it ain't like coming and calling *himself;* and you needn't read his letters unless you like. Well, 'India be it,' says Jack; 'that's as good a place as another;' though, in my opinion, he never expected to go there. He thought he had no chance whatever of pulling through, and so did I, for the fact is, Jack is a born fool."

"Did you say he was your brother, or only your half-brother?" inquired Mr. Byam Ryll, with an appearance of great interest.

"My very own brother, Sir," replied the unconscious Chandos, flattered to find such attention paid to him; "and as like to me as one thimble, I mean as one pea, is to another. Well, the strange thing is, the deuce alone knows how it happened, but *Jack got through.*" Here he took a bumper of port, as though in honor of that occasion. "It's a perfect marvel, but the best thing for *him* (as well as for me) in the world. Nobody ever went out under better auspices, for the governor of Bengal is our cousin, and Jack was to school with his private sec.: it's a first-rate connection. Our family has been connected with India for ever so long. I'll tell you how."

"It is a most admirable connection," observed Mr. Byam Ryll; "and the whole circumstances of the case will, I have no doubt, be interesting in the highest degree to the natives of Bengal. Your brother should embody them in a neat speech, and deliver it from the deck of the steamer before he lands."

It is probable that Mr. Frederick Chandos would have so far misunderstood the nature of this observation as to have accepted it as a compliment had not Carew burst into a series of wild laughs, which betokened high approval, and was one of his few tokens of enjoyment. He had evinced unmistakable signs of discontent and boredom before his intellectual henchman had thus struck in on his behalf; and he was really gratified for the rescue. Chandos was muttering some drunken words of insolence and anger; but Carew bore him down.

"Pooh, pooh! Old Byam was right!" cried he, with boisterous mirth. "I dare say all that long story of yours *may* interest those black fellows; but for me, I care nothing about it. It's all rubbish. Be quiet, you young fool, I say; it's too early yet for buffets. Here, bring the beaker."

This was a magnificent tankard, the pride of Crompton, which, at the conclusion of dinner, was always filled with port-wine, and passed round the table. It was lined with silver gilt, but made of ivory, and had a cover of the same, both finely carved. On the bowl was portrayed a Forest Scene, with Satyrs pursuing Nymphs; on the lid was the Battle of the Centaurs; while the stem was formed by a sculptured figure of Hercules. If the artist, Magnus Berg, who had fashioned it long ago in his own Rhine Land, had had foresight of the sort of company into whose hands his work was in these days to pass he could not have hit upon more apt devices. His Satyrs and his Centaurs had here their representatives in the flesh; while the thews and sinews of the son of Alcmene had their counterpart in those of the man who now stood up at the head of that splendid table, and drank such a draught as though the port were porter. It was a feat to hold it with one hand, and therefore Carew did so; but to empty it at a draught was, even for him, an impossibility, for it held three bottles of wine. Though the Squire could be acquitted of entertaining reverence for any thing human or divine, he had a sort of superstitious regard for his beaker, and believed that so long as he had it in his possession—like the "Luck of Eden Hall"—no great harm could happen to him. He attached all the importance of a religious ceremony—and, indeed, it was the only one he practiced—to the using of this goblet, and resented any levity during the process as though it were sacrilege. But to stand up after dinner, and much less to support this elaborate drinking-vessel, was not always an easy matter with the Squire's guests, and so it happened on the present occasion. The usage was, that one held the cover while his neighbor drank from the cup, after a ceremonious bow to him; and it fell to the lot of Mr. Frederick Chandos to perform this latter duty immediately after his host, and while there was still much wine in the goblet. Uncertain as to his footing, and trembling with irritation, as well as with the weight of his burden, he hesitated to drink. Perhaps, in his already wine-muddled brain, he had some vague idea of passing the vessel on, and thereby showing his displeasure; but, at all events, the hesitation was unfortunate for him, for, with a fierce ejaculation of impatience, Carew crammed the great cover on the young man's head, which, like the helmet of Otranto, came down over nose and chin. Maddened with the insult, Chandos dashed the contents of the goblet into what he thought was the Squire's face, but which was indeed the white cravat and waistcoat of his opposite neighbor; and then began a scene that Smollett alone could have described or Hogarth painted. It was as though a concerted signal had been given for a free fight among all the Squire's guests. The one art that was practiced among them was that of boxing, and almost every man present had a neat way of hitting out with one hand or the other, which he believed to be unique, and the effect of which he was most curious to observe. The less skillful with their fists used any other weapons that came handy. The dessert service of Dresden porcelain, elaborately enameled with views of the chief towns of Germany, had once been the marriage portion of a princess, and was justly held to be one of the rarest treasures of Crompton; but it was no more respected now than if it had furnished forth the table of Pirithous. The plates skimmed about like quoits, and all the board became a wreck of glass and china. Above the clamor and the fighting could be heard Carew's strident voice demanding his beaker, pouring unimaginable anathemas against any one who should do it damage, and threatening to unmuzzle and bring in his bear. The servants, not unused to such mad tumults, gathered in a mass at the doorway, and awaited with equanimity the subsidence of the storm among their betters. It came at last, and found the scene of contest not unlike a ship after storm—the decks all but clean swept, and the crew (who had broken into the spirit-room) exhausted.

Richard Yorke, who, with his two neighbors, had taken no part in the affray beyond defending himself from blows or missiles, was even more astonished at the general good-humor that now succeeded than at the fracas itself. If there had been any bad blood among the combatants, it seemed to have been spilled, for there was now nothing but laughter and applausive drumming of fists upon the table. The company were as pleased with their own performance as the holiday faces that greet with such exuberant joy the havoc upon the stage at pantomime time. The *habitués* of Crompton, indeed, were not unlike wild school-boys, with a Lord of Misrule for their master, and "give and take" for their one good precept. Nay, the rude outbreak had even a beneficial effect, for it cut short the orgie, which might, and probably would, have otherwise been prolonged for hours. There was no dissentient voice when Mr. Byam Ryll arose and observed, in demure accents: "Suppose, my dear friends, that we join the ladies."

CHAPTER VII.

YORKE REPORTS PROGRESS.

I TRUST it will not be imagined, and far less hoped for, by any reader of this sober narrative, that the phrase which concluded the last chapter implies that he or she is about to be introduced to bad company. The fair sex will not be without their representatives in our story, and that soon; but they will not be such as blushed unseen (if they blushed at all) in the bowers at Crompton. Mr. Ryll's suggestion, "Let us join the ladies," was only an elegant way he had, and which was well understood by his audience, of proposing an adjournment to the billiard-room. If that worthy old gentleman could be said to have had any source of income whatever, it was the billiard-table; and hence it was that he was always ready to proceed thither. Nor had he boasted without reason, a while ago, of his powers of self-denial, for he would often forego a glass of generous wine (when he felt that he had had enough), in order to keep his hand steady for the game at pool, which invariably took place at Crompton after dinner. His extreme obesity, though it deprived him of some advantages in the way of "reach," was, upon the whole, a benefit to him. His antagonists lost the sense of his superiority of skill in their enjoyment of the ridiculous and constrained postures in which he was compelled to place himself, and he was well content to see them laugh and lose. None but a first-rate player could have held his own among that company, whose intelligence had been directed to this particular pursuit for most of their natural lives; and even "Tub Ryll," as they called him, had to supplement his dexterity by other means to make success secure. His liveliest sallies, his bitterest jests, were all reserved for these occasions, so that mirth or anger was forever unstringing the nerves of his competitors, and diminishing their chance of gain. It was difficult to unstring the nerves of Parson Whymper, who ran him very close in skill, and sometimes divided the spoil with him; but on the present occasion he had a wordy weapon to baffle even that foe. This consisted in constant allusion to the latter's supposed reversionary interest in the living at Crompton, the incumbent whereof was ancient and infirm, and which was in the Squire's gift. This piece of preferment was the object of the chaplain's dearest hopes, and the last subject he would have chosen to jest upon, especially in the presence of its patron.

"Is he to have it, Squire, or is he not?" would be Tub Ryll's serious inquiry, just as it was the parson's turn to play on him, or, "Who backs the vicar elect?"—observations which seldom failed to cost that expectant divine a sovereign, for the play at the Hall table, although not so high as was going on in the Library with those who patronized cards, was for considerable stakes. Carew, who enjoyed, above all things, this embarrassing pleasantry, would return an ambiguous reply, so that the problem remained without a solution. But when the disgusted chaplain at last threw up his cue, in a most unusual fit of dudgeon, the Squire put the question to the company, as a case of church preferment of which he was unwilling to take the sole responsibility. "The sum," he said, "which had been offered to him for the next presentation would exactly defray the cost of his second pack of hounds, which his chaplain himself had advised him to put down; so the point to be considered—"

"The hounds, the hounds!" broke in this impatient audience, amidst roars of laughter. And nobody knew better than poor Parson Whymper that this verdict would be more final than that of most other ecclesiastical synods, and that he had lost his preferment. It was Carew's humor to take jest for earnest (as it was to turn into ridicule what was serious), and to pretend that his word was pledged to decisions to which nobody else would have attached the slightest weight; it pleased him to feel that his lightest word was law, or perhaps it was a part of the savage adoration which he professed to pay to truth.

Byam Ryll felt a genuine regret that he had pushed matters so far, though Whymper himself was to blame for having shown temper, and thereby precipitated the catastrophe. But he did not play the less skillfully on that account; and, moreover, had no rival to divide the pool with him.

"I would give five pounds if somebody would beat him," muttered the discontented parson within Yorke's hearing, who was standing aloof with his cigar watching the game.

"I think I *could*," said the young man, quietly, "if I *had* five pounds."

As the pool was two pounds, and the lives were one, this was exactly the amount of pecuniary risk to be run, and which want of the necessary funds had alone prevented the young man from incurring.

"Here is a fiver," replied the parson, softly.

"But I really have no money," remonstrated Yorke, though his fine face lit up for a moment with delight (for he was a gambler to the core), "nor any expectation of—"

"Yes, yes; you have expectations enough," answered the other, hurriedly. "You may give me that living yet yourself—who knows? Take a ball, man—take a ball."

So, when another game commenced, the young landscape-painter, who had spent at least as much of his short life at those boards of green cloth called "public tables" as in studying the verdant hues of nature, made one of the combatants, and not a little astonished them by his performance. He had the eye of a hawk, with the litheness of a young panther; and his prudence during the late debauch had preserved his steadiness of hand. Mr. Theodore Fane had the misfortune to be his immediate predecessor, and was "potted" at long distances.

"By Jove!" exclaimed he, sulkily, upon losing his last life by a double, "you must have lived by your wits, young gentleman, to have learned to play pool like that."

"I have," returned Yorke, without moving a muscle, and preparing to strike again. "You will come to do the same, if you play much at this game—but your sad end will not be protracted. You will starve to death with considerable rapidity."

"My dear Mr. Yorke," said Byam Ryll, approvingly, "you have won my heart, though I can't afford to let you win my sovereigns; I like you, but I must kill you off, I see."

"Unless—" said Yorke.

"Unless what?" inquired Ryll, as he made his stroke at Yorke's ball, which was quite safe, and grazed it with his own, which, gliding off another ball, found its way into a pocket. For once, he had really allowed himself to be "put off" his aim.

"Unless you commit suicide," replied the young fellow, smiling. "I was about to warn you of the danger of that kiss."

"You are worse than a highway robber, young Sir," said the annoyed old gentleman.

"That's true," returned Yorke, "for I take your money and your 'life.'"

The young fellow repaid his loan that night, besides putting half a dozen sovereigns into his own pocket; and there was other fruit from that investment.

Carew was delighted with his son's skill, though his wit was somewhat wasted on him. "Why the deuce did you not play in the first game?" said he, when the party broke up to adjourn to the hazard-table. "I suppose it was your confounded cunning" (and here his face grew dark, as though with some recollection of the past); "you wanted to see how they played before you pitted yourself against them—did you? How like, how like!"

"I had no money, Sir, until Parson Whymper lent me some."

"Oh, that was it—was it?" said the Squire. "Well, well, that was not your fault, lad, nor shall it be mine—here, catch," and out of his breeches-pocket he took a roll of crumpled notes and flung them at him; then suddenly turned upon his heels, with what sounded like a muttered execration at his own folly.

Yorke did not risk this unexpected treasure on the chances of the dice, but retired to his own room. It was a dainty chamber, as we have said, and offered in its appointments a curious contrast to his late sleeping-room in the keeper's lodge. He opened the door of communication to which the Squire had referred, and found himself in a sort of boudoir, in which, as in his own room, a good fire was burning. By the lover of art-furniture, this latter apartment would have been pronounced a perfect gem. Here also every article was of ebony, and flashed back the blaze from the red coals like dusky mirrors. Yorke lit the candles—huge waxen ones, such as the pious soul in peril sees in his mind's eye, and promises to his saint—and looked around him with curiosity. Like the little Marchioness of Mr. Richard Swiveller, he had never seen such things, "except in shops;" or rather, he had seen single specimens of such exposed in windows of great furniture warehouses, rather as a wonder and a show than with any hope to tempt a purchaser. On one hand stood an ebony cabinet, elaborately carved with fruit and flowers; it was divided into three parts, and their shut doors faced with plate-glass gave it the appearance of a tripartite altar with its sacred fire kindled. A casket almost as large glowed close beside it, enriched with figures and landscapes, and with shining locks and hinges, as he afterward discovered, of solid gold. A book-case of the same precious wood was filled with volumes bound in scarlet—all French novels, superbly if not very decorously illustrated. But the article which astonished the new tenant of this chamber most was the ebony escritoire that occupied its centre, with every thing set out for ornament or use that is seen on a lady's writing-table. It was impossible that such nick-nacks as he there beheld could be intended for male use, and still less for such men as were the Squire's guests. Did this chamber and its neighbor apartment usually own a female proprietress? and if so, why was *he* placed there? This idea by no means alarmed the young landscape-painter, who had no more *mauvaise honte*, nor dislike to adventures of gallantry, than Gil Blas de Santillane. He sat down at the escritoire, and, taking up a gilt pen with a ridiculous silk tassel, began a letter to the same person to whom that day he had already dispatched a missive; but this time it was not so brief: the day of brilliant dies and illuminated addresses had not as yet set in, so he wrote at the top of the little scented sheet, in a bold free hand, the word Crompton! and put a note of admiration after it. Had you seen his face as he did so, you would have said it was a note of triumph.

"My dear Mother,—*Veni, vidi, vici*—I have come, I have seen him, and I am at all events tolerated. The perilous moment was when I told him who I was. He said he was half disposed to set his bull-dog at me, but he didn't; on the contrary, he at once bid me exchange my bachelor's quarters for the two chambers I at present occupy, and which remind me of the *Arabian Nights*. I have never seen any thing like them; the furniture of both is of ebony; but the most curious part of the affair is, that they are evidently designed for a lady. Imagine your Richard sleeping under a coverlet of real Brussels lace! Every thing in the house, however, is magnificent, or was so once, before it was damaged by barbarous revel. Such orgies as I have witnessed to-night would seem incredible, if I wrote them; the *Modern Midnight Entertainment* of old Hogarth will supply you with the *dramatis personæ;* but the splendor of the surroundings immensely heightened the effect of it all. Carew and his friends might have sat for

Alaric and his Goths carousing amidst the wreck of the art treasures of Rome. Nothing that he has affords him any satisfaction; though, if it is of great cost, Chaplain Whymper tells me that he derives a momentary pleasure from its willful damage. This man and one other are the only persons of intelligence about Carew; but even they have no influence with him that can be depended on. If madness were always hereditary indeed, I might consider myself doomed. You were right there, I own; but you must needs allow that in undertaking this adventure contrary to your advice I have effected something. The chaplain is already speculating upon my future fortunes, and he knows his patron better than any body; at all events, if I am turned out of doors to-morrow (which I am aware is quite on the cards), I shall have three hundred pounds in my pocket, which Carew, with a 'Catch that,' threw me in notes, exactly as you throw a chicken-bone to *Dandy* as he sits on his hind-legs, though I did not 'beg' for them, I do assure you. The immediate cause of my being invited hither was as follows [here the writer described his exploit with the stags]. This, with our match at fisticuffs by moonlight, had greatly inclined Carew to favor me; yet, when the disclosure of my identity was made, I thought for a moment all my pains were lost. He resented the intrusion exceedingly; but then he had himself invited me to be his guest; and he holds his word as good as his bond. Indeed, by what the chaplain tells me, it will soon be held something better, for even his vast estate is crumbling away, acre by acre, beneath the load of lavish expenditure it has to bear. There must be much, however, at the worst, to be picked up among the *débris* of such a fortune.

"I am aware that it is in the last degree improbable that Carew will be persuaded to make a will in *any body's* favor at present. He imagines, I think, that the whole world is made for his sole enjoyment—it almost might be so, for all he sees to the contrary—and never dreams that he will die. But it is also certain that he will die early; and more than likely that he will come to grief, when he has lost his nerve, in one or other of the mad exploits which he will be too proud to discontinue. Then will your Richard become the most assiduous and painstaking of nurses that ever humored crack-brained patient. But there! I have made a dozen programmes of what is to happen, and this is but a specimen. Who can tell? I may be heir of Crompton yet, or I may come back to you to-morrow like a bad penny, and with what the vulgar describe as a flea in my ear.

"It will not surprise you to learn that you are personally held in great disfavor here, though the chaplain (who has heard all from the Squire's lips) speaks of you with due respect. The last thing that is desired at Crompton is, of course, the return of its lawful mistress. Carew himself is very bitter against you, which is doubtless owing to the good offices of grandmamma. The clock has just struck four, which bids me close this letter, though of all the Squire's guests, to judge by the wrangling that is going on in the Library below stairs, the first to retire will be your affectionate son, Richard Yorke.

"P.S.—I forgot to say that Carew made the most pointed inquiries as to whether I had any other profession than that of landscape-painting. Would it not be strangely comical if he should bestir himself to get me some Civil appointment! I almost fancied he must have been thinking of doing so, from some scraps of talk I heard him let fall at dinner. Curiously enough, by-the-by, who should have been sitting at his right-hand, but Frederick Chandos, Jack's brother! 'Good Heaven!' (you will say), 'suppose it had been Jack himself;' however, it was not."

CHAPTER VIII.

HOW BENEDICT BECAME A BACHELOR.

Notwithstanding the late hour at which Yorke retired to his sumptuous couch, he was up the next morning betimes. He was restless, and eager to explore the splendors of the house, that had been so nearly his inheritance, for it was not without a stubborn contest that the law had deprived him of what he still believed to be his rights. Nor had Crompton, in his eyes (as we have hinted), only the interest of Might-have-been; it had that of Might-be also. If not absolutely sanguine, he was certainly far from hopeless of fortune making him that great amends; at all events, while the opportunity was afforded him, which he well knew might be lost forever by his own imprudence, or through the caprice of another, he resolved not to neglect it. It was broad daylight, yet not a soul was stirring in all the stately place; nothing but the echo of his own footsteps, as he trod the corridor, and entered the great Picture-gallery, met his attentive ear. The collection of old masters at Crompton was varied and valuable; he could have spent hours among them with infinite pleasure, if the intoxicating thought that they all might be one day his own had not been present to mar their charms. He regarded them less as an admiring disciple, or a connoisseur, than as an appraiser. The homely life-scenes of Jan Stein, the saintly creations of Paul Veronese, the warmth of Rubens, and the stateliness of Vandyck, were all measured by one standard—that of price. The contents of this one room alone, thought he, "represent no moderate fortune."

When his eye strayed to the tall windows, and rested on the wooded acres which owned in mad Carew a nominal master, the beauty of dale and upland touched him not at all. "I wonder now," sighed he, "how much of this is dipped?" It was a good sign, he thought, that in one room he found a cabinet containing no less than fifty antique cameos; for, if the pressure of pecuniary difficulty had really begun to be severe, the Squire would surely have parted with what must have been in his view useless lumber, and was so easily convertible into cash. The Library offered a strange spectacle: chairs thrown down, and broken glasses, bore witness to the wildness of last night's revel; the splendid carpet was strewn with the ends and ashes of cigars, and with packs of cards; and on the table, scratched in all directions by the sharp spurs of fighting-cocks, still lay the dice and caster. The atmosphere was so heavy with the fumes of wine and smoke that Yorke was glad to escape from it, through a half-opened window, into the morning air.

How bright and fresh it was! How much there was of bracing enjoyment, of wholesome gayety, in the mere breath of it; how much of invigorating delight in the mere sight of the glittering turf, the beaded trees, to which the hoar-frost had lent its jewels! But such cheap luxuries are not only unknown to those who are sleeping off their debauch of the past night during the brightest hours of the day; they are also lost upon those who rise early in the morning, to follow the strong drink of greed and envious expectation. Richard Yorke enjoyed them not, save that he felt his lungs play more freely. A couple of gardeners were at work upon the lawn, of one of whom he asked the way to the stables, the report of the completeness and perfection of which had often reached him. The house and its furniture—nay, the house and its inmates—were of less consequence in the Squire's eyes than the arrangements of his loose-boxes. The old dynasty of Houyhnhnms was re-established at Crompton; the Horse bare sway, or was at least held in higher account than the Human. The Horse, the Hound, the Pheasant, the Bag-fox, and, fifthly, Man, were there the gradations of rank; and a compound being—half man, half brute—was, by a not unparalleled freak of fortune, the master of all. Carew had never fed his mares with human flesh, but there was a legend that he had rubbed a friend over with anise-seed, and offered that dainty morsel to his dogs. The victim was snatched away again, however, by some officious underling, who justified his interference upon the ground that the hounds would have been spoiled by such an indulgence; and the Squire had pardoned him. This was one of the stories about the Master of Crompton which divided the country into those who believed it and those who did not; but Walter Grange had told it to Richard as a characteristic fact.

The stables were indeed a marvel, not only of cleanliness and comfort, but, if it had been possible by any arts of daintiness to make them coxcombs, such would Carew's horses have become. They had looking-glasses in their own glossy coats, and yet it was not well for one of them to be an especial favorite with its master, for it more than once happened that he would ride such so often and so long that it fell under him, killed with kindness, overwhelmed with his oppressive favor. On such occasions, if the Squire happened to have been as devoted as usual to his brandy flask, he would shed copious tears, which many instanced as a proof that he was neither selfish nor cold-hearted.

The kennels were of vast proportions, hedged in by high palisades, through the interstices of which many a black muzzle now protruded, sniffing like ill-tempered women, or uttering shrill whines of despair. As Yorke, with his hands buried in his pockets, for they were cold, though his head was too well provided with clustering hair to be conscious of the absence of a hat, was contemplating this spectacle with cynical amusement, up strode the chaplain, wholesome and ruddy-looking.

"You are up betimes—as Crompton hours go—Mr. Yorke; I hope such good habits will not be undermined by evil associations. How I envy you your constitution, to be able to face this November mist with a bare head!"

"Nay, parson," rejoined the young man, "you must have risen early yourself to know that there *was* a mist. It's clear enough now all round. I suppose our impatient friends yonder," pointing to the kennel, where all the dogs, hearing the chaplain's voice, were now in full chorus, "will have their will this morning?"

"Yes; it is this pack's turn to hunt."

"I wish, for your sake, Mr. Whymper, that there was only one pack," observed Yorke, with good-natured earnestness.

"Ah, you are referring to that foolish talk about the living last night. Poor Ryll is quite broken-hearted about it this morning; and, in fact, he did do me an ill turn, though, I am sure, without intending it. It is the misfortune of a professed wit—and especially of a poor one—that he can not afford to be silent."

"You take it more good-humoredly than I should," said Yorke. "I should be inclined to charge something for a joke made at my own expense, where the loss was so considerable."

"You don't look of a very revengeful disposition, neither," returned the chaplain, critically.

"I have never experienced the feeling of revenge," answered the young man, frankly; "but I know what it is to feel wronged, and I think it is lucky that it is the law, and not an individual, that has done me the mischief—one can't have a vendetta against the law, you know. But, if it were a man, ay, though he were my own flesh and blood, he should pay for it—yes, sevenfold. I would not put up with injustice from any human being; and where I could, if the law would not help me, I would right myself with the strong hand."

It was curious to see the effect which this objectless passion wrought upon the young man's face, and even figure. His lithe limbs seemed to grow rigid; his right hand was clenched convulsively; his handsome Spanish countenance was lit up with a sort of dusky glow.

"My dear young friend," said the chaplain, quietly, "my profession, perhaps, ought to suggest to me some serious arguments against the disposition which you so unmistakably evince; but I will confine myself to saying that such a temper as yours is not to be kept for nothing. It is only men in your father's position who can indulge themselves in such a luxury, I do assure you. You'll come to grief with it some day."

Yorke laughed, good-humoredly. "What must be, will be. Let us hope there will be no occasion for the display of my fire-works. I suppose, what with his two packs of hounds and the rest of it, even my father will be brought to behave himself demurely, sooner or later."

"I should like to see Carew demure," said the chaplain, smiling; "although not reduced to that state by the extremities of poverty. Yes, as you say," he added, in a graver tone, "the pace at which he has been going these twenty years has begun to tell on his fortune. But it is not the dogs that will ruin him (as they ruined poor Ryll, with his few thousands), nor yet his hunters. It is his race-horses on the Downs yonder that will bring him to his piece of bread."

"I suppose so," said Yorke, sighing, not so much on Carew's account as on his own; "he backs a horse because it is his own. That is his confounded egotism."

"Your tie of relationship, Mr. Yorke, does

not, I perceive, make you blind to your father's foibles."

"Why should it?" rejoined the young man, passionately. "Am I to feel grateful to him for begetting me? What has he done to make me feel that I owe him aught? Do you suppose I thank him for being admitted here, unacknowledged, uninvited in my own proper person? For being permitted to take my fill at the common trough along with his drunken swine?"

"Nay, my friend," interposed the chaplain, coldly; "the food and wine are of the best; and we should never scoff at good victual. If you have so proud a stomach, why are you here? It embarrasses you to answer the question. Let me, then, shape the reply. 'I have a sense of my own dignity,' you would say, 'far keener than that of my father's flatterers and favorites; but, on the other hand, I humiliate myself for a much greater stake.'"

"*I* humiliate myself?" reiterated the young man, angrily.

"You take money that is not very gracefully offered for your acceptance, my young friend," said the chaplain, quietly.

"You saw him, did you?" cried Richard, hoarse with shame and passion.

"No; I did not; but I heard him swearing at you at the hazard-table for having emptied his pockets; and I am familiar with his mode of bestowing presents. You must forgive me, Mr. Yorke," added Parson Whymper, dryly; "but you ought to know that when a man has lost his own self-respect, he is naturally averse to the profession of independence in another."

"If you deem yourself a dependent, Mr. Chaplain," replied Yorke, bitterly, "you still permit yourself some frankness."

"Yes; that is one of the few virtues which are practiced at Crompton. You will find me speak the truth."

There was irony in Parson Whymper's tone; and yet the young man felt that he was not the subject of its cynicism. Was it possible that this hard-drinking, hard-riding, hard-headed divine was scornful of himself, and of his own degraded position? Yorke did not credit him with any such fine feeling. He had read of Swift at Temple's, and could understand the great Dean's bitterness against a shallow master and his insolent guests, but that a man should become despicable to himself, was unintelligible to him.

"Of course," continued the chaplain, smiling at his evident bewilderment, "I could have been as smooth-spoken as you please, my young friend; but I had estimated your good sense too highly to endeavor to conciliate you by such vapid arts."

"I thank you," said Yorke, thoughtfully. "I hope you were right there; I am sure at least that from your mouth I could hear home truths, which from another's would be very unpalatable. You are good enough to speak as though you would wish us to be friends. I am going to ask you, therefore, to do me a favor."

"I will do any thing that lies in my power; but do not, for your own sake, press me to influence your father—"

"No, no; it is not that," broke in the other, hastily. "It lies with yourself to grant my request. I wish to hear from you the true story of Carew's marriage with my mother."

"The *true story?*" echoed Parson Whymper. "Nay; I can not vouch for being possessed of that. I have only heard it from your grandmother: the counsel for the prosecution is scarcely a reliable authority for the facts of a case."

"And I have only heard the defense," said Yorke. "Let me now, for the first time, know what was urged upon the other side, and so weightily," the young man gloomily added, "that it made my mother an outcast, and myself a disgraced and penniless lad. You see, I know exactly what was the end of it all, so do not fear to shock me."

"There can be no disgrace where one has not one's self to blame," urged the chaplain.

"You think so?" broke in the other, bitterly. "What! not when one's mother is to blame, for instance? Well, please begin."

"I had much rather not," said the chaplain. "It would be much better for you to get the newspaper report of the case—I can tell you the exact date—and read both *pro* and *con.*"

"No report was ever published, Mr. Whymper; the case was heard with closed doors, or suppressed by Carew's influence. So much, perhaps—to judge by your face—the better for me."

"I think it would be better for you not to hear it, even now, Mr. Yorke," returned the chaplain, not without a touch of tenderness in his tone. "But, if you insist upon it, come to my private room, and let us breakfast together first, then we will have the story over our cigars."

Accordingly, the two repaired to the apartment in question—a very snug one, on the ground-floor, but so strewn with documents and letters that it resembled a lawyer's sanctum. The morning meal—which, in the host's case, consisted of a game-pie and a tankard of strong ale—having been here dispatched, and their cigars lighted, Parson Whymper began as follows:

"It must have been in the autumn of 1821 that Carew finally left school—the public school of Harton. He got into some difficulties with the authorities—refused, I believe, to apologize for some misdemeanor—so that he had to be privately withdrawn—"

"I beg your pardon there," remarked Yorke, hastily. "He was expelled, as I happen to know for certain."

"Very likely," said the chaplain, slowly expelling the smoke from his lips; "indeed, I should say most likely. But remember mine is professedly an *ex parte* statement. Mrs. Carew—I mean Mrs. Carew the elder—is solely responsible for it. Of course, she softened down the facts against her son, and I have no doubt made compensation for so doing by highly coloring the offenses of her daughter-in-law. I told you, you would not like the story. Is it still your wish that I should proceed with it?"

"Yes, yes," said Yorke; "go on. I was a fool to interrupt you." But the chaplain noticed that the young man held his open palm before his face, under pretense of shielding it from the fire, and that his cheeks grew scarlet as the tale went on, nevertheless.

"Carew was not seventeen then, when he left school for the house of a gentleman of the name of Hardcastle, in Berkshire, as his private pupil. It was understood that he was to have his particular care and attention, but not his exclusive services. There were one or two other pupils—

rather queer ones, as it would seem; but Mr. Hardcastle advertised in the newspapers for lads of position, but neglected education—young fellows, in short, who had proved unmanageable at home—and undertook to reform them by his system. It was no wonder, then, that Carew found some strange companions. The strangest of all, however, under the circumstances, was surely the tutor's niece, Miss Hardcastle herself."

"Why strangest?" interrupted Yorke.

"I think Mrs. Carew the elder meant to imply that this young lady, being possessed of great physical advantages, should have been the last person selected by Mr. Hardcastle as his housekeeper, and the companion of his pupils, and the more so since he was well aware, as it afterward turned out, that she had already succeeded in victimizing (such was Mrs. Carew's expression) one of these very lads. That was years ago, it is true; and it might well be imagined that a lady of the mature age of five-and-thirty might have outlived her charms; but in her particular case this was not so. Miss Hardcastle, as she was called, was still very beautiful, high-spirited, and an excellent horsewoman. She was also—if that had been necessary to obtain her purpose—well-read and accomplished. Being clever, good-looking, and not easily shocked, however, she was more than competent to secure the affections of young Carew. She was, nevertheless, as I have said, literally old enough to be his mother; and the idea of the affair having been a love-match, in the usual sense of the expression, was simply preposterous. That Miss Hardcastle was herself of this opinion seems evident from her having enjoined secrecy upon her youthful bridegroom. They lived together as man and wife, under Mr. Hardcastle's roof, for near six months before their marriage was proclaimed. Then young Mrs. Carew took a bold step: she persuaded her husband to bring her to his house, under the roof of which his mother was then residing. But they did not come (as one might have imagined) in the fashion of two runaway lovers, who seek forgiveness for their youthful ardor with penitence and submission. The bridegroom was full of wild mirth at having at last done something seriously to astonish the world. He was fond of his mother, after his own fashion; but so far from entreating her forgiveness, he did not even perceive any particular necessity for conciliation. The bride was full of triumph; she had not risked much, and she had won a great stake. It would have been better for her could she have borne her success with more modesty. Her mother-in-law was transported with rage, which she was too wise to exhibit. She knew her son far better than his new wife did; and she felt that opposition was for the present hopeless; but she took counsel with her son's guardian, and bided her time. It came at last, though very slowly. Carew was devoted to his spouse for a whole twelvemonth—a longer time than youth and beauty combined have ever enthralled him since. Even when her tender tones—for she had the sweetest voice that ever woman possessed—failed to thrill him, and her queenly form to charm, he would probably not have consented to take part against her, but for her own imprudence. She lost her temper with him upon a matter where it is difficult for the wisest of her sex to keep it: she grew jealous."

"Without cause?" inquired Yorke, gloomily. His cigar had gone out, though he still held it between his white lips.

"No; not without cause. That is a point, I fancy, about which my informant had her reasons for not being explicit."

"What!" cried the young man, indignantly. "She threw some one in her son's way, to divert his attention from his lawful wife?"

"Perhaps; I can't say for certain. I am not defending her, Mr. Yorke; but remember, she loved her son. She beheld him a victim to an artful woman. He was not in her eyes as he is in mine, and perhaps in yours. He had, she argued, capabilities of good, an affectionate and trustful nature; he was the best *parti* in the county, and had chosen his tutor's niece—a woman old enough to have borne him. Besides, she was *not* his lawful wife. The dowager had secretly taken legal opinion upon that matter, and was only waiting for an opportunity to test it. It was essential for this that her son should desire his own freedom; and at last he did so. I have told you the occasion. In the whirlwind of her wrath, your mother told Carew some home truths; above all, let him know she despised him, and had inveigled him into marriage. He had no other name for her, henceforth, but Serpent."

"I know," said Yorke. "Go on."

"It was within two months of your birth that this quarrel took place. Had you been born, and especially here at Crompton, I think the rupture would never have happened. Your grandmother felt that too, and did her utmost to precipitate matters, and, as you know, she was successful. Her daughter-in-law was compelled to leave the house, and an action was commenced in an ecclesiastical court. The validity of the marriage was contested on the ground of undue publication of the bans, both parties having a knowledge of the fact. I am a parson, you know, and this bit of law lies in my way. The bride appeared in the register as spinster, whereas she was the widow of an old pupil of her uncle's, whose surname you bear. It was not an easy victory by any means. The judge of the Consistory Court held that the inaccuracy in question was insufficient to invalidate the ceremony; but Carew, or rather your grandmother, appealed to the Court of Arches, and got the decision reversed. The marriage was therefore declared null and void. Very hard lines it was for you, Mr. Yorke; and—and that's the whole story."

"I thank you," said the young man, gravely. "I can easily imagine that it might have been told by other lips in harsher terms."

They were silent for full a minute, Yorke busying himself with the titles of the documents upon the table, written out in the chaplain's sprawling hand.

"Your mother must be a most remarkable woman," observed the latter, thoughtfully. "Is she still young-looking for her age?"

"Yes; very. What a queer docket is here! '*Tin Mine. Refused.*' What does that mean?"

"It is an application from one Trevethick, an inn-keeper, to purchase a disused mine at Gethin, on the west coast of Cornwall, which Carew has declined. Two thousand pounds was offered on the nail, a sum far beyond its value; but it is one of his crazes that his property there is very valuable, and it's evident that this Trevethick thinks so too—whereas it is only picturesque. For grandeur of position, Gethin Castle, or rather what is left of it, for it is a ruin, is indeed unequaled! You should take your sketch-book down there, some day. May I ask, by-the-by, are you only an amateur in that way, or a professional?"

"I am an artist by profession. I live by my pencil, save for what my mother allows me out of Carew's pittance. That is small enough, you know. Hollo! there are the hounds coming round to the front! I suppose Carew and the rest of them will soon be in the saddle?"

"And you have never made money by any other means?" pursued the chaplain, thoughtfully.

"Never. Why do you ask?"

"Well, it seemed so strange that a lad like you should find purchasers for his works," returned the chaplain, carelessly. "The Picture-gallery here will be of service to you, no doubt."

"Yes. I shall get my education at Crompton, if I get nothing else," said Yorke; "and indeed, as I have no desire to peril my neck out hunting, I shall set to work at once. Good-morning, Mr. Chaplain, and many thanks." And with a nod and a smile, the young man left the room.

Parson Whymper looked after him with a grave face. "I wonder whether Fane was right," he muttered. "He seemed quite positive; though, 'tis true, he owed him a grudge for potting him at pool. There was something wrong in that young fellow's face as he said 'Never,' when I asked him that question as to whether he gained money by other means. If he lied, the lying must have come from the mother's side. That woman must be a marvel. Well, I'm sorry, for I should have liked Richard Yorke to have had his chance here."

CHAPTER IX.

IN BLOOMSBURY.

It was the evening of the day after Yorke had listened to his own biography, and night had long fallen upon the shivering woods of Crompton; the rain fell heavily also upon roof and sky-light with thud and splash. It was a wretched night, even in town, where man has sought out so many inventions to defy foul weather and the powers of darkness. The waste-pipes could not carry off the water from the houses fast enough, choke and gurgle as they would; the contents of the gutters overflowed the streets; and wherever the gas-lights shone was reflected a damp glimmer. In a large room on the ground-floor of Rupert Street, Bloomsbury, sat a woman writing, and undisturbed by the dull beating of the rain without. She often raised her head, intermitted her occupation, and appeared to listen; but it was to the voices of her Past that she was giving heed, and not to the ceaseless patter of the rain. What power they have with us, those voices! While they speak to us we hear nothing else; we know of nothing that is taking place; there is no Present at all; we are living our lives again. If purely, so much the better for us; if vilely, viciously, there is no end to the contaminating association. It is to escape this that some men work, and others pray. The furniture of the room was peculiar to the neighborhood; massive, yet cheap. It had been good once; but long before it came into the hands of her who now owned it. There was the round bulging looking-glass; the side-board was adapted for quite a magnificent show of plate and tankards—only there were none; a horse-hair sofa, from which you would have seen the intestines protruding had it not been for the continuous gloom. If the sun ever visited Rupert Street, it shone on the other side of the way. On the mantel-piece were two of those huge shells in which the tropic deep is ever murmuring. Who that has taken lodgings in London does not know them? Who has not sometimes forgotten the commonplaces of his life in listening to those cold lifeless lips? If you take them up on their own tropic shore, they will tell you of the roar of London streets.

There were two articles in the room, however, which were peculiar to itself. The one was a human skull—to all appearance, the same as all other skulls, the virtue of which has gone out of them, though it had once belonged to no common man. The second object could still less be termed an ornament than the first, although it was a picture. It depicted a woman of frightful aspect, having but one eye, and a hare-lip; she was standing up, and appeared to be declaiming or dictating; while an old cripple, at a table beside her, took down her words in writing. If you had gone all over the rest of the house—and it was a large one—you would have found nothing else remarkable, or which did not smack of Bloomsbury. It was, indeed, nothing but a lodging-house, and the room we have described was the private apartment of its mistress. She might consult her own private taste, she considered, in her own room, else the skull and the picture occasionally rather shocked "the daintier sense" of the new lodgers, to whom the landlady gave audience in this apartment. She is as little like a lodging-house keeper, to look at, as can be imagined. Her cheeks are firm and fresh-colored, her teeth white and shining, her eyes quite bright, and her hands plump. To one who knows her age, as we do—she is fifty-three—she looks like an old woman who has found out the secret of perpetual youth, but has kept it for her own use, as, in such a case, every woman probably would do. There is only one piece of deception in her appearance; her black hair, which clusters over her forehead like a girl's, is dyed of that color: it is in reality as white as snow. By lamp-light, as you see her now, she might be a woman of five-and-twenty, penning a letter to her love. But she is, in fact, writing to her son; for it is Mrs. Yorke. Writing to him, but not thinking of him, surely, when she frowns as now, and leans back in her chair with that menacing and angry look. No; her anger is not directed against *him*, although he has left her and home, long since, upon an adventure of which she disapproved.

"You will gain nothing for yourself, Richard," was her warning; "and, perhaps, may wreck even *my* scanty fortunes." But, as we know, her son had taken his own way (as he was wont to do), and had so far prospered. She was writing a reply to the letter she had received from him from Crompton that very morning, and the task was one that naturally evoked some bitter memories.

"So he put him in the ebony chamber, did he?" they ran on. "Ay, that was *my* room once. What a pretty chime that serpent-clock had; and how often have I heard it in the early morning as I lay there—alone! If it had not been for that hateful woman, I might have been listening to it now! He seems as mad as ever, by Dick's account, and, I do not doubt, as brutal and as selfish! And yet it was *he* that suffered, *he* that was wronged, *he* that was to be pitied! His wife was the adventuress, forsooth! who deserved all she got. Oh, these men, these men, that treat us as they please, because they are so sure of sympathy, even from our fellow-slaves and sisters!"

She bent again to her occupation, but only for a minute. "All this is labor in vain, Dick," muttered she, laying down her pen; "the luck is gone both from you and from me. If I were thirty years younger, indeed, and might have my chance once more, I would tame your father yet. I ought to have beaten his meek-faced mother out of doors; I ought to have trained his bold-eyed girl to work my will with him. She should have been my accomplice, and not hers; but, now, what boots it that old age has spared me? Yonder is the only woman!"—she looked toward the picture—"who has found a way to win mankind, save as their toy. My reign has been longer than that of most; but it is over." She rose, and, holding up the lamp, surveyed herself, with a mocking face, in the round glass. "And this was once Jane Hardcastle, was it? *This* was her face, and *this* her figure! No drunkard, staggering home through such a night as this, could take me for her now! She had wits too; and better for me had I lost them with all the rest; then I should not have the sense to be so bitter! What a future she must once have had before her, if she had but known what men were made of! It is only when too late that such women discover what they have missed. This mad Carew was tinder to a flash of these bright eyes; and the fool Yorke, except in his wild creeds, as pliant as a hazel twig. I used to think yonder woman was an idiot, because she believed in a place of torment; but she was right there. Yes, Joanna," she continued, apostrophizing the picture, "I'm compelled to confess that you are right; for, being in hell, it is idle to deny its existence."

She placed the lamp once more upon the table, yet did not seat herself beside it, but walked hastily up and down the room. "To be young no more, to be poor and powerless, to have no hope in this world nor belief in a better, to have lost even belief in one's self—is not that to be in Gehenna? I am punished for my sins, men say. Hypocrites! liars! Why is *he* not punished? Why is he proud, and strong, and prosperous? Sins? If Judgment-day should come to-morrow, my soul would be as pure as snow beside that man's! ay, and beside most men's! Joanna here knew *that*—I suppose by inspiration; for how else should she? What's that?"

Amidst the pelting of the rain, which had increased within the last few hours rather than diminished, the pulling of the house-bell could be heard. Mrs. Yorke drew forth her watch—a jeweled trinket of exquisite beauty, one of the few relics of her palmy time. "Past midnight," she murmured, "and all the lodgers are within. Who can it be?"

The bell pealed forth again.

She went into the hall, where the gas was burning, and unlocked the door. At the same time somebody flung himself violently against it, but the chain was up.

"Who is it?" inquired she; and it was strange, at such a moment, to hear how very soft and musically she spoke, although, when talking to herself a while ago, her tones had been harsh and bitter as her mood.

"It is I, mother," returned the voice from outside.

She unhitched the chain and let him in. "I knew it would be so, Dick," said she, quietly.

Richard was pale and haggard, and shone from head to foot with the rain, which poured off his water-proof coat in streams.

"You were right, mother," said he, as he kissed her cheek. "No reproaches. Let me have food and fire."

She brought him socks and slippers, made a cheerful blaze, and set cold meat and spirits upon the table.

He ate voraciously, and drank his hot brandy-and-water, while Mrs. Yorke worked busily at an antimacassar, in silence.

"You are not disappointed at seeing me, that's one thing, mother?"

"No. Read that." She pushed across to him the letter she had been writing to him that evening, and pointed to this sentence: "You have my good wishes, but *not* my hopes—I have no hopes. I shall be surprised if I do not have you back again before the week is out."

"Just so," said the young man, cynically. "You have the pleasure, then, which your dear friend Joanna there never enjoyed, of seeing your own prophecy accomplished; and I, for my part, have three hundred pounds to solace myself with for what has certainly been a disappointment."

"I am glad you are so philosophic, Dick. It is the best thing we can be, if we can't be religious. How did it all happen?"

"I scarcely know the plot (for there *was* a plot), but only the *dénouement*. I had offended a certain Mr. Fane, toady-in-ordinary to Frederick Chandos."

"Ah!" cried Mrs. Yorke, shaking her head.

"Yes; you were right again, mother, there—the whole affair is a tribute to your sagacity, if you will only permit me to narrate it to you. I say that this fellow Fane, when walking with his patron's brother, stupid Jack, had me pointed out to him in town one day as the man who had 'pulled him through,' as he called it. Can you imagine how even such a fool as he could have been so mad? It was an act of suicide, which, so far as I know, fools never commit. Well, Fane was pretty certain of the identity of your humble servant, which he was, moreover, anxious to establish, because I had beaten him at pool, and given him the rough side of my tongue."

"Oh, Dick, Dick! have skillful hand and ready speech been only given you to make enemies?"

Richard laughed, and lighted a cigar.

"Well, sometimes, mother, the most prudent of us are carried away by our own genius. I am told that even you, for instance, lost your temper upon a certain occasion down at Crompton—gave a 'piece of your mind' to my father, which, it seems, he took as a sample of the whole of it. There, don't be angry: the provocation, it must be allowed, was in your case greater than mine; but then you pique yourself on your self-control! However, this Fane did hate me, and told the chaplain of his suspicions; the good parson was my friend, however, and all might have gone well, but for this oaf—this idiot Jack—coming down to Carew's in person. He could never get any coin out of 'Fred,' it appears, by letter; or, perhaps, he couldn't 'write!' But there he was in the big drawing-room when I went in last night, and Carew saw his jaw drop at the sight of me. He had not the sense to shut it even afterward, though I told him he had made a mistake, and gave him every chance. I could have persuaded him, indeed, out of his own identity—and much more mine—only that he appealed to Fane; and then the game was up. It would have made me laugh had I not been so savage. Carew turned us both out of the house together. His love of truth would not permit him, it seems, to harbor us. So Jack and I went to the inn, played *écarté* all night, and parted the best of friends this morning. But I'll be even with that fellow Fane—yes; by Heaven, I will, if it's a score of years hence!"

Perhaps the light satiric tone which the young man had used throughout his narrative was little in accordance with the feelings which really agitated him; but, at all events, his last few words were full of malignant passion.

"Be even, Dick, by all means, with every body," observed Mrs. Yorke, coolly, "but do not indulge yourself in revenge. Revenge is like a game at battledoor, wherein one can never tell who will have the last hit."

"At the same time, it is one of those few luxuries which those who have least to lose can best afford," said Richard, with the air of a moralist.

"It is not cheap, however, even to them," returned Mrs. Yorke, still busy with her antimacassar. "It may cost one one's life, for instance."

"And what then?" inquired Richard, carelessly.

"Nobody knows 'what then,' Dick. Our fanatic yonder had one opinion; our philosopher there"—she pointed to the skull—"another. Both of them know by this time, and yet can not tell us. It is the one case where the experience of others can not benefit ourselves."

This subject had no charms for Richard. When we are what is vulgarly called "in the sulks," and displeased (if we were to own it) with the system of universal government in this world, the next seems of but little importance. There may be a miscarriage of justice (that is, a thwarting of our particular wishes) even *there*. Perhaps Mrs. Yorke was aware that her son's clouded face did not portend religious or metaphysical speculation, for she abruptly changed the subject.

"And what are you going to do, Dick, now that this Crompton plan has failed?"

He did not answer, but stood with his back to the fire, moodily stroking his silken mustache.

"Richard"—she rose, and placed her plump white hand upon his shoulder—"it is very, very seldom that I ask a favor of you, but I am about to do so now. Promise me that you will never again undertake for another what you undertook for this man Chandos."

He laughed, as he had laughed before, in bitter fashion. "Why not? It was fifty pounds down; and apparently no risk: that is, no risk from the law, which has omitted to provide for the contingency. Next to being above the law is surely to be ahead of it. Besides, I am really a public benefactor. Without my help, the state would already have been deprived of the services of four young gentlemen, all of excellent families. Of course, such a calling has its disadvantages. It is very difficult to obtain clients. The offer of one's valuable assistance is liable to be declined uncivilly—it requires the talents of a diplomatist to convey it without offense—still, I possess those talents. Again, undoubtedly the profession is in itself temporary, can never be permanent; but then, has not nature especially favored me for it, after my mother's model? Shall I not be a boy at forty, and blooming at fifty-three? The idea of you being fifty-three, mother!"

As they stood together side by side it seemed, indeed, impossible that this young man could be her son, far less the offspring of her middle age. She smiled upon him sadly, patting his handsome cheek. "And is my Richard so full-grown a man," said she, "as to flatter, and not to grant?" It was impossible to imagine a more winsome voice, or a more tender tone.

"Nay, mother; I will promise, if you please," said the young fellow, kissing her. "And now, let us divide this Crompton spoil together." He pulled out his purse, and counted the contents. "There is Carew's three hundred, a few pounds I won at pool, and dull Jack's I O U for twenty—worth, perhaps, five. Come, we two are partners in the game of life, you know, and must share alike."

"No, Dick, no," returned his mother, tenderly; "it is enough for me to see you win." She shut the purse, and forced it back into his unwilling hand. "Some day, I trust, you will sweep away a great stake—though not as you gained this."

"Ah, you mean an heiress! You think that every woman must needs fall in love with me, because *you* have done so, mother."

His rage and bitterness had vanished, as though by magic; her tone and touch had spirited them away.

"Perhaps I do, dear. Go to bed, and dream of one. You must be very tired. I ought not to say that I am glad to see you back, Dick; yet how can I help it?"

CHAPTER X.

OVER THE EMBERS.

It was one of the peculiarities of Jane Yorke that she took but little sleep. The household had long retired, and she put the remains of her son's meal away with her own hands, then sat down by the fire, thinking. She had more subject for thought than most women; her life had been eventful, her experience strange. We know what her second husband—the man who repudiated her and her child—had been and was. Her first husband had been scarcely less remarkable. Leonard Yorke was a young man of respectable family, and of tolerable means. His parents were dead, and his relatives and himself had parted company early. They were sober, steady people, connected with the iron trade: a share in their house of business at Birmingham, carried on in the name of his two uncles, was the only tie between him and them, save that of kinship. They were strong Unitarians, strong political economists, strong in their rugged material fashion every way. They did not know what to do with a nephew who was a religious zealot, and thought all the world was out of joint; and they had characteristically sought for assistance in the advertising columns of the *Times*. Mr. Hardcastle therein proclaimed himself as having a specialty for the reduction and reform of intractable young gentlemen, and they had consigned Leonard to his establishment. It was the best thing that they could think of—for they were genuinely conscientious men—and they did not grudge the money, though the tutor's terms were high. Jane was then a very young girl—so young, indeed, that parents and guardians would scarcely have taken alarm had they been aware of her being beneath the same roof with their impressionable charges; and she was childish-looking even for her tender years. Leonard Yorke, gentle and good-humored, was moved with compassion toward the orphan girl, as guileless-eyed as a saint in a picture; he pitied her poverty, and, still more, the worldly character of her uncle and her surroundings. She was wholly ignorant of the spiritual matters which engrossed his being, and yet so willing to be taught. She sat at his feet, and listened by the hour to the outpourings of his fervid zeal. If she did not understand them, she was in no worse position than himself. His tongue was fluent. His words were like a lambent flame, playing with some indestructible material. His mind was weak, and devoted to metaphysical speculations—mysticisms: the *arcana cœlestia* of Swedenborg was Holy Writ to him. He believed in three heavens, and their opposites. Jane's endeavors were directed to make him believe in a fourth heaven. Childlike and immature in appearance, she was in character exceedingly precocious. Her intelligence was keen and practical. In very early years it had been instilled into her that her future welfare would depend upon her own exertions, and she never forgot the lesson. Her uncle was very generous to her; but he was not the man to have saved money for his own offspring, if he had had any, and far less for his niece; he spent every shilling of his income. Little Jane would secretly have preferred to receive in hard cash the sums which he lavished upon her in indulgences; she would have dispensed with her pony, and kept a steed in the stable for herself of another sort. The rainy day was certain to come some time or other to her, and she would have liked to have made provision for it—a difficult matter for most of us, and for her impossible. She was wise enough, even then, to know how Uncle Hardcastle would have received any suggestion of a prudential nature, and she held her tongue.

In Leonard Yorke, if she did not comprehend his doctrine of "perpetual subsistence," she perceived a provision for her future. At one-and-twenty, indeed, he made his pupil his wife, to the astonishment rather than the scandal of the neighborhood. They opined that it was only in the East, or in royal families who wedded by proxy, that brides ran so young. Jane Hardcastle, however, was in reality eighteen years of age.

Yorke Brothers, of Birmingham, had nothing to say against the match, but they objected to a Swedenborgian partner in the iron trade, and bought their nephew at a fair price out of the business. They did not offer to take him back again, when, five years later, he became a true believer in the faith of Mary Joanna Southcott and the coming of the young Shiloh. This lady, whose portrait, with that of her spiritual amanuensis, hung in Mrs. Yorke's sitting-room, had been her only rival in the affections of her husband. She had not been jealous of her upon that account, feeling pretty certain, perhaps, that the "affinity" between them was Platonic; but she had rather grudged the money with which he had so lavishly relieved the "perplexities" of "the handmaid." The amanuensis used to issue I O U's at Joanna's dictation, to be paid with enormous interest Hereafter, and Leonard Yorke was always ready to discount her paper. There was no one that subscribed more munificently than he did toward the famous "cradle," or looked more devoutly for its expected tenant. Even when that long-looked-for 19th of October had come and gone without sign, and two months later his poor deluded idol passed away into that future with which she had been so rashly familiar, he was faithful to her yet, and kept the "seal" which she had given him—his passport to the realms of bliss—as his dearest treasure. He had scarcely any other "effects" by that time, for, actuated by his too fervent faith, he had been living upon the principle of his fortune; and at five-and-thirty years of age Mrs. Yorke found herself a widow, with a stock of very varied experience indeed, but not much more of worldly wealth than she had had to start with. It was hard, after half a lifetime, to resume the same semi-relative, semi-dependent position under her uncle's roof which she had occupied before; but no better offered itself, and she was glad to accept it. Her natural attractions were still wondrously preserved to her; and, perhaps, on the occasion of her second nuptials (and the fact of her first was carefully concealed), her age excited less astonishment than her youth had done in the former instance.

Yet now at fifty-three, this woman, as remarkable for her talents as for her beauty, and who, if but for a brief period, had once stood "on fortune's crowning slope," found herself with little beyond a bare subsistence, which she received without gratitude from the hands of Carew. What she derived from her lodging-house defrayed the somewhat lavish expenditure of her son Richard. She was far, however, from complaining of his extravagances. She wished him to live like a gentleman, and not to soil his hands with ignoble pursuits. She felt a genuine pleasure—only known to mothers—in gathering toilsomely together what she knew he would lightly spend. She was for the present amply repaid by the reflection that her Dick was as handsome and well-appointed a young fellow as was to be seen in London, with an air and manner that would become a prince. It was only a question of time, she thought, when the princess should appear, be captivated, and raise him to the sphere for which she had taken care to fit him. In the mean time, it was only natural that he should enjoy himself after the manner of other youth of great expectations. She was not averse to his dissipations, for in them indeed lay his best chance of getting acquainted with young men of this class; nor, so far, had she been disappointed. It would be surprising to many a stately paterfamilias to learn how easily acquaintanceship, and even friendship, is contracted with his male offspring, if they be among the pleasure-seekers of the town. A young man of good address and exterior, with plenty of money in his pocket, does not require introduction. The club door soon flies open to him, but not that of the home. Richard was on tolerably intimate terms with Chandos, and other young men of the same class—but he had never been introduced to their sisters. It was here that Mrs. Yorke made her mistake: she thought she understood society because she had studied two exceptional phases of it. There is nobody more short-sighted than the Bohemian, who imagines he is a citizen of the world; his round of life may have no fence in the shape of convention, yet it is often very limited, and it is outside every other.

Mrs. Yorke judged of all men by her knowledge of her late husband and of Carew, and of women by herself. If it had not been for the artificialities of society, she might have been right; but they are powerful, and she knew little about them. In some matters she was exceedingly sagacious. She did not entertain the alarm which would have been felt by some mothers with respect to her son's morals, probably exposed to some danger by his mode of life; perhaps she had not their scruples; and yet it is strange to see how light those weigh, even with our severest matrons, when any question of "position" is in the other scale: they will not only permit their sons to herd with *roués*, provided they are persons of distinction, but even accept them for their sons-in-law. Mrs. Yorke, being daughterless, had no temptation to commit this latter crime, but she was not displeased to imagine her Richard a man of gallantry; he would in that case be less likely to fall a victim to undowered charms. "It is not your man-about-town who sacrifices his future in a love-match," was her reflection. On the other hand, no one knew better than herself what an easy prey to woman's wiles is a young gentleman without experience. It was for this reason, as well as because she loved to have her boy about her, that she had opposed Richard's going to Midlandshire. She knew Carew too well to hope that he would ever take into favor a son of hers, and she distrusted the country, with its opportunities for ensnaring youth into matrimonial engagements. Thirty years ago, in a fortnight of village life together, she would have backed herself to have got a promise of marriage out of the Pope; and she did not believe this to be one of the lost arts among young persons of her sex.

Thus Mrs. Yorke had strained every nerve to get the necessary funds to make town-life pleasant to her son, and yet she had not succeeded. It was not so much that he found his allowance insufficient, for he had various means of supplementing it, one of them (at which we have already hinted) a strange one enough; but the wayward fit was on him that takes so many of us in the early dawn of manhood; he was restless and eager for change, and the lessons which his mother had caused him to receive in landscape-painting furnished him with an excuse for wandering. She had had him taught to sketch, because it was a likely sort of accomplishment to aid the scheme of life which she had planned for him; and he had taken up with the art more seriously than with any thing else. But it was not in Richard's nature to apply himself with assiduity to any pursuit. Such callings as lay within his means and opportunities he was incapacitated for by education and temper. He could not have occupied any subordinate position that required respectful behavior—submission to the will of a master. He had had to put the greatest restraint upon himself during his brief residence at Crompton, and it was more than doubtful if he could have maintained his position there as a dependent in any case. He was gentle and good-humored, genial and agreeable, when pleased; but he had that personal pride which is as stubborn as any haughtiness of descent, and infinitely more inflammable. It was no idle brag when he told the Crompton chaplain that he would put up with injustice from no man (if he could help it), and would repay his wrong-doer sevenfold (if he got the chance). His sense of right was very acute and sensitive, especially as respected himself. All his passions were strong. Much of this might probably be said of any young gentleman of position accustomed to have his own way: lads of spirit (who can afford it) do not put up with slights; young noblemen in moments of exhilaration may even pitch into policemen; and generally, where there is no temptation to offend, much is forgiven. The danger in Richard Yorke's case was that his position was far from assured, while he had done some things which might prove great obstacles to his ever winning one. He had all the sensitiveness and impatience of one born to fortune, without the money.

Mrs. Yorke was too wise a woman not to be acquainted with her son's character. Her love for him was very great; as great and disinterested as that with which the most religious and well-principled of women regard their offspring; but it did not blind her to his faults. Her experience of life had not led her to expect perfection; her standard of morals was of very moderate height, and Dick came fully up to it; yet she felt that her son was headstrong, impulsive, and occasionally ungovernable. He had taken his own line in respect to his dealings with Chandos and with others, in spite of her urgent entreaties. Her opposition, though fruitless, had indeed been so strenuous that the subject was a sore one between them; and had the opportunity been less palpable, she would scarcely have ventured to revert to it that night. She had done so, however, and carried her point. He had passed his word to her that he would undertake no more such hazards, and Dick's word was as steadfast as Carew's. He was aimless and indolent; but as a mean man, who brings himself to perform some act of munificence, will effect it unsparingly, or a selfish man, "when he is about it," will be all self-abnegation; so, when he *had* made up his mind, his determination was rock. Mrs. Yorke then felt sure of her son so far, and rejoiced at it. But she was disturbed about him on other accounts. Perhaps, notwithstanding her assertion to the contrary, she may have had some scanty hopes of her son's success at Crompton; or perhaps his want of it placed before her for the first time the gigantic obstacles that lay in his social path. Were the times really gone by which she had known, wherein personal beauty, and youth, and grace of manner could win their way to any height? Or did she misjudge her own sex, while so sagacious an observer of the other? Her Dick was still very young; but his appearance should surely have done something for him even now; yet hitherto it had won him nothing but friendships of doubtful value, one of which, indeed, had just done him infinite hurt. Were girls with fortunes, then, as prudent and calculating as those who were penniless, as she had been? It did not strike her that they were infinitely more unapproachable; or rather, such was her estimation of her son's attractions, that she thought he had only to be seen in his opera-stall to become the magnet of every female heart. Had she been mistaken altogether in her plan for his future?

As she sat over the dropping embers of the fire, while the ceaseless rain huddled against the pane without, a terrible vision crossed her mind. She saw her son, no longer young, wan with dissipation and excess, peevish and fretting for the luxuries which she herself, old and decrepit, could no longer procure for him. She even heard a voice reproaching her as the cause of their common ruin: "Why did you humor me, woman, when I should have been corrected? Why did you bring me up to beggary, as though I had been a prince? why have taught me nothing whereby I could now at least earn my daily bread? Why did you let me lavish in my youth the money which, frugally husbanded, might now have supported us in comfort? Why did you do all this—you who were so boastful of your worldly wisdom?" For a moment, so great was her mental anguish, that she almost looked her age—not that the picture had any terrors for herself, but upon her son's account alone. She may not have been penitent, as good folks are, but her heart was full of another's woe, and had no room left for one selfish regret. She had (in her vision) ruined both; but it was only for dear Dick that her tears fell. If the guardian angel, which is said to watch for a time by every one of us, had not given up his disappointing vigil at poor Mrs. Yorke's elbow, a tremor of delight then stirred him limb and wing. Nay, perhaps in the Great Day, when all our plans shall be scrutinized, whether they have been carried out or not, this poor, impotent, fallacious one, which worldly Mrs. Yorke had formed for her son's future, will stand, perchance, when others which recommend themselves better to human eyes have toppled down, because built on the rotten foundations of self. There will certainly be many worse ones. She did not propose to sell her offspring, as match-making mothers do, to evil bidders. In her doting thought her Dick would make any woman happy as his wife. At all events, right or wrong, judicious or otherwise, her scheme must now be adhered to: it was too late to take up with any other. The vision of its failure had faded away, and she could think the matter out with her usual calmness.

The gray dawn creeping through the shutter-chinks found her thinking still; but ere the dull sounds of awakening life were heard above stairs, and before the coming of the sleepy, slatternly maid to "do the parlor," Mrs. York had arrived at her conclusion.

The early matin prime, she was wont to say, was always her brightest hour, but it found her, on the present occasion, white and worn, not with her long vigil, but because it was "borne in upon her," as poor Joanna used to say, that her son and she must part for his own good: so soon as the spring should come she would bid him go. London, where all was prudence and constraint, was no place to win the bride she sought for him. He should go forth into the country, where even heiresses were still girls, and win her, as troubadour of old, but with sketch-book in hand instead of harp. Not a promising scheme, one might say; but then, what schemes for a young man's future, who has no money, *are* promising nowadays? Moreover, it could be said of it (as can not be often said) that, such as it was, her Richard was by nature adapted for it; and—though this was a less satisfactory reflection—was adapted for nothing else.

CHAPTER XI.

THE GUIDE TO GETHIN.

It is the spring-time, that time of all the year when those "in city pent" desire most to leave it, if only for a day or two, and breathe the air of the mountain or the sea; the time when the freshest incense arises from the great altar of Nature, and all men would come to worship at it if they could. Even the old, who so far from the East have traveled that they have well-nigh forgotten their priesthood, feel the sacred longing; in their sluggish blood there still beats a pulse in spring-time, as the sap stirs in the ancient tree; but the young turn to the open fields with rapture, and drink the returning sunbeams in like wine. To draw breath beneath the broad sky is to them an intoxication, and the very air kisses their cheek like the red lips of love.

With his face set ever southward or westward, Richard Yorke has traveled afoot for days, nor yet has tired; neither coach nor train has carried him, and all the luggage that he possesses is in the knapsack on his back, to which is strapped his sketch-book, like a shield. He is striding across a heath-clad moor, with stony ridges, and here and there a distant mine-chimney—a desolate barren scene enough, but with sunshine, and a breeze from the unseen sea. It is classic ground, for here, or hereabouts, twelve centuries ago, was fought "that last weird battle in the west," wherein King Arthur perished, and many a gallant knight, Lancelot, or Galahad, may have pricked across that Cornish moor before him on a less promising quest than even his. How silent and how solitary it was; for even what men were near were underground, and not a roof to be seen any where, nor track of man nor beast, nor even a tree. There had been men enough, and beasts and trees too, in old times—heathen and ravening creatures, and huge forests; but it seemed, as the wayfarer looked around him, as though all things had been as he now beheld them from the beginning of creation. Richard, artist though he was by calling, had not the soul to take pleasure in a picture for the filling in of which so much imagination was required; and he turned aside to one of the stony hills, and climbed it, in hopes to see some dwelling-place of man. He was gregarious by nature, and, besides, he was in want of his mid-day meal.

There was feast enough before him for his eyes.

In front lay a great table-land, indented here and there with three chasm-like bays, which showed how high the cliffs were which they cut. In one, nestled a fishing-town, with its harbor; in another, a low white range of cottages hung on the green hill-side; and in the third, at sea, as it appeared, stood up an ancient castle, huge and rugged. This last object was of such enormous size that Richard rubbed his eyes like one in a dream. He had heard of Cornish giants, and certainly here was a habitation fit for the king of them. A lonely church upon the cliff-top beyond it, by affording him some measure of the probable size of this edifice, increased his incredulity. He looked again, and saw that it was not a castle, though the sun yet seemed to light up tower and battlement quite vividly, but only one isolated rock of vast size and picturesque proportions; upon the crown of which, however, there were certainly walls, and what looked to be broken towers. "That must be Gethin," said the young man, cheerily. "I must be at the end of my journey." Unless, indeed, he should take ship, there was not much more opportunity for travel. Before him stretched in all directions the limitless sea.

So magnificent had been the prospect that, when Richard descended and pursued his trackless way again along the moor, he half doubted whether that fair vision had not been a mere figment of his brain; the more so, since what view there was about him seemed now to contract rather than to expand; the horizon grew more limited; and presently nor sea, nor land, nor even sky was to be seen. There was no rain, but his hair and mustache were wet with a fog that was as thick as wool. By touch rather than by sight he presently became aware that he had left the heath, and was walking on down-land. Suppose he were nearing the verge of that line of cliffs which he had just seen, and should come to it before he was aware! As he paused, in some apprehension of this, all of a sudden a song broke upon his ear, like a solemn chant:

"Keep us, O keep us, King of kings,
Under thine own almighty wings."

He did not recognize the words, but the tone in which they were sung, though muffled by the dense atmosphere, struck him as especially sweet and earnest. The next instant, walking rapidly, with a light and graceful motion, the dim figure of a young girl passed in front of him, and the mist closed behind her, though he still heard her pious psalm. Richard stood like one enchanted. Was she an angel sent to warn him of his peril, or an evil spirit clothed in beauty and holiness to lure him on to it? He gave a great shout, and the harmonious voice, already faint, grew still at once. He cried out again: "I am a stranger here, and have lost my way; pray, help me."

Then once more through the mist came the young girl, this time without her song, and stood before him; she was very beautiful, but with a pale face and frightened eyes. "She is crazed, poor soul," thought Richard; and he smiled upon her with genuine pity. She put her hand to her side, as though in pain, or to repress some tumult of her heart.

"Where is it you wish to go, Sir?"

"To Gethin; where there is an inn, I believe. Is it not so?"

"Yes, Sir." Her words were sane and concise enough, but the tone in which they were spoken was tremulous and alarmed.

"You are not afraid of me, are you?" said Richard, in the voice that he had inherited from his mother.

"No, Sir, no," answered she, hurriedly; "only the fog was so thick, and I was startled. I did not expect to find any body here. It is very lonely about Gethin, and we do not in general see any of the quality who come to sketch and such like"—and she pointed to his port-folio—"until much later in the year."

"I am not the quality," rejoined Richard, smiling, "but only a wandering artist, who has heard of the beauties of Gethin. What has been told me, however, comes far short of the reality, believe me;" and he cast a glance of genuine admiration upon the blushing girl.

A slender fair-haired maiden she was, with soft blue eyes, over which the lids were modestly but attractively drooped. One who had a great experience of the sex—if not a very respectable one—has left on record a warning against eyelids. "A wicked woman," says he, "will take you with her eyelids."

It does not, however, require wickedness to ensnare a young gentleman by these simple means.

"I wish, my pretty damsel," said Richard, softly, "that I painted figures instead of landscapes, for then I should ask you to be my model."

It was not modesty so much as sheer ignorance which kept the young girl silent; she had never heard of a painter's model; but the tone in which her new acquaintance spoke implied a compliment, and she looked more confused than ever.

"Have you often so thick a fog as this at Gethin?"

"Not often, Sir; this is a very bad one, and you might have come to harm in it. Some folks believe that in such weather the Pixies come abroad, as they do at night, to mislead travelers who have lost their way; and, indeed, the cliff-top lies not a hundred yards in front of you."

"Oh, you think I was misled by a bad fairy, do you?" returned Richard, in an amused and bantering tone. "Well, at all events, I have now met with a good one; and may I ask what name she goes by?"

"My name is Trevethick, Sir," said the damsel, simply. "I am no angel, but I am going to the place you seek; it is this way, Sir."

It was evident that his banter had not pleased

her. The same tone that is found agreeable in the town does not always prove welcome in the country. She motioned with her hand to the southward, and began to walk so fast that Richard could not easily keep pace with her.

"But are there really fairies about here?" inquired he, seriously. "I am quite a stranger to these parts, and should be glad to learn all I can."

"Nay, Sir, I can not say; I have myself never seen one, though I know some who have, or say they have. There are tales of worse than Pixies told about that moor you have come across. You might have met the Demon Horse that tempts the tired traveler to mount him, and then carries him nobody knows whither; but, for certain, he is never seen again."

"Then the spirits about here are all bad, are they? I suppose to make up for the goodness and the beauty of the mortals, eh?"

"Nay, they are not all bad, Sir," continued the young girl, gravely; "the Spriggans, who guard the buried treasures of the giants, have often helped a poor man out of their store; or, at least, 'tis said so."

"And the giants—are they all dead?"

"Yes, indeed, Sir, long ago," answered the damsel; "though that they lived here once is true enough. There's Bonza's Chair, you must have passed before the fog came on, and could not but have noticed; and the hurling-stones he used to throw for pastime with his brother, they are to be seen still; but all that about his having such long arms that he could snatch the sailors from the decks of ships as they went by, is, in my judgment, but an old wife's tale, and I don't credit it. There, see, Sir; the fog is thinning; that is the castle yonder. When you see it thus in air it is a sign of storm."

The mist, instead of lifting, was growing less dense above, as it melted before the rays of the sun, and the ruin which Richard had seen from the hill-range was now once more visible, without the pedestal of rock on which it was placed. It was a glorious sight, though weird and spectral, and the young painter halted in mute admiration. The scene seemed scarcely of the earth at all.

"Most folks are pleased with that when they first see it," remarked his companion, with the flattered air of one who exhibits some wonder of his own to a well-pleased stranger. "You are very lucky, Sir; it is not often one gets so good a view."

"I am lucky, too, in having so fair a guide to show it me," said Richard, gallantly. "There is a church in air too: what is that?"

"That is Gethin church, Sir. It stands all by itself, a mile from the village; but folks say that the tower was first built for a landmark for the ships, and that the church and church-yard were added afterward."

"Then people die here, do they, even in this land of dreams?" said Richard, half to himself.

"Die, Sir? Oh yes," answered the young girl, sadly; "my own mother died two years ago, and lies buried there in yonder lonesome place. But it is not usual for Gethin folks to die so young, except by shipwreck."

"Are there many wrecks here, then?"

"Yes, Sir, and will be to all time; our church-yard is half full of drowned men. On the nights before storm, up yonder, you may hear them calling out each other's names."

"Have *you* ever heard them?"

"Not I, Sir, thanks be to Heaven. I would not venture there at night for the best cargo that ever came to Turlock."

"Where is Turlock?"

"The port there behind us, Sir; you can see the houses now, but not the harbor. It winds beneath the cliff, so that a ship can scarcely make it, save in smooth weather, though, when it once does so, it is safe enough. To see the great green waves rush in and turn, and turn, and waste themselves in their wild fury, as though they searched for it in anger—ah! it's an awful sight."

"That is in winter-time only, I suppose?"

"Nay, Sir; we have storms at other seasons. Whenever I see such a sign as the castle without the crag—it's all clear now, you see, because the wind is rising—then am I thankful that my father is no sailor. Most folk are such at Gethin that are not miners."

"Then your father is a miner, is he?"

"No, Sir, not now, though he once was. Every body knows John Trevethick about here, and why he don't work underground."

"How was that, then?" inquired Richard, with interest. "You must remember I am a stranger, and know nothing."

"Well, Sir, it was years ago, and before I was born. Father was just married, though he was not a young man for a bridegroom, and was down Turlock pit-hole with Harry Coe (Solomon's father), putting in shot for blasting. They had worked underground together for five-and-twenty years, and were fast friends, though Coe was an older man, and a widower, with Solomon almost of age. They were deep down in the shaft, and one at a time was all that the man at the windlass above could haul up; and they had put in their shot, and given them the signal. One was to go up first, of course, and then the second to light the match, and follow him with all speed. Now, while they were still both at the bottom, it struck Coe that the match was too long, and he took a couple of stones, a flat and a sharp one, to cut it shorter. He did cut it shorter, but at the same time kindled the match. Both shouted their loudest, and sprang at the basket, but the man at the windlass could not lift the double weight. You see, Sir, it was certain death to both of them, unless one should give way. Then Coe jumped out, crying to father: 'Go aloft, John. In one minute I shall be in heaven.' It was he who had caused the disaster, and therefore, as he doubtless thought, should be the one to suffer for it; besides, he reflected, perhaps, that he was an old man, and had no bride at home to mourn for him; still, it was a noble deed, and I never denied it."

"Denied it!" exclaimed Richard; "I should think not. Why should you?" and he looked up with wonder into his companion's face. It was one blush from brow to chin.

"Well, Sir," continued she, disregarding his interruption, "my father was hurried up; and as he looked over the basket the charge exploded, and the great stones flew up and blackened his face. In a minute more he was safe above-ground."

"But the poor man below?"

"He was dead, Sir. It could not have been otherwise. Father took it so to heart that he never did a day's work underground again. And when I was born, a few months afterward, I was christened Harry—though that's a lad's name—in memory of the friend that saved his life by the sacrifice of his own."

"He might well have done that, and even more," said Richard, "if more could have been done."

"That's just what father says, Sir," answered the young girl, quietly. "But when things have happened so long ago—before one was born—they don't come home to one quite so strong, you see. Father keeps not only his old gratitude, but his old tastes. He cares more for mines and machinery and such like than for any thing else; he is a better mechanic than any in Turlock, where I have just been to the watch-maker's to get him some steel springs. You should see the locks he makes, and the rings he turns. He will be so pleased if you ask him to show them to you."

"I shall certainly ask him to do so, if I get the chance," said Richard, eagerly. "Is that your house with the pretty garden?"

"No, Sir; that's the parson's. Nobody can get flowers to grow as he does. The next house at the top of the hill is ours."

"Why, I thought that would be the inn!" exclaimed Richard, looking at the little white-washed house, with its sign-board, or what seemed to be such, swinging in the rising breeze.

"It *is* the inn," said his companion, quietly, but not without a roguish smile. "Father keeps the *Gethin Castle*, although he has many other trades."

"And is that he, at the door yonder?" inquired Richard, pointing to a tall, thick-set man of middle age, who was standing beneath the little portico, with a pipe in his mouth.

"No, Sir, that is not father," replied the girl, with sudden gravity; "that is Solomon Coe."

CHAPTER XII.

A PERILOUS CLIMB.

"Is father in?" inquired the young girl of Solomon, as he stood in the doorway, without moving aside to let Richard pass into the house.

"No, he is not," returned the person addressed, his keen blue eye fixed suspiciously on the stranger. "As you were so long on your errand, he gave up his lock-work, and has gone off to the pit. He said he had never known you loiter so."

"I did not loiter at all," returned the maiden, indignantly; "if it had not been for the fog, I should have been home an hour ago; but one can't walk through wool as if it were air. You had the fog here yourselves, hadn't ye?"

It was strange to note the change in the girl's speech; not only were her air and tone quite different from what they had been—her modesty or shyness exchanged for a confidence and even a touch of defiance—but her phraseology had become blunt and provincial.

"Well, any way he was angered, Harry," returned Solomon, "until I told him of the new copper lode, as I whispered to you of this morning (you were the first to learn it, Harry), when off he set, in good-humor enough with all the world.—You'll come across John Trevethick, if you want him, young man, over at Dunloppel, though I doubt whether you will find him much of a customer—unless you are in the iron and steel line."

"I am in the knife-and-fork line just at present," answered Richard, good-humoredly; "and, if you will be good enough to move aside, I should like to order my dinner."

"I ax pardon," said Solomon, sulkily, withdrawing himself from the doorway. "I did not know I was hindering custom.—Who is this young spark, Harry?" added he, in a low tone, as the other entered the house.

"Well, he's a young gentleman, Solomon, as you could see very well if you chose," answered the girl, angrily. "He don't look much like a bagman, I think, any ways. I am sure father would not like you to treat his customers in that fashion."

"I am sure he wouldn't like your escorting such customers over Turlock Down alone."

"That's father's business, and not yours, at present, Solomon," retorted the girl, tartly; "and perhaps it never may be yours. You take as much upon yourself because of your new copper vein as if it was gold."

"Nay, don't say that, Harry," replied the other, with an admiring look, from which every trace of ill feeling seemed to have departed. "If it *were* gold, I should be more pleased upon your account than my own, you may depend upon it. You think I am jealous, now, of yonder bit of a lad, but—"

"I think nothing of the kind," answered Harry, impetuously.

"Well, well," returned Solomon, soothingly; "then we'll say no more about it. Trevethick wanted me to be away with him to pit, but I said: 'No; I'll wait for Harry, and bring her with me to Dunloppel.' It's a great find, my girl, and may be the making of us all."

"Nay, a walk to Turlock and back is enough for one day's work, Solomon; and, besides, I'm wet through with the fog, and must change my things.—Hannah! Hannah!" and, raising her voice to landlady pitch, she addressed some one within doors, "didn't you hear the parlor bell ringing?—So never mind me, Solomon; I dare say I shall hear enough about the lode when you and father come back;" and with that, and a careless nod of her shapely head, the young girl pushed past her disappointed swain, and ran up stairs.

The *Gethin Castle Inn* was a much better house of entertainment than might have been looked for in a spot so secluded from the world, and far from the great arteries of travel. A coast-road passed through the little village leading from Turlock to the now almost disused harbor at Polwheel, and that was the sole means of getting to Gethin save on foot or horseback. There was no traffic—to be called such—in the district. Dunloppel, always a productive mine, was, like its more famous brother, Botallack, situated on the sea-coast, so that neither road nor tramway had been created for its needs; the land about was barren, except in minerals; and not a tree was to be seen for miles. Indeed, with the exception of the parson's garden, there was scarcely a cultivated spot in the whole parish. The graceful sprays of the sea-tamarisk, however, flourished every where, in lieu of foliage, and in places where certainly foliage is seldom seen. Not only did it grow luxuriantly on banks and similar exposed positions, as though the roaring sea-winds, which cut off all other vegetation, favored and nourished it, but waved its triumphant pennant upon walls and house-tops. Stony places have a special attraction for this weed; and it takes root so readily that the story of its importation into Gethin might have had more foundation in fact than some other local legends equally credited. Only a few years back the plant had been unknown there, but a wagoner of the place, on his return journey, had plucked a sprig of it in some locality where it grew, to serve the purpose of a whip; and, when he reached home, had thrown it carelessly on the top of an earthen wall, where it had struck root, and multiplied.

The cliffs, and the sea, and, above all, the ruined castle upon the rock, were the sole attractions then which Gethin possessed—and that they *did* attract was an unceasing subject of wonder to its inhabitants. Whatever could the fine folk see in a heap of stones or a waste of water, to bring them there for hundreds of miles, was a mystery unexplained; but the villagers were no more unwilling than professional spiritualists to take a practical advantage of the Inexplicable. In the winter they reaped the harvest of the sea, or explored the bowels of the earth; in the summer they transformed themselves into "guides," and set up curiosity-shops of shells and minerals; while, to supply accommodation to the increasing throng of visitors, John Trevethick, who had always a keen eye for profit, had leased the village beer-house, and enlarged it to the dimensions of a respectable inn. Even now, however, the house exhibited a curious ignorance or disregard of the tastes of those for whose use it was built—the windows of all its sitting-rooms opened upon the straggling street, while the glorious prospect of cliff and ocean which it commanded behind was totally ignored. Thus Richard Yorke found himself located in an apartment which, though otherwise tolerably comfortable, might as well have been in Bloomsbury for the view which it afforded. The walls were ornamented by colored pictures of the Royal Exchange and of the Thames Tunnel, London; and upon the mantel-piece was an equestrian figure (in china) of Field-marshal the Duke of Wellington as he appears upon the arch of Constitution Hill. The only attempt at "local coloring" was found in the book-case—composed of two boards and a cat's cradle—in which three odd volumes of the "Tales of the Castle" had been placed, no doubt with reference to the grand old ruin whose tottering walls beckoned "the quality" to Gethin.

His simple meal of bacon and eggs having been dispatched, and gratitude failing to invest with interest the lean pigs that searched in vain for cabbage-stalks, or the dyspeptic fowls that were moulting digestive pebbles in the street without, Richard lit a cigar, and prepared to saunter forth. The fog had vanished; all the sky was blue and bright. The keen and gusty air increased in him that elasticity of spirit with which luncheon at all stages of their life-journey inspires mankind.

"I suppose," said he, looking in at the window of the room he had just left, and where Hannah, who was waiting-maid as well as cook, except "in the season," was clearing away the remnants of the repast, "one can get to the castle without a guide?"

"Nay, Sir; you must get the key first, for the man don't bide at the cottage, except in summer-time, and the gate has got spikes at the top. Miss Harry has got it somewheres, if you'll wait a minute."

Miss Harry herself brought it out to him. She had changed her attire for what was an even more becoming one than that she had worn before, and her bright brown hair was arranged with greater care, and perhaps with more view to effect.

"The guide has not begun his duties yet, Sir," she explained, with a smile; "and so we keep the key here. You can't fail to find the road; but the precipice-path is a bit awkward in a wind like this, and you must be careful to take the right one; the old ledge was broken in by the storm last month, and has an ugly gap."

"But why not show me the way yourself, Miss Harry?" pleaded the young fellow. "You know how easily I lose myself; and if I should come to harm, by taking the wrong turning, you would be sorry, I'm sure."

"Indeed I should, Sir," returned the young girl, simply; "and I doubt whether you will find any body else in the village. This news from the mine has taken them all off, it seems; and you wouldn't know rock from castle, unless you had one to tell you, they are so alike."

The fact was that Harry's conscience smote her for her wish to be of service to this handsome young fellow, since she had just refused to accompany Solomon to Dunloppel, on the score of fatigue. It was level walking, or nearly so, to the pit-mouth, and it was a climb of many hundreds of feet to the ruin. Still, she felt no longer tired, if she had done so a while ago, and the stranger *might* come to harm without a guide.

"But you're not coming without a bonnet?" exclaimed Richard.

"Nay, Sir; I should come home without one if I went up yonder in such a wind as this," answered she, laughing; "and I recommend you to fasten on *your* hat, if you wish to see it again."

"But you'll catch cold," urged Richard.

"We don't mind air at Gethin, Sir; and this shawl will cover my head, if that's all."

It really was Harry Trevethick's custom to go bareheaded in fine weather about her own home, though, perhaps, the consciousness that she never looked so well in even her Sunday head-gear, as with her own ample tresses for a covering, may have influenced her resolve. Chignons were unknown at that time, and never had the young man beheld such wealth of gold-tinged locks as that which blew about his fair companion's brow, and presently streamed out behind her, as they neared the cliffs, and met the full force of that Atlantic breeze. It blew freshly and shrilly enough up the winding gorge through which they had to descend to the foot of the castled rock; but by the time they reached the beach the wind had risen to a gale. They stopped a minute within shelter of a hollowed cliff to view the place. It was a noble spectacle. The great waves came roaring in, and dashed themselves against the walls of slate in sheets of foam, to fall back baffled and groaning. They had eaten the cliff away in two dark frowning spots, which his guide said were caverns, approachable at low-water; but the rock itself on which the castle stood defied them; they had only succeeded in insulating it, except for a narrow tongue of land, which now formed the sole access to it from the shore. Even without any historical or poetic association, the object before them—rising bare and sheer into the air to such a height—on which a swarm of gulls, shrunk to the size of bees, were clanging faintly, was grand and striking; but the place had been the hold of knights and kings a thousand years ago and more. The young girl pointed out to Richard where the main-land cliff had once projected so as to meet the rock, and showed him on the former's brow some fragments of rude masonry. "That was the ancient barbacan," she said, "once joined to the castle by a draw-bridge, as was supposed, which, when drawn up, left Gethin so that neither man nor beast could approach it without permission of its defenders. Even now, with none to hinder one, it is a steep and perilous way, especially in a wind like this. Perhaps it would be better not to venture."

"But you shall take my arm, Harry," said Richard; "only let me pin your shawl about your head first, lest those long locks of yours blind us both."

"I can do that myself, Sir, thank you," said Harry, austerely; then added, with a smile, to reassure him—for why should she be angry?—"you would only have pricked your fingers, as Solomon does. No man is clever with his hands, excepting father."

"And you say that to a painter, do you, Miss Harry—a man who lives by his handiwork?"

"I forgot that," said Harry, penitently; "besides, I was only saying what Solomon says."

"That was the gentleman who took me for a peddler, eh?" said Richard. "He is not quite so wise as his namesake—is he?"

"Oh yes, Sir; Solomon Coe has a long head: the longest, father says, of any in these parts. He has made his own way famously in the world—or, rather, under it, for he is a miner. He used to work in the coal-pits up Durham way, but—"

"Is that why he looks so black?" interposed Richard, laughing.

"Nay, Sir, I didn't notice *that*," said Harry, simply. "Very likely he was down Dunloppel this morning. It half belongs to him, father says; and if this lode turns out well, he will be very rich."

"And your father would be glad of that, would he not?"

"Yes, indeed, Sir; for Solomon is the son of his old friend and preserver, as I told you."

"But it would not please *you* quite so much—eh, Miss Harry?"

"Not so much as father—certainly not," answered the girl, gravely. "It seems to me folks are rich enough when they don't spend half they get; just as other folk—like Mr. Carew, who owns all about here—are poor enough, with all their wealth, who pay out of their purse twice what comes into it."

"Mr. Carew is known here for a spendthrift, is he, then?"

"Well, Sir, it's only gossip, for he has never set foot here in his life, I reckon; but, from what we hear, he must fling away his money finely. However, as father says, there's one excuse for him—he has neither chick nor child of his own. Eh, but you're looking white, Sir; Gethin air is apt to nip pretty sharp those who are not accustomed to it. You had best not try the castle to-day."

"Yes, yes; we will go at once," cried Richard, impatiently; and, drawing the girl's hesitating arm through his own, he moved rapidly along the wind-swept way. Under the circumstances, there really was some danger; but, had there been twice the peril, he would not have shrunk from it at that moment—the chance observation of the young girl about Carew's having no offspring had turned his blood to a white heat of wrath. Although his mother had studiously instilled in him how foolish it was to indulge in any expectations with respect to the Squire, he had always entertained some secret hopes in that quarter until he had proved their fallacy by experiment; and the failure of his expedition to Crompton rankled in his mind. He regarded his father with the bitterest resentment; he did not altogether forgive his mother for the share which she had had (through her misrepresentation of her own position in the register) in depriving him of his birth-right, and he felt himself at odds with all the world. He had come to Gethin partly on account of what Parson Whymper had told him of its picturesqueness, but chiefly because it was an out-of-the-way spot, unfrequented by that society with whom he had such good grounds for quarrel, and where he was not likely to have his pride wounded afresh by any reference to his position; and yet he had not been two hours in the place before the only person in it in whom he was likely to be interested had galled him keenly. He could not long be angry with her, however, for her involuntary offense, nor angry at all in such fair company. She clung to him, perforce, upon the narrow causeway, and shrank with him into whatever shelter was afforded, here and there, upon their toilsome path, when they took breath, and gathered strength together for once again confronting that pitiless blast. If either of them had known how fierce a gale was imminent, they would not certainly have ventured upon such an expedition; but, having done so, they were resolved to go through with it. Harry had plenty of courage, and fought her way with practiced eye and hand along the winding ledge; and Richard was not one to own himself vanquished by difficulties before which a woman did not quail. Twice and thrice, however, they were both driven back again round some comparatively sheltered corner by the mere fury of the wind, which battled with them as stubbornly as though it were the disembodied spirits of the ancient defenders of the place; and when, mechanically, and almost of necessity, Richard's arm sought the young girl's waist, whose garments made it more difficult for her to advance than for him, she did not reject its welcome aid. Then, just as his disengaged hand was clinging to a pinnacle of rock, his hat blew off, exactly as she had predicted, and his dark curls mixed with hers in wild confusion. Thus, foot by foot, they won their way, and reached at last the iron-spiked door, the only work of modern hands on that gray rock. This screened them from the gale; and, as they stood a while to rest beneath its shelter, she showed him what a handsome key her father had made for it, with cunning wards, more suitable for a banker's safe than for such ancient relics as they guarded, and told him how the gate was put there to exclude the summer visitors, who would otherwise enter without fee.

"Nay, but I will pay my fee," said Richard, gallantly; and, since their cheeks were almost touching as it was, the debt was easily discharged on her ripe lips.

"For shame, Sir!" cried the girl, indignantly; and there was something in her face and voice which showed him that her anger was not feigned. "I am sorry I brought you here, mistaking you for a gentleman. Here is the key, Sir; but I go back alone." And she freed herself roughly from his arm, and turned to go.

"For Heaven's sake, don't!" cried Richard, earnestly. "You may call me any thing you please, but do not let my rudeness prove your peril. I *was* rude, but, on my honor, I did not intend to be so. I meant no harm, although I see I have vexed you. Forgive me, pray; I did not mean to be either ungenerous or ungrateful. Is it thought so very wrong at Gethin—even with such great temptation—"

"Yes, Sir, it is," she broke in, vehemently; "and I was wrong to come with you."

"Nay, don't say that," pleaded the young fellow. "How could you be wrong to do so great a kindness to a stranger as you have done to me? It was my sense of it—my heartfelt sense, believe me, of the trouble and toil you have undergone for my sake; and I don't deny, Harry, your beauty too, of which I have never seen the like. But there, I am offending you again. Pray, come into the shelter; it makes me sick to see you in such danger;" and to make room for her, and at the same time to stand as much apart from her as possible, he stepped back, forgetting the scanty space on which he stood, and —fell!

A yard—a mile—he scarcely could say which, so overwhelming for the instant was his sense of peril! He only knew that he was flying through space. Then, suddenly, his feet found foothold, and his hands clung to the gray rock, and the driving wind beat on his body ceaselessly, and seemed to nail him where he clung.

Was it the scream of gull, or piercing cry of some spirit of the air, that rang through his brain? or was it, indeed, the agonizing shriek of a woman? He heard it plainly; but Harry never knew whether she had shrieked or not. She was aware of nothing except that this unhappy man was perishing—had, perhaps, already perished—for her sake; through fear for her safety, and his wish not to give her offense. She was on her knees upon the ledge, and craning over it with horror-stricken face the next instant, and could see him plainly. His feet had fallen upon that very part of the old path which the storms of last winter had torn and jagged away. A few jolting fragments of rock were all that was left of it—insufficient even for a practiced cragsman to make his way along on either side. His head—she could not see his face—was but a yard beneath her; but how could she get at him?

"I am here," she cried. "Be of good courage, Sir."

She had nothing to offer in the way of help at the moment; but she was well aware of what vital importance it was that he should not lose heart. She lay down with her face on the bare rock, and strove to reach him; but, even had her arm been long enough, he had no hand to spare to clasp her own. The whole force of the gale was full upon her, and carried her hair to windward like a whip.

"Do not come too near the edge, brave girl," cried Richard, beginning to be conscious of her efforts. "Is there no rope nor ladder?"

"Yes," answered the girl. "Keep heart. Do not look down. I must be five minutes gone—not more."

She was up, and with the gate-key in her hand, ere she had done speaking. Great Heaven! would that door never open? How her trembling hands missed the keyhole; and when the key was in, how the rusty wards opposed its turning. Then when the door was opened, it seemed as though the winds had husbanded their strength behind it for one wild sortie, with such fury did they rush out to beat her back. But she struggled in somehow, and on across the howling waste of cliff-top to a little hut of stone, which formed the covering of a well. There, as she expected, she found a rope coiled up, which was used to draw up water in an iron cup, to gratify the curiosity of visitors as much as to quench their thirst; for it was strange, indeed, to meet with fresh water there, the presence of which, no doubt, had caused the place to be chosen for a fastness in old time. With this she hurried back; and fixing one end firmly round the door-post, she looped the other in a slip-knot, and lowered it carefully to Richard. "Put this beneath your arms," she said; "the rope is strong and firmly fastened. You must climb up by it, hand over hand."

It was not so easy a task for the young artist as for a Gethin man; but he was strong and active; and where his chief difficulty lay, which was at the cliff-top, the girl's willing arms assisted him.

"You have saved my life, Harry," were his first words, when he stood in safety. "How shall I ever repay you?"

Then this brave girl, who had never faltered where action was necessary, began to sob and cry.

He took her hand and covered it with kisses. "I may kiss this," said he, plaintively, "may I not?"

She did not withdraw her fingers, but neither did she cease from weeping. Her grief seemed to be something more than that resulting from the tension of strong feelings suddenly relaxed.

"Let me go home, let me go home!" was her sole reply to all his entreaties that she should rest a while, and strive to calm herself. It was with difficulty that he could support her down the steep, so violently did she tremble. When they reached the foot of it she turned to Richard and murmured: "I have one favor to ask of you, Sir. Will you grant it to me?"

"Most certainly, dear girl. It would be gross ingratitude indeed if I did not."

"Then never speak," returned she, earnestly, "of what has occurred to-day. Never show by your manner that you feel—as you say—grateful for what service I have been able to be to you. Let not father nor Solomon ever know."

"It will be very hard, Harry, to keep silence—to owe you so great a debt, without acknowledging it," said Richard, tenderly; "but, since such is your wish, I will obey it."

"Thank you, Sir. And now I will go home alone. I was deterred by the wind, the steepness—any thing you please—from accompanying you up yonder; remember that. You will not mind waiting a while behind me?"

"Surely not," said Richard, wonderingly.

And the next moment she had hurried round an angle of the main-land cliff, and was gone.

CHAPTER XIII.

FISHING FOR AN INVITATION.

"What a strange girl!" muttered Richard, as he stood in the same hollowed rock, alone, where Harry and he had first taken shelter. "What a compound of strength and weakness—as my mother says all girls are, though I have never known them strong before! How eager she seemed to part company with me, and how anxious to get home without me—and I am never to speak of what has happened, to her father nor to Solomon! This Solomon is her unwelcome wooer, that is clear. He is neither young nor handsome—nor attractive in any way in her eyes, I reckon. And what a beauty she is, to be thrown away on such a boor!"

The recollection that the door at the top of the rock had been left open, and the key inside it, here flashed upon him. "She will be sorry about that key," he thought; "and glad and grateful to me if I go back and fetch it. The old man will be wroth with her for having trusted a stranger with such a treasure. This Trevethick must be an ingenious fellow, and a long-sighted one, no doubt. It was he who applied to Parson Whymper for a lease of the old mine, if I remember right. Perhaps the chaplain may help me to get it him, for I owe him something for his daughter's sake. The idea of his having such a daughter! What rubbish is this we artists talk of birth and beauty! Neither in life nor on canvas have I ever seen one so fair as this girl." He meditated for a moment, then cried out, angrily: "Heaven curse me, if I harm her! What an ungrateful villain should I be! If there be a Gehenna, and but one man in it, I should deserve to be that man!"

Then he began to climb the rock. He did not tarry this time for breath nor shelter, though the wind had no whit abated, but trod right on till he reached the spot where the catastrophe which had been so near fatal to him had occurred. "It was a narrow escape," mused he, looking down upon the place, not without a slight shudder. "What odd things come into the head when Death is whispering in the ear! If it had not been for my fair guide, where should I have been by this time? Beneath the sea, for certain. But what else? How strange it seems that if there is any 'else,' no one, from the beginning of time till now, of all the millions who have experienced it, should have come back to tell us! And yet there was a man who came back from the grave once. Who was he? I recollect his picture by Haydon; his talk must have been better worth listening to than that of most. Is nothing true that one hears or reads, I wonder? Here is where I kissed her! I wouldn't kiss her again, if I had the chance; I swear I would not. I am a good boy now—all morality, if not religion—for they do say that hell is paved with good intentions—which seems hard. If one is to be punished for one's wicked thoughts—even if they do not bear fruit—it is surely but reasonable that one's good ones—even if never carried into practice—should be set down on the credit side of the ledger."

With an exclamation of contempt or impatience, he turned from the dizzy sight of cliff and sea, and shouldered his way through the wind-kept doorway on to the open summit of the rock. It was a wild waste place indeed, yet not without ample indications of having been inhabited in days of old. Low but massive walls sketched out the ground-plan of many a chamber, the respective uses of which could only now be guessed at. But beneath one broken arch there was a heap of rude steps with a stone something on it, which Richard rightly imagined had once formed an altar. Man had worshiped there thirteen hundred years ago. Nay, not far off, and in the very centre of this desolate hold, there was a burial-ground, with a low wall of earth about it, which neither time, nor the curious barbarism which marks our epoch, had much defaced. The archæologists had been there, of course, and discovered evidence which had satisfied them of the presence of the remains of their fellow-creatures; but with that they had been content. The dead had, for the most part, been left undisturbed in their rocky graves, to await the summons in the faith of which—and perhaps even for it—they had died. For these were King Arthur's men (as Richard had read)—the warriors who had helped the blameless king "to drive the heathen and to slay the beast, to fell the forest and let in the sun."

The lonely desolation of the place, and its natural sublimity, combined with the recollection of his late deadly peril, tinged the young man's thoughts with an unusual seriousness; and yet he could not restrain the cynicism that was habitual to him whenever his attention was compelled to solemn subjects.

"Now, are these poor folks—whose creed must have been any thing but orthodox, by all accounts—all in eternal torments, I wonder, or only waiting to be so, for a few hundreds of years longer? Such was my mother's friend, Joanna's, comfortable creed, and it is shared, as I understand, by all the most excellent people. How much better (if so) would it have been for them to have been born and cradled on this rock as sea-gulls! Gad, to dwell here and fight for a king about whose very existence posterity is to be in doubt in this world, and then to go to the devil! What a nightmare view of life it seems! If, an hour ago or so, things had turned out otherwise with *me*, I should have solved the problem for myself. I almost wish I had. And yet it was not so when I was clinging tooth and nail to the cliff yonder; and these folks would not have died if they could have helped it, neither. There's something ugly in black Death that disinclines man to woo her. This wind bites to the marrow, and I'll go. I've seen

Gethin now, and there's an end." He turned, and walked as slowly as the blast would let him toward the gate. "And yet, if it was warmer, and summer-time," continued he, "I should like to sketch these things, or some of them, especially if Harry were with me." He came out, and locked the door, and once more stood in the shelter of it, with the key in his hand. "She'll be glad I went back for this, and know that it was done for her sake. If she had but money, now—this girl—and was a lady, and all that! Or if I could choose whom I would!" He began to descend slowly, step by step; the furious gale forgotten; his late escape from death unremembered; one thought alone monopolizing his mind—the thought that monopolizes all men's minds (or nearly all) at his age. It was here that his hat had blown off, and her soft curls had played about his face; it was there that he had first clasped her waist, and had not been rebuked. Then he fell to thinking of all that had happened between them during the few hours that were already an epoch in his life. Why had she looked so frightened at first seeing him? Had he seemed to come upon her as her "fate," as some girls say? He would ask her that some day—perhaps up yonder amidst the ruins. He had not missed the look of annoyance which she wore when Solomon had spoken to him so roughly, nor failed to couple it with the expressions she had before made use of with reference to Coe the elder, and the gratitude with which her father regarded his memory. This Solomon might be a suitor who was backed by the old man, but certainly not encouraged by Harry. Was she already engaged to him, tacitly or otherwise? It was impossible, being what she was, that she should not have been wooed by somebody.

Richard Yorke was not one of those exacting characters who demand that the object of their affections should never have attracted those of another; he was even reasonable enough to have forgiven her (if necessary) for having returned them, in ignorance of the existence of a more worthy admirer in himself. There are many more varieties of Love than even the poets have classified; and perhaps it is in despair of dealing with this Proteus that we elders so often ignore him in our calculations.

The day was darkening by the time Richard reached the village. Around the inn door were a group of miners, who stared at his bare head hard enough, but gave way to him civilly. They were talking and laughing loudly, and wiping their mouths with the backs of their hands. It was evident that somebody had been "standing treat" in the narrow passage; and leaning their elbows on the sill of the little bar window were more miners, each with his pint pot of ale.

"Here's luck to Trevethick and Coe," said one, "for a parting toast."

"Ha, ha, that's good!" cried another, in appreciation of this commercial epigram; "Trevethick and Coe; to be sure."

"Trevethick and Coe, and may the copper last!"

But one, emboldened by the liquor, or naturally more audacious than the rest, put his head and shoulders through the open window, and, making a trumpet of his two hands, whispered in a hoarse voice, audible to every one: "And is it to be Coe and Trevethick also, Miss Harry—eh?"

Then the window was slammed down with no gentle hand, and the men went out laughing heartily, and for the first time leaving room for Richard to pass in. He did not look toward the bar window, but, as though he had heard nothing, walked quickly past it into the sitting-room, which had been allotted to him. It was strange, since what he had just heard only confirmed the suspicions which he had already entertained, that the words should give him annoyance; but they certainly did so. What was more natural than that this inn-keeper's daughter should be engaged to marry her father's friend—a man apparently well-to-do, and with a prospect of doing better? What could be more unreasonable than for Mr. Richard Yorke, a young gentleman whose only hope in life was to marry a girl—or an old woman, for that matter—with a good fortune, to be irritated at such intelligence, especially after an acquaintance with this "Miss Harry" of about three hours at most? After a minute or two of reflection the idea seemed to strike even himself in the same light; for he gave a short sharp laugh, and said what a fool he was, and then lit his pipe. Even tobacco, however, that balm of hurt minds, did not altogether soothe him. He could think of nothing but this young girl, whose beauty had bewitched him, and to whose courage and presence of mind he owed his life. He had sworn to himself—and there was no necessity to repeat it—that he meant her no harm. Indeed, it would not be less than she deserved to ask her to be his wife. Perhaps, if this mine, in which her father had a share, should turn out well, she would not be so bad a match, even in point of money; but to this he did not attach much importance. He was indulging in a dream, which he fondly imagined was unselfish and honorable to himself in a high degree. Quite a virtuous glow seemed to mingle with his ardent passion; though the fact simply was (as it often is in such cases) that, for a personal gratification, he was prepared to barter his future prospects. He did not doubt but that what he contemplated would be for the benefit of this young girl; he must seem like an angel to her (for love does not always touch us with the sense of unworthiness); as, indeed, by comparison with this man Coe, he was. His mother would be a good deal "put out," it was true, but then she was too fond of him to be angry with him for long, far less to break with him. He was his own master, for some time to come, at all events, for he had two hundred pounds in his pocket.

What nonsense do the greatest philosophers sometimes discourse, when their topic is Self-interest! It is likely enough that self-interest actuates *them*, and in a supreme degree. When folks are by nature wise and prudent—or if their tastes are studious, and their vices few—or when, above all, the brain is seasoned, and the blood moves sluggishly in the veins, then men do act for their own advantage, and keep their eyes fixed on the main chance. But with most of us, especially when young, self-interest, properly so called, is often but a feather's weight in the balance of Motive. Revenge makes it kick the beam; and Passion; and even momentary Whim. It was one of the arguments advanced by Christian men in favor of slavery, that no man would ill-use his slave, because it was his own property; as though the lust of cruelty in a brutal nature were, while it lasted, not ten times as strong as the lust of gain. There are moments when a man is ready to part with not only his earthly prospects, but his hopes of heaven, rather than be balked of an immediate satisfaction: that of striking his brother to the heart, or growing rich by one stroke of fraud, or ruining forever the woman that loves him best; and there are many men, in no such desperate case, whose only guide is Impulse, and whose care for the morrow is dwarfed to nothing matched with the gratification of to-day. These are said to have no enemies but themselves, but they have victims; and, though not apt for plots, are often more dangerous than the most designing knaves.

Pipe after pipe smoked Richard Yorke as he sat over the fire in the deepening twilight, so deep in thought that it quite startled him, when, suddenly looking up, he found that all was dark. Then he rang the bell, and Hannah entered with the wished-for candles.

"Is your master in?"

"I'll see, Sir. Do you wish to see him?"

"Yes. First bring me a bottle of sherry and two glasses, then ask him to step in."

The serving-maid obeyed; and presently there was a heavy step in the passage, and in strode John Trevethick, a man of sixty years or so, but straight as a pine, and strong as an oak.

"Your servant, Sir," said he, in a gruff voice, and with no such inclination of the head as landlords use.

"Good-evening, Mr. Trevethick. I am afraid I'm putting you to some inconvenience by coming to Gethin so many weeks before the usual time."

"Nay, Sir; my house is open summer and winter."

"Now I wonder is this the natural manner of this boor," thought Richard, "or has he been already prejudiced against me by the other?—And an excellent house it is, Mr. Trevethick; I little expected to find so good a one down here, I promise you."

"Well, I built it myself, Sir," said the landlord; "so it don't become me to say much of that. It cost me a good bit of money, however; and it's hard to get it back, when one's season only lasts for a month or two."

"Ah! I'm the first swallow that you've seen this year, I dare say. Well, I hope I herald a lucky summer. Take a glass of your own sherry, will you?"

The landlord looked suspiciously at his guest: perhaps the phrase "your own sherry" smote his conscience, knowing the price he paid for it, and what it was, and what he meant to charge; but grunting: "Here's to you, Sir," he filled his glass, and smacked his lips over it slowly.

"Solomon has not set him against me," was Richard's conclusion. "The graceful manner of this Cornish giant is natural to him.—You have a fine castle here, Mr. Trevethick, and nobly placed. Indeed, I never saw the like before."

"So most folks say," answered the landlord.

"There is not much left of it, however," said Richard, smiling.

"Well, it 'll last my time, at all events, and I dare say yours," was the morose reply.

"Indeed it will, and that of many a generation to come. It is seldom one sees such massive walls. A good deal of trouble, however, seems to have been taken to prevent people from running away with them, to judge by this;" and he held up the key.

"Well, the castle is mine, Sir—or, at least, I pay my rent for it; and, I suppose, I can do what I like with my own. If there was no gate there, do you think any body would pay me for viewing the place? Not they. Why, there's some parties ain't even content with the key, but must have a guide too, or else they buttons up their pockets."

It was so impossible to misunderstand the bearing of this remark that Richard burst out into a good-humored laugh; he was really pleased because the landlord's hint assured him that he was in ignorance that he had had a guide. "I shall certainly pay my footing, Mr. Trevethick, the same as if I had had an attendant—of which, however, I should have been glad at one or two places; the wind did take my hat, and very nearly the rest of me. But what I meant by the trouble that was taken to secure your ruins from intruders was with reference not to the door, but to the key of it. Why, if it were a real castle, full of furniture, it could not be more effectually guarded. You must have good locksmiths hereabout, if that's a specimen of their work."

The icy landlord thawed again.

"Well, Sir, the fact is, I made that key with my own hands."

"You?" cried Richard, in affected astonishment. "Why, you must be a mechanical genius. Look at the work! look at the wards!" and he scrutinized them admiringly close to the candle. "Do take another glass, Mr. Trevethick."

"Nay, Sir; I've a friend in the parlor waiting for me," rejoined the landlord, dryly. He appeared already to regret having given way to that momentary feeling of self-esteem.

"I wish *I* had," observed Richard, smiling. "It's lonely work coming down here by one's self, and finding nobody to speak to."

There was a short pause, during which Richard was rapt in admiration of the key.

"Now, if his thick skin prove impervious to flattery," thought he, "then will I fly my last shaft into his very gizzard."

Mr. Trevethick's skin was quite compliment-proof, if an invitation into the bar parlor was to be the evidence of its having been pierced.

"You should come down in the summer-time, Sir," said he, coolly; "then you will find lots of folks to talk with. At present I am afraid you must put up with your own company." And the huge frame of the landlord was already moving toward the door.

"I am afraid so, indeed," said Richard, carelessly. "Parson Whymper ought to have known better than to send me down here at such a time as this."

John Trevethick stopped at once, and Richard saw reflected in the glass above the fire-place a look of intense interest. He could not have supposed so phlegmatic a face was capable of so much expression.

"Parson who, did you say, Sir? Whymper?"

"Yes; an excellent friend of me and mine; the chaplain of Mr. Carew, of Crompton. It was he who told me how I might fill my sketch-book with the beauties of Gethin; and added, that I should have a hearty welcome from one John Trevethick, if I gave his name."

"And that you shall, Sir," cried the landlord, returning to the table, and striking his broad palm upon it, to give emphasis to his words. "A friend of Mr. Whymper's should be always welcome here. How is he, Sir? And how is Mr. Carew?"

"I have seen neither of them since I was staying at Crompton three months ago or so," said Richard, coolly. "They were well enough then, though the Squire was doing his best, as usual, to exhaust his constitution and his purse; and the chaplain, as usual, also, was making things as straight as he could, and putting the skid on where he dared. But you know all about that, Mr. Trevethick, I dare say, almost as well as I do. I am sorry you won't take another glass of wine."

"I think I will, if you permit me to change my mind, Sir," said the other, suiting the action to the word. "Now, the idea of your being so intimate with Parson Whymper, and having staid at Squire Carew's! Why, the Squire's my landlord, and owns all about here—leastway, short of Dunloppel. It's unlucky that this copper should have cropped out just beyond him, as it were."

"There is no mine here belonging to him then, eh?"

"Well, no, Sir; not, properly speaking, a mine, there ain't;" and the well-practiced hand of the landlord shook as he put down the glass, so that it clanked against the bottle.

Richard Yorke laughed a short dry laugh, apparently at some reflection of his own.

"Well, I'm sorry you've got your friend, landlord, and therefore can not have a chat with me; for it is evident we should find something to talk about together."

"And I'm sorry too, Sir. Though, if you wouldn't be too proud to come into our bar parlor — but then I can scarcely ask a gentleman as has been used to Crompton to do that."

"Indeed, I shall be very pleased to come," said Richard, frankly. "I have nothing to be proud of, I assure you; and if I had, why should I not accept the company of an honest man?"

"Very good, Sir. There's only me, and my daughter Harry, and this friend of mine, Solomon Coe. If you'll please to walk this way."

"Let's take the bottle with us, and then, perhaps, Mr. Coe will help us to finish it."

And bearing that token of amity in his hand, John Trevethick led the way into the bar parlor.

CHAPTER XIV.

THE BAR PARLOR.

THE bar parlor of the *Gethin Castle* was a small snug apartment in the rear of the house, and therefore exposed to the full fury of the Atlantic winds, which were now roaring without, and enhanced, by their idle menace, the comfort of its closely drawn red curtains, and its ample fire, the gleam of which was cast back from a goodly array of glasses and vessels of burnished pewter. Upon a well-polished oak chest—the pride of the house, for oak was almost as rare at Gethin as among the Esquimaux—stood a mighty punch-bowl; and on the mantel-piece was a grotesque piece of earthen-ware, used for holding tobacco, about which some long clay pipes and peacocks' feathers were artistically arranged. A smell of nutmeg and lemons pervaded this apartment, and pleasantly accorded with its almost tropical temperature; and the contrast it altogether afforded to his own more stately but desolate "private sitting-room," with its disused air and comfortless surroundings, struck Richard very agreeably. On a chintz-covered sofa, in the most retired corner of this parlor, sat Solomon Coe and Harry Trevethick, and it was difficult to say in which of their countenances the most astonishment appeared when the young painter presented himself at the door. Harry's cheeks, which were not pale before, became crimson, though she neither moved nor spoke. But Solomon rose, and, with a frown, seemed to be asking of Trevethick the reason of this unexpected intrusion.

"This is a friend of Mr. Whymper's," said the landlord, setting down the sherry on the table; "and therefore, I am sure, the friend of all of us. That's my daughter Harry, Sir; and that" (and here he grinned) "is Solomon Coe, a very intimate friend of hers—as you may see. We are a family party, in fact, or shall be some day; so, pray, make yourself at home."

"I have seen Mr. Coe before," said Richard, frankly, and shaking that gentleman's unwilling hand; "and, though he took me for a bagman, I bear him no malice on that account."

"A bagman! Lor, Sol, what could you ha' been thinking about?" laughed Trevethick, grimly. "Why, this here gentleman has been stopping at Crompton with the Squire! But you mustn't mind Sol, Sir; his mind ain't free just now. Well, Harry, lass, why don't you get up and shake hands with the gentleman?"

"I have seen this young lady before, also," explained Richard. "It was she who was good enough to get me the key of the castle, which I have just returned, by-the-by, to your father," he added.

Harry gave him a look which showed him that his second pilgrimage up the rock was not unappreciated.

"Did you see the chapel, Sir, and the tombs?" inquired she.

"I hardly know, indeed," said Richard. "It was the climb itself that I enjoyed the most, and shall never forget as long as I live."

"Oh, but you must go properly over our ruins, young gentleman," said Trevethick, with the air of a proprietor. "My girl here, or Solomon, must show you them to-morrow, for they need a bit of explanation. Sol knows all about them. Don't you, Sol?"

"Oh yes; *I* know," answered Solomon, doggedly; "but nobody won't go up to the castle to-morrow, I reckon, with this sou'wester a-blowing."

"It is a wild night, indeed," said Richard, putting aside the curtain, and looking out through the shutterless window. "The clouds are driving by at a frightful speed."

"Ay, and it ain't only the clouds," said Trevethick, filling his pipe, and speaking with great gravity; "the Flying Dutchman was seen off the point not two hours ago."

"By old Madge, I suppose?" observed Solomon, derisively.

"Yes, by old Madge," retorted the landlord, sturdily. "She as knew our life-boat was lost last year with all hands long before she drove into Turlock Bay, bottom upward."

"But how was that?" inquired Richard, with interest.

"Well, Sir, it was this way," said Trevethick. "It was a stormy night, though not so bad a one as this is like to be, and the life-boat had gone out to a disabled Indiaman. She had been away three hours or more, when, as I was sitting in this very parlor, in came Madge, looking scared enough. She had been to Turlock on an errand for me. So, 'Sit down,' says I, 'and take a glass, for you look as though the wind had blown your wits away, old woman.' ''Tain't that, John Trevethick,' says she; 'but I'm near frightened to death. I've seen a sight as I shall never forget to my dying day. I have just seen our life-boat men—all nine of 'em. The Lord have mercy on their souls!' 'Well, why not?' says I. 'Why shouldn't you ha' seen 'em? They've got back sooner than we hoped for—that's all.' 'Nay,' said she; 'but I met 'em coming out of Gethin—away from home—the home they will never see again—all wet and white like corpses. They're drowned men, as sure as you stand there, John Trevethick.' And so it turned out, poor fellows!"

"And did you tell any body of this before you knew that they were drowned?" inquired Richard.

"Ay, that's the point," muttered Solomon, approvingly.

"No," said Trevethick. "I didn't believe the old woman, and I thought her story would be very ill taken; so I kept it to myself. But it turned out true for all that; the thing happened just as I say. John Trevethick ain't no liar."

"Of course you are stating what you believe to be the fact," said Richard, in a conciliating tone; "I don't doubt that."

"Just so; he's told it so often that he really does believe it," said Solomon, laughing. "But what seems curious is, that it is always Madge—a purblind old woman, as wants to be thought a witch—as sees these things—drowned sailors, and Flying Dutchmen, and so forth. I should like to know who else has ever had the chance?"

"Lots of folks," said the landlord, doggedly.

"Well, *you've* been here these forty years," said Solomon, "have *you* seen 'em? And Harry here has been at Gethin all her life, has *she* seen 'em?"

There was an awkward silence. Harry had turned very pale—in terror, as Richard thought, of the dispute between her father and Solomon becoming serious.

"That's naught to do with it," said Trevethick, sharply. "You're no Gethin man, Solomon, or you wouldn't talk so. Why, didn't Madge describe the very ship as was lost off Castle Rock, the night before we ever set eyes on her? and wasn't it printed in the paper?"

"In the next Saturday's paper: yes," replied Solomon, curtly.

"Nay, I heard the old woman with my own ears," said Harry, gravely. "There had been no wreck when she told me she had seen the schooner. 'The *Firefly*,' said she, 'will never come nearer home than Gethin Bay: you mark my words.' That was twelve hours, ay, and more, before she struck."

"Forgive me for interrupting," said Richard; "but I don't understand this matter. Is it supposed that a vessel announces her own destruction beforehand?"

"Sometimes," said Trevethick, gravely. "A ship is as well known here—if she belongs to this part of the coast—as a house is known in the Midlands. Well, if she's doomed, Madge—and it ain't only Madge neither—will see her days before she comes to her end. This *Firefly*, for example, belonged to Polwheel, and had been away for weeks."

"But still she was expected home?" interrogated Richard.

"Ay, that's it," said Solomon, once more nodding approval. "The old woman had that in her mind."

"Why so?" argued Trevethick. "What was the *Firefly* to her that she should think she saw her drive into the bay, and break to pieces against the rock out yonder? And why should she tell her vision to Harry?"

"That certainly seems strange, indeed," said Richard, "as showing she attached importance to the affair herself. It was a most curious coincidence, to say the least of it. But what is this Flying Dutchman, of which you also spoke? I did not know he ever came so far out of his proper latitude as this."

"He's seen before great storms, however," said Trevethick; "you ask the coast-guard men, and hear what *they* say. There's many a craft has put out to her from Gethin, and come quite close, so that a man might almost reach her with a boat-hook, and then, all of a sudden, there is nothing to be seen but the big waves."

John Trevethick had more to say to the same effect, to which Richard listened with attentive courtesy; while at the same time he held to the same skeptical view entertained by Solomon. Thus he won the good opinion of both men; and of that of the girl he felt already assured. He scarcely ever addressed himself to Harry, and as much as possible avoided gazing at her. If the idea of his paying any serious attention to her had ever been put into her father's mind, the intelligence that he had been the friend and guest of Carew's had been probably sufficient to dissipate it: the social position which that fact implied seemed to make it out of the question that he should be Harry's suitor. It only remained for him to disabuse Solomon of the same notion. This was at first no easy task; but the stubbornness with which his rival resisted his attempts at conciliation gave way by degrees, and at last vanished. To have been able to make common cause with him upon this question of local superstition was a great point gained. Solomon had a hard head, and prided himself upon his freedom from such weaknesses; and he hailed an ally in a battle-field on which he had contended at odds, five nights out of every seven, for years. Harry, as we have seen, shared her father's sentiments in the matter; and it was a great stroke of policy in Richard to have espoused the other side. He would, of course, have much preferred to agree with her—to have embraced any view which had the attraction of her advocacy; but it now gave him genuine pleasure to find his opposition exciting her to petulance.

She was not petulant with Solomon, but left her father to tilt with him after his own fashion.

From the superstitions of the coast they fought their way to those of the mines. Old Trevethick believed in "Knockers" and "Buccas," spirits who indicate the position of good lodes by blows with invisible picks; and, as these had more immediate connection with his own affairs than the nautical phenomena, he clung to his creed with even greater tenacity than before. So fierce was their contention that it was with difficulty that Richard could put in an inquiry as to whence these spirits came who thus interested themselves in the success of human ventures.

"I know nothing of that," said Trevethick, frankly, "any more than I know where that wind comes from that is shaking yonder pane; I only know that it is there."

"Nay, father, but *I* know," said Harry, with a little blush at her own erudition: "the Buccas are the ghosts of the old Jews who crucified our Lord, and were sent as slaves by the Roman emperor to work the Cornish mines."

"Very like," said Trevethick, approvingly, although probably without any clear conception of the historical picture thus presented to him. "It's the least they could do in the spirit, after having done so much mischief in the flesh."

The contradiction involved in this exemplary remark, combined with the absurdity of repentance taking the form of interest in mining speculations, was almost too much for Richard's sense of humor; but he only nodded with gravity, as became a man who was imbibing information, and inquired further, whether, in addition to these favorers of industry, there were any spirits who worked ill to miners.

"Well, I can't say as there are," said the landlord, with the air of a man who can afford to give a point in an argument; "but there's a many things not of this world that happen underground, leastway in *our* mines, for Sol there is from the north, and it mayn't be the same in those parts."

"It certainly is not," interrupted Solomon, taking his pipe out of his mouth to intensify the positiveness of his position.

"I say," continued Trevethick, reddening, "that down in Cornwall here there is scarce a mine without its spirit o' some sort. At Wheal Vor, for example, a man and his son were once blown to pieces while blasting; and, nothing being left of them but fragments of flesh, the engine-man put 'em into the furnace with his shovel; and now the pit is full of little black dogs. I've seen one of 'em myself."

Solomon laughed aloud.

Richard was expecting an explosion of wrath. The old man turned toward him quietly, and observed with tender gravity: "And in a certain mine, which Sol and I are both acquainted with, a white rabbit always shows itself before any accident which proves fatal to man. It was seen on the day that Sol's father sacrificed his life for mine." Then he told the story which Richard had already heard from Harry's lips, while Solomon smoked in silence, and Harry looked hard at the fire, as though—as Richard thought—to avoid meeting the glance of her father's hereditary benefactor.

"You are right to remember such a noble deed as long as you live," said Richard, when the old man had done. "My own life," added he, in a lower tone, "was once preserved by one whom I shall love and honor as long as I have breath."

He saw the color glow on the young girl's cheek, and the fire-light shine with a new brilliance in her eyes. Neither Trevethick nor Solomon had caught his observation; at the moment it was made the former was stretching out his great hand to the latter, moved by that memory of twenty years ago, and, perhaps, in token of forgiveness for his recent skepticism.

"Then there's the Dead Hand at Wheal Danes, father," observed Harry, in somewhat hasty resumption of the general subject. "That's as curious as any, and more terrible."

"Wheal Danes!" said Solomon. "Why, how comes that about, when nobody can never have been killed there? It's been disused ever since the Roman time, I thought?"

"Yes, yes; so it has," answered Trevethick, impatiently.

"But I thought you told me about it yourself, father?" persisted Harry. "How you saw the Thing, with a flame at the finger-tops, going up and down where the ladders used to be, and heard voices calling from the pit."

"Not I, wench—not I. That was only what was told me by other folks.—Take another glass of your own sherry before supper, Sir; and after that we will have a bowl of punch."

The hospitalities of Mr. Trevethick were, in fact, profuse, and his manner toward Richard most conciliatory.

"We'll be glad to see you, Sol and I, in our little parlor, whenever you feel in want of company," were his last words at parting for the night. And, "Ay, ay, that's so," had been Solomon's indorsement.

Harry had said nothing; but the tender pressure of his hand, when he wished her good-night, had not gone unreturned, and was an invitation more welcome than words. The events of the day, the conversation of the evening, had given him plenty of matter for reflection; but the touch of those soft fingers was more potent, and the dreams evoked by it swallowed up all soberer thoughts. He sat up for hours that night, picturing to himself a future altogether new to his imagination; and when he went to bed it was not to rest. His excited brain was fed with a nightmare vision. He thought that he was once more with Harry on the castled rock; his lips were pressed to hers; his arm was around her waist, just as they had been; but, instead of his slipping alone over the precipice, they fell together; and as they did so—not without a wild delight mingling with his despair—she was suddenly plucked away from him, and, as he sank headlong down, down, he saw that Solomon Coe had caught her in his arms, and, with her father, was looking down upon him with savage and relentless glee!

CHAPTER XV.

SOLOMON'S REMINISCENCES.

There are wild places yet in the world, and primitive folk. Even in England there are localities of which the phrase, "It is a hundred years behindhand," still holds good; and so it was with Gethin. Its wind-swept moors, its rock-bound coast, had inhabitants altogether differing from the men of fields and farms; to Richard, a man of pleasure from the town, they seemed a foreign race. They were rough in externals, but kindly and genial at heart; given to hospitality, and, though good at a bargain, by no means greedy of gain. Above all there were no beggars. The poorest Gethin man would open a gate for you, or walk a hundred yards out of his way to show you your road, without asking for, or even expecting, a coin. They were, however, as delighted as surprised to get it; and before the open-handed young artist had been a week in the place he had demoralized it by his largesses. As, however, his smile and his thanks always accompanied these presents, he was served more for love's sake than the money's, and enjoyed a popularity which can not be purchased, and which yet is impossible to be won by one who has nothing to give. He had the reputation among these simple folks, who knew how to be frugal themselves, of having a superfluity of wealth; his air and manner showed he had been always used to be lavish (as indeed he had), and nourished this delusion, which extended, though upon other grounds, to the tenants of the little inn.

John Trevethick and his friend Solomon would not have been much impressed with the expenditure of a few pounds by an improvident youth; but the former was well aware that the guests of Carew of Crompton were almost without exception very wealthy men, and he judged of Richard's social position accordingly. He had no idea that his landscape-painting was any thing else than an amusement—as it was practiced by half the young ladies and gentlemen who visited Gethin in the summer months; he took him for an amateur; and if he had seen his sketches, and been a judge of art, he would have been only fortified in his conclusion. He liked the young fellow upon his own account, though not so much as his handsome face and pleasant manners, combined with his desire to please, caused others to do; for Mr. Trevethick was not at all impressionable in such matters. Richard hated him in his heart for the scanty crop of regard he seemed to get out of him, notwithstanding all his pains; he had never made so continued an effort to make himself agreeable and with so small a result; but his self-love would have been more deeply wounded had he known that his own exertions would not have even gained him what they did, had they not been seconded by a hidden ally in the landlord's breast. Richard's desire to conciliate was fully reciprocated by Trevethick, who wished above all things to make friends with the friend of Parson Whymper; only conciliation was so much out of his line. The old man and the young had absolutely nothing in common except their love for Harry.

Upon the other hand, John Trevethick and Solomon Coe were cast almost in the same mould. Notwithstanding the former's superstition he was intelligent and shrewd enough in practical matters, and had, indeed, quite a genius for mechanics. Deprived of his underground occupation by the catastrophe with which we are acquainted, he had set his wits to work at home on the matters with which he had hitherto but physically concerned himself; and the labor of his head had proved more lucrative than that of his hand. He had invented several improvements in the working machinery of the mine which had so nearly proved his tomb; these had been adopted, with considerable profit to himself, in other places; and the money thus acquired he had not frittered away (as is usual in such cases) in speculative investments. In the interim between his giving up his trade and his reaping the fruits of his inventions he had tasted the bitterness of poverty, and that had made him very cautious. But he had a small share in Dunloppel, which seemed likely to turn out very profitable; and he had built the inn, the returns from which were more than sufficient to support him—indeed, it was rumored that John Trevethick had been laying by a pretty penny, and could hold his head much higher if he pleased. His pleasures were certainly not expensive, for they consisted in fancy iron-working, the results of which brought him in a considerable sum; and in occasionally getting drunk, which, being a publican, he could accomplish at the most reasonable figure. He was a hard unlovable man, and interesting only as statistics may be said to be as compared with literature—in a hard, practical way. If superstitious, he was by no means religious; and, though honest, he was grasping. He took time to resolve upon a matter; but, when once his resolution was fixed, his will was iron, and his heart was stone. It was certainly curious that one of Trevethick's character should have entertained so long and freshly his sentiment of gratitude even to a man that had saved his life at the expense of his own; but even this may have had its roots in egotism. Had the person saved been his wife or his daughter the feeling would not perhaps have been so enduring; and in carrying it out, as he fully purposed to do, by bestowing Harry's hand upon Solomon, he was certainly not uninfluenced by the fact that the latter was, pecuniarily speaking, an excellent match.

Like himself, his intended son-in-law was the architect of his own fortunes; but he had built them up in a different way. His youth had been spent in the coal-mines of the north; and, though no lucky stroke of the pick can there make one rich, as it can in other underground localities, his strength and skill had met with their full reward. And what he had gained he had not wasted. Pound after pound he had laid by, until enough had been saved for investment; and it was Solomon's boast in after-years that he had never got less than ten per cent. for any of it. It was all ventured on underground speculations, some of them hazardous enough—but all had prospered; and here John Trevethick's judgment, though the old man himself had not the courage to follow it, had been of great advantage to him. Every thing he touched turned, if not to gold, at least to tin or copper; and before the lode ceased to yield Solomon had sold his shares at a good premium, and placed the proceeds in another pit. He had sown, as it were, his money in the earth, and reaped a golden harvest. And now Dunloppel, his last venture, seemed likely to prove his best: and it was another strand in the strong bond between himself and Trevethick that the latter had also a share in that undertaking. There are some men with whom a common pecuniary interest is the most binding tie of sympathy of which their nature is capable; and never had the landlord of the *Gethin Castle* been more closely attached to his guest and son-in-law elect than at this time, when Richard Yorke proposed to himself to part them; as though a gilded summer skiff should thrust itself between two laden coal-barges, and bid them budge.

It was at least a week before Solomon Coe could be induced to open his lips before Richard, beyond the utterance of a few pithy sentences; not that the smouldering embers of jealousy had been fanned in the mean time—for Richard had been prudence itself in his behavior to Harry—but because the miner could not comprehend the young fellow, and therefore distrusted him. The light and airy manners, which were as natural to Richard as was John Trevethick's ponderous cunning or his own self-satisfied reticence, seemed to Solomon mere affectation, and even his appearance effeminate and dandified; but when he saw that he wore no other air when conversing with the pitmen of Dunloppel—an expedition undertaken with himself at Richard's special invitation—and marked how actively he climbed the tall, steep ladders, and how fearlessly he trusted himself to the rope, he acquitted him of such artful fopperies. Of Richard's intelligence he had formed a good opinion from the time when the latter had enlisted himself upon his side in the argument concerning superstition; and it flattered his vanity to find so sensible and accomplished a young fellow deferring to his opinion upon all practical points, and apparently desirous of obtaining his views upon them.

There was one subject, the experience of his early years, upon which Solomon was never averse to descant, could he once be got to talk at all; and it was a certain token—as one, at least, of the company well knew—that his prejudice against Richard was quite surmounted when Solomon began to unfold to him, over their punch in the bar parlor, the annals of his underground career. Often had he done so to Harry—like another Othello (and almost as swarthy) narrating his adventures to his Desdemona—but never had she been so pleased to listen as now, when she needed but to seem to hear, and, without the penalty of reply, could feed her eyes upon young Richard's listening face. It is hard when, in the race for woman's favor, one has to waste one's breath in making the running for one's rival.

And yet the talk of Solomon Coe was well worth listening to. He told of the great war which is always being waged by man beneath the earth against the powers of Water, and Fire, and Foul Air, and of the daring deeds he had seen wrought against them. He told of coal-pits that had been on fire from time immemorial, above which no snow would lie, by reason of the heat beneath, and where the grass of the meadows was always green. He told of others which had been suddenly inundated by a neighboring river, or by the waters from old workings, let in by a single unlucky blow, whereby scores and scores of strong men were overwhelmed, whose corpses floated about for months in the dark drowned pit before their fellows above-ground could get at them.

His speech was somewhat sullen and hesitating, and what he said was interrupted by whiffs of smoke and sips of liquor; but the nature of the subject was so absorbing that it needed no gifts of eloquence. It interested Richard in spite of himself; and Solomon was not indifferent to the flattery which the young artist's attention conveyed, and scarcely needed the entreaties of Trevethick to persuade him to throw off his native reticence. What he forgot, and had mentioned in former narrations, the landlord supplemented; and when "Sol" became technical and obscure the other performed the part of chorus or explainer. If the former had been some gifted animal, and the latter its proprietor, he could not have taken a greater pride in the exhibition of its talent than did the landlord in these narrations. Now he would look at Richard, and nod and wink, as though to bespeak his special attention to what was coming; and now he would wave his pipe, like a dumb orchestra playing slow music, to express the tremendous nature of a situation. Perhaps he was genuinely impressed by these thrice-told tales—perhaps he was endeavoring, by a feigned admiration for Sol's experiences and exploits, to justify his choice of a son-in-law not altogether suited to his Harry. To do the *raconteur* justice, he was by no means so egotistic as his aider and abettor, and Trevethick would express his regrets to Richard that it was so hard to get Sol to dismiss generalities and talk about himself. "It's on account of Harry being here, you see," explained he behind his horny hand, but in a tone perfectly audible to the other tenants of the bar parlor; "or else he would tell you how the timbering of the pit once fell upon him, so as nothing was free but his head and his left hand; and yet he never lost his wits in all his agony, but told the men where to saw and what to do; but he don't like to boast before the 'gal.'"

Then Richard, taking the hint, inquired of Solomon whether any incident particularly striking had ever happened to himself during his underground experience; and Solomon replied, with affected carelessness; "No, not as I know on; nothing particular."

Then Trevethick broke in with, "What! not when you was shut up in the seam at Dunston?"

"Oh yes, to be sure," said Sol, as though the recollection of the circumstance had only just occurred to him; "there was *that*, certainly; but it was when I was quite a boy. I was not quite seventeen when Dunston Colliery was drowned. The Gatton poured right in upon it, and they have not got the water out of it in places to this day. It was always said that the pit was being worked too near the river; but that was little thought about by those as was most concerned, and it never disturbed the head of a lad like me, of course. It was in the afternoon of the 12th of December, a date as I am not likely to forget, when the thing happened. Two mates—one old man and a middle-aged one—and myself were at work in a heading together, when suddenly we heard a noise like thunder. 'That's never blasting,' says one. 'The Lord have mercy on us,' cries the other; 'it's the river come in at last!' For, as I say, the risk was quite well known, though it was considered small, and made a frequent jest of. Nothing that ever I heard was equal to that noise; the waves in Gethin caverns here, during storm, are a whisper to it; the whole pit seemed to be roaring in upon us. We all ran up the gallery, which, fortunately for us, had a great slope, and crouched down at the end of it. We heard the water pouring in and filling all the workings beneath us, and then pouring in and filling ours. It reached our feet, and left us but a very limited space, in which the air was compressed, when the noise of the inundation ceased. There was a singing in our ears, so that we could scarcely hear one another speak. We knew that the whole mine had become a lake by that time, and that it would take months to drain her, if she was ever drained. We knew that we were buried alive hundreds of feet beneath the earth; and yet we did not quite lose heart. There was this gleam of hope: supposing that the next gallery, which was on a higher level than our own, was not also flooded, we could be got at through the seam. We did not know the fact that it was more than sixty feet of solid coal, and would have taken under ordinary circumstances at least four weeks to dig through; we only knew that, if a door of escape was to open any where, it must open there. We kept tapping with the heels of our boots at equal intervals against this wall."

"The miner's signal," explained the landlord, with a wave of his pipe.

"We felt that if we were once heard, and if hard work could do it, that our mates would save us yet; and we encouraged one another as well as we could. But presently the oil in our lamps gave out, and we were left in darkness; and then our hope grew faint indeed. We had knocked for four-and-twenty hours unintermittingly without any reply. We did not cease, however, to discuss the possibilities of escape. We knew that all was being done for us aboveground that could be done; that the surveys of the mine were well executed; and that it was known exactly where we were, if we were alive at all. There were more than a hundred men employed in the lower workings, and it was a certainty that not one of them could have escaped death; the attention, therefore, of the engineers would be concentrated upon those parts of the mine that might possibly be left above water.

"On the second night of our imprisonment we heard a distinct reply to our signal; the old man who was of our company began to weep for joy, though he was doomed, as it turned out, poor soul! never to see the light. 'We shall be saved,' he said; 'do not fear.' We knocked again, and again the reply was heard—they had found us out, and would never relax their efforts to save us. 'God bless them!' said we all. We laid our ears close to the rock, and presently heard the strokes of the pick, but not very distinctly. When the other said he was afraid the rock was thick, the old man cried out: 'No, it was not that; it was because we were dull of hearing.' The fact was, that the seam was not only thick, but very hard. It was strange, indeed, though sounds are easily transmitted through rocks of considerable thickness, how our feeble taps had been heard at all. Day after day, and each day a black night, went on; every hour was to be the last of our captivity, according to the old man; as for me, I was almost worn out, and heavy with sleep, but he was in constant motion, knocking and listening. Then suddenly we heard a splash in the water beneath us—he had lost his balance, slid down the inclined plane, and been drowned. He never stirred a limb nor uttered a cry. His fate discouraged and alarmed us two survivors exceedingly. If help was coming, we now felt it would never come in time. We dug into the shale with the handles of our lamps and with our fingers, to make our position more secure. We did not venture to speak of our late companion's fate to one another. Horror overwhelmed us, so enfeebled had we become through famine and fatigue. We had devoured our leather belts, and even crumbled the rotten wood of the timber-props in water, and eaten that; but we were now consumed by thirst, which we dared no longer quench. We were afraid to venture down as before for the water in which the old man had sunk to death; and it was that which had kept us alive."

"Don't forget about how you made a bucket of your boots, Sol," suggested Trevethick, gravely.

"Yes, at last we tied a string to a boot, and got the water up that way," continued Solomon; "but our stomachs turned against it."

"It was not so good as my punch," observed the landlord, parenthetically, and emptying his steaming glass.

"More dark days came and went, though, of course, we could not tell how many; then, all of a sudden, we heard a human voice, inquiring: 'How many are you?' 'We are three,' was our reply. We had not the courage even then to own that one of us had already been taken; death seemed still so near to us. The aperture which had thus let in the world upon us was also very small."

"And what was it you asked for first?" interrupted the landlord, with a nod at Richard, as much as to say: "Listen now; this is curious."

"What we wanted was light. 'Light above all things!' was our cry. But our deliverers could give us but little of that, for they had scarcely any themselves. They had been working in a narrow gallery, by means of five inclined driftways, at each of which only one man could ply his pick at a time, and where light and air could only be procured artificially. The coal was carried out in baskets as fast as it was hewn out: the atmosphere in which they thus toiled like giants, naked to the waist, was almost suffocating; yet, under these conditions, they had literally effected in four days, to save our lives, what it would have taken them four weeks to do, had they been working by the piece for wages. They had even been compelled to put up ventilators, and their lamps would only burn when close to these. They gave us broth through a tin pipe; but almost another day elapsed before the hole was large enough for them to carry us through it in their arms."

"And there was nobody else saved, was there?" inquired the landlord, with a triumphant look.

"There was not," said Solomon, expressing his tobacco smoke very slowly. "Out of a hundred and thirteen men who had been caught by the flood in Dunston, we two were the sole survivors."

Many other stories of the like sort had Solomon to tell, and for not one of them was he indebted to his imagination. His experience of life had been remarkable, and it had impressed itself upon his character. His will was as strong as that of Trevethick, but he had less of caution;

and he was at the same time both plodding and audacious.

It would not be well, thought Richard occasionally, to have either of these men for an enemy; and he was right. Unhappily, it was impossible to win Harry without a quarrel with, at least, one of them, and rather than lose her he was prepared to defy them both. If he could but have lifted a corner of the curtain that veils the future—well, even then, so mad was he by this time with the love of her, that he would almost have defied them still.

CHAPTER XVI.

SPRING-TIDE.

There is a beauty in woman that takes the stranger, and another the changeful charm of which wins its way deeper and deeper daily into the heart of man; but in the person of Harry Trevethick these two beauties were combined. Richard thought he had never seen any face half so fair as that which shone upon him through the mist on the first day when he came to Gethin; and when he had dwelt there for weeks he was of the same opinion still. Harry was innocent, tender-hearted, and gay, and so far the expression of her features told you truth; but it also told you more than that, which you must needs believe, though it was not the fact. Her face was not the index of her mind in all respects; it was rather like the exquisite and costly dial-plate of a time-piece the works of which are indifferent. Her air was spiritual; her voice thrilled your being with its sweet tone; her eyes were full of earnest tenderness; but she was weak of purpose, vacillating rather than impulsive, credulous, and given (not from choice, but fear) to dissimulation. That last fault Richard willingly forgave her, since it worked to his advantage; and to the others he would have been more than human had he not been blind. For Harry loved him. She had never said so; he had never asked her to say so; but it was taken for granted on both sides. They were thrown much together, for Dunloppel—a treasure-house, which proved richer and richer the more it yielded—monopolized the attention of both Trevethick and Solomon; they were in high good-humor, and not at all disposed for quarrel or suspicion. Harry had always been the mistress of her own movements, and she went, as usual, whither she liked, and Richard went with her.

The spring was advancing, and brought its soft hues even to the barren moors of Gethin, and bathed its gray rocks in sunshine. There was much to see that was worth seeing, and who so fit as Harry to point out these objects of attraction with which she had been familiar from her childhood? They strolled along the beach to Polwheel, and she showed him how the harbor there had been silted up through the wrath of the mermaids, or "merry maids," as she called them, still (under favorable circumstances) sometimes seen sitting on the slate cliff ledges beneath the clear blue sea. Far from ridiculing her superstitions, he led her on to talk of them; he did not much mind what she talked about so long as he could look at her and listen.

"But why were the Polwheel mermaids so cruel, Harry? I always imagine them bright and beautiful beings, with golden hair almost as long as yours, and with nothing to do but to comb it."

"That is so, when they are let alone," said Harry, simply; "but even the weakest creatures love revenge, and will get it if they can."

"And quite right too," interrupted Richard; "but for fear of that the strong would be more uncivil even than they are."

"Well, a mermaid was once cruelly treated by a Polwheel man—he fell in love with her, and deserted her—and then her sisters choked up the harbor bar."

"But how did he come to court the mermaid? That must have been difficult; though, if I saw you sitting under water yonder, I should certainly dive, and try."

"You would have no breath to make me pretty speeches then," said Harry, demurely. "This mermaid was, however, a changed child. A Polwheel woman was bathing her infant in the pool yonder beneath that arched rock, when it suddenly gave a cry of joy, and leaped from her arms into the sea. She thought it was drowned, but it came up the next instant more beautiful and bright than ever. She did not herself know but that it was her own child, but there were old folks in the town who knew that it was in reality a mermaid's changeling. She grew up to be a lovely woman, and the Squire of Polwheel at that time—for his race has died out since—fell in love with her; he treated her very ill, and she died broken-hearted, at Gethin, and was buried in our church-yard, where I can show you the tomb."

"And did no punishment overtake the scoundrel Squire?"

"Yes. After a great revel one night, he was returning home by the sands, and in the moonlight beheld a beautiful lady sitting by this same pool. She was so like his dead love to look at that he was frightened at first, but she smiled and beckoned to him, and then, clasping him in her arms, leaped into the sea, and drowned him; and in the storm that arose that night the merry maids filled up the harbor."

"That was hard upon Polwheel," observed Richard, "though the Squire only got what he deserved. He must have been a bad lot."

"But the mermaid was very foolish to believe him," added Harry—"very."

They visited the Fairy Bower, did these young people—the only spot about Gethin where trees grew; a beautiful ravine, with a fall of water, and a caverned cell beside it, where a solitary hermit was said to have dwelt. Notwithstanding which celibate association, it had a wishing-well besides, into which a maiden had but to drop a pin, and wish her wish, and straightway the face of her future husband was mirrored in the water. Through its clear depths you might see the bottom of the pool quite paved with pins.

"And does the charm always work?" asked Richard, laughing. "Try it to-day."

"No, no," answered Harry, gravely; "one must be quite alone for that, and beneath the moonlight."

On Morven Point, a grand old promontory, which pushed out many a yard to meet the encroaching waves, and battled with them long before they reached the main land, they sat and watched the sunsets; looked down upon the busy hive of men that worked upon the slate quarry beneath, or gazed upon the ships that tacked and wore to make Turlock Haven. There was a tower on this place, half ruined and with broken steps, up which they climbed together on one occasion, and stood supporting one another upon its dizzy top. There lay around them a splendid prospect of sea and land, but they were looking into one another's eyes, and yet they did not speak of that which was nearest to their hearts. It was a topic to be avoided as long as possible. They only enjoyed these blissful opportunities—they had only been permitted to thus stroll out together alone and unsuspected—upon the tacit understanding that no such thing as love could exist between them. If Harry had not plighted faith to Solomon, her engagement to him tacitly existed nevertheless, and it was under its ægis alone that they had been protected and indulged. It was a part of the character of the young girl to persuade herself that she was doing no harm so long as it was possible to entertain that delusion; and it was all one to Richard what their love was called so long as it *was* love. Else, as they stood alone together in the noonday stillness, his arm around her waist, as it had not been since that first afternoon upon the castled rock, he must needs have told her why the heart that pressed so close against her side was beating high. Just then, however, he dared not. Suppose that, by any possibility, he had mistaken her sentiments; suppose, that is, an extorted promise, or fear of her father's anger, or what not, should compel her to deny his suit, and cleave to Solomon; suppose even that her simplicity was such—and it was in some things marvelously great—that she had accepted his affection as that of a brother—a friend of her father's and of "Sol's"—but no; he felt certain that she loved him; suppose, at all events, for whatever reason, she was once again to reprove him for yielding to the temptation of her lips, he felt that such a rebuke must of necessity finish all. She could not forgive him twice, unless she gave him license to offend forever. He dared not, therefore, speak directly of that which both were thinking of; and yet he could not altogether ignore so sweet a subject.

"That is the moor yonder, Harry, over which I first came to Gethin—how long ago!"

"Has the time, then, hung so very heavy on your hands?" asked she, seriously.

"No, Harry, no; on the contrary, I have never been so happy; but when one has a new experience, however charming it may be, it seems to dwindle down one's past to nothing. I have had two lifetimes, as it seems to me—one elsewhere, and one here; and yet it is but six weeks since I met you first, Harry, out yonder, gleaming like a sunbeam through the fog."

"I remember it well," said Harry, with a slight shiver.

"But not to sigh about it, dear, I trust? You are not afraid of me *now*, as you were then? Do you recollect how scared you were when I called you back that day?"

"Yes, well," answered the young girl, earnestly. "I had a reason for being scared, though you would laugh at me if I told you what it was."

"Do I ever laugh at you, Harry, when you would have me serious?" asked Richard, reproachfully. "Come, tell me why you shrank from me—as you can not to-day, dear, for, see, I have got you close—and why your large eyes looked so wild and strange that I half thought you mad? Did you take me for a ghost?"

"No; but I had just seen what is far worse than any ghost. Did you not mark how pale I got that same night? I thought I should have fainted when I was asked" (it was Solomon who had put the question, but Solomon's name was never mentioned between these two young people) "if I had ever seen a spectre ship. I had seen one that very day—only a few minutes before I met *you*—and on this very cliff."

"Well, and what then?" said Richard, smiling. "Neither your father, nor any one in whom you have an interest, goes to sea. The Flying Dutchman did not concern you, I reckon, even if he did pay you a call."

"You do not understand," said Harry, seriously; "it was not that at all. But when the mists rise over Turlock sands, as they did that day, a black, square-rigged vessel glides across them, which bodes ill to those who see her; and *I* saw her as plain as I see *you*."

"But not so near," said Richard, fondly.

"She was coming from Turlock to the quarry yonder—"

"To fetch slates," interrupted the other—"nothing more likely."

"Nay, not she; no craft would have attempted that in such weather; and, besides, there was not a soul on board of her. She was sailing against what little wind there was, and against the tide."

"But even if this was so, Harry, what of it? What harm has come of it?"

"Nothing as yet; nor was I greatly frightened at the time. That omen bodes unhappiness to him or her who sees it, and I was already unhappy."

"Because I was not here to comfort you, Harry. Well, that is remedied."

She shook her head, and did not return the reassuring pressure of his hand. "Listen!" she said. "This misery comes through the person whom he who has seen the vision shall next meet; and I thought I knew who I should meet on my way home—one from whom"—she sank her voice to a whisper—"I already expected misery."

"You mean—" began Richard, eagerly.

"No matter whom I mean. It was not he who met me; that was *you*."

The hand which he held in his was cold as ice; her face was pale; and her limbs trembled under her.

"This is folly, Harry dear. Am I likely to do you harm, to make you miserable?"

"I do not know," said she. "I sometimes think you are."

He put the long hair back from her forehead, and gazed into her eyes, which were now fast filling with tears. "I love you, Harry, with all my heart," sighed he—"you know I do. And, though you are sometimes cold, and at others seem as though you purposely avoided me, I think you love *me*—just a little—too. Better, at all events, than the man with whom you yourself have just confessed you expect nothing but misery."

"Hush, hush!" moaned she. "If I said that, it was very wrong."

"It was the truth, Harry. How could it be otherwise? He is not a lover meet for such as you; he is twice your age, and rough and rude of speech even as a suitor. Do you think he will be more tender when he is a husband? He is no mate for you, Harry, nor you for him."

Again she shook her head, with a slow mournful movement, as though less in dissent from his statement than in despair of remedy.

"What!" cried he, "because his father was your father's friend, does that give him the right to be your husband?"

The young girl answered only with her sobs.

"Now tell me, darling—did you ever promise to be this man's wife in words?"

"Yes—no—I am not sure. Oh yes, I must be his; my father has set his mind upon it. Nay, do not smile at that; you don't know what my father is. He is not one to cross;" and, as if at the very thought of her stern parent's wrath, she lifted up her head from Richard's breast, and looked around in fear.

"But suppose I win him to my side, sweet Harry?"

"That you could never do," sighed she. "I tell you you don't know him."

"Nay; but I think I do, dear; and, if I could show him that it was to his own advantage to have me for his son-in-law, in place of—"

"You would not persuade him," interrupted the young girl, firmly—"not even if you were Carew of Crompton's heir."

The words she had used were meant to express exhaustless wealth—for with such was the owner of Gethin still credited in that far-away corner of his possession—but they startled and offended Richard. "I may not be Carew's heir," said he, haughtily; "but I have some power at Crompton, and I can exert it in your father's favor."

Harry shook her head. "He wants for nothing," she said, "that you can give him. He is wealthier than you imagine. He has two thousand pounds in notes, for which he has no use; they lie in the strong-box in my room. But there, I promised not to speak of that."

"I am not a burglar in disguise," said Richard, smiling, "and would make your father richer rather than rob him. But why should he keep so large a sum by him?"

"I do not know; but there it *is*, locked with a letter padlock which he made himself. No human being can open it, he says, who does not know the secret."

Richard was silent. Something else than love was occupying his thoughts, though his fingers were making marriage rings for themselves of Harry's golden hair. It is like entertaining angels unawares to find after one has fallen in love that it is with an heiress.

"Dear Harry," said he at last, "I think I shall take you from your father's willing hands; I have good hope of it, and better since I have heard you so despairing; but, at all events, you will be mine. Let me hear those sweet lips say so. Promise me, promise me, my darling, that you will be my wife."

He caught and clasped her close, and she did not repulse him.

"I dare not, Richard—I dare not promise you," she murmured.

"But if your father gives me leave?" whispered he, his lips to her warm cheek.

She uttered a soft cry of passionate joy that told him more than a hundred phrases of assent how dear he was to her, and hid her face upon his breast.

Oh happy hour, so bright, and yet so brief! Oh golden noon, already on the verge of eve and blackest night!

How often in the after-time did that fair and sunny scene recur to them, a bitter memory; how often was that first kiss of love renewed by cruel fancy and in mocking dreams, its sweetness changed to gall!

Better for one—better, perhaps, for both—if, clasped in one another's arms, they had fallen from that tall tower's top, and then and there had ended life and love together!

CHAPTER XVII.

WORKING ON A PIVOT.

Never had Richard been in such high spirits as on the evening of that day on which Harry had made confession to him of her love, and had promised to be his wife should her father's consent be gained. It was true that she had been far from sanguine upon the latter point; but Richard had his reasons for being of a different opinion. It would be better, every way, if he could obtain Trevethick's good-will; not that he at all shared in the girl's dread of his anger, but because it really seemed that if he married her from her father's roof he should be fulfilling his mother's injunctions in making alliance with an heiress. What with his two thousand pounds in gold, and his inn, and his lucky mine, it was plain that the old man would have no despicable sum to leave behind him; and yet, to do Richard justice, this only formed an additional incentive to a project upon which, at all events, he had long set his heart. He had resolved at all hazards to make the girl his wife. His love for her was as deep as it was passionate; and now that he was assured from her own lips of its being returned, his heart was filled with joy, and spoke out of its abundance. It had been hitherto his habit in that family circle round the bar-parlor fire to play the part of listener rather than of talker. He had mainly confined himself to the exhibition of an attentive interest in Solomon's stories, or in his host's sagacious observations with respect to the investment of capital, such as: "One couldn't be too cautious where one put one's money;" and, "Where the interest was high the risk was great, and where it was low it was not worth while to let it leave one's hand." Next to the subject of local superstition, "investment" was the favorite subject of debate between Trevethick and "Sol;" and Richard, whose ignorance insured his impartiality, had been the judicious scale-holder between them. But upon the present occasion it was the young artist who led the talk and chose the matter. He told them of the splendors of Crompton and of the marvelous prodigality of its owner, and they listened with greedy ears. To vulgar natures, the topic of mere wealth is ever an attractive one, and in the present instance there was an additional whet to appetite in the connection of Carew with Gethin. He was naturally an object of curiosity to his tenant Trevethick, and never before had the old man had the opportunity of hearing at first hand of the eccentricities of the Squire. In relating them Richard took good care to show by implication on what intimate terms he stood with him, and hinted at the obligation under which he had put him by throwing his park gate open so opportunely. The impression which he left upon his audience, and desired to leave, was, that Carew was indebted to him for having saved his life.

"Then it is likely the Squire would do any thing for you that you chose to ask him?" observed Trevethick, with the thought of his own debt to Solomon's father doubtless in his mind.

"Well, he certainly ought to do so," answered Richard, carelessly; "but, on the other hand, it is not very probable that I shall put him to the test."

"Just so," returned Trevethick, sucking at his pipe; "you're independent of the likes of him."

"Altogether," was Richard's reply.

The old man spoke no more, but sat in a cloud of smoke and thought for the rest of the evening. Even when "Sol" rose up to go—Harry having retired long since, for they kept very early hours at the *Gethin Castle*—the landlord did not, as usual, accompany him, but mixed himself another glass of his favorite liquor. As for Richard, it was not his custom to seek his bed until after midnight; so Trevethick and he were left to one another's company. It was an opportunity to which the latter had been looking forward for many a day, but which he had never desired so keenly as at that moment.

"Are you likely to be at Crompton soon again?" inquired the landlord, pursuing the subject of the evening's talk.

"I have no intention of going there at present," returned Richard. "The fact is, Mr. Trevethick, between ourselves, I am but a poor man in comparison with many of those I meet there, and their ways and habits are too expensive for me."

"Ay! gambling and such like, I suppose?" observed the landlord, cunningly. "It is 'Light come light go' with the money of that sort of folk, I reckon."

"Just so; and though my money comes light enough—that is, I have not to earn it, since my mother makes me an allowance—I don't choose to risk it at the card-table."

"Quite right, quite right, young gentleman," answered the other, approvingly. "But there are some prudent gentry even at Crompton, I suppose. Parson Whymper, for instance, he don't gamble, do he?"

"Certainly not; he is much too sagacious a man, even if he were rich enough, to play; but for him, indeed, some say the Squire would have come to the end of his tether before this. He manages every thing at Crompton, as you know."

"And yet Carew don't want money?" said the landlord, musing.

"Well, I have been his guest," returned Richard, smiling; "and it is scarcely fair of me to speak of his embarrassments. He does not certainly want it so much but that he can still afford to indulge his whims, Mr. Trevethick, if *that's* what you mean."

"That's just what I *did* mean," said the old man, frankly. "Six months ago or so I made a certain proposition to the Squire, which would have been exceedingly to his advantage to accept—"

"And not to yours?" interrupted Richard, slyly.

"Nay, I don't say that, Sir," answered the other. "But it was one that he ought to have been glad to accept in any case, and which it was downright madness in him to refuse, if he wanted cash. It was a chance, too, I will venture to say, that will never offer itself from any other quarter. Mr. Whymper acknowledged that himself."

"I know all about the matter, Mr. Trevethick: the Squire behaved like the dog in the manger to you. He won't work the mine himself, nor yet let you work it."

"For mercy's sake, be quiet!" cried the landlord, earnestly, and looking cautiously about him. "If you know all about it, you need not let others know. What mine are you talking about? Give it a name—but speak it under your breath, man." The old man leaned forward with a white moist face, and peered into Richard's eyes as though he would read his soul.

"Wheal Danes was the name of the place, if I remember right," said Richard. "Carew has a notion that the Romans did not use it up, and that it only wants capital to make it a paying concern. It is one of his mad ideas, doubtless."

Mr. John Trevethick was not by nature a quick appreciator of sarcasm, but he could not misunderstand the irony expressed in Richard's words.

"And is *that* what you came down to Gethin about?" inquired he, with a sort of grim despair, which had nevertheless a comical effect.

Richard could only trust himself to nod his head assentingly.

"Well," cried the other, striking the table with his fist, "if I didn't think you was as deep as the devil the very first day that I set eyes on you! So you are Parson Whymper's man, are you?" And here, in default of language to express his sense of the deception that, as he supposed, had been practiced on him, Mr. Trevethick uttered an execration terrible enough for a Cornish giant.

"I am not Mr. Whymper's man at all," observed Richard, coolly. "Mr. Whymper is *my* man—or at least he will be one day or another."

"How so?" inquired the landlord, his eyes at their full stretch, his mouth agape, and his neglected pipe in his right hand. "Who, in the Fiend's name, *are* you?"

"I am the only son and heir of Carew of Crompton," answered the young man, deliberately.

"You? Why, Carew never had a son," exclaimed Trevethick, incredulously; "leastways, not a lawful one. He was married once to a wench of the name of Hardcastle, 'tis true; but that was put aside."

"I tell you I am Carew's lawful son, nevertheless," persisted Richard. "My mother was privately married to him. Ask Parson Whymper, and he will tell you the same. It is true that my father has not acknowledged me, but I shall have my rights some day—and Wheal Danes along with the rest."

The news of the young man's paternity must have been sufficiently startling to him who thus received it for the first time, and would, under any other circumstances, have doubtless excited his phlegmatic nature to the utmost; but what concerns ourselves in even a slight degree is, with some of us, more absorbing than the most vital interests of another; and thus it was with Trevethick. The ambitious pretensions of his lodger sank into insignificance—notwithstanding that, for the moment, he believed in them; for how, unless he was what he professed to be, could he know so much?—before the disappointment which had befallen himself in the overthrow of a long-cherished scheme.

"Why, Mr. Whymper wrote me with his own hand," growled he, "that in his judgment the mine was worthless, and that he had done all he could to persuade the Squire to sell. And yet you come down here to gauge and spy."

"All stratagems are fair in war and business," answered the young man, smiling. "Come, Mr. Trevethick; whatever reasons may have brought me here, I assure you, upon my honor, that they do not weigh with me now, in comparison with the great regard I feel for you and yours. If you will be frank with me, I will also be so with you; and let me say this at the outset, that nothing which may drop from your lips shall be made use of to prejudice your interests. I have gathered this much for myself, that Wheal—"

"Hush, Sir! for any sake, hush!" implored the landlord, earnestly, and holding up his huge hand for silence. "Do not give it a name again; there is some one moving above stairs."

"It is only Solomon," observed Richard, quietly.

"I don't want Sol nor any other man alive to hear what we are talking about, Mr. Yorke," answered Trevethick, hoarsely. "You have gathered for yourself, you were about to say, that the mine is rich, and well worth what I have offered for it."

"And a good deal more," interrupted Richard. "Perhaps a hundred times, perhaps a thousand times as much. We don't make so close a secret of a matter without our reasons. We don't see Dead Hands, with flames of fire at the finger-tips, going up and down ladders that don't exist, without the most excellent reasons, Mr. Trevethick. What we wish no eye to see, nay, no ear to hear spoken of, is probably a subject of considerable private importance to ourselves. Come, we are friends here together; I say again, let us be frank."

Trevethick was silent for a little; he felt a lump rise in his throat, as though nature itself forbade him to disclose the secret he had kept so long and so jealously guarded. "I have known it for these fifty years," he began, in a half-choking voice. "I found it out as a mere lad, when I went down into the old mine one day for sport, with some schoolmates. The vein lies in the lowest part of the old workings, at a depth that we think nothing of nowadays, though it was too deep for the old masters of the pit. I remember, as though it was yesterday, how my heart leaped within me when my torch shone upon it, and how I fled away, lest my schoolfellows should see it also. I came back the next day alone, to certify my great discovery. It is a good vein, if ever there was one. The copper there may be worth tens of thousands, hundreds of thousands, millions!" Never had the numeration table been invested with such significance. Trevethick's giant frame shook with emotion; his eyes literally glared with greed.

"You have been there since?" observed Richard, interrogatively.

"Often, often," answered the other, hoarsely; "I could not keep away. But nobody else has been there. The place is dark and perilous; there are rats, and bats, and eerie creatures all about it. And folks are afraid, because of the Dead Hand and the Flame."

"*Your* hand and torch?"

"Yes. I did my best to keep the place my own; my thoughts were never absent from it for a day. And when I had earned a little money I put it by, and more to that, and more to that again, till I had got enough to make a bid for the lease of the old mine. But Carew was under age; so that fell through. I bided my time, and bid again; not much—not enough, as I fondly thought, to excite suspicion—but still what would seem a good price for a disused pit. Then I bid more and more; but Carew will neither sell nor let; and my money grows and grows in vain. I tell you I have laid by a fortune only to pour into his hand. It is ready for him to-night; there would be no haggling, no asking for time—it would be paid him in hard cash. How long, thought I, will this madman balk me with his whim? He will die some day in his cups, or break his neck in hunting, and I shall surely come in with my offer to his heir, and have my way at last, and win my prize. But now, after all my patience and my pains, I am overmatched by a Parson and a Boy." He spoke with uncommon heat and passion—not complainingly. His face was dark, and his tone violent, and even menacing. There was no mistake about his having accepted his companion's invitation to be frank.

"Mr. Trevethick," said Richard, gravely, "your disappointment would be natural enough, if your long-cherished plan had really failed; but you have misunderstood me altogether. I am grateful to you for confiding to me the whole of what I had already guessed in part; and you shall have no reason to repent your confidence. Your secret is safer now than it has ever been; for from my lips Mr. Whymper shall never have his suspicions with respect to Wheal Danes confirmed. I have been too long your guest, I feel myself too much the friend of you and yours, to act in any way to your disadvantage."

Trevethick looked at him inquiringly, suspicion and disfavor glowing in his dusky face. "But if your story is true, young gentleman, this mine will be your own some day?"

"It may, or it may not be, Mr. Trevethick. My father's intentions are not to be counted upon, as you must be well aware, for twenty-four hours. But if ever Wheal Danes is mine—" Richard hesitated a moment, while the landlord devoured him with his eyes.

"Well," cried he, impatiently, "what then?"

"I am willing to make over to you, as soon as I come of age, by deed, all interest that I may have in it—on one condition."

"Make over Wheal Danes to me by deed! What! at my own price?"

"For nothing; you shall have it for a free gift."

"But the condition? What is it that you want of me that is not money?"

"I want permission from you, Mr. Trevethick, to wed, that is—for I would not speak of love without your leave—to woo your daughter."

"To wed my daughter!" cried Trevethick, starting from his seat; "my Harry!"

"I say provided that my suit is not displeasing to her," answered Richard, not without a tremor in his voice, for the old man's face was terrible to look upon. Hatred and Wrath were struggling there with Avarice, and had the upper hand.

He rocked himself to and fro, then answered, in a stifled voice, "My daughter's hand is already promised, young man."

"It may be so, Mr. Trevethick, but not by her, I think; and that her heart has not been given to the man you have designed for her is certain. You may see that for yourself."

"I tell you I have passed my word to Solomon Coe that she shall be his wife," returned the other, gloomily, "and I am not one to go back from a bargain."

"One can only promise what is in one's power," urged Richard; "your daughter's heart is not yours to give. In backing this man's suit you have already redeemed your word to him. If he has failed to win her affections—and I think he has—let me try my chance. I am a fitter match for her in years; I am a gentleman, and therefore fitter for her, for she is a true lady. I love her a thousand times as much as he. As for Wheal Danes, I would give you twenty such, if I had them, for the leave I ask for, and the end I hope for."

It was curious to mark how the mere mention of the mine by name affected the old man; his wrath, which seemed on the very point of explosion, was checked and smoothed at once, like raging waves by oil; his brow, indeed, was still dark and frowning, but he resumed his seat, and listened, or seemed to listen, to Richard's impassioned pleading. His genuine feeling made the young fellow eloquent, and gave a tender charm to his always handsome face and winning tones.

Perhaps even the unsympathetic Trevethick was really somewhat touched; at all events, he did not interrupt him, but when he had quite finished took out his watch, and said, in a softened tone: "The hour is late, Mr. Yorke, and you have given me much to think about, to which I can not reply just now. Your communication has taken me altogether by surprise. I will answer neither 'Yes' nor 'No' at present. Good-night, Sir." He nodded, which was his usual salute at parting; but upon the young man's eagerly stretching out his hand, he took it readily enough, and gave it such a squeeze with his giant fingers as made Richard wince. Then, smiling grimly, he retired.

As his heavy step toiled up stairs Richard perceived a slip of paper on the floor, which had apparently fluttered out of the old man's watch-case. Upon it were written the three letters, B, N, Z. As he held it in his hand he heard the landlord's tread returning with unusual haste, and had only just time to replace the paper, face downward, on the sanded floor, before the other reappeared.

"I have dropped a memorandum, somewhere," said he. "It is of no great consequence, but— Oh, here it is!" He picked it up, and replaced it in the hollow of his great silver watch.

Richard, who was sitting where he had left him, looked up with a glance of careless inquiry. "Good-night again, Mr. Trevethick."

"Good-night, Sir." And again the landlord smiled in his grim fashion.

CHAPTER XVIII.

BY MOONLIGHT.

Richard sat over the fire, revolving his late conversation with Trevethick in his mind, and picturing to himself what would probably come of it. Although the declaration of his love for Harry had been thus suddenly made, it had not been made unadvisedly. Though he had not expected the opportunity for stating it would have offered itself so soon, he had planned his whole argument out beforehand, with Wheal Danes for its pivot. And, upon the whole, he felt satisfied with its effect upon his host. The latter had not surprised him (except by his frankness) in his disclosure respecting the rich promise of the mine. Richard's own observation, aided by the clew which Parson Whymper's few chance sentences had given him, had convinced him that Wheal Danes was a most coveted object in the landlord's eyes; and had it happened to have fallen into his own hands, he did really suspect enough to have had it searched for ore from top to bottom. Trevethick had therefore lost nothing by his revelation (as his sagacity had doubtless foreseen), while he had made a very favorable impression upon Richard by his candor. Cornish giants, thought the latter, might be rude and brutal, but duplicity was foreign to their character; it was not Blunderbore, but Jack the Giant-killer, who dug pitfalls, and pretended to swallow what he only put in a bag.

Trevethick had certainly shown strong disfavor to the young man's suit, backed though it was by such great pretensions; and it was evident that but for his hold upon him with respect to the mine, Richard would not have been listened to so patiently. However, his mouth had not been peremptorily closed at once (as he had expected it would have been), which was a great point gained, and the longer the old man took to think about the matter the more likely was self-interest to gain the day with him. Supposing Richard's representations to have been correct, he was certainly "a better match" for Harry than Solomon was; and he had no apprehension of their being refuted. Trevethick would in all probability write to Mr. Whymper to inquire into the truth of them—but what then? He would certainly make no reference to the mine; and as to Richard being Carew's lawful son, had not the chaplain himself (whom he could count on as a friend to say all that was to his advantage besides) admitted that, in his eyes, he was born in honest wedlock? At all events, there would be ample excuse for his having taken such a view of the case; while, as to his prospects, he had frankly confessed that he was, for the present, unacknowledged by the Squire. So long, in fact, as he could keep up the pretense of influence, either present or contingent, at Crompton, he felt his position with Trevethick tolerably secure.

In all this scheme of dark deceit his love for Harry was interwoven like a golden thread, and amidst all his plots and plans her glorious face would suddenly rise unbidden, and charm him from them. He had long since resolved to win her, but the late avowal of her love for him, and now his partial success to gain her father's favor, seemed to have made her his own already. How beautiful she had looked that day upon the tower, with the sunlight on her hair! How fresh and guileless were her ways! Her very weaknesses were lovable, and the cause of love. How touching was her simple faith in omens, and how pleasant to combat it, his arm about her dainty waist, as though to protect her from the shadow of harm! How pitiful her fear of her gruff father, and of this Cornish Solomon; and how sweet to calm it, kissing her tears away! Once more his loving arms embraced her—once more his lips touched her warm cheeks—when a sudden noise awakened him from his dream of bliss.

The parlor fire had long gone out. It was warm for the time of year; but had it been otherwise he would not have replenished it. The candles, too, had burned out, and the moon-beams were streaming through the window; but had it been dark he would scarce have been aware of it. The house had long ago been hushed in repose, and yet Richard felt certain that he had heard a movement in the passage.

A stealthy step, yet not that of thief or burglar; a fairy footfall, rather, which was music to his ear. His heart leaped up to tell him that on the other side of the door was Harry Trevethick. He held his breath, and trembled—not for fear. Was it possible that, knowing he was sitting there alone, she had come down of her own choice to bear him company? Had her father told her something—some glad tidings which she could not keep from her lover even for a night? Or, filled with sweet dreams of him, as he of her, had she risen in her sleep, and been drawn involuntarily toward him by the loadstone of love? But—hark! The bolt that fastened the house-door was softly drawn, and the latch gently lifted. What *could* that mean? Why was she thus going forth alone, and clandestinely, at midnight? His heart beat faster than ever. For an instant all that he had read or heard from his wild companions, and what he had himself believed until he came to Gethin, of the wiles and inconstancy of woman, flashed upon his mind. Had he, bred in the town, and familiar with all the ways of vice, been flattered and hoodwinked by a country wanton? Impossible. For, though there were no virtue in the world, he felt assured that Harry loved him, and him alone. She must be walking in her sleep. Softly, but very swiftly, he left the parlor, and hurried to the front-door. It was closed, but unfastened. He opened it, and looked out. All was as light as day, and yet so different. Every object in the street, every stone in the cottage opposite, stood out distinct and clear, but bathed in a pale and ghostly atmosphere. The distant murmur of the sea came to him like the sigh of one just freed from pain. Nothing else was to be heard; no human tread disturbed the midnight stillness; but along the winding road that led to Turlock he caught the far-off flutter of a woman's dress. She was going at rapid speed, and the next moment had turned the corner, but not before he had recognized his Harry; and, closing the inn door softly behind him, he started after her like an arrow from the bow.

The scene of this pursuit was strange and weird enough, had Richard possessed eyes for any thing but the object of it. The sky was without a cloud, and the sea—which showed on its cold blue surface a broad and shining path where the moon-beams lay—without a ripple. On shore there was even less of motion. The bramble that threw its slender shadow on the road moved not a twig. Nature, green and pale, seemed to be cast in an enchanted sleep, and even to suspend her breathing. From the point Richard had reached he could see the road stretching for a full mile, like a white ribbon, save in the middle, where it dipped between high banks. It led to Turlock only, but at this place a foot-path struck across the fields to the Fairies' Bower. To his astonishment, though indeed he had scarcely capacity enough for further wonder, Harry took this path; he saw her climb the stile, and then for the first time look round; he sank under the hedge, to hide himself; and when he cautiously looked forth again the girl had vanished. But he knew whither she was going now. He had assisted her across that very stile but a few days ago; he had walked with her through the hazel copse, and skirted the clear trout-stream by her side; and he could follow her now at utmost speed, and with less caution, for the path was green and noiseless. He could hear his heart beat—not from want of breath—as though in accord with the silver treble of the stream, as he sped along. Through the scanty foliage of the dell he saw her light dress gleam across the wooden bridge, but he himself stopped beside it, peering through the lattice of the branches upon her as she stood on the green bank of the Wishing-Well.

Never had moon-beams shone upon a sight more fair. Harry was attired as she had been on the previous evening, except that she wore a shawl, which also served her as head-gear, like a hood. This she now unfastened, and taking out the pin that had joined it together, held it above the well, which showed, as in a mirror, her leaning face and curving form, her wealth of hair, her frightened yet hopeful eyes, and the rise and fall of her bosom, filled with anxiety and superstitious awe. She had come to test her future—to foresee her fate—at Gethin Wishing-Well. For an instant she poised the pin, her lips at the same time murmuring some simple charm—then dropped it into the well's clear depths, and watched it fall. As she did so, another figure seemed to glide upon the liquid mirror, at the sight of which she clasped her hands and trembled. Superstitious as she was, Harry had only half expected that her foolish curiosity would be actually gratified. Moved by the avowal of Richard's love that morning, the obstacles to which seemed to her so formidable, she had wished to see her future husband, to know how fate would decide between him she loved and him whom her father had chosen for her, and yet she was terrified now that that which she had desired was vouchsafed her. She scarcely dared to look upon yonder shadowy form, although its presence seemed to assure her of the fulfillment of her dearest wish. It was the counterfeit presentment of Richard Yorke himself; bareheaded, just as she had seen him last in the bar parlor, but with heightened color, an eager smile, and a loving gratitude in his eyes, which seemed to thank her for having thus summoned him before her. The figure was at right angles from her own, but the face was turned toward her. She gazed upon it intently, looking for it to faint and fade, since its mission had been accomplished. She even drew back a little, as though to express content, yet there was the vision still, a glorious picture in its fair round frame of moss and greenery. Supposing it should remain there (her pale face flushed at the thought) indelibly and forever, to tell the secret of her heart to all the world! Then a whisper, that seemed to tremble beneath its freight of love, whispered, "Harry! Harry!" and she looked up, and saw the substance of the shadow, her lover, standing upon the little wooden bridge!

Though Folly be near kin to Vice, she does not acknowledge the relationship, and, to do Harry Trevethick justice, she would never have made a midnight assignation with Richard in the Fairies' Bower. She was more alarmed and shocked at the too literal fulfillment of her wish than pleased to see him there. She shed tears for very shame. Whatever reserve she had hitherto maintained, with respect to her affection for him, had now, she perceived, been swept away by her own act. The scene to which he had just been an unsuspected witness was more than equivalent to a mere declaration of love: it was a leap-year offer of her hand and heart. She had no strong-hold of Duty left to which to betake herself, nor even a halting-place, such as coy maidens love to linger at a little before they murmur, "I am yours."

There was nothing left her but revilings. She poured upon him a torrent of contumely, reproaching him for his baseness, his cowardice, his treachery in tracking her hither, like a spy, to overhear a confession that should have been sacred with him of all men. Whatever that confession might have been—and, to say truth, so utterly possessed had she been by her passionate hopes, her loving yearnings, that she knew not what she had merely felt, what uttered aloud —she now retracted it; she had no tenderness for eaves-droppers, for deceivers, for—she did not know what she was saying—for wicked young men. Above all things it seemed necessary to be in a passion; to be as irritated and bitter against him as possible. The copiousness of her vocabulary of abuse surprised herself, and she did not shrink from tautology. She only stopped at last for want of breath, and even then, as though she knew how dangerous was silence, she bemoaned herself with sobs and sighs.

Then Richard, all tenderness and submission, explained his presence there; showed how little he was to blame in the matter, and, indeed, how there was neither blame nor shame to be attached to either of them; spoke of his late interview with her father, gilding it with brightest hopes, and cited the marvelous attributes of the Wishing-Well itself in support of his position. He felt himself already her affianced husband; the question of their union had become only one of time. She was listening to him now, and had suffered him to kiss her tears away, when suddenly she started from his embrace with a muffled cry of terror. Some movement of beast or bird in the copse had made a rustling in the underwood, but her fears gave it a human shape. What if Sol should have followed them thither, as Richard had followed *her!* What if her father should have heard her leave his roof, as Richard had, or should miss her from it—and —oh shame!—*miss him!* "Home! home!" she cried. "Let me go home." And she looked so wild with fright that he durst not hinder her. Hardly could he keep pace with her along the winding path, with such frantic speed she ran. At the stile she forbade him to accompany her farther.

"What! leave you to walk alone, and at such an hour, my darling?" It was nearly two o'clock.

"Why not?" she cried, turning upon him fiercely. "I am afraid of none but you, and of those whom I should love, but of whom you make me afraid." Then up the white road she glided like a ghost.

Richard watched her with anxious eyes as long as he could, then sat upon the stile, a prey to apprehensions. To what dangers might he not have already exposed her by his inconsiderate pursuit! Suppose some eye had seen them on their way, or should meet her now on her return! Suppose her own fears should prove true, and her father had already discovered their absence! His thoughts were loyally occupied with Harry alone; but the peril to himself was considerable. It was impossible that he could satisfactorily explain his companionship with the inn-keeper's daughter at such a place and hour. The truth would never be believed, even if it could be related. She had got home by this time; but had she done so unobserved? Otherwise, it was more than probable that he should find two Cornish giants waiting, if not "to grind his bones to make their bread," at least to break them with their cudgels. In their eyes he would seem to have been guilty of a deliberate seduction, the one of his daughter, the other of his destined bride. Yet, not to return to Gethin in such a case would be worse than cowardice, since his absence would be sure to be associated with Harry's midnight expedition. He had hitherto only despised this Trevethick and his friend, but now, since he feared them, he began to hate them. Bodily discomfort combined with his mental disquietude. For the first time he felt the keenness of the moonlit air, and shivered in it, notwithstanding the hasty strides which he now was taking homeward. Upon the hill-top he paused, and glanced about him. All was as it had been when he set out; there was no sign of change nor movement. The inn, with its drawn-down blinds, seemed itself asleep. The front-door had been left ajar, doubtless by Harry; he pushed his way in, and silently shut it to, and shot the bolt; then he took of his boots, and walked softly up stairs in his stockinged feet. He knew that there was at least one person in that house who was listening with beating heart for every noise.

The ways of clandestine love have been justly described as "full of cares and troubles, of fears and jealousies, of impatient waiting, tediousness of delay, and sufferance of affronts, and amazements of discovery;" and though Richard Yorke had never read those words of our great English divine, he had already begun to exemplify them, and was doomed to prove them to the uttermost.

CHAPTER XIX.

RICHARD BURNS HIS BOATS.

It was strange enough that day after day and week after week went by without John Trevethick making any reference to the application his guest had made for his daughter's hand. His silence certainly seemed to favor it; and the more so since, notwithstanding what he knew, he put no obstacles in the way of the young people's meeting and enjoying each other's society as heretofore. Perhaps he had too strong a confidence in Harry's sense of duty, or in the somewhat more than filial fear in which she stood of him. Perhaps Richard's prudent and undemonstrative behavior toward the girl in the presence of others deceived him. But, at all events, the summer came and still found Richard under the same roof with Harry, and more like one of the family than ever. Tourists of the young man's own position in life, and even of the same profession, began to visit Gethin, and of course "put up" at the *Castle*, but he found nothing so attractive in their company as to withdraw him from that homely coterie in the bar parlor for a single evening. He was always made welcome there by both his host and Solomon; and without doubt, so far as the former was concerned, a less sanguine man than the young landscape-painter might have considered that his suit was tacitly acceded to.

Even Harry herself — to whom her father's conduct was surprising enough—had come at last to this conclusion. Only one thing militated against this pleasant view of affairs—it was certain that the old man had not yet opened his lips to "Sol" upon the matter. It was clear that the miner still considered himself in the light of Harry's accepted suitor. As a lover, he was fortunately phlegmatic, and did not demand those little tributes of affection in the shape of smiles and whispers, secret glances, silent pressures, which his position might have exacted; but he would now and then pay her a blundering compliment in a manner that could not be misinterpreted, or even make some direct allusion to their future settlement in life, which embarrassed her still more. The young girl, as we have hinted, was by no means incapable of dissimulation, but she naturally revolted against having to support such a *rôle* as this, and would have even run the risk of precipitating what might have been a catastrophe by undeceiving him. But Richard bade her have patience. He had strong reasons, if they were not good ones, for being well satisfied with the present state of affairs. In love, notwithstanding much savage writing to the contrary, it is the woman who suffers; it is she who is the small trader, who can least afford to wait, while man is the capitalist. Richard saw no immediate necessity for pressing the matter of his marriage, upon which his heart was, nevertheless, as deeply set as ever. He would not (to do him justice) have been parted from his Harry now for all the wealth of Carew. But he was not parted from her, and he did not wish to risk even a temporary separation by any act of impetuosity. Living was cheap as well as pleasant at the *Gethin Castle*, and it was of importance to husband his funds—to reserve as much of his resources as he could for the expenses of his honey-moon. So far, and no further, went his plans for the future. He knew that his mother would not refuse to offer them a home, even if his wife should come to him empty-handed; and the more he humored the old man, and abstained from demanding a decision, when it was clear the other preferred to procrastinate, the better favor he would have with him, and consequently the better chance of gaining a dowry with his daughter. Even if he should press matters, it was probable, he reasoned, that Trevethick had no decisive reply to give him. He had doubtless written to Mr. Whymper, and learned all that Richard had already divulged to him—and no more; that is to say, that he was, though an unacknowledged offspring of the Squire, in a very different position, at all events, toward him than that of a mere natural son. Trevethick could not have heard less—that is, less to his advantage—or he certainly would not have kept silence for so long.

Such was the state of affairs at Gethin. Harry with her two suitors; her father with his two expectant sons-in-law, each of whom had more or less of reason for his expectation. Though Richard might be satisfied with it, it was clear it could not last forever—nor for long. The day on which the change took place, though it was in no wise remarkable in other respects, he never forgot: every incident connected with it, though disregarded at the time, impressed itself upon his mind, to be subsequently dwelt upon a thousand times. It might have been marked in the hitherto sunny calendar of his life as the "Last day of Thoughtless Gayety. Here Love and Pleasure end."

It was fine weather, and there were more tourists at the inn than could be accommodated, so Richard had given up his private sitting-room to their temporary use. This, however, did not throw him more in Harry's society than usual, since their presence naturally much occupied her time. He had not, indeed, seen her since the mid-day meal which he had taken in the bar parlor; but she had promised, if she could get away, to call for him at a certain spot where he had gone to sketch—the church-yard on the hill. The attraction of the castled rock was such that few visitors sought the former spot, notwithstanding its picturesque and wild position. How the church maintained itself on that elevated and unsheltered hill, despite such winds as swept it in the winter, was almost a miracle: but there it stood—as it had done for centuries—gray, solitary, sublime. It was of considerable size, but small in comparison with its God's-acre, which was of vast extent, and only sparsely occupied by graves. The bare and rocky moor was almost valueless; it is as easy for one duly qualified to consecrate a square mile as an acre; and the materials of the low stone wall that marked its limits had been close at hand. In one or two spots only did the dead lie thickly; where shipwrecked mariners — the very names of whom were unknown to those who buried them—were interred; and where the victims of the Plague reposed by scores. Even Gethin had not escaped the ravages of that fell scourge; and, what was very singular, had suffered from it twice over; for, on the occasion of an ordinary burial having taken place many generations after the first calamity, in the same spot, the disease had broken forth afresh, and scattered broadcast in the little hamlet ancient death. The particulars of the catastrophe, so characteristic of this home of antique legend and hoary ruin, were engraven on a stone above the spot, which had never since been disturbed.

In a lone corner, as though seeking in its humility to be as distant from the sacred edifice as possible, was a quaint old cross. It was probably not so old by half a dozen centuries as the grave-mounds on the rock where the ruined castle stood, but it seemed even older, because there were words cut in its stone in a tongue that was no longer known to man. Seated on the low wall beside it, Richard was transferring to his sketch-book this relic of the past in his usual intermittent manner—now gazing out upon the far-stretching sea, here blue and bright, there shadowed by a passing cloud; now down into the village, which stood on a lower hill, with a ravine between. He had seen the post-cart come and go—for it came in and went out simultaneously at that out-of-the-way hamlet, where there was no one to write complainingly to the papers concerning the inefficiency of the mail service—and it was almost time for Harry to come and fetch him, as she had appointed. But presently the reason for her absence made itself apparent in the person of her father. It was not unusual for old Trevethick, at the close of the day, to call at the cottage in the ravine, which the guide to the ruin inhabited in the summer months, and see how business was doing in that quarter. If he had no eye for the picturesque, he had a very sharp one for the shillings which were made out of it; and Richard was not surprised to see the landlord descending the opposite hill. "This will keep Harry at home; confound him!" muttered the young man to himself, and then resumed his occupation. As there was now no one to watch for, he worked with more assiduity, and with such engrossment in his subject that he was first made conscious that he was not alone by the sudden presence of a shadow on his sketch-book. He looked up, not a little startled, and there was John Trevethick standing beside him, his huge form black against the sun.

"You may well be frightened, young gentleman," were his first ominous words; "it is only a guilty conscience that starts at a shadow."

Richard *had* a guilty conscience; and yet the remark that was thus addressed to him, unconciliatory, if not directly hostile, as it was, rather reassured him than otherwise.

Trevethick's presence there, for he had never made pretense of seeking Richard's society for its own sake—was of evil augury; his tone and manner were morose and threatening; his swarthy face was full of pent-up wrath; and yet it was obvious to the other that the secret was yet safe, the divulging of which he had most cause to fear. Had it been otherwise there would have been no mere thunder-cloud, but a tornado. "The post has brought some ill news from Crompton," was what flashed across the young man's brain; and the thought, though sufficiently uncomfortable, was a relief compared with that he had first entertained, and which had driven the color from his cheeks.

"I have no cause to be frightened, that I know of, either of you or any other man, Mr. Trevethick," observed Richard, haughtily.

"I hear you say so," was the other's grim reply; "but I shall be better pleased to hear you prove it."

"Prove what?"

"Two things—that you are not a bastard, nor a pauper."

Richard leaped down from the wall with a fierce oath; and for a moment it really seemed that he would have flung himself against his gigantic opponent, like a fretful wave against a rock of granite.

Trevethick uttered an exclamation of contempt. "Pick up your sketch-book, young man, or one of those pretty pictures will be spoiled by which you gain your bread. You've acted the fine gentleman at Gethin very well, but the play is over now."

"I don't understand you, Mr. Trevethick. If you must needs be insolent, at all events, be explicit. You have miscalled me by two names—Bastard and Pauper. Who has put those lies into your mouth, the taste of which you seem to relish so?"

Trevethick reached forth his huge hand, and seized the other's shoulder with a gripe of steel. It seemed to compress bone and sinew as in a vice; the arm between them was as a bar of iron. Richard felt powerless as a child, and could have cried like a child—not from pain, though he was in great pain, but from vexation and rage. It was maddening to find himself thus physically subjugated by one whom he so utterly despised.

"Keep a civil tongue in your head, cock-sparrow," growled the giant, "lest I wring your neck. You're a nice one to talk of lying; you, with your tales of son and heirship to the Squire, and your offers of copper-mines for the asking! Who told me how I had been fooled? Why, Carew himself! You thought I should write to the parson, eh?"

Richard certainly had thought that he would have written to the parson, but he strove to look as calm and free from disappointment as he could, as he replied: "It was quite indifferent to me to whom you wrote, Mr. Trevethick. There was only one account to give of my affairs; and it was the same I had already given to you. I told you that my father did not choose to acknowledge me for the present, and I have no doubt that your questioning him upon the matter has made him very bitter against me; the more so because he is well aware that he is fighting against the truth; he knows that he was married to my mother in a lawful way, and that I am the issue of that marriage. It is true that technical objections have been raised against it, but his own conscience warns him that they are worthless. Mr. Whymper will tell you the same."

"Never you mind Mr. Whymper," said the landlord, gruffly, but at the same time relaxing his grasp upon the young man's shoulder; "the parson needs all his cleverness to take care of himself in this matter, and will have no helping hand to spare for you. The Squire is in a pretty temper with you both, I promise you. Here's his letter, if you'd like to see what he says of you in black and white; not that there's much white in it, egad!"

It was a custom of the Squire of Crompton, unconsciously plagiarized from the Great Napoleon, to let all letters addressed to him in an unfamiliar hand answer themselves. They were not destroyed, but lay for weeks or months unopened, until the fancy seized him to examine their contents. He made, it was true, a gallant exception in the case of those whose superscription seemed to promise a lady correspondent; but that had not been the case with the communication from Trevethick, and hence the long interval that had elapsed before it was attended to. Trevethick's business letters had hitherto, as was the case with all tenants of Crompton estate, been addressed to the chaplain only, so that he was unaware of this peculiarity of Carew, and had naturally construed his silence into a tacit admission of the truth of Richard's statement.

If force of language and bitterness of tone could have made up for his previous neglect, the Squire's letter was an apology in itself. It was short, but sharp and decisive. "The grain of truth," he wrote, "among the bushel of lies that this young gentleman has told you is, that he was once a guest under my roof—I forget whether for two nights or three. He will never be there again—neither now nor after I am in my box" (this was the Squire's playful way of alluding to the rites of sepulture). "He has no more claim upon me than any other of my bastards—of whom I have more than I know of—and in fact less, for I may have deceived their mothers, whereas his played a trick on me. As to his expectations from me, I can only tell you this much, that I expect he will come to be hanged; as for interest, whatever he may have with my son of a she-dog of a chaplain, he has none with me; and as for money, so far as I know, he is a pauper, and likely to remain so as long as he lives." There were other sentences spurted from the volcano of the Squire's wrath, but to the same effect.

"A nice letter of recommendation, truly, and from his own father, of the young gentleman who asked me for my daughter's hand!" growled Trevethick. "You ought to be thankful to get out of Gethin with whole bones. If 'Sol' was to come to know of what you asked of me, I would not answer for even so much as that, I promise you."

"'Sol' might have known of it had you not chosen to keep it from him, for reasons best known to yourself," said Richard, quietly. "You have taken some time to make up your mind between us."

Trevethick winced; for the promise of the young man's interest with respect to Wheal Danes had, in fact, been the bait which had tempted him to temporize so long. He had never meant to give his daughter to Richard; but he had hoped to reap an advantage, present or future, out of the implied intention; nor did he know even yet in what relation Richard stood with Parson Whymper.

"At all events, it's made up now," answered the landlord, curtly.

"This letter has caused you to decide against me, then?"

"That letter? Well, of course it has. Not that there ain't a heap of other reasons; but that one's enough, I should think, even for you."

"It is just such a letter as I should have expected Carew to pen," observed Richard, coolly, "and does not alter the facts of the case as I stated them to you one whit. That my father is furious with me is clear enough; that is, because he is in the wrong, and feels it. He is angry, you see, even with Mr. Whymper, because he knows that his view of my case is such as I described to you. I confessed from the first that my interest at Crompton was a contingent one. You are treating me with great injustice, Mr. Trevethick."

"What! Have you so much brass left as to say that? You, that have asked my permission to pay court to my daughter, under the pretense that you were a fine gentleman, independent at present, and the heir-presumptive to one of the richest commoners in the kingdom! How durst you do it? You vagabond! you scoundrel!"

"You will be sorry for having said those words some day," said Richard, hoarsely; he was choking with rage, and yet it was necessary to restrain himself. He felt that this man would presently forbid him his house—would separate him from his Harry forever; and that would be like tearing out his heart-strings. Always audacious, there was nothing that he was not now prepared to say or do to avert this. "I tell you, Mr. Trevethick, this letter is full of lies, or rather it is written by a madman. I am not a bastard; I am not a pauper. I have an independence of my own, though, indeed, it is small compared with my expectations. My mother makes me a good allowance. I am a gentleman, and I have a right to be listened to by any man, when I ask leave to be his daughter's lover."

"Let us leave alone your gentility, Sir, and your mother's allowances," sneered the landlord, "since there is no means of gauging either the one or the other. As for your independent property—I don't believe you have a hundred pounds in the world; but it is easy enough to prove that I am mistaken there. Let me see the money down. Show me your three or four thousand pounds in gold, or notes that I know, for I must needs be particular with so clever a young gentleman; notes of the Bank of England, or of the Miners' Bank at Plymouth. Let me hold them in my hand, and then I shall feel that you are speaking the truth. At present, I tell you fairly, that if I saw a check of yours, I should look upon it as so much waste paper until I also saw it honored."

"Three thousand pounds is a large sum, Mr. Trevethick," said Richard, thoughtfully.

"Let us say two, then," returned the landlord, mockingly. "Sell out two thousand pounds of this independent fortune of yours, that has been invested in the Deep Sea Cockle Mine, or in debentures of the Railway in the Air. Let me see but two thousand pounds, Mr. Richard Yorke, and then—and not before—may you open your lips to me again respecting my daughter Harry." He turned upon his heel with a bitter laugh; while Richard, as white as the sketch-book he still held in his hand, remained speechless. A perilous thought had taken possession of his mind—a thought that it would have been better for him to have dropped down there dead than to have entertained, but it grew and grew apace within him like a foul weed. Had his life of selfish pleasure angered the long-suffering gods, and, having resolved upon his ruin, were they already making him mad? He ran after the old man, who did not so much as turn to look behind him, though he could not but have heard his rapid steps. "Mr. Trevethick, I will do it," he gasped out.

"Do what?" said the other, contemptuously, striding on. "Go hang yourself, or jump off Gethin rock into the sea?"

"I will get you the money that you speak of—the two thousand pounds. You shall have it in your hand, and keep it for that matter, if you please."

"What?" Unutterable astonishment stared out from the landlord's face. For the first time since the receipt of Carew's letter he began to discredit its contents. If this young fellow had really the immediate command of so large a sum, there was probably much more "behind him." He must either have a fortune in his own right, or if Carew had settled such a sum of money on him, he must have had a reason for it—the very reason Richard had assigned. And if so, Wheal Danes might be his to dispose of even yet. But Trevethick was not the man to hint a doubt of his foregone conclusions. "You have not got this money in your pocket, have you?" said he, with a short dry laugh.

"No, Sir; but I can get a check for it from my mother, in course of post."

"A check!" cried the other, contemptuously, all his suspicions returning with tenfold force. "I would not give one penny for such a check."

"I will get it changed myself, Mr. Trevethick, at Plymouth. The post has gone, but I will write to-morrow, and within the week—"

"You shall not stay here a week, nor another twenty-four hours," roared Trevethick. "I have been made a fool of long enough. I will not listen to another word."

But he did listen, nevertheless. No longer hampered by vague fears and difficulties, with which he knew not how to grapple, but with a distinct plan of operations before him, Richard's eloquence was irresistible. Deceit, if not habitual with him, had been practiced too often to lack the gloss of truth from his ready tongue. He actually had a scheme for procuring the sum in question, and when he possessed confidence himself, it was rarely, indeed, that he failed to inspire it in others. For the second time, the landlord of the *Gethin Castle* found himself in doubt; he was staggered by the positiveness of the young man's assertions, and by the force and flow of his glowing words. In spite of himself, he began once more to think that he might have been mistaken in condemning him as an impostor, after all; as Richard had said, Carew *was* scarcely sane, and when excited by wrath, a downright madman. His resolves, too, were as untrustworthy and fickle as the winds. Trevethick felt tolerably convinced that the money would, at all events, be forthcoming; and the sum—large in itself—seemed the earnest of much more. Last, but not least, there were the possibilities in connection with the mine. If he broke altogether with Richard, and turned him out of his house outright, might not his first act be to reveal to Parson Whymper, in revenge, all that he knew about Wheal Danes!

"Well, well, you shall stay at Gethin, then, till your check comes, young gentleman," said he, in a tone that was meant to be conciliatory. "I don't wish to be uncivil to any man, and certainly not to one who has been my guest so long. But you will keep yourself *to* yourself, if you please, in the mean time. The bar parlor will no longer be open to you, until you have proved your right to be there. And I don't mean to promise any thing certain by that, neither; but what with your fast talking and fine speaking I'm all in a buzz."

Honest John Trevethick did not, indeed, know what to think, what to believe, or what to propose to himself for the future. His brain, unaccustomed to much reflection, and dulled by pretty frequent potations, was fairly muddled. Most heartily did he wish that this young landscape-painter had never set foot in Gethin; but yet he could not make up his mind to summarily eject him. Upon the whole, he was almost as glad to temporize in the matter as Richard was himself.

In point of fact, Richard Yorke had won the battle, and was for the present master of the field; but what a struggle it had been, and at what a loss he had obtained the victory, you might have read in his white face and haggard eyes. As to whether it would be possible to hold the advantage he had gained was a problem he had yet to solve. He had committed himself to a policy which might—nay, very probably would—succeed; but if it should fail, there would be no escape from utter ruin. He had burned his boats, and broken down the bridge behind him.

CHAPTER XX.

ON THE BRINK.

For four more days, Richard Yorke continued at the *Gethin Castle*—to outward appearance, in the same relation with the landlord and his family as before, but in reality on a totally different footing. Trevethick had not found it practicable to exclude his late guest from the bar parlor; he could not do so without entering into an explanation with its other tenants, which he was not prepared for, or without devising some excuse far beyond his powers. Notwithstanding his bluff ways, he could tell a lie without moving a muscle; but he was incapable of any such ambitious flight of deceit as the present state of affairs demanded. He had, indeed, no aptitude for social diplomacy of any kind, and suffered his change of feeling toward the young landscape-painter to appear so plainly that even the phlegmatic Solomon observed it. He was rather pleased than otherwise to do so. He had acquiesced in the hospitality with which Richard had been treated, but without the slightest sympathy with it; and, in fact, he had no sympathies save those which were connected with his personal interests. It was evident enough that his father-in-law elect had had some reasons of his own—probably in relation to the property he held under Carew—for conciliating this young gentleman; and "Sol" had taken it for granted they were good, that is, substantial, ones. If these reasons no longer existed, the sooner this young gentleman was got rid of the better. It was true he had behaved himself very civilly; but his presence among them had been, on the whole, oppressive. "Sol" rather chafed at Richard's social superiority, though it was certainly never intruded, and, at all events, he preferred the society of his own class, among whom he felt himself qualified to take the lead. But the idea of jealousy had never entered into his mind. In his eyes Richard was a mere boy, whose years, as well as his position in life, precluded him from any serious intentions with respect to Harry, whom, moreover, Solomon regarded as his betrothed. If he had been married to her, he would certainly have forbidden her "gadding about" so much with this young fellow; but at present she was under her father's rule, and the old man knew very well what he was about. He was glad that there now seemed a prospect, to judge from the latter's manner, that the lad's intimacy with Harry, and the family generally, was about to end; but it might have lasted six months longer without "Sol's" opening his mouth about it, so prudently had Richard played his cards — so irreproachably behaved "before folk."

Solomon went, as usual, daily to look after affairs at Dunloppel, but Trevethick remained within doors, under pretense that the influx of guests, which was in fact considerable, demanded his presence. He took care that Richard and Harry should have no opportunity of meeting alone throughout the day; while in the evening he sat in almost total silence, sucking his pipe, and frowning gloomily—a wet blanket upon the little company, and the source of well-grounded terror to his daughter Harry.

Richard had told her how the matter stood; protested that he could get the money; and argued that when that was done, her father could have no excuse for forbidding his suit. But she knew the old man better than he, and trembled.

On the fifth day Richard received a letter, inclosing a check for two thousand pounds upon a London bank, from his mother, and, with an air of quiet triumph, showed it to his host.

"That is worth nothing here," observed Trevethick, coldly; "for all I know, the bank may not exist, or she may have no account there." But it was plain he was surprised, and disappointed.

"Notice has been sent to Plymouth, as I am here informed," said Richard; "so that I can get the check changed there, if you are still dissatisfied; which, you must pardon me for saying, I do not think you really are. Come, take my hand, and allow that you have behaved ungenerously. You're a man of your word, I know. This proves to you I am at least no pauper. I claim the right which you agreed to grant on that condition, to ask your daughter's hand, and demand of you to leave her, at all events, to grant it if she pleases. I affirm, once more, the truth of all that I have told you as regards myself. I am Carew's only son, begotten in lawful wedlock. He will acknowledge as much himself some day, even though he should delay it to his dying hour. If ever I come to possess it (and I think I shall), Wheal Danes shall be yours, without the payment of a shilling. Even now, I do not offer myself empty-handed. This is the sum that you yourself agreed I should show myself possessed of; but there is more where this comes from. I ask again, then, give me my fair chance with Harry: let her choose between me and this man Coe."

This was a wily speech; for Richard was recapitulating the very arguments which were presenting themselves to the old man's mind. True, he had promised his daughter to Solomon, and would much rather have had him for a son-in-law; but there were unquestionably great advantages in the position of this other claimant. Trevethick was not quite the slave to gratitude which he had professed himself to be, with respect to Coe's father. He did feel sincerely grateful; but he had himself exaggerated the feeling, with the very intention of making Harry understand that her fate was fixed. He had not been blind to the fact, that from the first she had never regarded "Sol" with favor as a suitor, and it was still possible to break off the match without disgrace, upon the ground of her disinclination to it. Above all, perhaps, he was actuated by the apprehension that Richard, if refused a hearing, would disclose the secret of Wheal Danes, and wreck the scheme upon which his heart had been set for near half a century. One word from him would divert the unsuspected wealth, over which he had so long gloated in anticipation, into another's hand. But he did not like the young man better for the precious knowledge which he alone shared with him; far otherwise; he hated him for it, and, without being a murderer in his heart, would have gladly welcomed the news that his mouth was closed forever by death.

"I wish such or such a one was in heaven," is a common expression, the meaning of which is of still more general acceptation. The idea, in fact, has doubtless flitted across the minds of most of us, though few, let us hope, would help to realize it; for, notwithstanding its agreeable form, it is not a benevolent aspiration. The reception of the individual in question into the realms of bliss has less interest with us than his removal from the earth's surface, and, consequently, from our path upon it. We may be very civil toward this person, and we often are; but we seldom desire him for a son-in-law. John Trevethick did not. But still less did he desire his open enmity; the longer, at all events, the declaration of war could be deferred the better.

"Come," urged Richard; "I am only demanding the redemption of your promise—one," added he, precipitately, "that it lies in your own power to redeem."

"The conditions, Mr. Yorke, have not yet been fulfilled," said Trevethick, pointing to the check. "I must see that money in bank-notes."

He had not the least doubt of the genuineness of the document; but his objection would at least give him the respite of another day or two, and a respite seemed almost a reprieve.

"As you will," answered Richard, with a faint smile. "It is a matter of perfect indifference to me, and only costs me a journey to Plymouth. If you will be so good as to let me have some vehicle to take me as far as Turlock, I will pack my carpet-bag and start at once."

The landlord nodded, and withdrew without a word.

Left to himself, the smile faded from Richard's face, and was succeeded by a look of the utmost dejection and disappointment. All had been going so well up to that very last moment, and now all remained to be done, just as though nothing had been done at all. The dangerous path that he had marked out for himself had to be trodden from first to last, at the very moment when he had seemed to have reached his journey's end by a safe short-cut. He knew that it was the smallest grain of suspicion, if not the mere desire to procrastinate, that had turned the scale in Trevethick's mind, and imposed this task upon him. The genuineness of the check had been *almost* taken for granted — entire success had been missed, as it were, by a hair's-breadth. And now he was as far from it as ever. Had he been but a little more earnest, or a little more careless in his own manner, all might have been well. The obstacle that intervened between him and his desire still stood there, though only by an accident, as though, after he had fairly blown it into the air, it had resettled itself precisely in the same spot.

Richard felt like some offender against the law who had been foiled in an ingenious scheme by the stupidity rather than the sagacity of him he would have defrauded; or, rather, like one who has been brought to justice by misadventure —through some blunder which Fate itself had suggested to his prosecutor. He was filled with bitterness and mortification, and also with fear. This miscarriage now imposed a necessity upon him, which he had contemplated, indeed, but never looked fairly in the face; he had always hoped it might be evaded. The only alternative that presented itself was to give up his Harry; this swept across his mind for a single instant— a black shadow that seemed to plunge his whole being in night—then left it firmly set upon its perilous purpose.

He did not seek to see her before he left; he could not trust himself so far even as to turn his head and wave her a good-by, as he started from the inn door, although he felt that she was watching him from an upper window. He was afraid of the anxiety that consumed him being visible to those loving eyes. She knew upon what errand he was going, but not the dangers of it. But he spoke cheerfully to Trevethick, who stood beneath the porch with moody brow, and testily found fault with horse and harness.

"The master's in a queer temper to-day, Sir," was the driver's remark, as they slowly climbed the hill out of the village.

"So it seems," answered Richard, absently.

The road they traveled was the same on which he had pursued Harry on that eventful night, now months ago; every object recalled her to him—the ruined tower on the promontory, the Fairies' Bower in the glen; but they suggested less of love than of the peril that, for love's sake, he was about to undergo. When they reached the point where he had met her first, on the margin of the moor, now bright with gorse and heather, and with its gray rocks sparkling in the sun, an overwhelming melancholy seized him. Was it possible that the omen which had alarmed her simple mind was really in the course of fulfillment? Was he, indeed, fated to be the cause of misfortune to her he loved so well? If evil should befall him, it was only too certain that it would include her in its consequences.

"You seem a cup too low, Mr. Yorke," said the driver, wondering at the young man's unusual silence; for his habit was to be brisk and lively with every body.

"We'll remedy that when we get to Turlock," answered Richard, good-naturedly, "by taking a glass of what you will together."

Accordingly, when they reached the little town, and while the post-horses were getting ready which were to take him on the next stage of his journey, Richard called for some liquor.

"Here's your good health, Sir," said the man, and added, in a roguish whisper, "and our young missus's too, Sir."

"By all means," said Richard, coolly. "But why couple hers with mine?"

"Well, Sir, it do come natural like, somehow," said the man, becoming suddenly stolid, on perceiving that his remark was by no means relished. "I suppose it's seeing you so much about together; but I meant no offense."

"I am sure of that," said Richard. It was on the tip of his tongue to pursue the subject, but he restrained himself. If he had already given occasion for gossip, he did not wish to provide fresh fuel for it in his absence from Gethin.

When a mile or two away from Turlock he produced the check which was the apparent cause of his irksome journey, and tearing it into minute fragments, scattered them out of the window.

Upon the second day he arrived at Plymouth, but too late for banking-hours, and drove to an hotel. He had had little to eat upon his journey, yet he now sent his dinner away almost untasted; on the other hand, though it was unusual with him to take much wine, he drank a bottle of Champagne and some sherry, then lit a cigar, and strolled out of doors. It was a beautiful evening; and he sauntered on the Hoe, gazing upon that glorious prospect of sea and shore which it affords, without paying regard to any thing, although all was as new as fair. His mind, however, took in every object mechanically, and often presented them to him again in after-years, just as it did that summer scene upon the ruined tower. Was it laying in provision for itself against the time, now drawing so nigh, when his physical eyes should have no more of such fair sights to feed upon? Or was the circumstance only such as attends all great changes and crises of our lives; for is not every feature of the face of Nature, upon the eve of any vital event, thus engraven on our recollection? Do we not note the daisies on the lawn forever, when for one instant we look out upon it from the darkened room wherein our loved one lies a-dying?

It presently grew too late for the ordinary signs and tokens of life; but Richard still paced to and fro, and gazed upon the darkening waters; he saw the light leap out upon them from the distant Eddystone, and from the craft in harbor, and from the houses that were built upon its margin: blue and red, and white and yellow.

There was one large vessel a great way off that he had not hitherto observed, but which now became conspicuous by its green light. Richard, vaguely interested in this exceptional beacon, inquired of a miserable-looking man, who had in vain been offering his services as cicerone, what it signified.

"Well, Sir, them colors as the ships show all mean something different; the red is from the floating powder-magazine, and the yellow is—"

"I said the *green* light," broke in Richard,

with his usual impatience of prolixity. "What is that vessel *there*, I say?"

"Oh, that's the convict ship, Sir; they say she is waiting until after the 'sizes, to take the drab-jackets to Portland."

Richard nodded, and threw the man a shilling; then walked hastily away into the town. The night was mild, but his teeth chattered, and he shook in every limb.

CHAPTER XXI.

THE MINERS' BANK.

As, though Richard had fasted long, he could not eat, so, though he was fatigued with the travel of the last two days, he could not sleep. He turned from side to side upon his pillow throughout the weary night, and strove to lose himself, and shut out thought, in vain, even for an instant. He got up and paced the room; and, when the streaks of dawn began to show themselves, drew up the blind, and looked forth. It was a very different scene from that he had been accustomed to contemplate at Gethin. In place of the waste of ocean, specked by a sail or two, whose presence only served to intensify its solitary grandeur, the thick-peopled city lay before him. But as yet there were no tokens of waking life; the streets were empty, the windows shrouded, and a steady drizzle of rain was falling, which gave promise of a wretched day. Even when the morning advanced, it was difficult to make out the individual buildings; but he had had the Miners' Bank pointed out to him on the previous day, and he thought he recognized it now. It was there that the business which he had proposed to himself was to be effected, and he gazed at it with interest. The wisest of us are simple in some things, and though so knowing in the ways of the world—that is, of *his* world—Richard knew nothing of banks whatever, and wondered whether he would have any difficulty in carrying out his object. He could not foresee any; it seemed to him that the banking folks would be glad to oblige him in the matter in question, since, if there was any advantage, it would be on their side. But there were six hours yet before he could perform this business, and since sleep was denied him, how was he to pass the time? There was a large book upon the drawers, which he had not hitherto observed, with the royal arms stamped upon it, and the name of the hotel inscribed beneath them. It did not look like a devotional work, but it was the New Testament—a work that was very literally new to Richard Yorke. He had seen it, of course, often; was acquainted by hearsay with its contents, and had joked about them. It is the easiest book in the world to make jokes upon, which, perhaps, accounts for its being so favorite a subject of ridicule with foolish persons. Shakspeare is also easy to make fun of, but the *soupçon* of blasphemy is in that case wanting, which, to many, forms the chief charm of witty converse. Richard looked at it as a dog looks at a stick; but he took it up, and opened it at random. "Having no hope, and without God in the world."

He was not a believer in sortilege. If the text he had chanced upon had been ever so applicable to his own condition, it would have made but little impression upon him, and this was not very pertinent in its application. He was by no means without hope. He had come to Plymouth full of hope, though disappointed at its not having been already exchanged for certainty. He had good hope of inspiring John Trevethick with confidence in his social position, and consequently of obtaining his consent to marry the woman who had now become indispensable to his happiness. He had even some hope of yet inheriting a portion of his father's great estate. He could not be accused of spiritual ambition. Any other sort of hope than that of being in a position to enjoy himself thoroughly had never entered into his mind. Just now, however, he was far from enjoying himself; he was a prey to anxiety, and any opportunity of forgetting it was welcome to him. Not without an effort to be interested, therefore, he reflected upon these words, which seemed rather to have been spoken in his ear aloud than merely to have caught his eye. He had already shut the book with contemptuous impatience, but he found himself, nevertheless, repeating: "Having no hope, and without God in the world," and pondering upon their meaning. He wondered at himself for taking the trouble to do so; but if he didn't do that, his thoughts would, he knew, be even less pleasantly occupied; so he let them slip into this novel channel. How *could* a man be without God in the world, if God was every where? as he had somewhere seen or heard stated, and which he believed to be the fact. It was one of the objections against the Bible, was his peevish reflection, that it was self-contradictory in its assertions, and unmistakably distinct only in its denunciations of wrath. Here was a case in point, and one which might justly be "taken up" by a fellow, if it was worth while. As for himself, he was no skeptic. Exeter Hall might have clasped him to her breast (and would) upon that ground. He was accustomed to use the name of the Creator whenever he wished to be particularly decisive; but for any other purpose he had never named it with his lips. Even as a child, his mother had never taught him to do so. She had never spoken to him on religious subjects except in humorous connection with the Heads of the two Churches to which her first husband had belonged—Emanuel Swedenborg and Joanna Southcott. If the expression "without God in the world" meant the living in it without the practice of religion, it certainly did have an application to himself, but also to every one else with whom he was acquainted. Of course he had known people who went to church—young men of his own age, whom their parents compelled to do so, and who envied him the liberty he enjoyed in that respect; and the poor folks at Gethin went to chapel. But, even there, shrewd fellows like Trevethick and Solomon did not trouble themselves to do so. True, Harry went! But then women, unless they were uncommonly clever, like his own mother, always did go to hear the parsons. Parsons, as a rule, were hypocrites. He had met one or two of them in town under circumstances that showed they had really no more "nonsense about them" than other people, but in the pulpit they were bound to cant. Look at Mr. Whymper, for instance—the best specimen of them, by-the-by, he had ever known—who could doubt that his mind was wholly set upon the main chance? To what slights and insolences did he submit himself for the sake of feathering his own nest; and how he had counted upon that fat living, of which the Squire had so cruelly disappointed him! Talk of religion! why, there was Carew himself, with thirty thousand a year, and did not spend a shilling of it on religion! True, he kept a chaplain, but only as a check upon his steward, to manage his estate for him. If there was really any thing in it, would not a rich man like him have put aside a portion of his wealth, by way of insurance—insurance against fire?—and here Richard chuckled to himself.

It was all rubbish, these texts and things. He would dress himself, and go out and take a walk, although it was so early. He had already heard sounds in the house, as though somebody was astir; so he rang the bell. It was answered by a sleepy and disheveled personage, whom he scarcely recognized for the sleek "night chamberlain," whose duty it was to watch while others slept, and who had given him a bed-candle not many hours before.

"What! still up, my man?" said Richard, gayly.

"Yes, Sir. The morning mail has but just come in; we had a passenger by it. I put him in the room under you; but he seemed a quiet one, and I didn't think he'd 'a disturbed you."

"He did not," said Richard. "I have been awake all night, and never so much as heard him. Can I have some hot water?"

"Not yet, Sir, I'm afraid; there's no fire alight at present. I can get you some brandy-and-soda, Sir."

"No, no," answered Richard, smiling; "I sha'n't want that; and as for the hot water, I can do without it; but, now you're here, just tell me, for I am quite a stranger to your town, isn't that high roof yonder," and he pointed to the object in question, "the Miners' Bank?"

"Yessir, that's it. Ah, if the morning was but a little finer, you would have a lovely view from this here window—half the town and a good slice of the harbor! There's a splendid building out to the left there, if the clouds would but lift a little. That's the County Jail, Sir."

"Indeed," said Richard, carelessly, and turned away. "Just take my boots down with you, as I shall want them as soon as you can get them cleaned."

The man did as he was bid. Directly he had left the room, Richard pulled down the window-blind, and staggered to a chair. Perhaps want of food and sleep had weakened him; but he sat down, looking very pale and haggard, like one who has received a sudden shock. Why should one man have answered him last night, "the convict ship," and now this fellow have pointed out the jail? It was only a coincidence, of course; but if there was ever such a thing as an evil augury, he had surely experienced it on those two occasions. "This is what comes of burying one's self at Gethin," thought he, smiling faintly at his own folly. "If I staid there much longer, I should begin to believe in mermaids and the Flying Dutchman." Jail! Why, if the very worst should happen, the matter would only require to be explained; he was in no real peril from the law, after all. Indeed, the very revelation which he most dreaded would only, by exposing the true state of affairs, precipitate his happiness. Trevethick would then be as eager as himself to hasten Harry's marriage.

Thus he reasoned until something of equanimity returned to him. Then he attired himself, buttoning his frock-coat carefully over his chest, and went down stairs. As he reached the next landing, a gentleman emerged from the room immediately beneath his own, like himself, fully dressed, and carrying his hat and great-coat. He was a small stout man, with bushy red whiskers, a good-natured face, and little twinkling black eyes. With a civil bow he made way for Richard to pass him, and then followed him down stairs into the coffee-room. It was a huge apartment, and quite empty except for their two selves. Most persons meeting in such a Sahara would have exchanged a salutation; and Richard, gregarious by nature besides, being eager to divert his thoughts, at once entered into conversation.

"You are the gentleman who arrived by the mail this morning, I conclude," said he, "otherwise you would scarcely keep such early hours."

"Just so, Sir," answered the other, smiling. "I thought it was not worth while to go to bed, but just gave myself a wash and brush up; and here I am, sharp-set for breakfast."

It was plain this man was not a gentleman, but Richard cared very little about that. He would have talked to the waiter, in default of any other companion.

"Well, I have been to bed," said Richard, smiling, "though something I took at dinner disagreed with me, and kept me awake all night. Do you mean to say you are not going to take any horizontal refreshment at all?"

"Well, no; I had some sleep in the coach, and a very little of that article does for me. If you eat and drink enough, as I do, it is astonishing how well you can get on without rest."

"Indeed," said Richard. "I should like to see the substitutes you take for what I have always found an indispensable necessity. Suppose we have breakfast together, and you shall order it."

"But not pay for it," stipulated the stout gentleman, in a tone that you might take as either jest or earnest. "We'll go shares in that, eh?"

"Unless you will allow me to be your host, we will certainly go shares," said Richard, wondering to himself whether in all Gethin so great a boor as this could be found above-ground or beneath it, or making his business on the waters, but rather amused nevertheless.

"I don't like misunderstandings," explained the little man, "nor yet obligations. It's not that I grudge my money, or have not as much of it as I want, thank Heaven!"

"Then you've got more than any body else I know," said Richard, laughing; "and I am acquainted with some rich men too."

"I dare say, Sir; you are a rich man yourself, I hope. You look like a young gentleman with plenty of money in your pocket."

At any other time Richard would not have been displeased by such an observation, which was, moreover, a perfectly just one. He looked from head to heel like a young man of fortune, and had been brought up as idly and uselessly as any such; but now he blushed and felt uncomfortable; and his fingers, in spite of himself, sought that breast-pocket which he had so carefully buttoned up, as though his companion's observation had had a literal and material meaning.

"Do you know Plymouth?" asked he of the stranger, by way of turning the conversation.

"Perfectly. Indeed, I live here; but I did not wish to arrive at home at such an unseasonable hour as the coach comes in. If, as a resident, I can be of any service to you, pray command me. But you don't eat, Sir."

Richard, indeed, was only playing with a piece of toast, while eggs and ham and marmalade were disappearing with marvelous rapidity down the throat of his companion.

"I am not like you," he answered. "Want of sleep produces want of appetite with me. With respect to Plymouth, you are very good to offer me your hospitality, but—"

"Services, Sir—services while in the town, I said," observed the little man. "Let us have no misunderstanding, nor yet obligation; that's my motto. Now, what can I do for you, short of that?"

"Well, I shall not greatly tax your prudence," rejoined Richard, this time laughing heartily, "though you must certainly be either a Scotchman or a lawyer, to be so anxious to act 'without prejudice.' The only information I have to ask of you is, at what time the bank opens; for I have got some business to do there, which I want to effect as soon as possible, and then be off."

"The bank! Well, there's more than one bank in Plymouth," observed the little man, scraping up the last shreds of marmalade on his plate. "They open at different hours."

"The Miners' Company is the one I want to go to."

"That opens at nine, Sir. It's on my way home, and I shall be glad to show it you."

"Thank you; but it was pointed out to me last night," said Richard, stiffly; for he preferred to effect the business which he had on hand alone. "It is still raining. What do you say to a cigar in the smoking-room?"

"With pleasure, when I have just written three words to tell my people of my arrival," answered the stranger; "however, I can do that as well there as here."

And so eager did he seem for Richard's society that he had pen and paper brought into the hotel divan, and from thence dispatched his note.

"Take one of my cigars," said Richard, good-naturedly, offering his case.

"No, no," replied the little man, shaking his head, and looking very grave; "you know my motto, Sir."

"A cigar," urged Richard, "is one of those things that one can accept even from a stranger without that sense of obligation from which you shrink so sensitively. Seriously, my good Sir, I shall feel offended if you refuse me this small favor."

"Sooner than that shall be, Sir, I'll take your cigar," said the little man. He held it up to the light, and sniffed at it with great zest. "This is no common brand, I reckon."

"Well, it is better than you will get out of the waiter's box, I dare say," answered Richard, smiling; for his cigars, like every thing else he had about him, were of the best.

"Now I'll tell you what I'll do. I'll put this in my pocket, if you'll allow me, young gentleman, for a treat when I get home. After an early morning breakfast, I generally prefer a pipe;" and he produced one accordingly from his pocket.

The room was melancholy to the last degree, being lit only from a sky-light; relics of the last night's dissipation, in the shape of empty glasses and ends of cigars, were still upon the small round tables; while a two-days-old newspaper was the only literature of which the apartment could boast.

"This place and hour would be dull enough, Sir, without your society," observed Richard, genially. "I don't think I was ever up so early in my life before, nor in such a den of a place."

"It's reckoned a good inn, too, is the *George and Vulture;* but the life of a hôtel, you see, don't begin till later on in the day."

"That's a pity," said Richard, laughing, "as I sha'n't have the opportunity of seeing it at its best. I hope to be away by 9.30, or 10 at latest."

"Ah," said the little man, "indeed!" His words were meaningless enough, but there was really a genuine air of interest in his tone. He was a vulgar fellow, no doubt; but Richard rather liked him, mainly because it was evident that the other was captivated by him. He had laid himself out to please John Trevethick and his friend Solomon for the last six months, without success, yet here was a man who had evidently appreciated him at once. If he was but a bagman, or something of that sort, it was only the more creditable to his own powers of pleasing; and his vanity—and Richard was as vain of his social attractions as a girl—was flattered accordingly. In his solitude and wretchedness, too, the society of this stranger had been very welcome.

"I am sorry," said Richard, when they had passed some hours together, and it was getting near nine o'clock, "that I am obliged to leave Plymouth so soon. It would have given me great pleasure if you could have come and dined with me; though, indeed, I fear I have already detained you from your family. It was the act of a good Samaritan to keep me company so long, and I thank you heartily."

"Don't mention it, Sir—don't mention it," said the little man, quite huskily. "I have only done my duty."

This courteous sentiment made Richard laugh. "Your duty to your neighbor, eh?" said he. "Well, I must now wish you good-by;" and he held out his hand with a frank smile. "Perhaps we may meet again some day."

"Perhaps so, Sir," said the other, knocking the ashes out of his pipe, and accompanying him into the hall.

At the hotel door Richard called a fly, as it was now raining heavily. "Shall I take you as far as the bank," said he, "since your road home lies that way? or is even that little service contrary to your motto?"

"I have got to see to my luggage," answered the other, evasively.

"Well, good-by, then."

"Good-by."

The vehicle rattled down a street or two, then

stopped before a building of some pretension, with a tall portico and a flight of stone steps before it. Another fly drove up at the same moment, but it did not attract Richard's attention, which was concentrated upon the business he had in hand, and made his heart beat very fast. He pushed his way through the huge swinging door, and found himself in a vast room, with a large circular counter, at which clerks were standing, each behind a little rail. He had never been inside a bank before, and he looked around him curiously. On the left was an opaque glass door, with "Manager's Room" painted on it; on the right was an elevated desk, from which every part of the apartment could be commanded; the clerk who sat there looked down at him for an instant as he entered, but at once resumed his occupation. Every body was busy with pen and ledger; men were thronging in and out like bees, giving or receiving sheaves of bank-notes, or heaps of gold and silver. Richard waited until there was a vacant place at the counter, then stepped up with: "I want to exchange some Bank of England notes, please, for your own notes."

"Next desk, Sir," said the man, not even looking up, but pointing with the feather of his quill pen, then scratching away again as though he would have overtaken the lost time.

There was a singing in Richard's ear as he repeated his request, and fumbled in his breast-pocket for the notes; then a silence seemed to fall upon the place, which a moment before had been so alive and noisy. Every pen seemed to stop; the ring of the gold, the rustle of paper, ceased; only the tick of the great clock over the centre door was heard. "Thief, thief! thief, thief!" were the words it said.

"How much is there?" inquired the clerk, taking the bundle of notes from Richard's hand; and his voice sounded as though it was uttered in an empty room.

"Two thousand pounds," said Richard. "Is there any difficulty about it? If so, I can take them elsewhere."

But the clerk had got them already, and was beginning to put down the number of each in a great ledger. Richard had not calculated upon this course of procedure, and had his reasons for objecting to it.

"80,431, 80,432, 80,433," read out the clerk aloud, and every soul in the room seemed listening to him.

"That will do," said another voice close to Richard's ear, and a light touch was laid upon his arm. Scarlet to the very temples, he looked up, and there stood the little red-whiskered man from whom he had parted not ten minutes before. A very grave expression was now in those twinkling black eyes. "I have a warrant for your apprehension, young man, upon a charge of theft," said he.

"Of theft!" said Richard, angrily. "What nonsense is this?"

"Those notes are stolen," said the little man. "Your name is Richard Yorke, is it not?"

"What's that to you?" said Richard. "I decline—"

Here the door of the manager's room was opened, and out strode Solomon Coe, with a look of cruel triumph on his harsh features. "That's your man, right enough," said he. "He'd wheedle the devil, if once you let him talk. Be off with him!"

The next moment Richard's wrists were seized, and he was hurried out between two men—his late acquaintance of the hotel and a policeman—down the bank steps, and into a fly that stood there in waiting.

"To the County Jail!" cried Solomon, as he entered the vehicle after them. Then he turned to the red-whiskered man, and inquired fiercely, why he hadn't put the darbies on the scoundrel.

"Never you mind that," was the sharp reply. "I'm responsible for the young gentleman's safe-keeping, and that's enough."

"Young gentleman! I am sure the young gentleman ought to be much obliged to you," replied Solomon, contemptuously. "Young felon, you mean."

"Nobody's a felon until after trial and conviction," observed the little man, decisively. "Let's have no misunderstanding and no obligation, Mr. Coe; that's my motto."

Here the wheels began to rumble, and a shadow fell over the vehicle and those it held: they were passing under the archway of the jail.

CHAPTER XXII.

LEAVING THE WORLD.

What wondrous and surpassing change may be in store for us when the soul and body have parted company none can guess; but of all the changes of which man has experience in this world, there is probably none so great and overwhelming as that which he undergoes when, for the first time, he passes the material barrier that separates guilt from innocence, and finds himself in the clutches of the criminal law. To be no longer a free man is a position which only one who has lost his freedom is able to realize; the shock, of course, is greater or less according to his antecedents. The habitual breaker of the law is aware that sooner or later to the "stone jug" he must come; his friends have been there, and laughed and joked about it, as Eton boys who have been "swished" make merry with the block and rod, and affect to despise them; the situation is, in idea at least, familiar to him; yet even he, perhaps, feels a sinking of the heart when the door of the prison-cell clangs upon him for the first time, and shuts him from the world. The common liberty to go where we will is estimated, while we have it, at nothing; but, once denied, it becomes the most precious boon in life. How infinitely more poignant, then, must be the feelings of one thus unhappily circumstanced, to whom the idea of such a catastrophe has never occurred; who has always looked upon the law from the vantage-ground of a good social position, and acquiesced in its working with complacence, as in something which could have no personal relation to himself!

Thus it was with Richard Yorke when, for the first time, he found himself a prisoner in the hands of Mr. Dodge, the detective, and his blue-coated assistant. For the time he felt utterly unmanned, and might have even fainted, or burst into tears, but for the consciousness that Solomon Coe was sitting opposite to him. The presence of that gentleman acted as a cordial upon him; the idea that he owed his miserable position to that despised boor wounded him to the quick, but at the same time gave him an outward show of calmness: he could not have broken down before that man, though he had been standing beneath the gallows-tree. Despondency would have utterly possessed him but for hate and rage—hate of his rival and all who might be concerned in this catastrophe, and rage at the arrest itself. For, though he had not the consciousness of innocence to support him, he had no sense of guilt. He had had no intention of absolutely stealing Trevethick's money; and yet he foresaw how difficult it would be to clear himself of that grave charge. He also looked back, and perceived for the first time the magnitude of the folly which he had committed. He felt no shame for it as a crime—he had not principle enough for that; but he recognized the extent of the imprudence, and its mad audacity; yet he was mad and audacious still. He had been brought up as much his own master as any youth in England, no matter how rich or nobly born; he had never known control, nor even (except during those few days at Crompton) what it was to control himself; and he could not realize the fact that he might actually come to share the fate of common thieves; to wear a prison garb; to be shut up within stone walls for months or even years; no longer a man, but a convict, known only by his number from other jail-birds. He did not think it could even come to his standing in the felon's dock, subject to the curious gaze of a hundred eyes, the indifferent regard of the stern judge, the— In the midst of these bitter thoughts, which were indeed disputations with his fears, the fly had stopped at the jail gate, and Mr. Dodge, with a cheerful air, observed: "We must get out here, if you please, Mr. Yorke."

Richard hesitated; he was mistrustful of his very limbs, so severely had the sight of those stone walls shaken him.

"Your young friend does not seem much to like the idea of lodging here," said Solomon, with a brutal laugh.

"That is fortunate," answered the detective, dryly, "since he will not have to do so. In my profession, Mr. Coe, we hold it a mean trick to kick a man when he is down.—This way, Sir, if you please." For, at the sound of Solomon's voice, Richard was up and out in a moment. "It is merely a form that you have to go through before we go before the beak."

"A form?" asked Richard, hoarsely; "what form?"

"We shall have to search you, Sir; that's all."

"That's all," echoed Solomon, with a grin.

Richard's face changed from white to red, from red to white, by turns.

"Mr. Coe will stay where he is," said Dodge, peremptorily, as he led the way into a little room that opened from the gate-keeper's parlor.

"I thank you for that, Mr. Dodge," said Richard, gratefully.

"Not at all, Sir. If you have any thing of a compromising nature about you—revolvers or such like—that's my business and the beak's, not his.—Officer do your duty."

Richard was searched accordingly. He had no revolver; but what astonished himself more than it did the searcher was that a cigar was found loose in his breast-pocket.

"Why, this must be the one that I gave to you this morning, Mr. Dodge."

"Just so, Sir. I put it back again as we came along. You know my motto. When you come to be your own master again—which I hope 'll be soon—then I'll smoke it with you with pleasure; they'll keep it for you very careful, you may depend upon it, and baccar is a thing as don't spoil. That's a pretty bit of jewelry now—*that* is." Mr. Dodge's remark referred to a gold locket, with the word "Harry" outside it, written in diamonds; and within a portrait of her, which he had executed himself. "That's a token of some favorite brother, I dare say?"

"Yes," said Richard. "Might I keep that, if you please; or, at all events, might I ask that it should not be shown to the man in yonder room? It's my own, Mr. Dodge," added he, earnestly, "upon my word and honor."

"No doubt, Sir; no doubt. There's no charge against you except as to these notes. I must put it down on the list, because that's the law; but you can keep it, and welcome, so far as I am concerned; though I am afraid the Cross Key folks will not be so very easy with you."

"The Cross Key folks?"

"Well, Mr. Yorke, it's no use to hide from you that you will be sent to Cross Key; that's the nearest jail to Gethin, I believe. I am afraid the beak will be for committing you; the sum is so large, and the case so clear, that I doubt whether he'll entertain the question of bail. You have no friends in Plymouth, either, you told me."

"None," said Richard, sadly; "unless," he added, in a whisper, "I can count you as one."

"Officer, just fetch a glass of water," said Dodge; "the prisoner says he feels faint.—Look here, young gentleman," continued he, earnestly, as soon as they were alone, "this is no use; I can do nothing for you whatever, except wish you luck, which I do most heartily. I am as helpless as a baby in this matter. I can only give you one piece of good advice: when the beak asks if you've any thing to say, unless you have something that will clear you, and can be proved—you know best about that—say, 'I reserve my defense;' then, as soon as you're committed, ask to see your solicitor; send for Weasel of Plymouth; your friends have money, I conclude. Hush! Here's the water, young man; just sip a little, and you'll soon come round."

Not another word, either then or afterward, did Mr. Dodge exchange with his prisoner. Perhaps he began to think he had acted contrary to the motto which was his guide in life in the good-will he had already shown him. Perhaps he resented the favorable impression that the attractions and geniality of his acquaintance at the hotel had made upon him as unprofessional. At all events, during their drive from the jail to the office where the magistrate was sitting—it was not open at the hour when Richard had been arrested, or he would have been searched there—Mr. Dodge seemed to have lost all sympathy for his "young gentleman," chatting with the officer quite carelessly upon matters connected with their common calling, and even offering Mr. Coe a pinch from his snuff-box, without extending that courtesy to Yorke. Nay, when they were just at their journey's end, he had the want of feeling to look his prisoner straight in the face, and whistle an enlivening air. The melody was not so popular as it has since become, or perhaps Mr. Dodge had doubts of his ability to render it with accuracy, but, as if to inform all whom it might concern what it was that he was executing, he hummed aloud the fag-end of the tune, keeping time with his fist upon his knee, "Pop goes the weasel, pop goes the weasel."

Richard understood, and thanked him with his eyes. He had no need, however, to be reminded of the good-natured detective's word of advice. The ignominy which he had just undergone had had the effect of revealing to him the imminence as well as the full extent of the peril in which he stood. Henceforward he could think of nothing—not even revenge—save the means of extricating himself from the toils which every moment seemed to multiply about him. The time for action was, indeed, but short; if he was ever (for it already seemed "ever") to be free again, the means must be taken to deliver him at once. The assizes would be held at Cross Key—he had heard the Gethin gossips talk of them, little thinking that they would have any interest for him—in three weeks. Until then, at all events, he must be a prisoner; beyond that time he would not, dared not, look.

Within ten minutes Richard Yorke stood committed to Cross Key Jail.

He followed his friend's counsel in all respects. But the messenger dispatched for Mr. Weasel returned with the news that that gentleman was out of town; he was very busy at that season—there were other folks in difficulties besides our hero, urgent for his consolation and advice as to their course of conduct before my Lord the Judge. Mr. Dodge, however, assured Richard, upon taking leave, that he would dispatch the attorney after him that very night.

The road to Cross Key was, for many miles, the same which he had lately traveled in the reverse direction; yet how different it looked! He had been in far from good spirits on that occasion, but how infinitely more miserable was he now! The hills, the rocks, the streams were far more beautiful than he had ever thought them, but they mocked him with their beauty. He longed to get out of the vehicle, and feel the springy turf, the yielding heather, beneath his feet; to lave his hands in the sparkling brook, to lie on the moss-grown rock, and bask in the blessed sun. Perhaps he should never see them any more — these simple everyday beauties, of which he had scarcely taken any account when they were freely offered for his enjoyment. He looked back on even the day before, wherein he had certainly been wretched enough, with yearning regret. He had at least been a free man, and when should he be free again? Ah, when! He was, as it were, in a prison on wheels, guarded by two jailers. Escape would have been hopeless, even had it been judicious to make the attempt. His only consolation was, that Solomon Coe was no longer with him to jeer at his dejected looks. He had started for Gethin with the news, doubtless as welcome to Trevethick as to himself, of the prisoner's committal. What would Harry say when she came to hear of it? What would she not suffer? Richard cast himself back in his seat, and groaned aloud. The man at his side exchanged a glance with his companion. "He is guilty, this young fellow." "Without doubt, he's booked." They had their little code of signals for such occasions.

The day drew on, and the soft sweet air of evening began to rise. They had stopped here and there for refreshments, but Richard had taken nothing; he had, however, always accompanied his custodians within doors at the various halting-places. He was afraid of the crowd that might gather about the vehicle to look at the man that was being taken to prison. There was nothing to mark him as such, but it seemed to him that nobody could fail to know it. He welcomed the approach of night. They still traveled on for hours, since there was no House of Detention at which he could be placed in safety on the road; at last the wheels rumbled over the uneven stones of a little country town; they stopped before a building similar, so far as he could see by the moonlight, to that to which he had been taken at Plymouth: all jails are alike, especially to the eyes of the prisoner. A great bell was rung; there was a parley with the keeper of the gate. The whole scene resembled something which Richard remembered to have read in a book; he knew not what, nor where. A door in the wall was opened; they led him up some stone steps; the door closed behind him with a clang; and its locks seemed to bite into the stone.

"This way, prisoner," said a gruff voice.

Door after door, passage after passage; a labyrinth of stone and iron. At last he was ushered into a small chamber, unlike any thing he had ever seen in his life. His sleeping-room at the keeper's lodge at Crompton was palatial compared with it. The walls were stone; the floor of a shining brown, so that it looked wet, though it was not so. His jailer-chamberlain pointed to a low-lying hammock, stretched upon two straps between the walls. "There, tumble in," he said; "you will have your bath in the morning. Look alive!"

Richard obeyed him at once. "Good-night, warder," said he.

"Night!" grumbled the other; "it's mornin'. A pretty time to be knockin' up people at a respectable establishment. If you want any thin'—broiled bones, or deviled kidneys"—for the man was a wag in his quaint way—"ring this 'ere bell. As for the other rules and regulations of her Majesty's jail, you'll learn them at breakfast-time."

The door slammed behind him.

How the doors *did* slam in that place! And Richard was left alone. If, instead of the metal ewer of water that stood by his bed-head, there had been a glass of deadliest poison, he would have seized it greedily, and emptied it to the dregs.

CHAPTER XXIII.

THE LETTER LOCK.

On the day that Richard left Gethin, which was itself an incident to keep the tongues of its gossips wagging for a good week, another occurrence took place in that favored neighborhood, and one of even more absorbing interest—the workings of Dunloppel were suspended. This, of course, was not a wholly unexpected catastrophe. The new vein, after giving an exceedingly rich yield for some months, had of late, it was whispered, evinced signs of exhaustion, although the fact was not known that for several weeks the undertaking had been carried on at a loss. Neither Trevethick nor Solomon, who were the principal proprietors, was the sort of man to play long at a losing game, or to send good money after bad; so, for the present, the pit was closed. But Solomon believed in Dunloppel; contrary to his custom, he had not disposed of a single share when the mine was at a premium, and his stake in it was very large.

Only a few minutes after Richard had departed for Plymouth with his check, Solomon returned to the inn with thoughtful brow.

Trevethick was moodily smoking his pipe in the porch, still balancing the rival claims of his sons-in-law elect, and dissatisfied with both of them. He did not share Solomon's hopes, and he detested losing his money above every thing. "Well, you've packed off all those fellows, I hope, that have been eating me out of house and home for these three weeks?"

"I've closed the mine, if that's what you mean," said Solomon. "But" (he looked cautiously up at the windows of the inn, which were all open—the guests were out in search of the picturesque, and Harry was on the tower, straining her eyes after Richard) "I want to have a word with you in private, Trevethick."

"Come into the bar parlor, then," grunted the landlord, for he did not much relish the idea of a confidential talk with Solomon just then, since it might have relation to a matter about which he had not fully made up his mind to give him an answer.

"Is that young painter fellow out of the way, then?" asked Solomon. "We have never had a place to ourselves, it seems to me, since *he* came to Gethin."

"Yes, yes, he's far enough off," answered Trevethick, more peevishly than before, for Sol's remark seemed to foreshadow the very subject he would fain have avoided talking about. "He's gone to Plymouth, he is, and won't be back these five days."

"Umph!" said Sol. If he had said, "I wish he would never come back at all," he could not have expressed his feelings more clearly.

"Well," growled Trevethick, when they were in his sanctum, and had shut the door, "what is it now? Bad news, of course, of some sort."

It was a habit with Trevethick, as it is with many men of his stamp, to have a perpetual grievance against Providence—to profess themselves as never astonished at any bad turn that *It* may do them—and, besides, he was on the present occasion desirous of taking up a position of discontent beforehand, so that the expected topic might not appear to have produced it.

"No; it's good news, Trevethick," said Solomon, quietly—"the best of news, as it seems to me; and I hope to bring you over to the same opinion."

"He's got some scheme for marrying Harry out of hand," thought the harassed landlord. "How the deuce shall I put him off?"

There was not the slightest excuse for doing so; if Solomon had been of a less phlegmatic disposition, he might have married her a year ago, young as she was. "Read this," said he, producing a letter from his pocket, "and tell me what you think of it. It's old Stratum's report upon the mine."

"Ay, ay," said Trevethick, diving into his capacious pocket for his silver spectacles. As a general rule, he was wont to receive all such reports with discredit, and to throw cold water upon Sol's more sanguine views; but it was several minutes before he could get himself into his normal state of dissatisfied depression, so much relieved was he to find that his daughter was not to be the topic of the conversation.

"Here's the plan," continued Solomon, "which accompanied the letter. I got it just after I dismissed the men; and, upon my life, I'd half a mind to set them on again. But I thought I'd just have a talk with you first."

"Ay," said Trevethick—"well?" He was quite himself again now—crafty, prudent, reticent; about as unpromising a gentleman to "get on with," far less get the better of in a bargain, as a Greek Jew. But Solomon was quite accustomed to him.

"Stratum feels confident about the continuation of the lode, you see; and also that the fault is not considerable. We shall not have to sink fifty feet, he thinks, before we come on the vein again."

"He *thinks*," said Trevethick, contemptuously. "Is he ready to sink his own money in it?"

"It's no good asking him that," said Solomon, coolly, "because he's got none. But I have always found Stratum pretty correct in his judgment; and, as for me, I believe in Dunloppel. The question is, Shall I go on with it single-handed, or will you go shares?"

"If it's so good a thing, why not keep it yourself, Sol?"

"Because my money is particularly well laid out at present, and I don't want to shift it."

"That's just the case with mine," said Trevethick, from behind the plan.

"I thought you might have five hundred pounds or so lying idle, that's all," returned the other. "I'd give six per cent. for it just now."

"Oh, that's another thing. Perhaps I have. I'll see about it."

"If you could get it me at once, that would be half the battle," urged Solomon. "There are some good men at the mine whom I should not like to lose. If I could send round to-night to tell them not to engage themselves elsewhere, since they're opening so many new pits just now, that would be a relief to my mind."

"Very good; you may do that, then. I'll write for the money to-morrow."

So blunt, straightforward, and exceedingly unpleasant a man as John Trevethick was, ought to have been the very incarnation of Truth, whereas that last observation of his was, to say the least of it, Jesuitical. There was no occasion to write to any body for what he had got above stairs, locked up in his private strong-box. But he did not wish all the world to know that, nor even his *alter ego*, Solomon Coe.

Trevethick, although a close-fisted fellow, was no miser in the vulgar sense. He kept this vast sum at hand, partly because he had no confidence in ordinary securities, and partly because he wished to be in a position, at a moment's notice, to accomplish his darling scheme. If Carew should happen to change his mind, it would be because he was in want of ready money, and he would be in mad haste to get it. His impatience on such occasions brooked no delay on the score of advantage; and the man that could offer him what he wanted, as it were, in his open hand, would be the financier he would favor in preference to a much less grasping accommodator, who might keep him waiting for a week. It was not so much the tempting bait of ready money that caught the Squire as the fact of his wishes being obeyed upon the instant. He had not been used to wait, and his pride revolted against it; and many a time had a usurer missed his mark by not understanding with how great a bashaw he had to deal in the person of Carew of Crompton. Trevethick was aware of this, and indeed the chaplain had given him a hint to keep the proposed purchase-money within easy reach, in case the Squire's mood might alter, or his necessities demand his consent to what Mr. Whymper honestly believed to be a very advantageous offer. Otherwise, Trevethick was not one to keep a hoard in his house for the mere pleasure of gloating over it. He had not looked into his strong-box for months, nor would he have done so now, but for this unexpected demand upon it. It was safe enough, he knew, in his daughter's room; and as for its having been opened, that was an impossibility; the padlock hung in front of it as usual, and it would have taken a man half a lifetime to have hit upon its open sesame by trial. He was justly proud of that letter lock, which was his own contrivance, invented when he was quite a young man, and had been perforce compelled to turn his attention to mechanics, and he considered it a marvel of skill. It was characteristic in him that he had never revealed its secret even to his daughter. Indeed, with the exception of Harry, nobody at Gethin—save, perhaps, Hannah, when she dusted her young mistress's room—had ever set eyes upon it, nor, if they had, would they have understood its meaning.

It was therefore without the slightest suspicion of its having been tampered with, that, an hour or two after the conversation just narrated, Trevethick repaired to his strong-box, with the intention of taking from it the sum of money required by Solomon. The padlock was like a little clock, except that it had the letters of the alphabet round its face instead of figures, and three hands instead of two; this latter circumstance insured, by its complication, the safety of the treasure, but at the same time rendered it useless —unless he broke the box open—to the possessor himself if by any accident he should forget the letter time at which he had set it; and accordingly Trevethick was accustomed to carry a memorandum of this about with him; even if he lost it, it would be no great matter, for what meaning would it convey to any human being to find a bit of paper with the letters B, N, Z upon it? Harry, as we have said, was out of the house, so his daughter's room was untenanted. He went to a cupboard, and took down the box from its usual shelf, with the same feeling of satisfaction that an old poet recurs to his first volume of verse; he may have written better things, and things that have brought him more money, but those spring leaves are dearest to him of all. So it was with Trevethick's spring lock. He adjusted the hands, and the padlock sprang open; he lifted the lid, and the box was empty; the two thousand pounds in Bank of England notes were gone.

He was a big bull-necked man, of what is called (in the reports of inquests) "a full habit of body," and the discovery was almost fatal to him. His face grew purple, the veins in his forehead stood out, and his well-seasoned head, which liquor could so little affect, went round and round with him, and sang like a humming-top. He was on the very brink of a fit, which might have "annihilated space and time" (as far as he was concerned), "and made two lovers happy." But the star of Richard Yorke was not in the ascendant. The old man held on by the shelf of the cupboard, and gradually came to himself. He did not even then comprehend the whole gravity of the position; the sense of his great loss—not only of so much wealth, but of that which he had secured with such toil, and laid by unproductively so long for the accomplishment of his darling purpose—monopolized his mind. Who *could* have been the thief? was the one question with which he concerned himself, and the answer was not long delayed. It was the coincidence of amount in the sum stolen with that which Richard had gone to Plymouth to realize, that turned his suspicions upon the young artist. Why, the scoundrel had fixed upon that very sum as the test of his possessing an independence for a reason that was now clear enough: it was the exact limit of what he knew he could lay his hand upon. But how *did* he know?—or, rather (for the old man's thoughts were still fixed upon the mechanical mystery of his loss), how did he open the padlock? Then there flashed upon his mind that incident of his having dropped the memorandum out of his watch-case in the bar parlor in Richard's presence, and the whole affair seemed as clear as day. It was Richard's intention to change the notes at Plymouth for the paper of the Miners' Bank, or for gold, and then to exhibit it to him in its new form as his own property. He did not believe that the young artist intended to steal it; but he was by no means less furious with him upon that account—quite otherwise. He piqued himself upon his caution and long-headedness, and resented every deception practiced upon him even more than an injury. Moreover, he felt that but for Solomon's unexpected request for the loan the plan would have succeeded. In all probability, he would not have discovered his loss until it had been too late—he would not have known how to refuse the young man leave to become his daughter's suitor; and once his son-in-law, he could scarcely have prosecuted him for replacing two thousand pounds' worth of bank-notes in his strong-box by notes of another kind. Exasperated beyond all measure as Trevethick was, it did credit to his sagacity that even at such a moment he did not conceive of Richard Yorke as being a common thief. But he concluded him to be much worse, and deserving of far heavier punishment, as a man that would have obtained his daughter under false pretenses. He went down stairs, taking the box with him, to seek his friend. Solomon had just returned from the cottage over the way, where he had been giving orders to one of the best miners to still hold himself engaged at Dunloppel, and had bidden him tell others the same. He was in high spirits, and was twirling about in his large hands Mr. Stratum's diagnosis of the mine.

"You may put that away and have done with it," said Trevethick, hoarsely; "I have no money to lend you for that, nor nothing else. This box held two thousand pounds of mine, but it's all gone now."

"Two thousand pounds!" exclaimed Solomon, too amazed at the magnitude of the sum to realize what had happened to it. "Two thousand pounds in a box!" He had always suspected that the old man kept something in a stocking-foot, and had often rallied him upon his unnecessary caution with respect to investments; but this statement of his appeared incredible.

"What does it matter if it was twenty thousand, when I tell you it's gone," said Trevethick, sullenly. "That limb of the devil, Yorke, is off with every shilling of it."

"Do you mean to say *he's* stolen it?" inquired the other, even more astonished than before.

"He's taken it to Plymouth with him, that's all."

Solomon Coe was a man of action, and prompt in emergencies, but for the moment he was fairly staggered. He had no liking for Richard, but such a charge as this appeared incredible; it seemed more likely that the old man had repented of his late offer of the loan of five hundred pounds, and had invented this monstrous fiction to excuse himself.

"Where was the box kept?" asked Solomon, dryly.

For a moment or two Trevethick was silent.

"It is as I suspected," thought the other; "the old man is making up the story as he goes on."

But the fact was that this question had gone to the very root of the matter, and opened Trevethick's dull eyes wide. In his chagrin at his loss (though he did believe it would be temporary), and irritation at his sagacity having been set at naught, he had overlooked the most serious feature of the whole catastrophe. How had Yorke come to the knowledge that the strong-box was kept in Harry's room? and under what circumstances had he obtained access to it?

"Where's Harry?" exclaimed Trevethick, starting up with a great oath; for it flashed upon him that she had fled with Richard. "Where's my daughter?"

"I saw her in the village just now," said Solomon, "talking to old Madge. She had been for a stroll out Turlock way, she said. But what's the use of vexing *her* about the matter? Women are much best kept in the dark when one don't want things to be talked about. The more quiet you keep this story, the more chance you'll have of getting your money back, you may depend upon it. It was in notes, of course?"

"Yes, in notes," answered the other, with a vacant look, and drumming on the table with his right hand.

"Come, come, Trevethick, you must keep your head," remonstrated Solomon. "I'll act for you quick enough, if you'll only supply me with the means. It's a great loss, but it should not paralyze a man. You've got a memorandum of the numbers of the notes?"

"Yes, yes; I have somewhere."

"Well, go and fetch it, while I order out a horse. I can get to Plymouth before wheels can do it, and shall catch this scoundrel yet. He'll be going there to change the notes, I reckon?"

"Yes, yes," said Trevethick; "he'll be at the *George and Vulture;* so he said."

"Good," replied Solomon. "I'll get a warrant from old Justice Smallgood on my way. Rouse up, man, rouse up; you shall have your money back, I tell you, and see this rascal lagged for life into the bargain."

"If I could only get him hanged!" answered the old man, fiercely—"if I could only get *him* hanged, Sol, I'd let the money go, and welcome!"

Solomon stared after him, as he left the room and tramped up stairs in search of the list of notes, with a ludicrous expression of wonder. In *his* eyes, no revenge at present seemed worth so extravagant a price. But Trevethick had his reasons, or thought he had, for this excess of hate; his slow-moving yet powerful nature resembled the python—it was exceedingly tenacious when its object was once grasped, and it was apt to glut itself.

CHAPTER XXIV.

A HARD ALTERNATIVE.

SOLOMON had ridden off, and was half-way to Turlock before Trevethick felt himself sufficiently collected to summon Hannah, and bid her send for her young mistress. He could not go in search of her himself and speak what he had to ask: no bird of the air must carry her reply, no wind of heaven breathe it, if it was such as he feared. There must be no "scene" in public to let loose the gossips' tongues. He sat in the bar parlor, with his huge head leaning on his hands, brooding over his wrongs, and waiting for her—for the daughter by whose wicked connivance, as he thought, he had been despoiled of his hard-earned gains. He did not reproach himself for having thrown her so much with Richard, in order that the latter might be kept in good-humor, and apt to forward his plans as to Wheal Danes. He "wondered at their vice, and not his folly." As to there being any thing beyond a flirtation between the young people, he did not suspect it; but even as matters were, he was bitterly enraged against Harry, and would have strangled Richard out of hand if he could have got near him. It was evident to him that this fellow had been courting his daughter, though he knew she was plighted to another, and had wormed out of her the secret of his hoarded wealth. Six months ago she would not for her life have dared to tell what she knew he wished to hide; and now this young villain had wound himself so cunningly about her that she had no will but his, and had even helped him to rob her own flesh and blood. His heel was on that serpent's head, however, or would be in a day or two, and *then*— The old man ground his teeth as though his enemy were between them.

"Well, father, here I am; Hannah said you wanted me."

Harry's voice was as calm as she could make

"SHE DRAGGED UPON HIS ARM,"

it, but her young limbs trembled, and her face was very pale.

"Come here—nearer!" cried Trevethick, hoarsely, seizing her by the wrist. "Do you know that you are the only creature but two—but one, I may say, for gratitude ain't love—that I have ever loved in this world—that I have worked for you, planned for you, and for you only, all my life?"

"Yes, father; and I am very grateful for it," answered she, submissively.

"No doubt," sneered the old man; "and the way you show how much you feel it, the way you show your duty and your love to your father in return, is to put a thief—a lying, cheating thief—in the road to rob him!"

"You must be mad, father!" exclaimed Harry, in blank amazement. "I know no thief!"

"You know Richard Yorke, you wicked, wanton wench!" interrupted Trevethick, passionately. "And how could *he* have heard of yonder box except through you? Of course you'll lie; a lie or two is nothing to one like you. But here's the proof. The padlock has been opened, the money taken. Who did it? Who could have done it, except him, or you?"

"As I am a living woman, father, as I hope for heaven," answered Harry, earnestly, "I did not do it, and I do not know who did."

"You didn't, and you don't! The thing's incredible. Reach here that Bible." He still held her by the wrist. "You shall swear that, and be damned forever! What! you never told that villain where my money lay?"

"I did tell Mr. Yorke that, father. Pray, pray, be patient. It was long ago; we were talking together about I know not what, and it slipped from me that you kept money in a strong-box. That was all."

"All," said the old man, bitterly, and flinging her arm away from him, the wrist all black and bruised with his angry clutch. "What more, or worse, could you have told than the one secret I had bid you keep? You told him the exact sum, too, I'll warrant? Two thousand pounds!"

"Yes, father, I did. It was very wrong, and I was very sorry directly I had done it. But I knew the secret would be safe with a gentleman like Mr. Yorke."

"A gentleman! A cheat, an impostor, a common rogue!"

"Oh no, oh no, father!"

"But I say 'yes.' To-morrow he will have the handcuffs on him! What! Have you tears for him, and none for me, you slut! Perhaps you *showed* him where the box was kept, as well as told him! Did you, *did* you?"

There was something in Harry's frightened face that made her father rise and lock the door.

"Speak low!" said he, in an awful voice; "you have something to tell me. Tell it."

"Only that I love him, father—oh, so much!" pleaded Harry, passionately. "Indeed, indeed, I could not help it! I tried to love Sol, because you wished it, but it was no use; I felt that even before Richard came. We walked every day together for weeks and weeks, and he was so different from Sol, so bright and pleasant, and he loved me from the first, he said. He told me, too, that you had listened with favor to his suit, or, at all events, had not refused to listen—that there was good hope of your consenting to it, and without that hope he knew he could not win me. I only promised to be his on that condition. Speak to me, father; pardon me, father! Don't look at me so. He never meant to thieve, I am sure of that. You asked of him some warrant of his wealth, some proof that he could afford to marry me. You would not have done that had you set your face utterly against him. And I think—I fear—though Heaven is my witness that I knew nothing of it until now, that he took this money only to bring it back to you again, and win your favor. It was an ill deed, if he has really done it, which even yet I do not credit; but it was done for my sake; then for *my* sake, father, pity him, pardon him!" She had thrown herself upon her knees beside the old man's chair; her long hair had come unfastened, and trailed upon the sanded floor; her hands were clasped in an agony of supplication. No pictured Magdalen ever looked more wretched or more beautiful.

"You have more to tell?" said the old man, harshly.

She shook her head, and uttered a plaintive moan.

"Then *I* have," continued he. "You say you love this man; now *I* hate him! I do not regret that he has robbed me, since, by that act, he has placed himself in my power, and I mean to use it to the uttermost; but for his cozening me to my face, as he has done so long, and for his smooth, false ways, and for his impudent tales, which I had half believed, and for his audacious attempt to pluck you from the hand for which I had designed you, I *hate* him. I tell you," cried out the old man, fiercely, "if this villain had fifty lives, and the law would help me to them, I would exact them all! If he stood here, I would brain him with yonder staff; and if my curse could follow him beyond the grave—as my vengeance shall to the grave's brink—he should perish in eternal fire! *Hate* him? I almost hate you for having loved him; and if I thought you would dare to cross me further by holding to him now, I'd drive you from my door this very hour. You will never see him more; but I shall, once. This mouth shall witness against him to the uttermost; these ears shall hear the judge pronounce on him his righteous doom."

"No, no," gasped the young girl, faintly. "If you do not hate me yet, I pray you to unsay those words. When you curse Richard, father, you are cursing you know not whom." She dragged upon his arm, and brought his ear down to the level of her mouth, and whispered in it.

The old man started to his feet, and pushed her from him with a hideous oath; then made as though he would have unlocked the door and thrown it wide, to drive her, as he had so lately threatened, from his roof. But there was a noise of many feet and chattering and laughter in the passage without, which showed that some of the tourist guests had just come in. Only a plank intervened between that little knot of giddy pleasure-seekers, with their jokes and small-talk, and the father and daughter in their agony.

"Mercy! mercy!" cried the wretched girl.

Trevethick clapped his hand upon her little mouth, with, "Hush, fool! hush!" and she felt thankful that he called her by no worse name.

"Forgive me—pity—pardon," murmured she.

"Listen!" said he, in a stern whisper. "Obey me now, you wicked, wanton slut, or I proclaim your shame before them all; one minute will decide your fate! Be stubborn, and you shall go forth through yonder door, discarded, friendless, infamous, to beg your bread, or win it how you will; be tractable, and even yet you shall have a father and a home. Make choice, and quickly; and having made it, be you sure of this, that it shall hold. Do you hear me, trollop?"

"I hear! I hear!" she murmured, shuddering. "I will obey you now, and ever."

"Then marry Solomon Coe—at once—within the month."

"Oh, father, mercy!"

His fingers were on the door, and the key grated in the lock.

"The sea-air makes one famish," said a gay voice outside.

"It's lucky," laughed another, "for there is sure to be nothing for dinner but the inevitable ham and eggs."

In another instant the final barrier between herself and public shame would have been withdrawn by that relentless hand.

"I promise—I promise—spare me!" cried the unhappy girl, and fell fainting on the floor.

The old man drew a long, deep breath, and wiped his forehead. His victory had not been lightly won. He lifted his daughter up and carried her to the sofa; then raised the little clumsy window, rarely opened, and propped it with a stick, so that the breeze might blow upon her tear-stained cheek. How white and worn and emptied of all joy it looked! As he gazed upon her, a touch of pity stole into her father's face. He poured out a little spirits in a glass, and put it to her lips. "Take a sup of this, and you'll be better, child."

She opened her heavy eyes, and shook her head.

"You said you would have mercy, father, if I promised?"

"Yes, yes; all shall be forgotten. We will not even speak of it to one another."

"And you will pardon *him?* You will not hurt my Richard?"

"Your Richard!"

"Yes, for he was mine once. You will not bear witness against him before the judge? Is he not punished enough in losing me? Am *I* not punished?"

"Silence!" exclaimed the old man, in a terrible voice. His hand, trembling with passion, had struck against the strong-box, and at its touch his wrath broke out in flame. "That man is dead to you henceforth! You gave your promise without conditions. Moreover, his fate is in the hands of the law, and not in mine."

CHAPTER XXV.

AN UNEXPECTED GUEST.

Six days had come and gone since her lover's departure from Gethin, but no tidings of him had reached Harry's ears. Solomon had returned on the second day, and been closeted with her father for some hours, doubtless in consultation about Richard; but not a word had been spoken of him, in her presence, by either. She dared not mention him to her father, and still less could she apply for information to his rival, her now affianced bridegroom. How much, or how little, her father had disclosed concerning him to Sol she did not know; but the latter had evidently closed with the terms which she had in her late strait accepted on her own part. The bans had been put up in the church upon the hill, and in a month she would be this man's wife. She had been congratulated upon the coming event by all the neighbors. Some had slyly hinted—little guessing the pain they gave to that sore heart—at her late "goings-on" with that young gentleman-painter; they had almost suspected at one time that he would have supplanted her old flame; but they were glad to see matters as they were. Solomon was a steady, sagacious man, as every body knew, and would get on in the world; and what he gained he would not waste in foolish ways. Such an old friend of her father's, too. Nothing could be more fitting and satisfactory in all respects. Solomon, notoriously a laggard in love, was likened to the tortoise, who had won the race against the hare.

To have to listen to all this well-meant twaddle was misery indeed. Perhaps, upon the whole, good honest dullness does unknowingly inflict more grievous wounds than the barbed satiric tongue.

To think, to picture to herself the condition of her lover—deplorable, she was convinced, from the grim satisfaction upon Solomon's face when he first came back—was torture. She could not read, for her mind fled from the page, like breath from a mirror; there was nothing for it but occupation. She busied herself as she had never done before with the affairs of the house, which afforded some excuse for escaping from Sol's attentions, naturally grown somewhat pressing, now that his wedded happiness was drawing so near. The *Gethin Castle* was not, however, very full of guests. It had been wet for a few days, and rain spoils the harvest of the inn-keeper even more than that of the farmer. One night, when it was pouring heavily, and such a windfall as a new tourist was not to have been expected by the most sanguine Boniface, a lady arrived, alone, and took up her quarters in the very room that Richard had vacated. Trevethick himself was at the door when she had driven up and asked with some apparent anxiety whether she could be accommodated. She was wrapped up, and thickly veiled, but he had observed to his daughter what a well-spoken woman she was, and an uncommon fine one too, though her hair was gray. She had inquired whether there were any letters waiting for her, addressed to Mrs. Gilbert; but there was no letter.

Harry took in the new arrival's supper with her own hands. It was the time when she would otherwise have been expected in the bar parlor, to sit by Solomon's side, and feel his arm creep round her waist, more hateful than a serpent's fold. A fire had been lit in the sitting-room, on account of the inclement weather, and Mrs. Gilbert was standing beside it with her elbow on the mantel-piece. She watched Harry come in and out, without a word, but the expression of her face was so searching and attentive that it embarrassed her. Under other circumstances she would certainly have delegated her duties to Hannah, but to evade Solomon's society she would have waited on the Sphinx. She brought in each article one at a time, and when there was nothing more to bring inquired deferentially whether there was any thing else that she could do for the lady.

"Yes," said Mrs. Gilbert, gravely; the voice was soft, but the manner most earnest and impressive. "I want five minutes' talk with you; can I have it secure from interruption?"

"Certainly, madam," answered Harry, trembling, she knew not why.

"Close the door, girl. Come nearer, and away from the window; we must not be overheard."

Harry was constitutionally timid, and it struck her that this poor lady was not in her right mind. She hesitated. The other seemed to read her thoughts.

"I am not mad, child," said she, sorrowfully, "though I have trouble enough to make me so. You are the daughter of the landlord of this inn, I think?"

"Yes, madam."

"And I am the mother of Richard Yorke."

She was standing in the same position, and had spoken coldly and as sternly as such a voice as hers could speak, when something in the young girl's face caused her whole manner to change. With a sudden impulse she turned toward her, and held out both her arms; and Harry threw herself into them with a passionate cry, and sobbed as though her heart would break.

"Hush! hush!" whispered the other, tenderly; "we must not weep now, but act!"

But the girl still sobbed on, without lifting up her face. Tears had been strangers to her heated eyes for days, and she had longed in vain for one sympathizing breast on which to lay her head. "I have been his ruin," she murmured; "but for me he would never have done wrong. How you, who are his mother, must hate me!"

"No, Harry, no!" answered the other, putting aside those rich brown locks, and gazing upon the fair shut face attentively. "I do not wonder at his loving you; for such beauty as yours many a man would lose his soul! I did hate you until now. But you love my Richard truly, as I see; and we two can not afford to be enemies. We must work together for his good to avert the ruin of which you speak, for it is imminent. He has sent me to you, for he can not come himself. He is in prison, Harry!"

"In prison! O Heaven, have mercy!"

She sank down on her knees, and covered her face with her hands.

"Yes, Harry, think of it. Our Richard, so bright, so dear, within prison walls! He may pass his life there for what he has done for your sake, unless you help him."

"Help him? I would die for him!"

"Calm yourself. Sit down. To grieve is selfish where one can do better; when all is lost it is time enough for that. All *will* be lost a fortnight hence, unless we bestir ourselves. Hush! I hear a step in the passage. Who is that?"

"It is Sol, madam—Solomon Coe."

"The man you are to marry, is it not?"

A stifled groan was the girl's reply.

"I can not speak what I have to say here," said the other, thoughtfully. "Is there no other place? Stay. I can be ill—overfatigued with my journey—and you will come and tend me in my own room presently. That can be managed, can't it?"

"Yes, madam, yes."

"Then wipe your eyes—be a brave girl. Think of Richard, and not of yourself—think of him, when yonder boor is clasping the hand that once rested in his—think of him, when those alien lips press yours at parting, and be strong! If I were in your place, he would find that I had not deserted him in his trouble."

"Desert him, madam? I? Oh, never!"

"To be weak is to desert him, girl—to let yonder man and your father suspect that any friend of Richard's is beneath this roof is to desert him—to weep when there is need to work is to desert him. Did I not tell you I was his own mother; and yet *I* shed no tears! Look up, and learn your lesson from me."

The faces of the two women were indeed in strong contrast—the younger, yielding, feeble, despairing; the elder, calm, patient of purpose, and inflexible. Her cheeks were plump, and radiant with health; her form erect and composed; her eyes, indeed, betrayed anxiety, but it was from want of confidence in the person she addressed, not in herself; the white hair seemed to fitly crown that figure, so full of earnestness and firmness.

"I will do my best," cried the young girl, "though I know I am but weak and foolish. Pity me, and pray for me. I am going to the torture, but I will be resolute. Tell Hannah—the servant-maid—that you wish me to attend you in your room. Send for me soon, for mercy's sake! How I long to know how I can help our Richard!"

As she left the room Mrs. Gilbert's face grew dark. "A fool! a dolt!" she muttered, angrily. "How could he risk so much for such a stake! Oh, Richard! Richard!"—her voice began to falter at that well-loved name—"was this to have been the end of all my hopes? What fatal issue, then, may not my fears have end in! my beautiful, bright boy! The only light my lonely life possessed! to think of you as like yourself, and then to think of you as you are now!" She looked around her on the sordid walls, the vulgar ornaments upon the mantel-piece, the wretched ill-chosen books; then listened to the splash of the rain in the unpaved street. "And this was Paradise, was it, my poor boy, because this girl dwelt in it! I ought to have known that there was danger here. His letters few and short and far between, his patient tarrying in so wild a place, should have been enough to warn me. But not of this; in no nightmare dream could I have conceived this unimaginable peril. Ah, me! ah, me!" She sat down at the untasted meal, and strove to eat. "I must be strong, for Richard's sake," she murmured. But she soon laid down her knife and fork to muse again. "This Trevethick is a hard, stern man, I see. There is no hope in his mercy. The only path of safety is that which the lawyer pointed out; but will this puling girl have the heart and head to tread it? Will she not faint, as she nearly did just now, and lose her wits when my Richard most requires them? And then, and then?" As if unable to continue such reflections, she rose and rang the bell, which Hannah answered.

"Bring me a bed-candle, girl; I will seek my room at once; and please ask Miss Trevethick to look in upon me before she retires herself, for I feel far from well."

"Yes, ma'am." Hannah thought within herself that the new arrival looked uncommon fresh and well considering her years, and that her young mistress had far more need of rest and "looking to" than she; but, nevertheless, she gave the message; and Harry, at her usual time for going to rest, repaired to the new-comer's room accordingly.

"Are they gone to bed, those men?" inquired Mrs. Gilbert, anxiously, as soon as the door was closed.

"No, madam; my father and Solomon always sit up together now till late."

"Ay; plotting against my boy, I doubt not. Well, let us, then, counterplot. Who sleeps on either side of this room?"

"No one, madam. Both rooms are empty at present; the last visitor, except yourself, left us this evening."

"And the servants?"

"They have retired long ago up stairs."

"That's well. Sit here, then, close to me, and listen. You know that Richard is in prison, placed there by your father and that other man on a false charge. They know as well as I or you that he had no intention of committing the crime of which he stands accused, and yet they both mean to swear the contrary."

"Oh, madam, they will surely not do that!"

"But I say 'Yes;' they want revenge upon him. I know them better than you, who have known them all your life; or perhaps you say they will not, because you hope so. Is it possible," she broke forth, impatiently, "that in such a strait as this, girl, you can encourage such delusions! You are like the fool in the Scripture, of whom it is written, that though thou shouldst bray him among wheat with a pestle, yet will not his foolishness depart from him."

"I know I am not like you, madam," answered Harry, piteously. "Richard has often told me how wise and brave you are; but yet my love for him is as great as yours can be. Whatever you think fit that I should do to help him, that shall be done. Trust me; it shall, indeed."

"That's well said, girl. Be you the hand, and I the head, then, of this enterprise, and we shall conquer yet. I say again, that if they could, these men would swear my Richard's life away. They might as well do that as what they mean to do, and deprive him of his liberty; cast him for years into prison, and herd with the worst and basest of mankind; to work under a task-master with irons on. Do you understand, girl, what it is to which, unless we can hinder them, these wretches would doom him?"

"Yes, yes, I do," she murmured, shuddering. "It is horrible, most horrible! God help us!"

"We must help ourselves," answered Mrs. Gilbert, sternly.

"Yet God is surely on our side, and for the truth, madam. If they swear falsely—"

"You must swear also," interrupted the other, angrily; "you must meet them with their own weapons, if you would defend the innocent against them. As it is, the law is with them, and will prove the instrument of their vengeance. The notes were found upon his person; he strove to change them, that he might pass their substitutes more easily. He counted upon your father not missing them from his strong-box until it was too late. The case is clear against him that he stole them."

"Great Heaven!" cried Harry, clasping her hands in agony; "and yet he did not mean to steal them."

"Of course not; nay more, he did *not* steal them, for *you gave them to him.*"

"*I* gave them to him? Nay, I never did."

"You did—you did, girl; you acquiesced in his plan for obtaining your father's consent to your engagement; you undertook to supply him temporarily with the money requisite to establish his pretensions as a man of fortune. Or, if you did *not*"—and here her voice assumed an intense earnestness—"your Richard, the man you pretend to love, will be a convicted felon—a prisoner for all the summer of his life, and for the rest an outcast!"

Harry was silent; her hands were pressed to her forehead, as though to compel her fevered brain to think without distraction. "I see, I see," she murmured, presently; "his fate hangs upon my word. 'So help me, God,' is what I have first to say, and then say *that!*"

"Why not?" rejoined the other, stoutly. "Will not these men, too, call God to witness what they know to be a lie? Will not *He* discern the motive that prompts *you*—desire to see a wronged man righted, the innocent set free—and the motive that prompts *them*—malicious hate? Or do you deem the all-seeing eye of Heaven is purblind? I tell you this, girl, if I were in *your* place, and the man I loved stood *justly* in such peril, I would swear a score such oaths to set him free! Yet here, with justice on your side and truth, and Heaven itself, you hesitate; you shrink from uttering a mere form of words, the spirit of which is contrary to the letter, and for conscience sake, forsooth, will let your lover perish! *Your* lover! yes, but you were never *his*, although he thinks so. I will go hence, and tell him that you refuse to speak the thing that alone can save him from life-long wretchedness; I will go and tell him that the girl for whose sake he has brought this load of ruin on himself will not so much as lift it with her little finger! You fair, foul devil, how I hate you!" She drew herself up to her full height, and regarded the wretched girl with such contemptuous scorn that even in her abject misery she felt its barb.

"I have not earned your hate," said Harry, with some degree of firmness, "if I have earned your scorn; nor is it meet that you should so despise me, because I fear to anger God."

"And man," added the other, with bitterness. "You fear your father's wrath far more than Heaven's."

That bolt went home: the unhappy girl did indeed stand in greater terror of her father than of the sin of perjury; and the idea of affirming upon oath what she had but a few days before so solemnly denied to him was filling her with consternation and dismay. Still the picture that had just been drawn of the ruin that would assuredly befall her Richard, unless she interposed to save him, had more vivid colors even than that of Trevethick's anger. Let him kill her, if he would, after the trial was over, but Richard should go free.

"I will do your bidding, madam," said she, suddenly, "though I perish, body and soul."

"You say that now, girl, and it's well and bravely said; but will you have strength to put your words to proof? When I am gone, and there are none but Richard's foes about you, will you resist their menaces, their arguments, their cajolements, and be true as steel?"

"I will, I will; I swear it," answered Harry, passionately; "they shall never turn me from it. But suppose they prevent me from leaving Gethin, from attending at the trial at all?"

"Well thought of!" answered Mrs. Gilbert, approvingly; "she has some wits, then, after all, this girl. As for their forbidding you to give evidence, however, Mr. Weasel, who is Richard's lawyer, will see to that. You will be subpœnaed as a witness for the defense. You will say, then, that it was you who opened the strong-box, and took out the notes, and gave them into Richard's hand."

"But how could I open the letter padlock?"

"Good, again!" answered the other; "you have asked the very question for which I have brought the answer. Now, listen! Have you access to your father's watch at times when he does not wear it?"

"Yes; he does not always put it on—never on the day he goes to market, for instance. He comes back late, you see."

"Just so; and sometimes, perhaps, not altogether sober. Very good. Now, you once opened that watch from curiosity, and saw a paper in its case with B N Z upon it. Those letters formed the secret by which the lock was opened. You tried it, just in fun at first, and found they did. Do you understand?"

"I do," said Harry.

"You will not forget, then, what you have to say; or shall I recapitulate it?"

"There is no need," groaned Harry. "I shall remember it forever, be sure of that, and on my death-bed most of all." With a wearied look on her wan face, and a heavy sigh, the young girl rose to go. "Good-night, madam. We need not speak of this again to-morrow, need we?"

"Surely not, child. My mission here is done. The rain is falling still, and that will be a sufficient excuse for my departure. I had a sick headache to-night—remember that—but it will be better after a night's sleep."

"Do you sleep?" asked Harry, simply. "Ah me, I would that *I* could sleep!"

"Of course I do. Is it not necessary for Richard's sake that I should be well and strong? I could weep all night and fast all day, if I let my foolish heart have its own will. It is easy enough to grieve at any time; one has only to think to do that. Sleep, child, sleep, and dream of him as he will be when you have set him free; then wake to work his freedom. I will tell him that you will do so. Press your lips to mine, that I may carry their sweet impress back to him. One moment more. Do not get your lesson by heart, lest they should doubt you; but hold by this one sentence, and never swerve from it: 'I gave Richard Yorke the notes with my own hand.' That is the key which can alone unlock his prison-door. Good-night, good-night."

CHAPTER XXVI.

MR. ROBERT BALFOUR.

An author of sensitive organization has always a difficulty in treating the subject of prison life. If he avoids details, the critics do not ascribe it to delicacy, but to incompetence; if, on the other hand, he enters into them, they nudge the elbow of the public, and hint that this particular phase of human experience is his specialty—that he "ought to know," because he has been "through the mill" himself. This is not kind, of course; but the expression, "a little more than kin and less than kind," is exceedingly applicable to the critic in relation to his humble brother, the author. We will take a middle course, then, and exhibit only just so much of Cross Key as may be seen in a "justice's visit."

Twenty years ago, the system of treatment of prisoners before trial incarcerated in her Majesty's jails was not so uniform as it now is. In some they were permitted few privileges not enjoyed by the convicts themselves; in others a considerable difference was made between the two classes. The establishment at Cross Key leaned to the side of indulgence. Its inmates who were awaiting their trial were allowed to wear their own clothes; to write letters to their friends without supervision (though not without the suspicion of it on their own part); and to mingle together for some hours in a common room, where that unbroken silence which pervades all our modern Bastiles, and is perhaps their most terrible feature, was not insisted upon. In this common room Richard Yorke was sitting on the afternoon following his incarceration. The principal meal of the day had been just concluded, and himself and his fellow-guests were brooding moodily over their troubles. The platters, the block-tin knives, so rounded that the most determined self-destroyer could never job himself with them into Hades, and the metal mugs had been removed, and their places on the narrow deal table were occupied by a few periodicals of a somewhat depressing character, though "devoted to the cultivation of quiet cheerfulness," and by a leaden inkstand much too large to be swallowed. The prisoners — upon the ground, perhaps, of not needing the wings of liberty for any other purpose — were expected to furnish (from them) their own pens. There were but half a dozen of these unfortunates; all, with two exceptions, were of the same type—that of the ordinary agricultural criminal. Ignorant, slouching, dogged, they might have fired a rick, or killed a keeper, or even—sacrilegious but unthinking boors—have shot a great man's pheasant. They did not make use of their privileges of conversation beyond a muttered word or two, but stared stupidly at the pictures in the magazines, wondering (as well they might) at the benevolent faces of the landlords, clergymen, and all persons in authority therein portrayed, or perhaps not wondering at them at all, but rather pondering whether Bet and the children had gone into "the House" or not by this time, or whether the man in the big wig would be hard upon themselves next Wednesday three weeks.

One of these two exceptions was, of course, our hero, who looked, by contrast with these poor, simple malefactors, like a being from another world, a fallen angel, but with the evil forces of his new abode already gathering fast within him. His capacities for ill, indeed, were ten times theirs; and the dusky glow of his dark eyes evinced that they were at work, though they did but ineffectually reflect the hell of hate that was beginning to be lit within him. It flamed against the whole world of his fellow-creatures, so mad he was with pride and scorn and rage; his hand should be against every man henceforth, as theirs was now against him; his motto, like the *exeunt* exclamation of the mob in the play, should be: "Fire, burn, slay!" He was like a spoiled child who for the first time has received a severe punishment—for a wonder, not wholly deserved—and who wishes, in his vengeful passion, that all mankind might have one neck in common with his persecutor, that (forgetting he is no Hercules) his infant arms might throttle it off-hand. The love which he still felt for Harry and his mother, far from softening him toward others, rather increased his bitterness of spirit. They, too, were suffering wrong and ill-treatment, and needed an avenger. His fury choked him, so that he had eaten nothing of what had been set before him, and he now sat leaning with his elbows on the bare boards, staring with heated eyes at the blank wall before him, and feeding on his own heart.

"This is your first time in quod, I guess, young gentleman," observed a quiet voice beside him.

Richard started. He had thrown one contemptuous glance upon the company when they first assembled, and had decided that they possessed no more interest for him than a herd of cattle; buried in his own sombre thoughts, he had lost consciousness of their very presence, as of that of the warder, who was pacing up and down the room with monotonous tread. But now that his attention was thus drawn to his next neighbor, he saw that he differed somewhat from the rest; not that he was more intelligent-looking—for, indeed, there was a reckless brutality in his expression which the others lacked—but there was a certain resolution and strength of will in his face, which at least told of power. But it was the tone of voice, which, coming from such a man, though it was a gruff voice enough in itself, had something conciliatory and winning in it, that chiefly attracted Richard. Perhaps, too, the phrase "young gentleman" flattered his vanity. We can not throw off all our weaknesses at a moment's notice, no matter how stupendous the crisis in our fortunes, any more than, though our boat be sinking under us, we can divest ourselves of our clothes with a single shrug; and sympathy and deferential respect had still their weight with Richard Yorke. Perhaps, too, his nature had not yet even got quit of its gregariousness, and he was not sorry to have his acquaintance sought, though by this hang-dog thief.

"I have never been in prison before, if that is what you mean," returned he, civilly.

He who asked the question was a stout-built, grizzled fellow, of about fifty years. He was dressed like a well-to-do farmer, but his accent smacked of London rather than the country; and his hands, Richard observed, were not so coarse and rough as might be expected in one used to manual labor, though his limbs and frame were powerful enough for the most arduous toil. His gray eyes looked keenly at Richard from under their bushy brows, as he propounded a second inquiry:

"What are you in for? Forgery or embezzlement, I reckon—which is it?"

"Neither," answered Richard, laconically, a bitter smile parting his lips in spite of himself.

"Well, now, that's curious," observed the other, coolly. "If it was not that you were sent here with the rest of us, and not shut up by yourself, I should have guessed 'Murder' outright, for you were looking all that a minute ago; and since it could not be murder, I thought it must be one of the other two."

"I don't know what I am here for," said Richard, gloomily, "except that the charge is false."

"Oh, of course," rejoined the other, with a grim chuckle; "it's always false the first time, and as often afterward as we can get the juries to believe us. I'm an old hand myself, and my feelings are not easily wounded; but I have never yet disgraced myself by pleading guilty. It's throwing a chance away, unless you are a very beautiful young woman who has put away her baby, and that I never was, nor did."

"Beauty in distress mollifies the court, does it?" inquired Richard, willing to be won from his own wretchedness by talk even with a man like this.

"Mollifies!—yes, it makes a molly of every body. I have known a judge shed tears about it, which he is not bound to do unless he has the black cap on—that always set him going like an onion. Why, I've seen even an attorney use his pocket-handkerchief because of a pretty face in trouble; but then she was his client, to be sure. Talking of attorneys, you'll have Weasel, of course?"

Richard nodded an affirmative.

"Quite right. I should have him myself, if there was a shadow of a chance; but, as it is, it's throwing good money out o' winder. I wish you better luck, young gentleman, than mine is like to be; not that you want luck, of course, but only justice."

Richard did not relish this tone of banter, and he showed it in his look.

"Come, come," said the other, good-humoredly, "it is a pity to curdle such a handsome face as yours with sour thoughts. Let us be friends, for you may be glad of even a friend like me some dirty day."

"It is very likely," answered Richard, bitterly. "I see no fine days ahead, nor yet fine friends."

"I hope you will see both," answered the other, frankly. "The first time one finds one's self provided for so extra careful as this," with a glance at the iron bars across the low-arched windows, "the prospect always does seem dark. But one learns to look upon the bright side at last. Is the figure very heavy that you're in for? Excuse my country manners: I don't mean to be rude, nor do I ask the question from mere curiosity; but you don't look like one to have come here for a mere trifle."

"The amount in question is two thousand pounds."

"No whistling there!" cried the warder, peremptorily, for the "old hand" had not been able to repress an expression of emotion at this announcement. He looked at Richard with an air of self-complacency, such as a gentleman of the middle classes exhibits on suddenly discovering that he has been in familiar converse with a person of title, or a small trader on being brought into unexpected connection with a merchant prince. The gigantic character of the "operation" had invested this young man with an increased interest in the stranger's eye.

"That's a great beginning," said he, admiringly, "and could scarcely have happened with a poor devil like me. One requires to be born a gentleman to have such opportunities. Now, I don't mind telling *you*," here he sank his voice to a whisper, and looked cautiously about him, "that I was forty years of age before I ever got such a haul as yours. I've done better since, but it's been up-hill work, for all that."

"It doesn't seem to have been very hard work," said Richard, with a meaning glance at the other's hand.

"Well, no, I can't say as it's been hard; a neat touch is what is wanted in my profession."

"Why, you're not a pick—" Richard hesitated from motives of delicacy.

"A pickpocket? Well, I hope not, Sir, indeed," interrupted the other, indignantly.

"Then what *are* you?" said Richard, bluntly.

As a coy maiden blushes and hangs her head in silence when asked the question which she is yet both proud and pleased to answer in the affirmative, so did Mr. Robert Balfour (for such was the name of our new acquaintance) pause and in graceful confusion rub his stubble chin with his closed fist ere he replied: "Well, the fact is, I have been in the gold and precious stone line these thirty years, and never in the provinces until this present summer, when I came down here, as a Yankee pal of mine once put it, 'to open a little jewelry store.'"

"With a crowbar?" suggested Richard, with a faint smile.

"Just so," said the other, nodding; "and it so happened that yours truly, Bob Balfour, was caught in the very act."

"And what term of punishment do you expect for such a—"

"Such a misfortune as that?" answered Mr. Balfour, hastening to relieve Richard's embarrassment. "Well, if I had got the swag, I should —considering the testimonials that will be handed in—have been a lifer. But since I did not realize so much as a weddin' *ring*, twenty years ought to see me through it now."

Twenty years! Why, this man would be over seventy before he regained his liberty!

"Great Heaven!" cried Richard, "can you be cheerful with such a future before you! and at the end of it, to be turned old and penniless into the wide world!"

A genuine pity showed itself in the young man's look and tone. A minute before he had thought himself the most wretched of human beings; yet here was one whose fate was even harder, and who met it without repining. Community of trouble had already touched the heart which he had thought was turned to stone.

"Are you sorry for me, young gentleman," inquired the convict, in an altered voice, "you who have got so much trouble of your own to bear?"

"I am, indeed," said Richard, frankly.

"You would not write a letter for me, though, would you?" inquired the other, wistfully. "I should like to tell—somebody as I've left at home —where I am gone to; and the fact is, I can't write; I never learned how to do it."

A blush came over Bob Balfour's face for the first time; the man was ashamed of his ignorance, though not of his career of crime. "If it's too much trouble, say so," added he, gruffly. "Perhaps it was too great a favor to ask of a gentleman born."

"Not at all," said Richard, hastily, "if the man will bring us pen and paper."

"Hush! the *officer*, if you please," said Balfour. "They like to be 'officered,' these gentry, every one of them. Some friends of mine always addresses 'em as 'dogs;' but that's a mistake, when they has to watch you."

Mr. Robert Balfour spoke a few respectful words to the warder, and the requisite materials were soon laid upon the table. Richard dipped his pen in the ink, and waited for directions. "It's only a few words," muttered Mr. Balfour, apologetically, "to my old mother. Perhaps you have a mother yourself, young gentleman?"

"I have." He had written to her guardedly the previous day, before he left Plymouth, to tell her the same sad news which he was now, as he supposed, about to repeat for another, and to urge her to repair to Cross Key at once.

Mr. Balfour beat softly on the table with his forefinger for a moment, and then, as though he had found the key-note of the desired composition, dictated as follows:

"My dear Mother,—When this comes to hand, I shall have took your advice, and started for the New World. There's a ship a-sailing from Plymouth in a day or two, and my passage in her is booked. I didn't like to come back to town again, for fear I should change my mind, and turn to the old trade. The post is queer and doubtful, they tell me, in these far-away parts; but you shall hear from me whenever I have an opportunity. All as is mine is yours, remember; so, use it. I have no need of money myself, for there's a place being kep for me, out yonder, in the carpentering line. Hoping this finds you well, as it leaves me, I am your dutiful son, Robert Balfour."

"Then you don't tell her any thing about what's happened to you?" said Richard, wonderingly.

"Why should I? The poor soul's over seventy, and will never see me again. It's much better that she should have a pretty picture to look at than such a reality as this; ain't it?"

"Well, I suppose it is."

This delicate feeling on the part of Mr. Balfour jarred upon Richard. *He* had taken no pains to break the news of his imprisonment to *his* mother; on the contrary, he had painted the wretchedness of his position, with a view to set forth the urgent necessity for help, in its most sombre colors. Of course there was a great difference in the two cases, an immense difference; but still he resented this exhibition of natural piety, as contrasting unpleasantly with his own conduct.

The other, however, had no suspicion of this. His thoughts, just then, were far away; and the subject of them gave an unwonted softness to his tone as he observed: "I thank you for this, kindly, young gentleman. Here's the address—Earl Street, Spitalfields. It's her own house; and she will have enough, and to spare, while she lives, thank the Lord! Well, that's done with; and if Bob Balfour can do you a good turn for it, he will. Hello, you're wanted."

"Richard Yorke!" repeated the warder, loudly. "Can't you hear?"

Richard had heard well enough; but the idea that it was his mother who had come to see him had for the moment unmanned him; he well knew how proud she had been of him; and how was he to meet her now, disgraced, disheartened, in prison, a reputed thief! But the next instant he reflected that her arrival could not be possibly looked for for some days; perhaps it was Trevethick, who had, in the mean time, learned all, and was come to announce his willingness to withdraw from the prosecution; perhaps Harry herself was with him; perhaps—

But there was no time for further prognostication; a second warder was at the door, beckoning impatiently, and Richard rose at once. The dull faces of the rest were all raised toward him with a malign aspect; they feared that some good news was come for him, that they were about to lose a companion in misfortune. Only one held out his hand, with a "Good luck to you, young gentleman; though I never see you again, I shall not forget you."

"Silence there!" cried the officer in charge, as Richard passed out into the stone passage. "You ought to know our ways better than that, Balfour."

CHAPTER XXVII.

ATTORNEY AND CLIENT.

In a hall of stone stood a room of glass, and in that room the inmates of Cross Key Jail were permitted to have access to their legal advisers. They were not lost sight of by the jealous guardians of the place, one of whom perambulated the hall throughout the interview; but though he could see all that passed, he could hear nothing. Mr. Weasel of Plymouth was very well known at Cross Key as being a frequent visitor to that transparent apartment, and those prisoners whom he favored with his attentions were justly held in high estimation by the warders, as gentlemen who, though in difficulties, had at least some considerable command of ready money. He was waiting now, with his hat on (which he always wore, to increase his very limited stature), in this chamber of audience; and so withered up he looked, and such a sharp, shrunk face he had, that Richard, seeing him in the glass case, might have thought him some dried specimen of humanity, not alive at all, had he not chanced to be in the act of taking snuff; and even that was ghostly too, since it produced the pantomimic action of sneezing without its accompanying sound.

"Mr. Richard Yorke, I believe?" said he, as soon as they were shut up within the walls of glass. "I am glad to make your acquaintance, Sir, though I wish, for your sake, that it happened in another place. You'll excuse my not offering you my hand."

Richard drew back his extended arm and turned crimson.

"Don't be offended, Sir," said the lawyer; "but the fact is, the authorities here don't like it. There are some parties in this place who employ very queer legal advisers; and in shaking hands, a file or a gimlet, and a bit of tobacco, are as likely to pass as not. That warder can see every thing, my dear young Sir; but he can no more hear what we say than he can understand what a couple of bumble-bees are murmuring about who are barred up in a double window. We can therefore converse with one another as much without reserve as we please, or rather"—and here the little man's eyes twinkled significantly—"as *you* please. What I hear from a client in this ridiculous place is never revealed beyond it, except so far as it may serve his interests. If Mr. Dodge (to whose favor, as I understand, I owe this introduction) has told you any thing concerning me, he will, I am sure, have advised you to be quite frank and candid."

"There was no necessity for such a warning, Mr. Weasel, in my case, I do assure you," answered Richard, earnestly. "I have nothing to conceal from you with respect to the circumstances of my position: they are unfortunate, and doubtless very suspicious; but I am as innocent of this disgraceful charge—"

"Hush, hush! my dear Sir; this will never do. It is mere waste of time, though it might have been much worse. Good Heavens! suppose you had been guilty, and told me *that!* you would have placed me in the most embarrassing situation, as your professional adviser, it is possible for the human mind to conceive. What I want to know is *your* story, so far as these two thousand pounds found in your possession are concerned. Whether it is true or not, does not matter a button. I want to know whether it *seems* true; whether it will seem true to a judge and jury. You have thought the matter over, of course; you have gone through it in your own mind from beginning to end—now please to go over it to me."

The little man whipped out a note-book, leaned forward in his chair, and looked all eye and ear, like a terrier watching at a rat-hole.

After a moment's pause, Richard stated his case pretty much as we are already acquainted with it; the little lawyer interrupting him now and then by a gesture, but never by a word, in order that he might set down a point or a memorandum.

"Very good," said Mr. Weasel, when he had quite finished. "That's your story, is it?"

"It's the truth, Sir."

"Hush! my dear young Sir. We shall have enough of that—the truth, the whole truth, and nothing but the truth—a fortnight hence. What you and I have to consider are the probabilities. Why did you go to Plymouth, more than any other place, to change these notes?"

"Because I had heard there was a Miners' Bank there, and Trevethick had mentioned the notes of that company as being as good, in his opinion, as those of the Bank of England. I thought it would be easier to get the Mining notes in exchange for those of the Bank of England, than others of the same bank."

"The check which you showed this Trevethick was not, then, a *bonâ fide* piece of paper, eh?"

"It was not," said Richard, casting down his eyes.

"Very good," answered the lawyer, so cheerfully that you would have thought his client had cleared himself of the least suspicion upon *that* score, at all events. "Now, where did you get it?"

"My mother sent me a blank check, at my request, and I filled it in."

"That check is destroyed, you say—you burned it, of course?"

"No; I tore it up, and threw it out of the window of the carriage."

"The devil you did!" said Mr. Weasel, in perturbation. "That is not the way to destroy checks. Had your mother an account at the bank on which it was drawn?"

"Of course," said Richard, simply.

"There is nothing 'of course,' Mr. Yorke, in this matter," answered the lawyer, gravely. "Are you quite sure?"

"Quite. She has always had an account there; though to no such amount as two thousand pounds."

"It is a large sum," muttered the lawyer, thoughtfully, "but still they have not lost one penny of it. In case things went against you, Mr. Yorke, would an appeal to the prosecutor be likely to be of service?"

"Certainly not," answered Richard, hastily. "I would not accept mercy at his hands; besides, it is not a question of mercy."

"It may come to that," observed the other, gravely. "We must not deceive ourselves, Mr. Yorke."

"Good Heavens! do you believe, then, that I took this money with intent to steal it?"

"What my belief is is of no consequence, one way or the other; but my opinion is that the jury will take that view, if they hear your story as you tell it. The fact is, you have left out the most important incident of all: the whole case will hinge upon the young lady's having given you these notes with her own hand. It is evident, of course, that she sympathized with you in your scheme," pursued the lawyer, rapidly, and holding up his finger to forbid the protest that was already rising to Richard's lip: "nothing could be more natural, though most imprudent and ill judged, than her behavior. She had no more idea of stealing the money than you had; how should she, since it was in a manner her own, she being her father's sole heiress. You and I see that clearly enough, but to a jury used to mere matters of fact, motive has little significance unless put into action. What we want, and what we must have, is evidence that you got these notes, not only for this girl's sake, but from her fingers. Nobody can hurt *her*, you know. Trevethick could never prosecute his own daughter; indeed, the whole affair dwindles down to a lover's stratagem, and there is no need for prosecuting any body, if we can only put Harry Trevethick into the witness-box. Now can we, Mr. Yorke, or can we not? that's the question."

Richard was silent; the lawyer's argument struck him with its full force. He had no scruples on the matter for his own part, but he feared that Harry might entertain them—they would be only too much in keeping with her credulous and superstitious nature.

"If I could talk to her alone for five minutes," muttered Richard, uneasily.

"That is impossible," said Mr. Weasel, with decision. "We can only play with such cards as we hold. I could go to Gethin myself, though it would be most inconvenient at this busy time, and refresh this young woman's memory; but it is a delicate task, and would be looked upon by the other side with some suspicion. Now, is there no judicious friend that can be thoroughly depended upon—a female friend, if possible, since the affair may require tact and sympathy—to effect this little negotiation? Think, my good Sir, think."

"Why, there is my mother herself!" ejaculated Richard, suddenly. "She is the wisest of women, and the very one to conduct this matter, if properly instructed."

"Is she, now, is she?" said the lawyer, cheerily. "Come, come, that's well, and I begin to see a little light. Let her go down to Gethin, where, as I conclude, she is not known, and see Miss Trevethick herself. I should like to see her beforehand, however; indeed, that is absolutely necessary."

"In my note to her, yesterday, I asked her to call at your office in Plymouth on her way hither," stammered Richard. "I thought it better—that is, in the first instance—that she should hear from you how matters stood."

Mr. Weasel took a copious pinch of snuff, and shut his eyes, as though he were going to sneeze. Whenever a client got upon an embarrassing topic Mr. Weasel took snuff, to obviate the necessity of looking him in the face; while, in case of any compromising disclosure, Mr. Weasel sneezed, to obviate hearing it.

"In a case of this kind, Mr. Yorke, not a moment is to be lost. I should advise your mother's going direct to Gethin from my house, and making sure of this young lady's evidence. There is even a possibility—I don't say it is probable, but there is just a chance, you see—that she may be subpœnaed *by the other side.*"

"Just so," assented Richard, so naïvely that a smile flitted across the little lawyer's face.

"Under these circumstances, then, this is what we will do, my dear young Sir: Mrs. Yorke will go to the *Gethin Castle* as a guest, and, as I shall venture to suggest, under another name; she will then find an opportunity of speaking to Miss Trevethick without awakening her father's suspicions; and when she comes to Cross Key, she will have, I trust, some good news to bring you, something to talk about (although you must be very careful and guarded, mind that, for you will not be left alone together, as we are) besides mere regrets and lamentations; don't you see, don't you see?"

Richard saw exceedingly well, and felt more grateful to the lawyer for devising such an arrangement than he would like to have confessed; nevertheless, he did thank him heartily.

"Not at all, not at all, my dear young Sir," drawing on one of his gloves, in signal of departure. "In a case like this, we must consult feelings as well as array our facts; we must bring heart and head to bear together. Speaking of head reminds me, by-the-by, of the subject of counsel. I propose to instruct Mr. Smoothbore, who leads upon this circuit; I gather from your letter that there will be no difficulty with respect to funds."

"Whatever may be necessary, Mr. Weasel, for my defense will be, you may rest assured, forthcoming. My mother—"

The smile disappeared from the lawyer's face with electrical rapidity. "Pardon me, my young friend," said he; "but as a professional man, I only deal with principals in these matters. The word forthcoming is a little vague. Counsel are paid beforehand, you must remember."

We must not be angry with Mr. Weasel, who was really a good sort of man after his kind. He was naturally cautious, and if he had been the most trustful of mankind his experience would have taught him prudence. He did like to see his money down; and really, as to Mr. Yorke, all he knew of his pecuniary position was with relation to that blank check, the history of which was not of a nature to inspire confidence.

"I was about to observe," said Richard, haughtily, "that my mother would satisfy all claims; but, in the mean time, there were over a hundred pounds in notes and gold which were found upon me when I was searched at Plymouth. If you doubt me, you have only to make inquiries."

"My dear young Sir," returned the lawyer, earnestly, "this is not courteous, this is not kind. I never doubted you from the first moment that I saw you; no one with any knowledge of mankind could do so. Professional etiquette compelled me to remark that I could treat with principals only, that is all. Let me see," added he, consulting his note-book, "have I any thing more to say? Yes, yes. With respect to this young lady, Miss Harry Trevethick—I did not like to interrupt you at the time, but I see I have made a memorandum—is she pretty?"

"She is very, very beautiful," said Richard, earnestly, the remembrance of her beauty giving a tenderness to his tone.

"That's capital!" nodded the lawyer. "Old Bantam is our judge this session, and he likes a pretty face. So do we all, for the matter of that, I hope. You are young and good-looking yourself, too; Smoothbore will make something of *that*, you may depend upon it. 'Gracious Heavens, is the iron arm of the law to sunder these happy lovers for a mere indiscretion, and make their bright young lives a blank forever?' He'll give them something like that, Sir, in a voice broken by emotion, and bring you off with flying colors."

"I don't care about the colors, if he only brings me off," said Richard, grimly.

"A very natural remark, my dear young Sir, for one in your present situation; but three weeks hence, as I both hope and believe, you will not be so easily satisfied; the more we have, the more we want, you know—except in the matter of time. I have very little to spare of it just now, and must therefore take my leave."

Mr. Weasel had put on his other glove and his hat, and, with a cheerful nod, had actually placed his fingers on the door-handle, when he suddenly turned round, and said: "By-the-by, I had almost forgotten a little form of words, which in your case I am sure will be *but* a form, and yet I do not like to omit it. I never leave a client in your position without asking him the question; so you must excuse me, my young friend, and not be offended."

"I am not in a position to be very sensitive about what is said to me," answered Richard, bitterly. "Pray ask whatever you please."

Mr. Weasel looked cautiously round, to see that the warder was not too near, and lowered his voice to a whisper. "Is this little affair your first, my dear young Sir? I mean," added he, "have you ever been in trouble with the law before?"

"Certainly not," replied Richard, smiling.

"I had anticipated your answer," said the little lawyer, gayly; "but I thought it right to make quite certain. Because, if the affair should happen to reach a stage where the question of 'character' is mooted (though it won't get so far as *that*, I trust, in our case), one doesn't like to be taken altogether by surprise, do you see? You have been a landscape-painter, you say. A most innocent and charming occupation, I am sure, and one which Smoothbore will make the very most of. The case altogether will afford him such opportunities that he really ought to do it cheap. And you've never been any thing else, have you? never had any other calling, or obtained your livelihood by any other than quite legal and permissible means—eh? What, what? You have not been quite frank and candid with me, my dear Sir, I fear."

"It is really not of much consequence," said Richard, hesitating.

"You must allow me to be the judge of that, Mr. Yorke," said the other, gravely, taking off his hat once more and one of his gloves. "Imagine yourself a good Catholic, if you please, with Father Weasel for your priest."

The confession lasted for some minutes.

"I think you will admit that what I have told you has not much bearing upon the matter in hand," said Richard, when he had finished.

"None at all, none at all—that is, I hope not," answered the other, thoughtfully. "But what an interesting revelation it is! What a nice point as to whether the matter is an offense against the law or not! How prettily Smoothbore would treat the subject, if it chanced to come in his way!" He looked at Richard with admiration. "You're a most remarkable young man, Sir; I wish that circumstances permitted of my shaking you by the hand. Good-morning, my dear Sir. You may depend upon my not permitting the grass to grow under my feet. When your mother comes she will have good news for you. Good-morning."

The warder took possession of Richard, while Mr. Weasel, followed by the young man's longing eyes, was ushered to the opposite door, on the other side of which was liberty. But the lawyer's mind was still within the prison walls, though his legs were free, and walking up the street of the little town toward his inn.

"Now, that is really a most remarkable young man," he murmured to himself. "A most ingenious young fellow, upon my word. The idea of his having invented a new crime! Why, bless my heart, it's quite an epoch—quite an epoch!"

CHAPTER XXVIII.

THE IRON CAGE.

So long as Richard had had Mr. Weasel to bear him company, half his troubles—so elastic was his nature, and so apt for social intercourse—seemed to have been removed; but now that that brisk, confident voice was heard no more, and the stone passages only echoed to the tread of the warder and himself, his spirits sank even lower than they had been before. Alone in his comfortless cell, he went over the lawyer's talk anew, and it was strange how the sparks of comfort died out of it. It was clear that in the first instance his companion had taken a gloomy view of his case, that he looked upon Richard's own story with utter disbelief, and was convinced it would not hold water before a jury. His remark about the money having been recovered must have had reference to a possible mitigation of the sentence, and therefore took conviction for granted. Nor, upon reconsideration of the case with calmness—the calm of loneliness and despair—was, Richard himself admitted, any other conclusion to be arrived at by a stranger. Those who were acquainted with his rash and impulsive character and reckless ways would understand that he had no serious intention of robbing Trevethick—except, that is, of his daughter; even Trevethick himself must be aware of that; though, with that same exception before his eyes, it was more than doubtful whether he would acknowledge it. Smarting with the sense of the deceit that Richard had practiced (almost with success) upon him, he might conceal his real impression of the affair, and treat it as a common felony. Taking the brutality of Solomon's manner to him when he was arrested as an index of his prosecutor's purpose, he felt that this was what would happen; and if so, what chance would he have against such evidence? Would the judge and jury be persuaded to believe that he had acted with the romantic folly that had in reality possessed him? And if not, to what protracted wretchedness might he not be doomed!

His old hopes, in short, lay dead within him, and he felt that his late adviser had been right in suggesting the evidence of Harry Trevethick as the only means to secure his acquittal. He did not look beyond *that* for an hour. Life for the next three weeks would have but one event for him—his trial and its result. The little attorney, whom he had seen but once, the suasive barrister, of whom he had only heard, were from henceforth the two persons upon earth who had the most interest for him of all mankind. If *they* failed him, all was lost. If they succeeded, all, or what had now become his all, was gained. He thought of Harry only as the being upon whose testimony his fate depended; he did not picture her to himself in any other character, though perhaps he would have refused to part with her even at the price of that liberty which had become so precious in his eyes. She would surely not refuse to say the half-dozen words which were the "open sesame" that alone could set him free! He thought of his mother, not so much as such—the truest and most unselfish friend he had—as the person best qualified to win Harry over to speak those words. He was no longer ashamed to see her; his heart was so full of anxious fear that there was no room for shame; but he was glad that the lawyer had recommended her to visit Gethin before coming to Cross Key. What he thirsted for was hope, a gleam of sunshine, a whisper of good news. If his mother had not that to give him, let her stay away. He did not wish his heart to be melted within him by regrets and tears; if there was no hope, let it harden on, till it was as hard as adamant, for the hour, that, however long delayed, must come at last—of vengeance! He thought of Solomon Coe as one of a dominant race thinks of the slave who has become his master, and was his murderer in his heart ten times a day. He thought of him as the man who would marry Trevethick's daughter, his own Harry, while he (Richard) rotted in jail.

Such were the bitter reflections, creeping fears, and meagre hopes which consumed him when he was alone, that is to say, for five-sixths of the day and all the weary night. In the society of Balfour he found, if not solace, at least some respite from his gnawing cares. The importance which this man had attached to the recovery of stolen goods as mitigating the punishment of crime, and to good looks in the case of a female witness or prisoner, corroborated as it had been by the judicial experience of Mr. Weasel, gave him confidence in the convict's intelligence; or, at least, in his judgment with respect to the matter on which Richard's thoughts were solely concentrated. He was never weary of asking this man's opinion on this point and on that of his own case, the details of which he fully confided to him. Balfour, on his part, gave him his best advice, and whatever comfort he could. He did not resent, nor even seem to be aware of the fact, that the position in which he stood himself awoke no corresponding sympathy in Richard. He had taken a fancy to this young fellow, so different from any companion that he had ever known; was flattered by his confidence; and felt that enthusiasm toward him which friendship, when it exists between two persons of widely different grades, sometimes begets in the inferior.

A week passed on, and then, at the same time and place as before, Richard was summoned from his fellow-prisoners. He turned pale in spite of himself, as he rose from the table to meet for the first time, since disgrace had overwhelmed him, his mother's face.

"Don't give way, my young master," whispered Balfour, good-naturedly, "for that will only make the old woman fret."

Richard nodded, and followed the warder, who on this occasion led the way through a different door. "It ain't Mr. Weasel this time," said the latter, in answer to his look of surprise; "it's a private friend, and therefore we can't let you have the glass box." He ushered him into what would have been a stone court-yard, except that it had a roof also of stone. In the middle of this, running right across it, was a sort of cage of iron, or rather a passage some six feet broad, shut in on either side by high iron rails; within this paced an officer of the prison; and on the other side of it stood a female figure, whom Richard at once recognized as his mother. It was with this iron cage between them, and in the presence of an official, that prisoners in Cross Key Jail were alone permitted to receive the visits of their friends and kinsfolk. It was no wonder that in an interview under such restrictions, Mr. Weasel should have recommended caution.

To do Richard justice, however, that was not the reflection that now passed through his mind. For all his selfish thoughts and calculations, he had really yearned to cast himself on his mother's breast, and feel once more her loving arms around him; to whisper in her ever-ready ear his sorrow for the past, his anxieties for the future; and when he saw that this was not to be, the heart that he would have poured out before her seemed to sink and shrink within him. In this material obstacle between them he seemed to behold a type of the dread doom that was impending over him—separation from humanity, exclusion from the world without, a life-long entombment within stone walls. He put his hand and arm through the bars, mechanically, to touch his mother's fingers, and when he found he could not reach them, he burst into tears. It was only by a great effort that Mrs. Yorke could maintain her self-control; but she, nevertheless, did do so. Her face was calm, and her eyes, though full of tenderness and pity, were tearless; only her low, soft voice gave token of the woe within her in its tremulous and faltering tones.

"Dear Richard," it said, "my own dear Richard, take heart; a few days hence, and you will be folded in your mother's arms; not to stray from them again, I trust, my boy, my boy!" She pressed her forehead with its fine white hair against the cruel bars, and seemed to devour him with her loving eyes. "All will yet be well," she continued; "your innocence can not fail to be established, and this dreadful time will be forgotten like an evil dream."

"Have you been to Gethin, mother?"

"Yes, dear; I only came from thence this morning. Harry sent you her best love. Your faith in her, she bade me tell you, is not misplaced; *she will be in the witness-box, for certain.*" This last sentence was uttered in the French tongue, and very rapidly.

"I am very sorry, ma'am," interrupted the official, who had retired to the further extremity of the cage, "but my orders are to prohibit conversation between prisoners and their friends in a foreign language."

"I will take care not to transgress again," said Mrs. Yorke, with a sweet smile; "your consideration for us I am sure demands all obedience."

"Has Mr. Weasel made his arrangements, mother?"

"Yes, all; the subpœna will be sent to Gethin to morrow. He is most confident as to the result."

"And what does Mr. Smoothbore say? Have you seen *him?*"

"No, dear, no. But the matter on which I went to Gethin having been satisfactorily arranged, we may consider that is all settled. Your counsel has no doubt of being able to establish your innocence, notwithstanding the malice of your enemies."

"But what is he like, this Smoothbore?"

"Well, the fact is, Richard, we have not got him, but another man, Mr. Balais—quite his equal, Mr. Weasel assures me, in all respects."

"Not got him!" cried Richard, impatiently. "Why, Weasel told me Smoothbore led the circuit. Why have we not secured him?"

"He has been retained by the other side," answered Mrs. Yorke, in a tone that she in vain endeavored to render cheerful. "To say the truth, Richard, the prosecutor is exhibiting the utmost vindictiveness, and straining every nerve for a conviction. Money, which he was said to be so fond of, is now no object with him, or at least he spares none. But he can not bribe twelve honest men, nor a righteous judge."

"I knew it," exclaimed Richard, stamping his foot on the stone floor. "Those sullen brutes, Trevethick and the other, would have my life, if they could. There is nothing that they would stick at, be assured of that—and do you put Weasel on his guard—to work my ruin. How could he be such a dolt as to let them be beforehand with him, when he himself said there was not an hour to be lost!"

"Indeed, Richard, all was done for the best. One could scarcely expect Mr. Weasel to advance so large a sum as was required, without security; and he did communicate with Mr. Smoothbore as soon as he had satisfied himself upon that score. He assures me Mr. Balais is quite as clever a counsel. Indeed, I should not have told you of the change, had you not pressed the question so directly."

"Tell me all, mother; tell me every thing; I adjure you to keep nothing back. To think and guess and fear, in a place like this, is worse than not to know the worst. Trevethick is a miser, and yet you say he is spending with a lavish hand. How is it you know that?"

"Why, Mr. Smoothbore's clerk is a friend of Mr. Weasel's, and he hears from him that his master has never received so large a retaining fee as on this occasion. The sum we offered, two days afterward, though larger than is customary, was, he said, but a trifle compared with it."

"You have something else to tell me yet, mother—I see it in your eyes. If you go away with it untold, you leave me on the rack."

"There is nothing more," answered his mother, hesitatingly, "or almost nothing."

"What is it?" cried Richard, hoarsely—"what is it?"

"Well, merely this: that thinking that no money should be spared to help you in this dreadful trouble, Richard, and having but a very little of my own, I—I forgot my pride and steadfast resolution never to ask your father—"

"You did not apply to Carew for money, surely?" ejaculated Richard, angrily. "To let him know that I was here was ruin."

"It may have been ill judged, indeed, dear Richard," replied his mother, quietly; "but it was not ill meant. Do you suppose it cost me nothing to be his suppliant? Do you suppose I have no scorn nor hate, as you have, for those who have wronged me and you? If fury could avail to set you free, your mother would be as the tigress robbed of her young. It is an easy thing enough to fume and foam; it is hard to have to clasp the knees of those whom you despise, in vain."

"He refused you, then—this man?"

"He did, Richard. He told me—what I had not learned from you; I do not say it to reproach you, dear—what it was that had so long detained you at Gethin. He mentioned, in coarsest terms, your love for Harry, and how you had misrepresented yourself to Trevethick as the heir of Crompton in order to win her. He expressed a callous indifference to your present peril, and added something more in menace than in warning respecting that affair with Chandos which caused you to leave his roof. Since it seemed you had made no secret of the matter to Mr. Weasel, I showed him Carew's note; and his opinion is that Trevethick has spies at work to track your past. This may or may not injure you. Mr. Weasel thinks that it will not; but it shows the rancor with which this case is pressed by Trevethick—a malice which we are altogether at a loss to understand."

Richard ground his heel upon the stone without reply, while his mother looked at him in gravest sorrow.

"Your time is almost up, ma'am," said the warder; "there's only a minute more."

"You told her how much depended on her, mother, did you?" said Richard, rousing himself in the effort.

"Yes, dear. She will not fail us, never fear. Keep heart and hope; and as for me, you will be sure that not a moment of my waking thoughts is wasted upon aught but you. I shall see you again, once more at least, before your—before the trial comes on; and Mr. Weasel will be here next week again. Is there any thing, my own dear boy, that I can do for you?"

"One moment, mother. Carew has not punished *you* on my account, I trust? He has not cut off—"

"The annuity? Yes; he has stopped that."

"May he rot on earth, and perish everlastingly!"

"Hush, hush, dear; pray be calm; there is no need to fret. I can support myself without his aid; indeed I can; and perhaps he may relent when he gets sane, for he was like a madman at my coming to Crompton. Mr. Whymper will do all he can, I am sure. How cruel it was of me to heed your words, and tell you— Look to him, warder, look to my son!" she screamed.

Richard had indeed turned deadly pale, and though his fingers still mechanically clutched the iron rail, was swaying to and fro; the warder unlocked the passage-gate, and ran to him just in time to save his falling headlong on the pavement.

"Are you a man," said the agonized woman, "or iron like this"—and she beat against the railing passionately—"that you will not let a mother kiss her son when he is dying?"

"Nay, nay, ma'am; it's not so bad as that," said the warder, good-naturedly; "see, he's a-coming round agen all right. I've seen a many took like that. In half a minute he'll be himself again. It's his trouble as does it, bless you. If you'll take my advice, you'll spare both your son and yourself the pain of parting, and leave him as he is. I'd go bail for it, it's just a faint, that's all."

"Let me kiss him once," implored the unhappy woman. "Oh, man, if you have ever known a mother's love, let me kiss him once! Here is a five-pound note—take it, and leave me still your debtor—but one kiss."

"Nay, ma'am, I can't take your money; of which, as I couldn't help hearing you say, you have not got too much to spare. But you shall kiss your bonnie boy, and welcome;" and with that the stout warder took the unconscious lad up in his arms, and bore him within the passage; and his mother put her lips between the bars and pressed them to his forehead once, twice, thrice.

"There, there, ma'am; that will do," muttered the man, impatiently; "and even that is as much as my place is worth. Now, just tap at yonder door, and they'll let you out."

Mrs. Yorke obeyed him without a word. She had heard the heavy fluttering sigh that betokened Richard's return to consciousness, and knew that the worst was over; unless, indeed, the coming back to life might not be the worst of all.

CHAPTER XXIX.

IN THE COURT-HOUSE.

It is proposed by some elevators of the public mind to make us all philosophers, and to abolish the morbid interest which mankind at present entertains in the issues of life and death. They hold it weakness that we should become excited by incident, or enthralled by mystery, and prophesy a future when intelligence shall reign supreme, to the extinction of the vulgar passion for sensation. In the mean time, however, the sympathetic hopes and fears of humanity remain pretty much as they have been within all living memory; and one of the greatest treats that can be provided for the popular palate is a criminal trial. There are many reasons why this should be the case; the courts of law are free, and a sight that can be seen for nothing is of itself attractive, since we are, at all events, not losing our time and money too. Again, the most popular drama, the most popular novel, are those to which the dénouements can not easily be guessed; and in the court-house we see drama and novel realized with the verdict of the jury and the sentence of the judge—a matter of anxious speculation to the very last. Where theatres and books are rare the passion for such scenes is proportionally stronger, and perhaps there is no periodical event which so deeply stirs the agricultural interest—speaking socially, and not politically—as the advent of the Judges of Assize.

At Cross Key, at all events, there was nothing else talked of for weeks beforehand; and the case which above all others was canvassed, and prejudged, and descanted upon over all sorts of boards—from the mahogany one in the dining-room at Cross Key Park to the deal tripod which held the pots and pipes at the road-side beer-house—was that of Richard Yorke, the young gentleman-painter, who had run away with old John Trevethick of Gethin's hoarded store. The rumor had got abroad that he had almost run away with his daughter also, and this intensified the interest immensely. The whole female population, from the high-sheriff's wife down to the woman who kept the apple-stall in the market-place, was agog to see this handsome young Lothario, and especially to hear the evidence of his (clandestinely) betrothed, who was known to have been subpœnaed for the defense.

There were innumerable biographies of the prisoner to be had for nothing. He was a nobleman in disguise; he was the illegitimate son of the prime minister; he was indirectly but immediately connected with royalty itself; he could speak every European language (except Polish), and painted landscapes like an angel; he had four thousand a year in land, only waiting for him to come of age, which carried with it half the representation of a Whig borough; he had not a penny in the world, but had hitherto supported himself in luxury by skillful forgeries; young as he was, he was a married man, and had a wife (three times his age) alive. All these particulars were insisted upon and denied forty times a day. The least scraps of trust-worthy intelligence concerning him were greedily devoured. The turnpike-man who had opened gate to let him through on the night he came to the jail was cross-examined as to his appearance and demeanor. The rural policeman of the district (who had never had a chance of seeing him) was treated to pots of ale, and suddenly found himself the best of company. The *Castle* at Gethin was thronged by local tourists, who, under pretense of being attracted by the scenery, came to stare at Harry, and, having seen her, retured to Cross Key with marvelous stories of her charms. As the time drew on the applications for admittance to the court-house made the life of the under-sheriff a burden, and caused the hearts of his subordinates (who got the half-crowns) to sing for joy.

The unhappy Richard was wholly ignorant of all this excitement. When he pictured the court-house to himself, as he often did, he only beheld a crowd of indifferent persons, who would pay no more attention to his own case than to that of Balfour, or any other that might follow or precede it. He saw himself taken out in custody, and carried in some conveyance, such as he had arrived in, through the gaping street; but the idea of that ordeal gave him no uneasiness. Those who saw him would forget him the next moment, or confuse him with some other in the same wretched plight. His mind always reverted from such reflections, as comparatively trivial, to the issue of the trial itself. Indeed, that thought might be said to be constant, though others intruded on it occasionally without obscuring it, like light clouds that cross the moon. As to the details of the scene of which he was about to be so prominent an actor, he knew nothing; for the warders never opened their lips to him, except officially, and Mr. Balfour had never happened to come to grief in the course of his professional practice in that particular locality before.

But the fact was that the jail of Cross Key, though situated in so out-of-the-way a spot, was a model establishment in its way, and built upon the very highest principles of architecture, as connected with the administration of the criminal law. No prisoner was ever taken out of it for trial at all, but was conducted by an underground passage into the court-house itself—indeed, into the very heart of it, for a flight of steps, with a trap-door at the top, led straight into the dock, in which he made his appearance like a Jack-in-the-box, but much more to his own astonishment than to that of the spectators.

Imagine the unhappy Richard thus confronted, wholly unexpectedly, with a thousand eager eyes! They devoured him on the right hand and on the left, before him and behind him; they looked down upon him from the galleries above with a hunger that was increased by distance. Even the barristers in the space between him and the judge turned round to gaze at him, and the judge himself adjusted his spectacles upon his nose to regard him with a searching look. Not a sound was to be heard except the monotonous voice of the clerk reading the indictment; it was plain that every one of that vast concourse knew him, and needed not that his neighbor should whisper, "That is he." Was his mother there? thought Richard, and above all, Was Harry there? He looked round once upon that peering throng; but he could catch sight of neither. The former, with a thick veil over her features, was, indeed, watching him from a corner of the court; but the only face he recognized was that of his attorney, seated immediately behind a man with a wig, whom he rightly concluded to be Mr. Sergeant Balais.

There was a sudden silence, following upon the question, "How say you, Richard Yorke, are you guilty of this felony, or not guilty?" The turnkey by the prisoner's side muttered harshly behind his hand, "They have called on you to plead."

"Not guilty," answered Richard, in a loud, firm voice, and fixing his eyes upon the judge.

A murmur of satisfaction ran softly through the court-house. His hesitation had alarmed the curious folks; they were afraid that he might have pleaded "Guilty," and robbed them of their treat. Not a few of them, and perhaps all the women, were also pleased upon his own account. He was so young and handsome that they could not choose but wish him well, and out of his peril.

Then Mr. Smoothbore rose, and was some time about it. He was six feet four inches high, and it seemed as though you would never see the last of him. ("Oh, Jerryusalem, upon wheels!" was the remark that Mr. Robert Balfour muttered to himself when some hours afterward *he* found himself confronted by the same gigantic counsel, instructed specially by the crown to prosecute so notorious a marauder.) The twelve men in the box opposite at once became all ear. Some leaned forward, as though to anticipate by the millionth of a second the silvery accents of Mr. Smoothbore; others leaned back with head aside, as though to concentrate their intelligence upon them; and the foreman held his head with both his hands, as though that portion of his person was not wholly under control, but might make some erratic twist, and thereby lose him some pregnant sentence. These honest men did not know Mr. Smoothbore, and thought (for the first five minutes) that they could sit and listen to him forever; before they had done with him they began to think that they should have to do it.

Far be it from us to emulate the prolixity with which the learned counsel set forth his case; it must be conceded that he did not hang over it; his words ran as smoothly as oil, and with perfect distinctness, and if any body missed his meaning, it was not for want of its being sufficiently expressed. To a listener of average ability, however, he became insupportable by repetition, which is, unhappily, not exclusively "the vice of the pulpit." We will take care to avoid his error. It will be sufficient to say that when he had finished Richard stood accused not only of having stolen two thousand pounds from John Trevethick, but of having compassed that crime under circumstances of peculiar baseness. He had taken advantage of his superior education, manners, and appearance, to impose himself upon the honest Cornishman as the legitimate son of his landlord, and secured within that humble home a footing of familiarity, only the better to compass a scheme of villainy, which must have occurred to him at a very early period of their acquaintance. Indeed, Mr. Smoothbore hinted that the prisoner's profession of landscape-painting was a mere pretense and pretext, and that it was more than probable that, having heard by some means of Trevethick's hoard, he had come down to Gethin with the express intention of becoming possessed of it, which his accidental discovery of the secret of the letter padlock enabled him to do. In short, by artful innuendo at this or that part of the story, Richard was painted as a common thief, whose possession of such faculties as dexterity and *finesse* only made him a more dangerous enemy of society. There had been rumors, Mr. Smoothbore admitted, of certain romantic circumstances connected with the case, but he was instructed to say that they were wholly baseless, and that the matter which the jury would have to decide upon was simply an impudent and audacious robbery, committed in a manner that he might stigmatize as being quite exceptionally void of extenuation.

The speech for the prosecution immensely disappointed the general public, already half-convinced, in spite of themselves, by Mr. Smoothbore's impassioned clearness and straightforward simplicity, while it pleased the jury, who were glad to hear that the matter in hand was, after all, an ordinary one, which would necessitate no deprivation of victuals, nor absence of fire and candle. The witnesses for the prosecution appeared, as usual, in an order in inverse ratio to the interest and importance of their respective testimonies—the clerk of the Miners' Bank into whose hands the notes had been paid, policemen, Mr. Dodge, and others, who only repeated what we already know. Even the appearance of Solomon Coe was marked by nothing especial, save to the eyes of the accused. In the triumphant bearing of this witness, and in the malignant glance which he had shot toward him ere he began his tale, Richard read that the charge against him was to be pushed to the bitter end. It was in this man's power, more than in any other's (save one), to extenuate or to set down in malice; and there was no doubt in his rival's mind (though his rancor took so blunt a form that it might well have been mistaken by others for outspoken candor) which of the two courses Solomon had chosen. He showed neither scruple nor hesitation; every word was distinct and decisive, and on one occasion (though the repetition of it was forbidden by the judge) even accompanied by a blow with his sledge-hammer fist in the way of corroboration. It seemed that the story he had to tell was, after all, a very plain one.

When John Trevethick, who was the last witness examined for the prosecution, strode into the box, this feeling was intensified. His giant frame and massive features seemed, somehow, to associate themselves with a plain story; and his evidence was as much in consonance with his counsel's speech as evidence could be with pleading.

But when he had quite done with his unvarnished tale, and when Mr. Smoothbore had given him a parting nod in sign that *he* had done with him, Sergeant Balais rose, for the first time, with an uplifted finger, as though, but for that signal of delay, the honest landlord would have fled incontinently, and hanged himself, like another Judas.

"You have a daughter, I believe, Mr. Trevethick?" and the Sergeant looked at the jury, with elevated eyebrows, as though he would have said, "If we can get even that admission out of this hoary miscreant, we may consider ourselves fortunate."

And indeed John Trevethick did hesitate for one instant ere he replied. He had not even looked at the prisoner before, but at that question he gave an involuntary glance toward him, and met Richard's answering look. When two men are fighting, each with his hands upon the throat of the other, not for dear life, but for the longed-for death of his foe, it is possible that in their faces some such inextinguishable lurid fire of hatred may be seen burning as then flashed from witness-box to dock, from dock to witness-box; but scarcely under any other circumstances could such a look of deadly malice be exchanged between man and man. It passed, however, in an instant, like the electric fire, and was gone, leaving no trace behind it.

"I *have* a daughter," replied Trevethick; and as he spoke his face, though somewhat pale, became as blank and hard and meaningless as a wall of stone.

"This man is about to perjure himself," thought the experienced Mr. Balais; and he looked around him with the air of one who was convinced of the fact.

"The prisoner at the bar was, I believe, your daughter's lover, was he not?"

"Not that I knew of."

"Not that you know of?" repeated Mr. Balais. "Will you venture to repeat that?"

"The witness said *knew*," interposed the judge, demurely, and ordered a sky-light to be closed, the draught from which inconvenienced him. Every body looked at the officer of the court who pulled the string and shut the sky-light, as though it had been the most ingenious contrivance known to man. Not that it was a relief to them to do so, but from that inexplicable motive which prompts us all to observe trivial circumstances with which we have nothing whatever to do, on any occasion of engrossing interest. Even Richard regarded this little process of ventilation with considerable concern, and wondered whether the judge would feel himself better after it.

"Oh, you didn't know of this attachment between the prisoner and your daughter at the time it was going on under your roof, but you knew of it afterward, did you? You read of it in the papers, I suppose, eh?"

"I heard of it, after the robbery was discovered, from my daughter herself."

"And, upon your oath, you did not know of it before then?"

"I did not."

"Nor suspect it even, perhaps?"

"Nor even suspect it."

Mr. Balais smiled, shrugged his shoulders. His principles of oratory were Demosthenean; his motto was "Action, action, action." His friends on circuit called him the Balais of action. He had had some experience of the depravity of human nature, said the shrug, but this beat every thing, and would be really amusing but for its atrocious infamy. Good Heavens!

"Then you never had any conversation with the prisoner with reference to your daughter at all?"

"Never."

Mr. Balais bent down and interchanged a word or two with Mr. Weasel behind him.

"Now be so good as to give me your best attention, Mr. Trevethick, for upon my next question more may depend than you may be aware of. If you have any regard for your own interests you will answer it truly; for as sure as—"

"Is this necessary, Brother Balais?" interrupted the judge, scratching his forehead with his forefinger, and looking up at the sky-light, as though that matter was not satisfactorily settled even yet.

"My lud, I am instructed that nothing less than a conspiracy has been entered into against my unfortunate client."

The judge nodded slightly, shivered considerably, and made a mental note to complain of that infernal draught before he should dismiss the grand jury.

"I ask you, Mr. Trevethick," continued the counsel, solemnly, "whether or not, in a conversation which you held with the prisoner upon a certain day last month, you mentioned two thousand pounds as the sum you must needs see in his possession before you could listen to any proposition of his with respect to your daughter's hand?"

"I did not."

"You never spoke of that particular sum to him at all?"

"Never at all."

It was Mr. Balais who looked up at the sky-light this time—as though he expected a thunder-bolt.

"The notes, of which we have heard so much, as being hoarded in this ingenious box of yours—and that you are a very ingenious man, Mr. Trevethick, there is no doubt—this box, I say, was kept in a certain cupboard, was it not?"

"It was."

"And now, please to look at the jury when you answer me this question: Where was this particular cupboard situated, Mr. Trevethick?"

Into the landlord's impassive face there stole for the first time a look of disquiet, and his harsh, monotonous voice grew tremulous as he replied, "The cupboard was in my daughter's bedroom."

"That will do, Mr. Trevethick, *for the present*," observed Mr. Balais, with emphasis; "though I shall probably have the opportunity of seeing you another time"—and he glanced significantly toward the dock—"*in another place.*"

CHAPTER XXX.

FOR THE DEFENSE.

WHEN Mr. Balais rose again it was to speak for the defense, and he addressed the jury amidst an unbroken silence. So rapt, indeed, was the attention of his audience that the smack of a carter's whip, as he went by in the street below, was resented by many a frown as an impertinent intrusion; and even the quarters of the church clock were listened to with impatience, lest its iron tongue should drown a single sentence. This latter interruption did not, however, often take place, for Mr. Balais was as brief in speech as he was energetic in action. He began by at once allowing the main facts which the prosecution had proved—that the notes had been taken from Trevethick's box, and found in the prisoner's possession, who had been detected in the very act of endeavoring to change them for notes of another banking company. But what he maintained was, that this exchange was not, as Mr. Smoothbore had suggested, effected for the purpose of realizing the money, but simply of throwing dust in the prosecutor's eyes. He had changed the notes only with the intention of returning his own money to Trevethick under another form. Even so young a man, and one so thoroughly ignorant of the ways of the world and of business matters as was his client, must surely have been aware, if using the money for himself had been his object, that it could be traced in notes of the Mining Company as easily as in notes of the Bank of England; nay, by this very proceeding of his, he had even given them a *double* chance of being traced. He (Mr. Balais) was not there, of course, to justify the conduct of the prisoner at the bar. It was unjustifiable, it was reprehensible in a very high degree; but what he did maintain was that, even taking for granted all that had been put in evidence, this young man's conduct was not criminal; it was not that of a thief. He had never had the least intention of stealing this money; his scheme had been merely a stratagem to obtain the object of his affections for his wife. This Trevethick was a hard and grasping man, and it was necessary for the young fellow to satisfy him that he was possessed of certain property before he would listen to any proposition for his daughter's hand. His idea—a wrong and foolish one, indeed, but then look at his youth and inexperience—was to impose upon this old miser, by showing him his own money in another form, and then, when he had gained his object, to return it to him. Mr. Balais was, for his own part, as certain of such being the fact as that he was standing in that court-house. Let them turn their eyes on the unhappy prisoner in the dock, and judge for themselves whether he looked like the mere felon which his learned friend had painted him, or the romantic, self-deceiving, thoughtless lad, such as he (Mr. Balais) felt convinced he was. They had all heard of the proverb that all things were fair in love as in war. When the jury had been young themselves perhaps some of them had acted upon that theory; at all events, it was not an unnatural idea for young people to act upon. Proverbs had always a certain weight and authority of their own. They were not necessarily Holy Writ (Mr. Balais was not quite certain whether the proverb in question was one of Solomon's own or not, so he put it in this cautious manner), but they smacked of it. This Richard Yorke, perhaps, had thought it no great harm to win his love by a false representation of the state of his finances. He could not see his way how otherwise to melt the stony heart of this old curmudgeon, who had doubtless—notwithstanding the evidence they had heard from him that day—encouraged the young man's addresses so long as he believed him to be Mr. Carew's lawful heir. The whole question, in fact, resolved itself into one of *motive;* and if there was not a word of evidence forthcoming upon the prisoner's part, he (Mr. Balais) would have left the case in the jury's hands, with the confident conviction that they would never impute to that unhappy boy—who had already suffered such tortures of mind and body as were more than a sufficient punishment for his offense—the deliberate and shameful crime of which he stood accused. He had lost his position in the world already; he had lost his sweetheart, for they had all heard that day that she was about to be driven into wedlock with his rival, a man twice his age and hers; he had lost the protection of his father—his own flesh and blood—for since this miserable occurrence he had chosen to disown him; and yet here was the prosecutor, who had lost nothing (except his own self-respect, and the respect of all who had listened to his audacious testimony that morning), pressing for a conviction, for more punishment; in a word, for the gratification of a mean revenge. If he (Mr. Balais) had nothing more, therefore, to urge in his client's defense, he would have been content to leave the jury to deal with this case—Englishmen, who detested oppression, and loved that justice only which is tempered with mercy. But as it so happened, there was no need thus to leave it; no necessity to appeal to mercy at all. He had only to ask them for the barest justice. He was happily in a position to prove that the prisoner at the bar had no more stolen this two thousand pounds than their own upright and sagacious foreman.

A sigh of relief was uttered from a hundred gentle breasts. "We are coming to something at last," it seemed to say. A hundred fair faces looked at Mr. Balais—who was growing gray and wrinkled, and found every new performance of his pantomime harder and harder—as though they could have kissed him, nevertheless. "Yes, gentlemen of the jury, that money was given to him by the prosecutor's daughter with her own hand."

A murmur of satisfaction ran round the court-house.

There *was* a romance—a love-story—in the case, then, after all.

Mr. Balais concluded a most energetic speech with a peroration of great brilliancy, in which Richard and Harry were exhibited like a transparency in the bright colors of Youth, and Hope, and Passion, and finally sat down amidst what would have been a burst of applause but for the harsh voice of the usher nipping it in the bud by proclaiming silence.

There was no need for his doing that when Mr. Balais jumped up to his feet again, as though he were on springs, and called for Harry Trevethick. The judge was taking snuff at the time; and such was the stillness that you could hear the overplus falling on the paper before him on which he wrote down his notes. There was a minute's delay, during which every eye was fixed upon the witness-box, and then Harry appeared. She was very pale, and wore a look of anxious timidity; but a bright spot came into her cheeks as she turned her face to the prisoner in the dock, and smiled upon him. From that moment Richard felt that he was safe. Guarded as he was, and still in peril, he forgot his danger, and once more resolved that he would cleave to this tender creature, to whom he was about to owe his safety, to his life's end.

Harry was simply yet attractively attired in a pale violet silk dress, with a straw bonnet trimmed with the same modest color. It was observed, with reference to this and to the innocence and gentleness of her expression, that she looked like a dove; and a dove she seemed to Richard, bringing him the signal that the flood was abating, the deep waters of which had so nearly overwhelmed both soul and body. Even the judge, as Mr. Weasel had foretold, regarded her through his double glasses with critical approval; for a most excellent judge he was—of female attractions.

Mr. Balais smiled triumphantly at the jury. "Did I not tell you," he seemed to say, "that my client is guiltless in this matter? Here is Truth herself come to witness in his favor. Bless her!" Richard's feverish eyes were fixed upon her; he knew no God, but here was his spring in the wilderness, his shadow of the great rock in a weary land. As for her, she looked only at the judge, expecting—poor little ignoramus—that it was he who would question her.

"You are the daughter of John Trevethick, of Gethin?" said Mr. Balais.

This interrogatory, simple as it was, made her color rise, coming from that unexpected quarter.

"Yes, Sir."

"He keeps an inn, does he not; the"—here Mr. Balais affected to consult his brief, to give her time to recover herself from her modest confusion—"the *Gethin Castle*, I believe?"

"Yes, Sir."

"The prisoner at the bar has been staying there for some months, has he not?"

She stole another look at Richard: it spoke as plainly as looks could speak, "Oh yes; that is how I came to know and love him." But she only murmured, "Yes, Sir."

"Speak up, Miss Trevethick," said the counsel, encouragingly; "these twelve gentlemen are all very anxious to hear what you have to say." The judge nodded and smiled, as though in corroboration, as well as to add, upon his own account, that it would give *him* also much pleasure to hear her.

"Was the prisoner staying in the inn as an ordinary guest, or did he mix with the family?"

"He was in the bar parlor most nights, Sir, along with father and me and Solomon."

"He was in the bar parlor most nights," repeated Mr. Balais, significantly, for he was anxious that the jury should catch that answer—"'with father and me and Solomon.' And who introduced him into the parlor?"

"Father brought him first, Sir, on the second day after he came to Gethin."

"Father brought him in, did he? Now, that is rather an unusual thing for the landlord of an inn to do, is it not? To introduce a young man whom he had known but twenty-four hours to his family circle, and to the society of his daughter, eh?"

"Please, Sir, I don't know, Sir."

"No, of course you don't, Miss Trevethick; how should you? But I think the jury know. You have no idea, then, yourself, why your father introduced this young gentleman to you so early?"

"Father said he was a friend of Mr. Carew's, of Crompton, who is father's landlord."

"Just so," said Mr. Balais, with another significant glance at the attentive twelve. "Mr.

Trevethick had already discovered that this youth was of a good social position, and likely to prove an excellent match. 'Will you walk into my parlor?' said the spider to the fly; 'I have the prettiest daughter that ever you did spy.'"

Every body tittered at this except Mr. Smoothbore and his solicitor; even the judge blew his nose.

"Now, not only did the prisoner at the bar spend most nights in the bar parlor, but, as I am given to understand, he spent most days there, or, at all events, in your society, did he not?"

"Father and Solomon were away most days, Sir, and so we were left a good deal together."

"Just so. Your father took care to be away most days, did he, in order that you should be left a good deal together?"

Mr. Smoothbore started to his feet. "My lud, I submit," etc.; meaning that this was a mode of interrogating the witness that he could *not* submit to for an instant.

"Very good," said Mr. Balais, smiling. "I will not put the question in that form, then. The form is of very little consequence. You were left together, however, and the consequence was that you two young people fell in love with one another, eh?"

Harry was crimson. "I—he—we;" and there she stuck.

"I am very sorry to embarrass you, my dear young lady, but I am necessitated to press this question. Did you fall in love with one another or not?"

No answer. Harry was thinking of Solomon, to whom she was to be married within ten days, and hung her head.

"Come, did he fall in love with *you*, then? There was ample apology for it, I am sure, and he ought to have been ashamed of himself if he hadn't. Now, did he 'court' you? I think you must know what that means."

No answer. Every eye was upon her, the judge's double glasses included. They might have been burning-glasses, she felt so hot and frightened.

"Come, did this young gentleman ever give you a kiss?"

"Yes, Sir," murmured poor Harry, almost under her breath.

"Did you say 'Yes' or 'No?'" inquired the judge, dipping his pen in the ink.

"I said 'Yes,' my lord," said the unhappy Harry.

"There were more kisses than one, now, I dare say," said Mr. Balais, with a wink at the jury; "and they were not all on one side, eh?"

No answer.

"Some of them were on the other side, were they not? I don't mean on the other cheek, for I have no doubt he was perfectly indifferent as to that."

Again there was a little titter.

"She is your own witness, Brother Balais," observed his lordship, "but it seems to me you are giving her unnecessary pain."

He had a very tender heart, had the old judge, where a young and pretty woman was concerned —otherwise he was a Tartar.

"My lud, it is absolutely necessary to prove that my client's passion was reciprocated. Did you ever return one of these many kisses, Miss Trevethick?"

"Yes, Sir."

"Did you ever meet him alone at night in a place, I believe, called the Fairies' Bower?"

"Yes, Sir."

"Yes," repeated Mr. Balais, recapitulating these facts upon his fingers; "you were left alone with him all day; you met him alone at night, away from your father's roof; you returned his kisses; and all this without the slightest suspicion—if we are to believe his evidence —being aroused upon the part of your parent. Now, Miss Trevethick, you were aware that your father kept a large sum of money—these two thousand pounds—in his strong-box, were you not?"

"I was, Sir."

"Did you ever speak to the prisoner at the bar about it?"

"I think—yes, I did, Sir, on one occasion," and here Harry's voice fluttered and faltered. No one noticed it, however, except the prisoner; if any neighbor eyes had watched him narrowly —but they were all fixed upon the witness—they would have seen his face whiten, and his brow grow damp. Why should she have laid that stress upon "on one occasion?"

"You told him that the two thousand pounds were in the box in the cupboard in your bedroom?"

"I did, Sir."

"The fastening of the box was not an ordinary lock, I believe. It was what is called a letter padlock?"

"Yes, Sir."

"Did you ever open it?"

"No, Sir."

A great bell seemed to be suddenly set tolling in Richard's brain—it was the knell of all his hopes.

"You had never opened it at that time, eh?" continued Mr. Balais, cheerfully. "But you learned the secret afterward?"

"I—yes—I did."

"Do you remember the letters that did open it?"

"Yes, Sir."

"What were they?"

"B, N, Z."

"Very good. We have heard from the counsel for the prosecution that they were so; and that Mr. Trevethick kept a memorandum of them on a piece of paper that fitted into his watch-case. Did he always carry that watch about with him?"

"Not always. When he went out to market, and was likely to be late, he sometimes left it at home."

"In his own room, I suppose, where you or any body else could get at it?"

"I suppose so, Sir."

"You *suppose?* You know he did, do you not? Did you not open the watch-case yourself, and so discover the means of unlocking the box?"

"No, Sir," said Harry, faintly; and once more she turned her eyes to Richard. It was a true and tender glance, one would have said, and accompanied by an attempt at a smile of encouragement. But if it had been a glance of a gorgon, it could not have had a more appalling effect; it literally seemed to turn him into stone.

"COME, DID THIS YOUNG GENTLEMAN EVER GIVE YOU A KISS?"

"Recollect yourself, Miss Trevethick," said Mr. Balais, earnestly; "you are getting confused, I fear. Now please to give me your attention. You say that you knew that the letters B, N, Z were those which formed the key of the letter padlock, and yet that you did not open your father's watch-case. How, then, did you become possessed of the secret?"

No answer. Harry caught her breath convulsively, and turned deadly pale. She could never tell how Mrs. Yorke had endeavored to suborn her.

"Well, well, this is a matter of very little consequence—though I see my learned friend is making a copious note of it," said Mr. Balais, gayly. "The main point is what, as you have told us, did occur—that you found out the secret somehow. When you got it, I suppose you opened the box?"

No answer, save from Mr. Smoothbore, who observed, tartly: "You have no right to assume that, Sergeant."

"Let the young woman have a glass of water," suggested the kindly judge.

"My lord, my lord!" cried Harry, with sudden passion, "he is not guilty. Richard did not mean to steal the money; indeed he did not. He only wished to get possession of it that my father might believe him to be a man of wealth. He did but—"

"Endeavor to compose yourself, young woman," interposed the judge. "The learned counsel will only ask what is necessary."

"Take your time, Miss Trevethick, take your time," pursued Mr. Balais, in his blandest tones. "The question is, how the prisoner became possessed of this money. Now, tell us, did you not give it him with your own hands?"

The bell was still tolling in Richard's brain, and yet he could hear the buzzing of a fly against a window of the court-house, and the careless whistle of some lad in the street without. It was the same tune that the keeper at Crompton had been wont to whistle in his leisure moments at home; and his mind reverted with a flash to the glades of the stately park, the herds of deer, the high-mossed gate, which he had shut in the face of the hounds when they were chasing Carew's carriage. Was it the bang of the gate, or had Harry really answered in a firm voice, that resounded through the silent court-house, "No, Sir?"

"What!" said Mr. Balais, raising his voice a little. "Do you mean to say, then—and recollect that the fate of the prisoner at the bar may depend upon your reply to this question—that Richard Yorke did not become possessed of these notes by your connivance, through your means, at all?"

"No, Sir, no," answered Harry, passionately; "I can't say that; indeed, Sir, I can not. But he is innocent—Richard is innocent—he never meant to steal them. O God, help me!" In her excitement, and not because she wished to do so, she had turned about, and once more caught sight of the prisoner at the bar. It was her turn now to shrink appalled and petrified. It was not reproach that she saw pictured in that well-loved face, but downright hate and loathing. "He will never, never forgive me!" cried she, with a piteous wail; and then scream followed scream, and she was borne out in haste, and a doctor sent for.

Cross-examination was, of course, quite out of the question; and, indeed, Mr. Smoothbore was much too sagacious a man to wish to exercise that privilege. The failure of the witness for the defense had proved the case of the prosecution.

It was Mr. Smoothbore who could now best afford to praise the innocence and candor of the unhappy Harry. Was it not evident that that tender creature had been tampered with, and almost persuaded to perjure herself, for the sake of the prisoner at the bar—almost, but, happily for the ends of justice, not quite persuaded! Her natural love of right had conquered the ignoble passion with which she had been inspired by this unscrupulous man. What words could sufficiently paint the baseness of the conduct of the accused! Was it not clear that he had endeavored to escape scot-free, at the sacrifice of this poor girl's good name? *She*, forsooth, was to proclaim herself thief, to save his worthless self! It was not for Mr. Smoothbore—Heaven forbid!—to exaggerate such wickedness, but was it possible that the phrase, "Young in years, but old in vice," had ever had a more appropriate application than in the present case! For the credit of human nature, he trusted not. The point upon which his learned friend had mainly relied having been thus proved *wholly* untenable—the fact of Richard's taking the money having been incontestably brought home to him—it only remained for him (Mr. Smoothbore) to notice what had been said with respect to motive. If the prisoner at the bar had even had the intention, which had been so gratuitously imputed to him, of returning this money to the prosecutor, when once the object of his supposed scheme had been effected, he would be no less guilty of the crime that was laid to his charge. It was possible, indeed, in such a case, that there might be extenuating circumstances, but those would not affect the verdict of the jury, however they might influence his lordship's sentence after that verdict had been truly given. And this he would say, after what had just occurred in that court—after the painful scene they had just witnessed—the breaking down of that innocent girl in an act of self-sacrifice, culpable in itself, but infinitely more culpable in him who had incited her to do it—for he could not for an instant suppose that the prisoner's legal advisers could have suggested such a line of defense: taking all this into consideration, he, Mr. Smoothbore, would confidently ask the jury whether the prisoner at the bar was to be credited with merely a romantic stratagem, or with a crime the heinousness of which was only exceeded by the means by which he had striven to exculpate himself from it, and to evade the ends of justice.

When Mr. Smoothbore had thus concluded a lengthened and impassioned harangue, he sat down, wiping his hands upon his handkerchief, as though implying that he had washed them of the prisoner for good and all, and that a very dirty job it had been; while the judge rose and left the court, it being the hour appointed to his system, by nature, for the reception of lunch.

CHAPTER XXXI.

THE SENTENCE.

Richard remained in the dock. The warder who had charge of him gave him the option of retiring, but he preferred to stay where he was till all was over. He had at last caught sight of his mother, straining her loving eyes toward him—with still some hope in them—from a distant corner of the gallery; and he kept his gaze fixed upon that spot. They had all the world against them now, these two, so clever, and yet so wholly unable to combat with inexorable fate. Harry's evidence, and especially the manner of it, had not needed Mr. Smoothbore's fiery scorn to turn all hearts against the accused. To the great mass of spectators it seemed as though Richard would have made the girl change places with himself, and become a vicarious sacrifice for his worthless self.

The majesty of the law having withdrawn itself, a hum of many voices filled the court-house; a munching of biscuits, a sipping of flasks. The silence of suspense no longer reigned. The struggle was virtually over, and the victim was only waiting his doom. It was hoped it would be a severe one. The spectators were pitiless, and had turned their thumbs toward their breasts. As to the verdict there was no doubt. Those who knew the character of the judge opined that this young gentleman would "get it hot," notwithstanding that this was his first offense. Odds were taken that he would have fourteen years. "At all events," said one of the small officials, in answer to eager inquiries, "more than he could do on his head." With this enigmatical reply of the oracle its astonished questioners were compelled to be content.

"Silence in the court—si-lence." The judge had returned. It was thought by some that it was in the prisoner's favor that the judge had lunched. They were mistaken, or perhaps a fatal economy had provided African sherry. His charge was scarcely less dead against the prisoner than had been Mr. Smoothbore's closing speech. As for the motive, upon which such stress had been laid by the counsel for the defense, that might be a plea for a recommendation to mercy, if the jury believed it, but it could not affect the question of the prisoner's guilt. That the stolen property had been found in the possession of the accused there was no sort of doubt. If the prisoner at the bar had not himself taken it out of the prosecutor's strong-box, who had?

Such was the form in which the case was left for the jury.

"It's U P," whispered Mr. Weasel behind his hand to Mr. Balais. Mr. Balais nodded indifferently; the case was over so far as he was concerned, and he was not going to employ significant action gratuitously. That would have been waste of power indeed at his age. The jury did not leave the box; they laid their heads together, like a hydra, and "deliberated" for half a minute; that is to say, the foreman whispered, "We can return but one verdict, I should say, gentlemen;" and the eleven answered, "But one."

"We find the prisoner guilty, your lordship."

His lordship nodded approval. "In my opinion, gentlemen, you could not have done otherwise. Hem!" Then that common phrase, "You could have heard a pin drop," might have been used with respect to that vast assemblage. That "hem!" was a very fatal sign with Mr. Justice Bantam, as the bar well knew.

"I'll take you six to five in sovs he gives him seven years," whispered one learned gentleman to another, without moving his lips.

"It seems to me you are rather fond of a good thing," returned the other, scornfully, but with a like precaution.

"Hem!" said the judge again. "Is there any one in court able to give any information concerning the antecedents of the prisoner?"

"We have no witnesses to character, my lud," said Mr. Balais, gravely; "we had hoped it would not have been necessary."

"There *is* a witness in court, please your ludship, a detective of the A division of metropolitan police, I believe," observed Mr. Smoothbore, "who knows something of the prisoner."

"Let him stand up," said the judge.

Here was an extra excitement—an additional attraction, which had not been advertised in the bills—and the public evinced their satisfaction accordingly by craning and crowding. Richard turned his heated eyes in the direction of this new enemy. He had no hope of seeing a friend. The individual in question was unknown to him. He was a tall, quiet-looking man, whose face might have been carved out of box-wood, it was so hard and serious, but for its keen eyes, which seemed to meet his own with a look of recognition.

"I know the prisoner at the bar; that is to say, I have seen him on a previous occasion, when he passed under the name of Chandos, and on other occasions, as I believe, under other names. From information received I attended a competitive examination, under the authority of government."

"Do you mean that you were employed by the government, or that the examination was a government one?" interrupted the judge.

"You'll hear something now," whispered Mr. Weasel to Mr. Balais, "by Jove!"

"Both, my lord," explained the witness. "It had come to the knowledge of the government that there had been several cases of personation in the competitive examinations recently instituted both for the military and civil services. Not only were young gentlemen, who had apparently passed with credit, found grossly ignorant of the subjects which they had previously been examined upon, but their physical appearance was sometimes such as would have seemed to have disqualified them: it appeared incredible that they should have passed the preliminary medical examination. One was humpbacked; another almost blind. It was understood that some systematized scheme of imposture, of mispersonation, was at work to produce these results, and I was instructed to inquire into it. I did so. I came to the conclusion that only one person was concerned in the matter—the prisoner at the bar. I had had my suspicions of him for some time. I had seen him on three separate occasions as a candidate at public examinations. His nomination was correct and genuine, but (as I have since discovered) it had been issued to another person. He succeeded in every instance in obtaining the appointments in question for his employers, who received them in due course, though they have, I believe, since been canceled. In the case of Chandos, a letter was written, by the supposed successful candidate, to the authorities of the government branch—the India Board—under which he was to serve, so grossly misspelled that the fraud was at once suspected. In this instance the guilt was brought home to the prisoner by the confession of the young man Chandos himself, who paid over to him a considerable sum of money for the service in question. But I am now in a position to prove that on several other occasions the prisoner has committed the same offense; and, in short, if he may be said to have a calling, it is that of personating, at competitive examinations, young gentlemen of small ability, who are thus enabled to secure situations and appointments which they could otherwise never obtain."

Mr. Justice Bantam had his prejudices, but he had a fair and honest mind.

"This is a most unlooked-for communication, Brother Balais," said he, doubtfully; "and it is not permitted you to cross-examine upon a point of character."

"I am sorry to say, my lud," returned Mr. Balais, after a hurried conversation with the little attorney, "that my client is not in a position to dispute the evidence just adduced. He prefers to throw himself upon the mercy of the court, on the ground—a very tenable one, I think—of his youth and," he was going to add "inexperience," but, under the circumstances, he thought it better not—"of his extreme youth, my lud; my unhappy client is barely eighteen years of age."

"Very good," said Mr. Justice Bantam, looking as if it could not be worse. "Hem! Prisoner at the bar: after a careful and fair trial, in which you have had the benefit of the best legal aid, you have been found *guilty* of the charge of which you are accused. In that verdict I cordially concur. The offense was a very serious one; but the endeavor which you have made to screen yourself, at the expense of that beautiful and innocent young girl, is, in my opinion, still more heinous and contemptible than the crime itself. Having made yourself master of her affections, you used your power to the utmost to effect her moral and social hurt. You would have had her perjure herself, and proclaim herself guilty of a crime she did not commit, in order that you might yourself escape justice. Nobody who heard her evidence—who saw her in yonder box—can doubt it. Still, as your counsel has just remarked, you are but a youth in years, and I looked about me in hopes to find some extenuating circumstances in your past career—some record of good—which might have justified me in inflicting on you a more lenient sentence than your offense had earned. I had no other purpose in asking whether any thing was known of your previous career. The reply to that question has astonished and shocked me, as it has shocked and astonished every right-thinking person in this court who heard it. We knew to what base purpose you had used the comeliness and youth and good address with which nature had endowed you; and now we have learned how evilly you have misused your talents—with what perverted ingenuity you have striven, at so early an age, to set at naught those precautions by which your country has lately endeavored to secure for itself efficient public servants."

"That's neat," whispered a learned friend to Mr. Balais, reverently shutting his eyes, as though in rapt admiration.

"Very," returned that gentleman. "He's bidding for the Lord Chief Justiceship."

"In the whole course of my legal experience, young man," continued the judge, "I have never seen a case which seems to me to call for more exemplary punishment than yours. The promise of your future is dark indeed—bad for yourself, and bad for that society which, though so fitted to adorn and benefit it, you have chosen to outrage. I will not, however, reproach you further; I will rather express a hope that when you return to the world after your long probation—and it will be as long as I am able to make it—you may be a wiser and better, as well as a much older man. The sentence of the court is, that you be kept in penal servitude for the space of twenty years."

CHAPTER XXXII.

BROODING.

NOT a syllable of the judge's exhortation was lost upon the prisoner at the bar. He listened to it as attentively as one who is waiting for the thunder listens to the muffled menace that precedes it, and the fall of each big drop of rain. When the words of doom smote upon his ear a solemn hush succeeded them; and then one piteous, agonized shriek, and a dull fall in the gallery above.

"This way," said a warder, sharply; and Richard was seized by the arm, and hurried through the trap-door, and down the stairs, by the way he had come. It seemed to him like descending into hell itself.

Twenty years' penal servitude! It was almost an eternity of torment! worse than death! and yet not so. He already beheld himself, at the end of his term of punishment, setting about the great work which alone was left him to do on earth—the accomplishment of his revenge. He had recognized his mother's voice in that agonized wail, and knew that her iron will had given way; that the weight of this unexpected calamity had deprived even her elastic and vigorous mind of consciousness—had crushed out of her, perhaps, even life itself. Better so, thought he, in his bitterness, if it had; there would then be not a single human creature left to soften, by her attachment, his heart toward his fellows—none to counsel moderation, mercy, prudence.

If the view taken by the judge had even been a correct one, as to "motive," Richard had been hardly dealt with, most severely sentenced; but in his own eyes he was an almost innocent man—the victim of an infamous conspiracy, in which she who was his nearest and dearest had treacherously joined. After flattering him with false hopes, she had deserted him at the eleventh hour, and in a manner even more atrocious than the desertion itself. He knew, of course, that it was mainly owing to her evidence, to which he had looked for his preservation, that his ruin had been so complete and overwhelming; but what he hated her worst for was for that smile she had bestowed upon him as she entered the witness-box, and which had bade him hope where no hope was. He could not be mistaken as to that. She had known that she was about to doom him by her silence to years of misery, and yet she had had the devilish cruelty to smile upon him, as she had often smiled, when they had sat, cheek to cheek, together! Since they had done so, he could never lift his hand against her (he felt that even now)—never strike her, slay her, nor even poison her; but he would have revenge upon her for all that. He would smite her, as she had smitten him, no matter how long the blow might be in falling: if her affections should be entwined in any human creatures, against them should his rage be directed; he would make her desolate, as she had rendered him; he would turn their love for her to hate, if it were possible, and, if not, he would destroy them. As for her father—as for that stone devil Trevethick—it choked him to think that nature herself might preserve him from his wrath, that the old man might die before his hour of expiation could arrive. But Solomon Coe would live to feel his vengeance. His hatred was at white heat now; what would it be after twenty years of unmerited torture? To think that this terrible punishment had befallen him through such contemptible agencies—through such dull brains and vulgar hands—was maddening; and yet he must needs feed upon that thought for twenty years, and keep his senses too, that at the end they might work out his purpose to the uttermost. There was plenty of time to plan and scheme and plot before him, and henceforth that should be his occupation. Revenge should be his latest thought and his earliest, and all night long he would dream of nothing else. His wrath against judge and jury, and the rest of them—though if he could have slain them all with a word he would have uttered it—was slight compared with the vehemence of his fury against those three at Gethin. Rage possessed him wholly, and, though without numbing him to the painful sense of his miserable doom, rendered him almost unconscious of what was going on about him.

When he found himself in his cell again he had no recollection of how he had got there; and the warder had to repeat his sharp command, "Put on these clothes," before he could get him to understand that he was to exchange his garments for the prison suit that lay before him. It was a small matter, but it brought home to him the reality of his situation more than any thing that had yet occurred. With the deprivation of his clothes he seemed to be deprived of his individuality, and, in adopting that shameful dress, to become an atom in a congeries of outcasts. From henceforth he was not even to bear a name, but must become a number—a unit of that great sum of scoundrels which the world was so willing to forget. That he was to suffer under a system which had authority and right for its basis made his case no less intolerable to him; he felt like one suddenly seized and sold into slavery. That his master and tyrant was called the Law was no mitigation of his calamity; nay, it was an aggravation, since he could not cut its throat.

"It is no use, young fellow," said the warder, coolly, as Richard looked at him like some hunted beast at bay. "If you was to kill me and a dozen more it would do you not a morsel of good; the law has got you tight, and it's better to be quiet."

Richard uttered a low moan, more woeful than any cry of physical anguish. It touched his jailer, used as he was to the contemplation of human misery. "Look here," said he; "you keep up a good heart, and get as many *V G*'s as you can. Then you'll get out on ticket-of-leave in fifteen years: it ain't as if you were a lifer."

He meant it for consolation; but this unvarnished statement of the *very best* that could by possibility befall poor Richard seemed only to deepen his despondency.

"Why, when you've done it," pursued the warder, "you'll be quite a young man still—younger than I am. There's Balfour, now; he's got some call to be down in the mouth, for he'll get it as hot as you, and he's an old un, yet he's cheery enough up yonder"—and he jerked his head in the direction of the court-house—"you may take your 'davey he is. You get *V G*'s."

"What are those?" said Richard, wearily.

"Why, the best marks that can be got; and remember that every one of 'em goes to shorten your time. You must be handier with your room, to begin with. You might be reported by some officers for the way in which that hammock is folded, and then away go your marks at once; and you must learn to sweep your room out cleaner. We couldn't stand *that* in one of our regulars, you know;" and he pointed to some specks of dust upon the shining floor. "As for the oakum pickings which will be set you to-morrow, I'll show you the great secret of that art. Your fingers will suffer a bit at first, no doubt, but you'll be a clever one at it before long. Only buckle to, and keep a civil tongue in your head, young fellow, and you'll do."

"Thank you," said Richard, mechanically.

"If you'll take my advice, you'll set about something at once; sweepin', or polishin', or readin' your Bible. Don't brood. But you will do as you like for this afternoon, since you won't begin regular business till to-morrow."

The warder looked keenly round the cell, probably to make sure that it afforded no facilities for suicide; but the gas was not yet turned on, and if it had been, his prisoner was unaware that by blowing it out, and placing the jet in his mouth, more than one in a similar strait to his own has found escape from his prison woes forever.

"I'll bring you some supper presently," he added; and with a familiar nod, good-naturedly intended for encouragement, he slammed the iron door behind him.

That he should have become an object of pity and patronage to a man like this would in itself have wounded Richard to the quick had he not been devoured by far more biting cares, and even now it galled him. His twenty years might possibly, then, by extremity of good luck, be curtailed by five. By diligent execution of menial drudgery; by performing to some overlooker's satisfaction his daily toil; by careful obedience and subservience to these Jacks in office, themselves but servants, and yet whose malice or ill-humor might cause them to report him for the most trifling faults, or for none at all, and thereby destroy even *this* hope—he might be a free man in fifteen years! He would, even then, he was told, be still a young man. But that he would never be young again Richard was well aware. Within these last three weeks—nay, within that last hour, he had already lived a life, and one that had aged him beyond the power of years. High spirits, pleasure, hopefulness, love, and all the attributes of youth, were dead within him for evermore. For the future he was only to be strong and vigorous in a will that could not have its way for fifteen years at earliest.

Through the grating of his narrow window a few rays of the setting sun were streaming in, and fell upon the bare brown wall behind him. What a flood of glory they were pouring on the woods of Crompton, now in their autumn splendor—on the cliffs at Gethin—on the copse that hid the Wishing Well—on the tower where he had first clasped Harry in his arms! He saw them all, and the sunset hues upon them became suddenly blood-red. He was once more at Gethin, and in imagination taking his revenge upon old Trevethick, and for the moment he was almost happy. "Pity on his gray hairs?" No, not he—though the gallows loomed before him, though hell yawned for him, he would slake his thirst in the life-blood of that perjured villain; and as for her, he would drag her by the hair to look upon her father's corpse. Where was she? Ah, with Solomon upon the castled rock; and see!—he had pushed him from the edge, and there he hung exactly as he himself had hung when Harry had preserved him! How long would a man hold on like that, even a strong man like Coe, on such a narrow ledge, with the gulls screaming about him? Not twenty years—no, nor fifteen!

The clatter of the trap in the door of his cell, as it fell in and formed a table, awoke him from this gloating dream. "Supper," said the warder, looking in at him through this orifice. "What! you're still brooding, are you?—that's bad;" then marched on to the next cell.

Some gruel and bread stood upon this little improvised side-board. If they had been the greatest luxuries imaginable, he could not have swallowed a morsel. The sunlight had faded away; his dream of retribution was over; he seemed to be touching the utmost verge of human wretchedness. Was it possible to kill himself? His neckerchief had been taken away; but he had his braces. The gas-pipe was the only thing to which he could attach them, and it would never bear his weight. He had read somewhere of some poor wretch who had suffocated himself by turning his tongue inward. Had he determination enough for such a device as that? Plenty. His will was iron; he felt that; but it was set on something else than suicide—that afterward, or death or life of any kind, he cared not what; but in the first place, and above all things, Vengeance! In the mean time, there were twenty years in which to think upon it! Twenty years!

The bar dined with the judge that night at Cross Key, and talked, among other things, "shop."

"A curious case that of that young fellow, Yorke," said one. "I wonder whether he has been playing his game long with these competitive examinations? That Chandos must be a queer one, too—son of Lord Fitzbacon's, is he not?"

"I dare say," answered another, carelessly. "It is only vicariously that the juvenile aristocracy ever get an appointment in these days, having no wits of their own. This conviction will be a great blow to them."

"Very good, Sharpshins! but you'd better not let old Bantam hear you, for he dearly loves the Swells. By-the-by, what a pretty girl that witness for the defense was, who turned out to be for the prosecution, eh?"

"Yes, she upset her lover's coach for him nicely. Is it true, I wonder, that the little traitress is going to marry that dull, heavy fellow whom Smoothbore had such work to pump? Gad! if I had been she, I'd have stuck to the other."

"Yes; but kissing goes by favor. She marries him next week, I hear. Is there any thing of interest at Bodmin?"

"Nothing of interest to *me*, at all events. Smoothbore and Balais get all there is between them, confound them! I say, just pass that claret."

Not another word about Richard. The judge himself had forgotten him except as a case in his notes. The jury forgot him in a week. A murder of a shipwrecked sailor happened soon afterward on that coast, and became the talk of the country-side in his place. The world went on its way, and never missed him; the rank closed up where he had used to march, and left no gap.

Richard Yorke was out of the world.

CHAPTER XXXIII.

IN COUPLES.

WHAT tender-nurtured boy, newly-arrived at school—that Paradise when looked back upon from afar, that *Inferno* of the present—has not awakened from sweet dreams of home with a heavy heart? Who has not pictured to himself the weary months that must elapse before he once more regains his freedom and his friends? The burden (one may say) is light, but then the back is also weak that bears it. It is a genuine woe. Something of this, but tenfold in intensity of wretchedness, did Richard feel when he awoke for the first time a convicted felon. He had dreamed that Carew was dead, and left him heir of Crompton; his mother and he were there, and Harry as his wife. The splendor of the house, the beauty of the grand domain about it, were as vividly presented to him as when he saw them with his eyes; and they were all his own. The hope of his youth, the desire of his manhood, were gratified to the uttermost; yet through all ran an undercurrent which mirrored a portion of the present reality. In the marshy pond where he had fought the Squire by moonlight lay two bodies; it was shallow, as it really had been, and he could see their faces as he peered into the water: they were those of Coe and Trevethick. He kept them there, and would not have the pond dragged; but would go thither and gloat upon them for half a summer's day. The mansion was full of gay folks—his old town companions invited to visit him, and behold his greatness (as he had often imagined they should be): Tub Ryll was *his* jester now, and Parson Whymper his "chaplain." They were all playing pool as usual, and he was just about to make an easy hazard, when somebody jogged his elbow. It was the warder of the jail.

"Come, come—this won't do," said he, gruffly. "You must jump up when the bell rings, or we shall quarrel. Fold up your hammock, and clean your room."

Even the school-boy does not begin on his first morning to reckon on his chimney almanac, "One day gone; twenty-four hours nearer to the holidays;" and how should Richard make that cheerful note, who had twenty years of prison life before him, save one day!

He did as he was ordered, wearily, with a heart that had no hope: it seemed to the warder that his air was sullen.

"If this happens again, young fellow, I report you; and then good-by to your *V G*'s."

He did not mean to be brutal; but Richard could have stabbed him where he stood. There were times to come when the temptation to commit such an act was to be very strong within him; and when no thought of punishment, far less of right, restrained him, but that of his projected vengeance always did. Every rough word, every insult, every wrong, was treasured up in his mind, and added to the long account against those who had doomed him to such a fate. It should be paid in full one day; and in the mean time the debt was out at compound interest.

He took his sordid meals, his cocoa, his bread, his gruel, not because he had ever any appetite for them, but because without them he should lose his strength. He must husband that for the long-expected hour when he might need it; when the moment had arrived to strike the blow for which his hand was clenched ten times a day. His hate grew every hour, and, like a petrifying spring, fell drop by drop about his heart, and made it stone. In the mean time, a fiend in torment could alone imagine what he suffered. He spoke to no one but his warders and the chaplain; for now he was a convict, there was no communication with his fellows; only once a day for an hour and a half he took his monotonous exercise in the high-walled prison-yard. Tramp, tramp, tramp, each half a dozen paces behind the other, with an officer on the watch to see that the limit was preserved.

"Keep your distance, you there, unless you want to be reported."

Richard did not want that; but at times his temper was like a devil unchained, and it got the better of him, and even of his treasured purpose; he sometimes returned a sharp answer. This weakness was almost the only feeling within him that reminded him that he was human. He was put on bread and water within the first fortnight; then cursed his folly for thus postponing the one object of his life, and amended. His case was quoted to the visiting justices as an exemplification of the efficacy of cutting short a prisoner's supplies.

While exercising one day he recognized Balfour, who happened to be on the opposite side of the ever-moving circle: the old jail-bird, without glancing toward him, threw his open hands out twice. By this he conveyed to him that his own sentence was also twenty years. During the nine months that Richard remained at Cross Key, this was all that happened to him which could be called an incident. At the end of three months his mother essayed to visit him, but he would not see her. She had been ill, it seemed, ever since that dreadful day of the trial, and was only just convalescent; she had had lodgings in the town, within a hundred yards of him, ever since: it was something, poor soul, to know that she was near him, however inexorably separated. "It would please him," she wrote, "to learn that, through Mr. Whymper's intercession, Carew had continued her pension. She had money enough, therefore, and to spare, but intended to go on with her business of lodging-house keeping in a new quarter of London, and under another name (that of Basil), that she might save, and her Richard find himself a rich man when he regained his liberty. In fifteen years—she had discovered that his time could be remitted to that extent—there would be quite a little fortune for him. In the mean time, she thought of him night and day." But there was something else in the letter. "She confessed that in her agony at his dreadful doom, she had written to his prosecutor to adjure him to appeal for mercy to the crown, and he had refused to do so." This news had driven Richard almost to frenzy. He had written her such a letter as the prison authorities had refused to send, and now he would not see her.

He wrote again; more moderately, however, to bid her never mention Trevethick's name again, nor Coe's, nor Harry's, if she wished him to think of her as his mother: they were dead to him, he said, *for the present.* To be brief, Richard never saw his mother after his conviction. He wished to harden his heart, and not to have it melted within him; and perhaps his fury at her having appealed to Trevethick was purposely exaggerated with this object. His recollection of "the cage," it must be remembered, was also not such as to make the idea of an interview attractive; moreover, that his mother should see him in his convict dress, kept within iron bars like a wild beast, seemed to him to afford a triumph to his deadly enemies.

In the tenth month, Richard, with the other convicts, was transferred to Lingmoor, one of the great penal settlements. They were "removed," for some portion of the distance, in vans, like furniture, or, we might rather say, in caravans like wild beasts; but for some miles they traveled by railway. They were handcuffed and chained together two and two, as pointers are upon their journeys, except that the connection was at the wrist instead of the neck. Silence was strictly enjoined, but this one opportunity of conversing with their fellow-creatures was not to be let slip. Richard's other half was a notorious burglar called Rolfe; this man had passed a quarter of a century in jail, and was conversant with every plan of trickery and evasion of orders. His countenance was not at all of that bull-dog type with which his class is falsely though generally credited; he had good features, though somewhat hard in their expression, and very intelligent gray eyes. It was their very intelligence, so sharp, so piercing, and yet which avoided your gaze, that showed to those who studied such matters what he was. After one glance at Richard he never looked at him again, but stared straight before him, and talked in muttered tones unceasingly, and with lips as motionless as those of a ventriloquist. He was doing fourteen years for cracking a public-house, and had cracked a good many private ones, concerning the details of which enterprises he was very eloquent. When he had concluded his autobiography he began to evince some interest in the circumstances of his companion. Richard, however, did not care to enlighten him on his own concerns, but confined his conversation to the one topic that was common between them—jails. Rolfe gave him a synopsis of the annals of Lingmoor, to which he was bound not for the first time. It was a place that had a bad reputation among those who became perforce its inmates; tobacco, for which elsewhere convenient warders charged a shilling an ounce, was there not less than eighteenpence: such a tariff was shameful, and almost amounted to a prohibition. A pal of his had hung himself there—it was supposed through deprivation of this necessary. It was "a queer case;" for he had "tucked himself up" to the bars of his cell by his braces, the buckles of which had left livid marks upon his neck. His Prayer-book had been found open at the Burial of the Dead, and it was understood that he had read that service over himself before taking leave of the world. He had also written his will with a point of the said brace-buckles upon the brick of his cell. He himself (Mr. Rolfe) had been called as a witness at the inquest, and had thereby obtained two hours' relaxation from labor; but upon the whole he would rather have been working with his gang—the affair had quite upset him; and, since its occurrence, the inmates of Lingmoor were forbidden to use braces.

"Were there any escapes from Lingmoor by any other means?" inquired Richard.

"Escapes?" Mr. Rolfe's countenance assumed a more solemn vacuity than ever. It was an indiscretion of his young friend to shape that word with his lips while a warder sat in the same carriage. Yes, there had been such things even at Lingmoor. But it was a difficult job, even for one used to cracking cribs. The outer wall was not to be scaled without a ladder, and ladders were even more difficult to procure than tobacco. Even if you did get over the outer wall, the space around the prison was very bare, and the sentries had orders to shoot you fleeing. If you got to Bergen Wood, two miles away, you might be safe so far, but it was a dangerous business. Nobody had ever done it yet without "putting somebody out."

This was a euphemism for murder, as Richard was by this time "old hand" enough to know.

"Warders?" inquired he indifferently; for he had already learned to value that objectionable class at a low figure.

"Hush! Yes; you must kill 'a dog' or two before you say good-by to Lingmoor, unless you can put them to sleep." (Bribery.) "There was a man once as had to kill his pal to do it."

"How could that help him?" Richard felt no interest whatever in these narratives as stories; but since they referred to escapes they were entrancing. The convict who is cast for death thinks of nothing but a reprieve; the "lifer" or the long-termer, thinks of nothing but an escape—and (sometimes) vengeance.

"Well, it was curious. There was a 'Smasher'" (utterer of counterfeit coin) "named Molony in for life there—a thin-shanked, shambling fellow, as Smashers mostly are—mere trash. He had got a file, this fool, and dared not use it—kept it as close as though it were 'bacca,' and waited for his chance, instead of making his chance for himself. Damme, if *I* had a file!"

Mr. Rolfe's feelings of irritation were almost too much for him; he turned up the whites of his eyes, so that persons who were unacquainted with his views upon religious subjects might have supposed him to be engaged in some devotional exercise.

"Next door to this fellow—though it seemed a long way off, for the cell was in an angle of the prison—there was one of the right sort; name of Jeffreys. No prison in England could have held *him* if he had had a file. With a rusty nail as he had picked up he dug through his cell wall, and came out one night, all of a sudden, upon the Smasher—thought he was out of doors, poor beggar, through this cursed angle, you see, and after all had only changed his room."

"That must have been the devil," observed Richard.

"It *was*," said Mr. Rolfe, significantly.

"'Why, how on earth did you do it?' asked the Smasher. At least I suppose he did, for the conversation was not reported, as you shall hear. 'With a mere nail, too. Why, *I*'ve got a file, and yet I never thought of that.'

"'A file!' cried Jeffreys. 'Let's look. Give it to me.'

"But Molony wouldn't give it him. The case was this, you see. If Jeffreys could have filed his irons off, and then the window-bars, he could have made a push for it; but he couldn't wait for the other; the night was too far gone for that—there was only time for one to free himself and get away. The Smasher was willing enough to make an effort now; the other's pluck had put a good heart into him. But since he had been there so long, and never moved a hand to help hisself, Jeffreys thought he might stop a little longer; it seemed to him dog-in-the-manger like to be refused the file—at least that's my view of what he thought; though he's been blamed a good deal for what afterward happened."

"But what did happen?"

"Well, they got to high words; the t'other wouldn't give up the file; and when Jeffreys tried to get hold of it, what did the aggravation Smasher do—for you see he was used to bolting half-crowns and such like—but *swallow the file!*"

"Why, that must have killed him?" observed Yorke.

"So Jeffreys concluded," returned Mr. Rolfe, coolly; "and indeed that was his defense when his trial came on. He pleaded that Molony was dead already. 'I did not put the file down his throat, though I did deprive him of it afterward. I was obliged to do it.' He made an anatomy of him with the nail, in fact, just as the surgeons do with their dissecting-knives, though not so neat, in order to get at the file. An ugly job, I call it; but it was a very pretty case, the lawyers said, as to whether murder had been done or not."

"But did this Jeffreys get off?"

"Upon the trial—yes; but not from the prison. He got into the yard all right, and climbed the wall by making steps of the file and the nail; but, in dropping on the other side, he broke his leg, and so they nabbed him. It's a very hard nut to crack, is Lingmoor, *I* can tell you."

With these and similar incidents of prison-life, Mr. Rolfe regaled his companion's ears. The sound of this man's voice, muffled as it was, notwithstanding the nature of his talk, was pleasant to Richard after so many months of enforced silence. After long starvation the stomach is thankful for even garbage; and so it is with the mind. Moreover, any thing would have seemed better than to sit and think during that hateful journey. The railway part of it was by far the worst. To be made a show of at the various stations—every one curious to see how convicts looked in their full regimentals, chained and ironed; to behold the other passengers who were free; to see the happy meetings of lovers and friends, of parents and children; and the partings that were scarcely partings at all compared with his own length of exile from all mankind: these were things the bitterness of which Richard felt to the uttermost; his very blood ran gall. His friend Balfour was among his fellow-travelers, but they did not journey in the same van nor railway carriage. Had it been otherwise Richard might have felt some sense of companionship; whereas the contact of this man Rolfe seemed to degrade him to his level, and isolate him from humanity itself. At the same time, he shrank with sensitiveness from the gaze of the gaping crowd. It is so difficult, even with the strongest will to do so, to become callous and hardened to shame except by slow degrees: every finger seemed to point at him in recognition, every tongue to be telling of his disgrace and doom; whereas, in simple fact, his own mother would scarcely have known him in such a garb, and with those iron ornaments about his limbs; his fine hair cropped to the roots; his delicate features worn and sharpened with spare diet and want of sleep; above all, with those haggard eyes, always watching and waiting for something a long way off—almost, indeed, out of sight at present, but coming up, as a ship comes spar by spar above the horizon, taking shape and distinctness as it nears. There were nineteen years and three months still, however, between him and *it*.

CHAPTER XXXIV.

OUT OF THE WORLD.

THIS tedious, shameful travel came to an end at nightfall. Their way had lain all day through landscapes of great beauty, though about to lose the last remnants of their autumn splendor; but when they left the rail, the woods, and glens, and rivers were seen no more. All was dreary moorland, where winter had already begun to reign. A village or two were passed, among whose scanty population their appearance created little excitement: such sights were common in that locality. They were on the high-road that leads to Lingmoor, and to nowhere else. The way seemed as typical of their outcast life-path as a page out of the *Pilgrim's Progress*. Vanity Fair, where they would fain have tarried if they could, was left far behind them, while to some of them the road was doomed to be the veritable Valley of the Shadow. They were never to see the world, nor partake of its coarse and brutal pleasures—the only ones they cared for, or perhaps had experienced—any more. How bare, and desolate, and wretched was the prospect! There was no living thing in sight; only the wild moorland streams hurried by, as if themselves desirous to escape from the barren solitude. Not a tree was to be seen save Bergen Wood, which Richard's companion indicated to him, as they neared it, by a movement of the eyelid. It had been the tomb of many a convict, who had striven for freedom, and found death. As they emerged from it, Lingmoor prison presented itself, solid, immense, and gloomy, as though it were built of steel—"Castle of Giant Despair." Its guarded gate was swung back, and all were marched into a paved court-yard, where their names were called over, and their irons removed. Then each was stripped and searched, and another uniform substituted for that they had worn at Cross Key. The old hands seemed to take a pride in knowing what was about to be done beforehand; in being recognized by the warders, though their greeting was but a contemptuous shrug; and in threading the windings of the stone labyrinths with an accustomed step. Richard was ushered into a cell the exact counterpart of that he had lately inhabited; and yet he regarded it with the interest which one can not fail to feel in what is to be one's home for years.

Home! Frightful misnomer for that place, warm and well-ventilated as it was, and supplied with the latest products of civilization. The gas was burning brightly; fresh cool water flowed at his will; at his touch a bell rang, and instantly, outside his door, an iron plate sprang out, and indicated to the warder in what cell his presence was required. "How clean and comfortable!" says the introduced-by-special-order visitor, to his obsequious acquaintance the governor, on observing these admirable arrangements. "How much better are these scoundrels cared for," cries the unthinking public, "than are our honest poor!" It is not, however, that the convict is pampered; but for this unkindly care he would not be able to endure the punishment which justice has decreed for him. Science has meted out to him each drop of gruel, each ounce of bread, each article of clothing, and each degree of warmth. Not one of all the recipients of this cruel benevolence but would gladly have exchanged places with the shivering tramp or the work-house pauper. To cower under the leafless branches of Bergen Wood, while the November night-blasts made them grind and clang, would have seemed paradise compared with that snug lodging; nay, the grave itself, with its dim dread Hereafter, has been preferred before it.

Life at Lingmoor was existence by machinery—a monotony that sometimes maddened as well as slew. To read of it is to understand nothing of this. The bald annals of the place reveal nothing of this terrible secret.

Richard rose at five at clang of bell, cleaned out his cell, and folded up his bed more neatly than did ever chamber-maid; at six was breakfast—porridge, and forty minutes allowed for its enjoyment; then chapel and parade; then labor—mat-making was his trade, at which he became a great proficient. His fingers deftly worked, while his mind brooded. At twelve was dinner—bread and potatoes, with seventy minutes allowed for its digestion; then exercise in the yard, and mat-making again till six in summer, and four in winter; prayers, supper, school till eight; when the weary day was done. On Sunday, except two hours of exercise and chapel, Richard was his own master, to brood as much as he would. There were also no less than three holidays in the year, on which it has been whispered with horror that the convicts have pudding. There was, however, no such excess at Lingmoor.

As for society, there was the chaplain. This gentleman could make nothing of Richard, though he tried his best. It was evident to him that the young man had something on his mind; if he would only confide in his spiritual adviser, he assured him comfort could be administered. But no confidence ever took place. It was a most distressing case; here was a youth of superior position, and well educated, as obstinate and stubborn as the most hardened criminal in the establishment. His Bible was never opened. One of his warders had expressed his opinion that No. 421 was vindictive, but he (the chaplain) was bound to say he had observed nothing of that. The remarks in his note-book respecting 421 were these: "Richard Yorke—aged twenty, looks ten years older; reserved and cynical; a hopeless infidel, but respectful, uncomplaining, and well-mannered."

Richard had been reported more than once for "inattention to orders," and had lost some of his good marks accordingly. The cause of this was one over which he could now be scarcely said to have control. He had become so absent and *distrait* that he sometimes hardly knew what was going on about him. The perpetual brooding in which he indulged had, in fact, already postponed the accomplishment of the very object which enthralled his thoughts. The effect of this was serious; and he had good reason for the apprehension which seized him, that his wits might leave him before that day of liberty arrived, which was still so many years distant. On account of his previous calling, which was described in the prison books as landscape-painter, he had been put to a handicraft trade; but he now applied for barrow-work, and the surgeon seconded his application. This change of occupation, which was destined in some respects to be beneficial, proved at the outset most unfortunate. The outdoor toil was mostly spade and barrow labor on the moor, on which the convicts worked in gangs—each gang under supervision of two warders, armed with sword and musket. The first face that Richard's eyes lit on, when he found himself in the open, with the free air of heaven blowing on him, and already, as it seemed, bearing the seeds of health and hope, was that of Robert Balfour. In his joyous excitement he sprang forward and held out his hand; the other hesitated—for the old cracksman was prudence itself—then, as if with an incontrollable impulse, grasped the offered fingers, with an "I am right glad to see you, lad." The next instant they were both in custody, and marched back to the prison, charged with the high crime and misdemeanor of conversation, which at Lingmoor was called "colloguing," "conspiracy," and other terrible terms. Brought before the authorities upon this serious charge, Richard at once confessed himself alone to blame; the fresh air had, in a manner, intoxicated him, after his long confinement within stone walls; and the sight of his old acquaintance had caused him to forget the rules. On the offense-list being examined, it was found, however, that No. 421 was a good deal in the habit of forgetting. His cell-warder gave him but an indifferent character; and Richard, in a fury, committed the fatal indiscretion of rebutting this latter accusation by a countercharge of tyranny and ill-usage. The next instant he could have bitten his tongue out—but it was too late; he felt that he had made an enemy of this body-servant, who was also his master, for the remainder of his term. An "old hand," unless he is a professional garroter (in which case he is generally too much respected to be ill-used), is always careful to keep on good terms with his attendant; otherwise—since a warder's word, if it be not law, is at all events worth that of ten prisoners—there may be no end to your troubles. This is not because warders are not as a class a most respectable body of men, but simply because you can't get all the virtues for a guinea a week. A strict and impartial sense of justice is especially a rare and dear article—even governors have sometimes been deficient in it. Most men have their prejudices, as women have their spites; and a prejudice against a fellow-creature is a thing that grows. Richard's warder was no tyrant—only a sullen, ignorant fellow, in a false position; he had an almost absolute power over his fellow-creatures, and like many—perhaps like most who have ever possessed such a thing—it was too much for him.

"I am a tyrant, am I?" said he, significantly, as he marched Richard back to his cell after sentence was decreed. "Very well; we'll *see.*"

Richard got bread and water for three days certain, and, what was far worse, another "monstrous cantle" might be cut out of that period of remission which began to be all the dearer in his eyes the more problematical it grew. Garroters, as we have said, were respected at Lingmoor; they are so ready with their great apelike hands, and so dull-brained with respect to consequences; yet Richard's warder, when he brought his bread and water, with a grin, that night, was probably as near to death by strangling as he had ever been during his professional experience. It was not that he was on his own account the object of his prisoner's wrath, but that by his conduct he had, as it were, supplemented the inexpiable wrong originally committed, and earned for himself a portion of the undying hate which was due elsewhere. "I may kill this brute some day," thought Richard, ruefully, "in spite of myself." And he resolved on the first opportunity to communicate a certain secret which was on his mind to a friendly ear; so that *that* at least should be utilized to the disadvantage of his foes, in case incontrollable passion should one day compel him to sacrifice a lesser victim, and make his great revenge to fail. It had not once entered into his mind that he could *forego* his purpose, but only that circumstances might render it impossible.

The occasion for which he looked was not long in coming. His days of punishment concluded, he was once more marched out upon the moor, and again found himself in Balfour's company. Not a sign passed between them this time, but as they delved they talked. "I fear you have been suffering for my sake," said Richard.

"It is no matter. My shoulders are broad enough for two," returned the other, kindly. "I am right glad to see your face again, though it is so changed. You have been ill, have you not, lad?"

"I don't know. Something is wrong with me, and I may be worse—that is why I want to speak to you. Listen!"

"All right. Don't look this way, and sink your voice if either of these dogs comes to leeward."

"If you get away from this place, and *I* don't—"

"Now, none of that, lad," interrupted the old man, earnestly. "That's the worst thing you can get into your head at Lingmoor, if you ever want to leave it. Never *say* die, nor even *think* it. I am three times your age, and yet I mean to get out again and enjoy myself. It is but fifteen years now, without counting remission—though I've got into disgrace with my cursed watch-dog, and sha'n't get much of that—and you must keep a good heart."

"I shall keep a firm one," answered Richard, "never fear. I wish to guard against contingencies, that's all. If I die—"

"Damned if you shall," said Balfour, sturdily, quite innocent of any plagiarism from Uncle Toby.

"Very good," continued Richard, coolly. "If you get out of this before me, let us merely say, I have something to tell you which may be of service to you. There's a man in Breakneckshire called Carew of Crompton—"

"I know him: the gentleman born as put on the gloves with Bendigo at Birmingham?"

"Very likely; at all events, every body knows him in the Midlands. He will go to the dogs some day, and his estate will be sold. You have saved money, you tell me; if the chance occurs, you can't invest it better than in the lot called Wheal Danes, a mine in Cornwall."

"I believe you every word," said Balfour; "but a mine would be rather over my figure, wouldn't it? I have only got eight hundred pounds."

"That would be plenty. It's a disused mine, and supposed to be worked out. There's only one man in England that knows it is not so, except myself. He will come or send to the auction, expecting to get it cheap; but do you bid two hundred pounds beforehand, and get it by private contract. Say you want the place—it's close to the sea—for building purposes; they'll laugh at you, and jump at your offer. The fee-simple is not supposed to be worth five shillings an acre. It will turn out a gold mine to whoever gets it."

"Wheal Danes," repeated Balfour, carefully. "I'll remember that; and what is more, lad, I'll not forget the man as told me of it. It's not the profit that I am speaking on: that will be yours, I hope, as it should be in all reason, and not mine; but it's the confidence." The old man's voice grew husky with emotion. "Damme, I liked *you* from the first, as was natural enough; but there was no reason why you should take a fancy to an old thief like me more than any other among this pretty lot here. The first as speaks of secrets is of course the one as runs the risk, but I will do what I can to show myself honorable on my side. You have trusted me, and I'll trust you."

"Have you any plan to get away from this?" whispered Richard, eagerly. "All that I have shall be yours: I swear it."

"Nay, lad; your word's enough," returned the other, reproachfully. "And I don't covet nothing of yours; indeed I don't."

"I was a brute to talk so to you, Balfour," answered Richard, penitently. "But you don't know how I crave for freedom: it makes me mad to think of it."

"Ay, ay; I know," sighed the old fellow. "It used to be so with me once; but now it only comes on me when my term is nearly up. One gets patient as one gets old, you'll find. No; I've no plan just now; though, if I ever have, I promise you you shall be the man to know it. It's another matter altogether that I meant to tell you about. You've given me an address to remember: let me give you another in exchange for it—No. 91 Earl Street East, Spitalfields. That's where mother lives, if the poor soul is alive to whom you wrote for me from Cross Key. She'll be dead, however, long before you or I get out of this, that's certain, or I should not be telling you what I do; for one's mother is the best friend of all friends, and should come first and foremost. Well, the money will do her no good; and if any thing happens to me, I have neither chick nor child to inherit it. I am speaking of this eight hundred pound, lad. If I get into the world, I shall want it for myself, for I doubt my limbs will be too stiff for work by that time; but if not, then you shall have it—every shilling. I am digging my own grave, as it might be, with this spade, and making my will, do you see?" said the old fellow, smiling.

"I thank you for your kind intentions," returned Richard, absently; "it's very good of you, I'm sure." His hopes of some scheme of present release had been excited by the old man's manner, and this faint and far-off prospect of a legateeship seemed but of little worth.

"I may not have another chance to tell you about it," resumed Balfour. "It is five years now since you and I spoke together last, and it may be another five years before such good luck happens again; so don't forget 91 Earl Street East. It's under the middle stone of the back kitchen, all in golden quids. You needn't mind it being 'swag;' and as for those whose own it is by rights, I could not tell you who the half of it belonged to, if I would. It's the savings of an industrious life, lad," added Mr. Balfour, pathetically; "and I should be sorry to think, if any thing happened to me, that it should lie there useless, or be found accidental like, and perhaps fall into the hands of the bluebottles. Your memory's good, my lad, I dare say, and you won't forget the number nor the street."

"My memory is very good, friend," returned Richard, slowly; "and I have only two or three things else to keep in it. And you, on your part, you will not forget the mine?"

"Nay, nay; I've got it safe: Wheal Danes, Wheal Danes."

"Silence, down there!" roared the warder; and nothing but the squeak of the barrow-wheel and the clean slice of the spade was heard in all that throng of involuntary toilers.

CHAPTER XXXV.

BASIL.

It is nineteen years since Richard Yorke stood in the dock at Cross Key and heard the words of doom. Almost a whole generation of his fellow-creatures has passed away from the earth. Old men have died, young men have become old, and babes have grown to be young men. There are but some half dozen persons in the world who, if reminded of him by some circumstance, can recollect him dimly. There are two who still keep him in their thoughts continually, just as he was—like a picture which bears no longer any resemblance to its original—and even these never breathe his name.

Here is a young fellow walking with his mother along Oxford Street who is not unlike him, who might be himself but for those nineteen years; and the girl that walks upon the other side of him might also be Harry Trevethick. Youth and beauty are not dead because Richard Yorke is dead, or as good as dead. The name of this girl is Agnes Aird, a painter's daughter, who is also a teacher of his art. The lad is her father's pupil, and has learned beneath his roof a lesson not included in the artistic course; you may know that by the way in which his eyes devour the girl, the intonation of his voice when he addresses her, the silent pressure of the arm on which her fingers rest. Charles Coe is in love with Agnes, and in all his studies of perspective beholds her, a radiant figure beckoning him on to a happy future. His pencil strays from its object to portray her features—to inscribe her name beside his own. Mr. Coe, his father, exceedingly disapproves of this projected alliance, and has forbidden the young people to associate. This ukase, however, can scarcely be obeyed while the whole party are inmates of Mr. Aird's residence, who "lets off" the upper part of his house as furnished apartments, which the Coes have now inhabited as lodgers for some weeks. Solomon (now a very well-to-do personage, and a great authority on metalliferous soils) has come to town on business, and left to his wife the choice of a residence; and she, to please her son, had chosen the artist's dwelling, upon whose door-plate was inscribed the fact that he was a professor of drawing. Solomon was not displeased that his son's tastes lay in that direction; it might be useful to himself hereafter in the matter of plans and sections; but he is violently opposed to this ridiculous love affair, which is to be stamped out at once. To that end he has instructed Mrs. Coe to look for lodgings in a distant quarter, and it is on that errand that we now behold her. It is characteristic of the Harry whom we once knew that she permits these young people to accompany her—and one another—on the very quest that has their final separation for its object. She can not resist making them happy while she can; and she can refuse her Charley nothing. Moreover, Solomon is in the City, looking after his mining interests, and need never know.

In appearance, however, Harry Trevethick is greatly changed. She is but seven-and-thirty, yet has already passed into the shade of middle life. Her hair, though still in profusion, is tinged with gray; her features are worn and sharp; her brow is wrinkled; and in her once trustful eyes dwells a certain eager care, not mere distress or trouble, but an anxiety which is almost Fear.

The three are now in one of the streets which unite Cavendish Square with Oxford Street, as a busy babbling rill connects the unruffled lake with the roaring river. It is composed both of shops and private houses, the latter of which in some cases deign, notwithstanding their genteel appearance, to accommodate visitors by the week or month.

"This is the sort of locality your father wished for, Charley," remarked Mrs. Coe, looking about her; "it seems central, and yet tolerably quiet. Let us try this house."

The name of "Basil," without prefix, was engraved upon the door-plate; and in a corner of the dining-room window lurked an enameled card with "Apartments" on it.

"There is no need to drag Agnes and you in," Mrs. Coe went on, as they stood waiting for the bell to be answered. So Charles, well pleased, was left outside with the young girl, while his mother "went over the house." In a few minutes, however, she reappeared, and in a somewhat hurried and excited tone observed, "I think this place will do, my dears; but there is a good deal to talk about and settle, which will take me some time. Therefore I think you had better go home together, and leave me." Then, without waiting for a reply, she retired within and closed the door.

"How very curious!" exclaimed Agnes, wondering.

"Oh, not at all," said the young man, cheerfully; "my mother likes to do things for herself, and I dare say has not a very high opinion of our judgment in domestic matters. You don't seem over-pleased, it seems to me, Agnes, at the notion of a *tête-à-tête* with your humble servant;" and Mr. Charles pouted, half in fun and half with annoyance.

"No, no; it is not that, Charles," answered the girl, hastily. "You know I have no pleasure equal to that of being with you; but I don't like your mother's looks; she had such a strange air, and spoke so differently from her usual way. I really scarcely like to leave her."

"My dear Agnes, you don't know my mother," returned Charles, laughing. "One would sometimes think she had all the care of the world upon her shoulders when every thing is going as smooth as oil. You don't appreciate the grave responsibility of taking furnished lodgings for a week certain. Come along, you little goose." And, drawing her still hesitating arm within his own, he marched away with her.

Yet Agnes had reason for what she said; and Charles, somewhat selfish as he was, would have foregone his flirtation and remained by his mother's side had he seen her the moment after the house door had shut her in.

With a throbbing heart, and a face as white as the handkerchief she passed over her damp brow, she leaned against the wall of the passage, ere, with trembling steps, she approached the open parlor door. An aged woman stood in the centre of the room, with hair as white as snow, but with a figure straight as a poplar, and drawn up rigidly to its full height.

"Why do you come back again?" cried she, in accents soft as milk, yet bitter as gall. "Why do you cross my threshold, you false witch, when there is nothing more to blight and blast? Did you think I should not know you, that you dared to come? I should know you among all the fair-faced fiends in hell."

"Mercy, mercy, Mrs. Yorke!" cried Harry, feebly; and she fell upon her knees, and made as though she would have clasped the other's garments with her stretched-out arms.

"Don't touch me, lest I strike you," answered the old woman, fiercely, "as, nineteen years ago, I would have struck you on your cruel lips, and spoiled the beauty that was the ruin of my boy! May *you* have sons to perish through false wantons, and to pine in prison! May *you* be desolate, and without heart or hope, as I am! Go, devil, go, and rid me of your hateful presence!"

"Hear me, hear me, Mrs. Yorke!" pleaded the other, with clasped hands. "Strike me, spit upon me, if you will, but only hear me! Abject as I look, wretched as I feel—as I knew I must needs look and feel—I have longed for this hour to come, as my boy longs for his bridal morning!"

"May he wake the next to find his bride a corpse; or, better still, to find her false, like you."

"I am not false; I never was; Heaven knows it!" cried Harry, passionately. "I do not blame you for your bitter words. I have earned your curses, though I meant to earn your blessing."

"My blessing!" Contempt and hatred struggled for the mastery in her tone. "Richard, Richard! in your chains and toil, do you hear this? This woman meant to earn my blessing!"

"Upon my soul—whose salvation I would have imperiled to save him—I did my best, although it seemed my worst," cried Harry. "That I was weak and credulous and fearful is most true; but indeed, indeed, I was faithful to your son. My father—he is dead, madam, and past your judgment" (for the fury in the other's eyes had blazed up afresh at the mention of him)—"deceived me with false hopes; for fear alone—though I was timid too—would never have caused me to break the promise I had passed to you. He said, if I disgraced myself and him by the perjury I contemplated, that he would thrust me from his door forever; that in the lips of all the world my name would become another word for shame and infamy; that even the man I loved would loathe me when I had thus served his turn. I answered him, 'No matter, so I save my Richard.' Then he said, 'But you will not save him; you will ruin him, rather, by this very evidence you purpose to give. We have proof enough of this Yorke's guilt, no matter what you swear; and we have proof, besides, of his having committed other offenses, if we choose to adduce it. All you will effect is to make yourself shameful.' Then I hesitated, not knowing what to think. 'The case is this,' argued my father: 'I have no grudge against this young scoundrel, since the money has been all recovered, and I don't want revenge—else, as I say, I can easily get it. But I'll have him taught a lesson; he must be punished for the wrong he has done, but not severely. Before the judge passes sentence, I, the prosecutor, will beg him off: such an appeal is always listened to, you know, and I will make it. But if you dare to speak for him, as I hear you mean to do—if you, my daughter, call yourself thief and trollop to save his skin, then shall he rot in jail! He shall, by Heaven! His fate hangs on my lips, not yours.'"

"Can this be true?" mused the old woman.

"It *is* true, so help me Heaven!" cried Harry. "I was a fool, a poor, weak, shuddering fool, but not a traitress. If you were in court, and saw me look at him—the smile I gave by which I meant to assure him all was well, however ill it seemed— You *did* see it; I see you did. You do believe me. Oh, thank Heaven—thank Heaven!"

She began to sob and cry, and caught hold of the old woman's hand and kissed it, while the other stood silent, still in doubt.

"Oh, madam, pity me. That you have suffered torments for long years is plain to see, and yet you have not, though he was your son, been tortured as I have. You could not have freed him by a word as I could; and oh, I did not utter it! I seemed to be his judge, his jailer, the cause of all his woes, to the man I loved—and loved beyond all others! I hated my own father for his sake. I"—she shuddered—"I was married to Richard's rival. You at least have been alone, not companioned night and day by one who helped to doom him. Your case is hard and bitter—but mine! not our own Richard, in his chains and toil, has suffered what *I* have suffered! Look at me, madam, and tell me if I speak truth or lie."

"Yes, yes," mused Mrs. Yorke, in tender tones, and passing her fingers over the other's silvering hair and haggard face; "I do—I must believe it. I should not have known you to-day had you not called me by my name. You must have mourned for him indeed. Is this the cheek he loved to kiss? Is this the hair a lock of which I took to comfort him in prison? Poor soul—poor soul!"

"How is he, madam?" whispered Harry, hoarsely. "Is he well? Is he free?"

"Not yet, Harry. In a year hence he will be. I had a letter only yesterday. But you must never see him; and if you really love him—I speak it for his sake, not theirs—you must never let him set eyes on your husband or your boy."

"I do not wish to see him; it would be too terrible to bear," groaned Harry.

"But he must not see *them*," insisted the other, gravely. "You must put the sea between yourselves and him, or there will be murder done. His wrath is terrible, and will be the destruction of both them and him. The hope of vengeance is the food he lives upon, and without which he would have perished years ago. Even if you persuaded him, as you have convinced *me*, that you yourself are innocent of his ruin, that would only make him firmer in his purpose against your husband. He will have his life-blood, and then his own will pay for it. If I had not seen you, I meant to see this man, and give him warning six months before Richard left the prison."

"Solomon would never heed it," exclaimed Harry, "nor even believe it if I told him."

"He will believe *me*," said the other, composedly. "You must bring him here that I may tell him. Your Solomon must be a fool indeed not to hearken when a mother warns him against her own son. Mind, I do not blame my Richard, woman!" continued Mrs. Yorke, with sudden passion; "he has had provocation enough; it is but right to kill such vermin, and I could stand by and smile to see him do it. But they must be kept apart, I say—this man and Richard

—lest a worse thing befall him than has happened already."

"Never to see him more!" moaned Harry, covering her face with her hands; "never to tell him I was not the wretch I seemed! only to fear him as an enemy to me and mine—"

"Ay, and to himself," interrupted the other, gravely. "If you would not inflict far more on him than you have done already; if you would not—as you will, if you neglect my warning—designedly bring him to a shameful death, as you have involuntarily doomed him to a shameful life, keep these two men apart. If you love this son of yours, remove him from the reach of mine."

"Great Heaven!" cried Harry, shuddering, "would he harm my boy—my innocent boy?"

"Ay, as he would set his heel upon his father—the viper and his brood. It is no idle menace he has breathed so cautiously that the whisper might well escape even another ear than mine, in every letter for these many years. He thirsts for liberty, not for his own sake, but for the slow-ripening vengeance it shall bear. He will have it, unless we save him from himself by saving them from him, as sure as yonder inky cloud will fall in storm. The thought of it was full grown in his mind when he wrote from Cross Key: '*They are dead to me, those three, at present*,' and forbade me ever to mention them by name; and since then he has thought of nothing else. The day of retribution is about to dawn. I say again, beware of him."

"But he must be mad to cherish—"

"Perhaps he is," interrupted the old woman, coldly; "he will not be less dangerous on that account to those who made him mad."

There was a long silence. Then Harry, in submissive tones, inquired what Mrs. Yorke would have her do.

"Bring your husband hither," returned she. "Take the rooms up stairs, and leave the task of telling him his peril to me: the sooner it is done the better. There is but a year at most—not much too long to sell his goods, and get him away across the world, erasing every footstep behind him. If he leave one—no matter how slight the clew—Richard will track him like a blood-hound."

"We will come here at once—to-morrow," cried Harry, eagerly.

"Good. My name is Basil now, remember; not that it is likely," she added, bitterly, "that you will call me Yorke from habit; it is not a household word with you, I reckon."

"It is never breathed," said Harry, simply; "but, oh, madam, I *think* of him, indeed I do! He was my first love, and my last; and though he should kill me for the crime, of which I have shown myself guiltless, I should pray God bless him with my latest breath. Yet he must curse *me* forever! He must never know but that I was the willing agent of his ruin!"

"'Tis true, I dare not mention your name, Harry," said Mrs. Yorke, sadly; "and, if I told him, all the knowledge of the deception practiced on you would only make him the more bitter against your husband—the man who, by connivance in your father's cruel falsehood, obtained you for his wife, while his rival pined in prison. I do not blame you for your marriage—I know the force of stern necessity too well. But do not imagine that Richard could forgive you: he never, never could."

"I know it, I know it," sighed Harry, shuddering; "and yet he would pity me if he did but know what my life has been—almost as much as I have pitied *him*. But you, madam, *you* at least have forgiven me; you believe me; you will not refuse to bless me, as his mother, before I go."

"I believe you, and therefore I forgive you," answered Mrs. Yorke, with tenderness; "and if I believed in blessings, and had the power of bestowing them, you should have your wish. From henceforth we two are friends—though I never thought to kiss your cheek again, Harry—and must work together for the good of him we love in common. You will be here to-morrow for certain, then?"

"Without fail we shall."

CHAPTER XXXVI.

THE OMEN.

Mrs. Coe was as good as her word, and her husband and son were Mrs. Basil's lodgers within four-and-twenty hours. Solomon Coe was not very particular as to furnished apartments, and left such arrangements wholly to his wife. On the other hand, he confided to her but little respecting his affairs, nor was she, on her part, curious to inquire into them. Man and wife had few things in common, and affection was not one of them. Solomon had married Harry with the full consciousness that another was preferred before him; the disclosures at the trial, and the subsequent gossip of his neighbors, had placed that fact beyond a doubt. But he was not to be balked of the bride that had been promised him so long; nor, above all, should his rival enjoy even the barren victory of Harry's remaining unwedded for his sake. There are marriages born of pique and spite on man's part as well as woman's; and Solomon's was one of them, although he reaped, of course, material advantages besides. Trevethick had survived more than ten years, during which he had largely increased his savings; and at his death all these had reverted to his daughter and her husband. The wealth that had thus poured in upon Solomon through Harry's means did not purchase for her any new regard; he had never ill-treated her, in a material sense, but he had spoken ash-sticks, though he had used none. On the slightest quarrel, that "jail-bird friend of yours" had been thrown in her face, and the cowardly missile was still cast at her upon occasion. The birth of their child had not cemented their union. As he grew up his character showed itself as foreign to that of his father as was his personal appearance. He was slight in figure, delicate in appearance (though not in constitution), and fastidious in taste. His choice of an artist's calling was not so objectionable to Solomon as might be imagined; he had not sensitiveness enough to abhor it from association, and, as has been said, he thought it might be made to co-operate with his own commercial schemes. But the artist nature was in antagonism to his own, and Charles and his father were not on affectionate terms with one another.

The wayward, handsome lad was, on the other

hand, adored by his mother. Her intelligence, not naturally acute, was quickened to see his faults, not indeed as such, but as possible causes of misfortune to him. His too lively impulses, his indecision, his love of pleasure, were all sources of apprehension to her, though scarcely ever of rebuke. She saw in Agnes Aird, his tutor's daughter—so simple, yet so sensible and sterling, so faithful, pure, and true—the very girl to make her son a fitting wife; an antidote for what was amiss in him; her honest heart a sheet-anchor to hold him fast, not in the turbid ocean of excess, for her Charley was too good to tempt it, but through that sparkling sea of gayety in which he was too apt to plunge. She was beautiful enough even for him to mate with; she was better born and better trained than he; for old Jacob Aird was none of those irregular geniuses of the pencil, addicted to gin-punch and Shelley, and selfish to the core, but a plain honest man, who had brought up his daughter well—in tastes a lady, but housewifely and wisely too. As for the inequality of wealth between them, her son would have enough for both; and it was certain that Agnes did not love him for his expectations, for they were unknown alike to her and him. Harry had never led him to believe that he would be a rich man; her love, as we have said, had made her wise in all that concerned Charley; and as for his father, he was naturally reticent in such matters. He did not spend one fifth part of his income. His habits were as inexpensive as they had been in the old days at Gethin; and if the village folks had ever hinted to the young fellow of his father's wealth, he had no conception of its real extent. The idea itself, too, would have had no great interest for him; he liked to have money for the pleasure of spending it, but it was never the object of his thoughts; he was too careless, too much the creature of the hour, to forecast his future. His mother gave him all she could, but he was aware that it was obtained with difficulty; the cost of his very education, which he had received at a school near Turlock, had, he knew, been grudged; his father had often grumbled that it was money thrown away, for, "Look at me," said he; "I taught myself." There was always, in short, a tightness in the Coe money market that augured any thing but pecuniary prosperity.

The very fact of their having taken lodgings at Mr. Aird's house, situated as it was in Soho, a respectable but far from fashionable locality, argued but moderate means, and placed the artist out of all suspicion of setting his pretty daughter as a matrimonial snare for Charley. She was pretty enough and good enough, the old man justly thought, for him or for his betters; and though he regarded the good-will which the young people evidently entertained for one another with favor, he saw in it neither condescension nor advantage. Solomon, much engaged in business affairs away from home, and estimating, besides, the power of love at a low rate, was not seriously alarmed at the growing attachment between his son and Agnes, nor would have been had it advanced much farther. He thought he had only to say "No," to put a stop to it at any point. Still he had determined to place the boy out of the reach of such temptation as a pretty girl living beneath the same roof must always offer to susceptible youth; and hence it was that Mrs. Coe had engaged new lodgings. But even now, so lightly did his father think of the matter, that Charley was still to be permitted to visit at Mr. Aird's daily, and take his drawing-lessons as heretofore.

An excuse for the change of residence had been afforded in the fact that Soho was too far from the parks, in which alone Mrs. Coe took pleasure in walking. She was quite unaccustomed to town life, and the roar and tumult of the streets annoyed and even alarmed her. In some respects, indeed, she was even a more nervous, timid creature than she had been as a girl; the warning just received from Mrs. Yorke had not fallen upon her altogether unexpectedly, though she could not have been said to be prepared for it. A vague apprehension of Richard's vengeance had haunted her whole married life; she did not fear for her own safety; something told her that his anger would scorn to harm herself; that it would pass over her head like a flaming sword, and smite her husband and her boy; and as face after face passed by her in the crowded street, she would shrink and tremble, thinking that that of Richard Yorke would come one day, and recognize her own, and track it home. Was he not fated to work their common ruin? Did not the spectre ship cross Turlock Sands before she met his face for the first time? Though so mature in years, Harry was indeed as superstitious as ever. A curious instance of this occurred on the day that the Coes moved into their new lodgings. The mother and son had arrived first—Solomon being engaged in the City until evening—and Charley had strolled into the ground-floor parlor, while the landlady (whom he had not yet seen) was engaged with his mother up stairs in the distribution of the luggage. Above the chimney-piece hung that striking if not attractive portrait of Joanna Southcott and her amanuensis, with which we are already acquainted; and it tickled the young man's fancy amazingly. He concluded it was a family group—the likeness, perhaps, of Mrs. Basil and her late husband engaged in making out their weekly accounts. "I will beg Agnes not to be jealous of our charming landlady," thought he, and took out his note-book with the intention of transferring the likeness for that young lady's amusement. While engaged in this occupation the door opened, and in stepped Mrs. Basil and her new tenant. In his alarm and haste he stepped back suddenly, and overthrew a little table, on which were some ornaments, he knew not what, which rolled to his mother's feet. She uttered a cry of horror; and the landlady herself stood still, regarding him with a face of astonishment, and even terror.

"Is that—your—son?" exclaimed she, clutching his mother by the arm.

But Mrs. Coe did not seem to hear her.

"Look, look!" cried she; "the skull, the skull! Oh, is it not a frightful omen!"

"I am really very sorry," said Charley, picking up the article in question; "it was very stupid of me, Mrs. Basil."

"Don't mention it, young Sir," said the landlady, who had apparently recovered from her sudden tremor; "the skull is no worse for its roll, you see; he was fortunately a hard-headed gentleman who originally owned it."

"Indeed," said Charley, taking it from her

hand with some curiosity, "it seems a curious ornament for a sitting-room. May I ask whom it belonged to when it had flesh about it?"

"It is the skull of Swedenborg," answered Mrs. Basil. "A near relative of mine was a disciple of his, and left it to me as a most precious relic."

"But how the deuce did he get possession of it?" inquired the young man.

"Well, not very fairly, as it seems to me," smiled the landlady. "While your mother sits down and rests herself—for I am afraid you have frightened her a bit—I'll tell you the story."

"Yes, yes," said Mrs. Coe, faintly; "I shall be better presently; don't mind me."

"Well, the tale runs thus, Sir. Swedenborg was buried in the vault beneath the Swedish embassador's chapel in Princes Square, Ratcliffe Highway; and a certain theologian having once affirmed that all great philosophers took their bodies with them into the world of spirits, and that this gentleman had done the like, leave was obtained to settle this point by actual examination. The body was found, and the theologian confuted, but no trouble was taken to solder on again the lid of the coffin. A thieving Swede, attending a funeral of one of his countrymen in the same vault, remarked this circumstance, and stole the skull, with the intention of selling it to some disciple of the great philosopher's; and I am ashamed to say that he found a purchaser in my respected relative: and that's how I became possessed of Swedenborg's skull."

"Very curious, though rather larcenous," observed the young man, laughing. "And this good lady over the mantel-piece, who is she?"

"That's Joanna Southcott. But, my good young gentleman, I will answer all your questions another time. Your mother and I will have enough to do to arrange matters before your father comes home. You will excuse my freedom, Sir."

"Certainly," said Charley, rather amused than otherwise with the landlady's bluntness. "I know I'm in the way just now; so I'll step out for half an hour or so. I am sorry I frightened you, dear mother."

He stooped and kissed her fondly; and then, with a smile and a nod at Mrs. Basil, stepped into the little passage and out of doors, and, whistling, passed the window down the street.

"Your son has a light heart," said Mrs. Basil, looking at Harry very earnestly. "How old is he?"

"Eighteen—or a little less."

"He looks his age *at least*," observed the other, emphatically.

"Yes; dark people always do."

"And your husband is dark, like him, I remember."

"Yes; his complexion is swarthy, though he is not slim, like Charles."

Mrs. Coe, still in the arm-chair into which she had first sunk, here closed her eyes; either the faintness of which she had complained was coming on again, or she did not wish to meet the other's searching gaze.

There was a long pause, during which Mrs. Basil went to the cellaret, and pouring out a glass of sherry, put it to her tenant's lips.

"Do you feel better now?" said she, when Harry had drunk it.

"Yes, yes; much better. But that skull—oh, horrible! it rolled from him to me. What an omen on your very threshold! Heaven guard my Charles from evil!"

"This is weakness, Mrs. Coe. The skull is harmless; and it rolled because your son upset it."

"Yes, my son," gasped the other, trembling. "It is for him I fear. It augurs death—death—death!"

There was a ring at the front-door, decisive, sharp, and resonant.

"Great Heaven!" cried Harry; "if it should be he himself! Hide me away; put me out of sight." Her terror was piteous to behold: she shook in every limb.

"It is the post," said Mrs. Basil, contemptuously; and she was right. The servant brought in a letter for her mistress.

"I don't know the hand," mused she. "Black-bordered, and black-sealed too." She opened it without excitement, and read it through: it was but a few lines.

"Your omen has proved true for once, Mrs. Coe," said she, in quiet tones. "This speaks of death."

"Whose death?" cried Harry.

"My husband's, Richard's father. Carew of Crompton died last night."

There was no sorrow in the aged woman's face: a gravity, unmixed with tenderness, possessed it. Carew was naught to her, and had been naught for twoscore years. But the tide of memory was at its flow within her brain; and because the Past *is* Past it touches us. This man had loved her once, after his own scornful manner, when he was young, and before power and selfishness had made him stone. He had been the father of her only son, and now he was Dead.

"I am so sorry," said Harry, not quite knowing what to say.

"There is no need for sorrow," replied the other, quietly. "Let us go up stairs and finish our work."

CHAPTER XXXVII.

WITCHERY.

Carew of Crompton was really dead, as men said, "at last," not that he had been long dying, or was an old man, but that he had eventually succumbed to one of those deadly risks to which he had so often voluntarily exposed himself. On the occasion which had been fatal to him he had started from home one frosty morning at the gallop, with a cigar in his mouth, the reins on his horse's neck, and both his hands in his pockets, and had been pitched off and broken his neck within half a mile of his own door. His chaplain, who had dispatched the news to Mrs. Basil, had been riding by his side at the very moment. "He was a good friend to me," was the laconic remark that poor Parson Whymper had added to the bare intelligence.

To judge by the regretful excitement in the Midlands, Carew might have been a good friend to every body. The news was at once telegraphed to town, and appeared in the evening papers. The public interest in his mad freaks had of late years grown somewhat faint—his extravagances were, perforce, on a less splendid scale—but his death revived it. "So that mad Carew has killed himself, after all," was the observation frequently overheard that evening, as acquaintance met acquaintance on their homeward way from business. "Well, he's had his whack of most things," was the reply of the philosophers; "He has not left much to tempt his heirs to be extravagant, I reckon," of the cynics; "He was a deuced good fellow at bottom, I believe," remarked those who were secretly desirous of earning the same eulogium for themselves; "He was altogether wrong at top," answered the charitable.

Solomon Coe came home to his new abode in such a state of elation that it even made him communicative to his wife. Mrs. Basil happened to be with her in the drawing-room, but he only acknowledged her presence by a hasty nod. "Well, what d'ye think, Carew of Crompton, that was your father's landlord and mine"—Solomon never said "ours" with reference to property—"has broken his neck at last!"

Of course the very name of Carew was a sore subject between man and wife, on account of Richard Yorke's connection with him; but it suited Solomon's purpose on this occasion to ignore that circumstance. It would be necessary for some time to come to allude to the Crompton property more or less, and it was just as well to begin at once; it was also less embarrassing to do so in the presence of a third person.

"Yes, Solomon, I knew Mr. Carew was dead," said Harry, gravely. The next instant she turned scarlet with the consciousness of her thoughtless indiscretion.

"Oh," grunted her husband, annoyed at what he deemed her sulky manner, when he himself was so graciously inclined to be conciliatory, and also displeased to find his news anticipated, "you've been buying an evening paper, have you? You must have more money than you know what to do with, it seems to me."

Harry was thankfully accepting this imputation in silence, when Mrs. Basil's soft voice was heard. "No, Sir; it was I who told your good lady. I had a letter from Crompton by the afternoon's post."

"The devil you did!" cried Solomon, turning sharply upon her. "How came that about?"

"I was housekeeper at Crompton, Sir, in old Mrs. Carew's time, for some years, and one of the servants wrote to let me know of the accident."

"Housekeeper, were you?" said Solomon, with interest. "That must have been a good place, with deuced good pickings, eh?"

"Solomon, Solomon," remonstrated his wife, in a low voice, "Mrs. Basil is quite a lady. Don't you see that you offend her?"

It is more than probable that, under ordinary circumstances, Mr. Coe would have resented this rebuke with choleric vehemence; but he had his reasons for being good-humored in the present instance. "You must excuse my country manners, Mrs. Basil," said he. "As my wife will tell you, I must always have my joke; but I mean no offense. So you were housekeeper at Crompton, were you? Well, now, that's curious, for Mrs. Coe's father and I myself, as you heard me saying, have had a great deal to do with Carew. You knew him well, of course?"

"Yes, Sir; I did."

"And the place too, of course. It was a very fine one, was it not? Plenty of pictures, and looking-glasses, and things?"

"It was very richly furnished."

It was curious to mark the difference of manner between questioner and respondent. Solomon, usually so reticent and reserved, was grown quite voluble. Mrs. Basil, on the other hand, naturally so apt in speech, seemed to reply with difficulty. She was weighing every word.

"The estate, I suppose, was out of your beat; you did not have much to do with that?"

"I used to walk in the park, Sir, most days."

"Ay; but the property generally? The friend who writes you to-day don't say any thing about *that*, I suppose—whether any of it is to be sold or not, for instance?"

"The report—of course, being a servant, she can only speak from report—is that Mr. Carew's affairs are in a sad state. Every thing, I believe, is to be sold at once. The whole estate is said to be—I don't know if I use the right term—mortgaged."

"Just so," replied Solomon; "yes, yes. That is so, no doubt." There was a slight pause; Mrs. Basil courtesied, and was about to leave the room. "Stop a bit, ma'am," said Solomon. "My wife tells me that you are a lone woman—a widow. Perhaps you'd like to take a bit of dinner with us to-day?"

Harry began to think her husband was intoxicated. He did get occasionally so when any particularly good stroke of business was in course of progress, and on such occasions his manner was unusually affable; but she had never seen him half so gracious as at present. Hospitality, though he did sometimes bring a mining agent or a broker home to dinner, was by no means his strong point. Mrs. Basil looked doubtfully at her dress, which, though homely, was perfectly well-made and lady-like, and murmured something about its being almost the dinner-hour, and there being "no time."

"Oh, never mind your gown" (which, by-the-by, Solomon pronounced "gownd"); "we're quite plain people ourselves, as my wife will tell you. You shall take pot-luck with us. Where's Charley? That boy's always late."

But at that very moment the young gentleman in question entered the room, at the same time as did the servant with the announcement that dinner was on the table.

The astonishment of the domestic at seeing her mistress taken down to the dining-room by the new lodger was only exceeded by that of Charley, as, with his mother on his arm, he followed the strangely assorted pair. "I knew she was a witch," he murmured, "with her human skull and her Joanna Southcott; but this beats old Margery's doings at Gethin."

"Hush, hush!" whispered his mother, for Charley's high spirits and audacity always terrified her when exhibited in his father's presence: "they have found they have a common acquaintance, and so made friends."

"Father didn't know Swedenborg, did he?" answered the young man, slyly. "My belief is, he has fallen in love with her. I saw a black cat on the stairs. She can make any body do it, as I was telling Aggey" (the young rogue had been to Soho since the morning); "I shall be the next victim, no doubt. It's no use saying to myself, 'Thou shalt not marry thy grandmother.' Her charms are too powerful for the rubric. You'll see she'll not say grace."

Mr. Charles was right in that particular of his diagnosis of their new guest. Mrs. Basil did treat that devotional formula, which Mrs. Coe never omitted to pronounce, in spite of her husband's contemptuous shrugs, with considerable indifference. She sat opposite to Charley, and more than once, when he looked up suddenly, he caught her gaze fixed earnestly upon him. Those wondrous eyes of hers yet shone forth bright and clear; her cheeks were still smooth; and, though her brow had many a wrinkle, they were the footprints of thought and care, rather than of years.

The conversation, as was natural where the company and the guest were strangers to each other, turned upon the topics of the day, and the objects in the room, some of which, as we know, were sufficiently remarkable. At Charley's request Mrs. Basil once more narrated the story of the skull; and then epitomized, with caustic tongue, the biography of poor Joanna. Up stairs, she said, she had one of that lady's "seals"—a passport to eternal bliss—which she would bestow as a present upon the young gentleman opposite. Her cynical humor delighted Charley, and won the approbation of his father—not the less so, perhaps, since he saw it annoyed his wife.

Poor Harry was a simple well-meaning woman in her way, and, had the circumstances of her life been less exceptional, would have earned the reputation of a good creature and steadfast chapel-goer. But our lives do not always fall in the places most suitable to our dispositions; the restive are often compelled to run in harness; and the quiet low-action goers, who would welcome restraint, are left without guide, and with no course marked out for them. Thus it was with Mrs. Coe. The situation in which Fate had placed her it was altogether beyond her powers to fill. She knew that Mrs. Basil was rapidly ingratiating herself with her husband, and so far was furthering their common plan; but, notwithstanding its supreme importance, she shrank from the means that were bidding fair to accomplish her own end. She shuddered at her husband's vulgar ejaculations of assent and approval; at her son's thoughtless laughter; at this woman's sparkling and audacious talk, which seemed so purposeless, and yet was so full of design and craft. She had feared her and shrank from her at Gethin, and she feared her now. And yet how necessary was her assistance! Of her own self she was well aware that she could do nothing to avert that coming peril from her husband and her son, the shadow of which had darkened all her married life, and was now deepening into blackest doom. It was absolutely necessary that Mrs. Basil should obtain the confidence of Solomon, and perhaps of Charley also, and yet this unlooked-for and swift success of hers was far from welcome to poor Harry. It really almost seemed that there was truth in what her son had spoken in jest—that there was witchcraft in it.

Solomon was now talking earnestly to Mrs. Basil in low tones, while Charley looked toward his mother with raised eyebrows, and a comic expression, which seemed to say, "She's got him, you see; I did see a black cat on the stairs."

If she could have overheard her husband's talk, it would still have been inexplicable to her.

"Then you think this sale at Crompton will take place directly after the funeral?"

"I should certainly imagine so—yes."

"There is something—you needn't tell my wife, because I wish it to be a surprise for her—that I should like to buy at it; something I have long had my eye on."

"Some piece of furniture, I suppose. Well, you must be prepared to give a good sum, I fear. From the curiosity of the thing—the reputation, I mean, of poor Mr. Carew—it is likely things will fetch more than their price."

"Perhaps so. But I should like to know, as soon as possible, when the sale comes off. From your connection with the place, you will be able to get news of this before the general public—I mean the exact date."

"No doubt. I will write to-morrow, and beg that the information may be sent me."

"I should feel much obliged if you would, Mrs. Basil."

"I'll write this very night. You wish to know the day on which the sale of the furniture may be fixed?"

"Yes; and of all the other things: of the estates as well, for instance; there may be some land that may prove a good investment. Don't make a fuss about it, but say you have a friend who is interested. The catalogue of effects, with the dates appointed for the sale of each, will, of course, be settled down there. I want to have an early copy."

"That is very simple," said Mrs. Basil, making a memorandum in her pocket-book: "you shall be among the very first to get one, Mr. Coe—you may rely on that."

CHAPTER XXXVIII.

OVER THE ROOF.

Richard Yorke is still at Lingmoor; and though but a twelvemonth intervenes between him and freedom—or perhaps partly because of it—prison life is growing insupportable. It is the last year of "a long term," as all "old hands" will tell you, which is the most trying. Impatience becomes more incontrollable as the limit of suffering is neared; and just as, after a tedious and dangerous illness, the convalescent will rise too soon, and risk a relapse in his feverish desire to be well, so a prisoner will often make some wild endeavors to escape, when, if he did but wait a little—a span of time compared with that in which he has lain captive—his jealous doors would open of themselves to let him pass in safety. But there are other reasons which are pressing Richard toward flight, and goading him (as he feels) to madness if he remain quiescent. He has quarreled with all about him, and has suffered for it; and he is now menaced with worse things. His sullenness, his brooding ire, have long transformed his nature; civility, and even obedience, have become impossible for him. He kicks, as it were, against a chevaux-de-frise of steel. He has been starved on bread and water, and grown thin and fierce.

He has been put, and not for nothing, into the dark cell for hours, to brood, as usual, and has come forth a more reckless devil than he went in.

His warder and he are open foes. That cross-grained official has taken a strong antipathy to him, which is more than reciprocated; and every time he enters his cell sets foot, though unconscious of the fact, on the very threshold of the grave. He is the keeper of one who is almost a madman; but the latter is sane on one point yet—he knows to whom his vengeance is mainly due; and while that knowledge lasts his lesser foe is safe from him—safe, that is, at present; but a provocation may be given which would compel this long-suffering victim—in years scarce a middle-aged man, in appearance gray and withered as the oldest within those prison walls—to give his passion way, and slay him. If something should take place, which this warder himself has prophesied would happen, it will be so; and all Richard's hoarded hate would then be useless, since it would have no heir. There has been flogging in the prison—an unusual punishment, and only inflicted for great offenses, or for continued contumacy and bad conduct. A conspiracy was discovered, and seven of the ringleaders received three dozen lashes each, in presence of all the inmates of the jail. It was a punishment perhaps deserved and necessary, but sickening enough to witness. Richard's warder stood beside him, and while the cat was descending on one wretch's naked back, observed in a grim whisper: "Do you take warning, my man; for if you are reported again, the governor says you are to have a dose of the same medicine."

Whether the man spoke truth or not, Richard believed him. It was more than probable that he *would* be reported, and by the very voice that uttered the menace. In a twelvemonth's time there were three hundred and sixty-five opportunities, ten times told, of its being fulfilled. If such a sentence was ever passed upon him, as it was almost sure to be, Richard was well resolved that it should not be carried out; rather should this man die, and he himself, his slayer, be hung for it. His desire for vengeance upon those who had blasted his young life so cruelly was as strong as ever—nay, stronger, fiftyfold; but he knew that he could never bear the lash. Somehow or other, therefore, at all risks, he must escape from Lingmoor.

Robert Balfour was to be set free in a few days, his conduct, though not good, having earned that much of remission. Richard was not envious of him, yet the contrast of their two positions made him perhaps more desperate and reckless. Of late months the old man had been admitted to certain privileges accorded to such as have almost worked out their time, or who are otherwise recommended for them. He had been employed as "a cleaner," then as "a special"—in which position he was permitted to work out of doors without an attendant warder, and even (in his particular case, for he was growing very old and feeble) to have leave of absence for an hour or two. On some occasions it was his duty to bring round the prisoners' meals; and then he saw Richard, and could even exchange a word or two with him alone. This happened upon the afternoon of the day when the public flogging had taken place.

"Balfour," said Richard, earnestly, "will you do me a favor?"

"Yes, lad, any thing," replied the old man, softly. The word "lad" seemed so inapplicable to that gray-headed, care-lined face, which he had known so young and comely, that the misuse of it touched the speaker. "You know I will."

"Even though you should run a risk," said Richard, "within a day or two of your freedom?"

"Ay; for your sake, I would do that and more."

"God bless you, if there be a God!" answered those haggard lips. "Ask leave to go to the village to-morrow, and get me a file."

"Hush!—the warder."

The conversation thus interrupted was resumed next day.

"Here is the file," said Balfour; "hide it in your mattress. But, lad, you will be mad to use it. I pray you be patient. It is only a twelvemonth now."

Richard shook his head, with a ghastly smile. "I must try," said he.

"Nay, nay; you will be retaken and flogged, lad; think of that."

"I shall never be retaken, Balfour, at least alive."

It was easy enough to read in Richard's face the corroboration of his words.

"Have you any plan?" asked the old man, disconsolately.

"I have. From my window here I see an open shed, with a coil of rope in it. I shall file my bars, and get that rope to-night; climb back again here, and over the roof. I have calculated the distance from outside. I feel sure I can reach the parapet with my finger-tips as I stand upon the window-ledge, then let myself down into the exercising-yard upon the west side."

"The walls about that yard are sixty feet high, lad."

"There is a spout in the north corner which will help me up; and if I reach the top without a broken neck, I make fast my rope, and slide on to the moor. From thence, no matter how dark it is—and it will be pitch-dark, I reckon—I can make Bergen Wood. No power on earth shall stop me. If you told the warder yonder of my plan this moment, I should still escape—in another and more certain fashion." To look at him and read the resolute despair in his white face was to have no doubt of that.

"What must be must be," sighed the old man. "But for *my* sake, lad—for mine, who love you as a father loves his own son—be patient till to-morrow. This is my last day at Lingmoor. To-morrow I shall be free. I'll come at night to the wall of the west yard, and throw a rope over the north corner, close by the spout you mention. It shall be made fast on my side, and if you do but lay hold of it, the rest is easy. Your scheme, as it now stands, is hopeless. No squirrel could climb that spout, far less a man reduced as you are;" and he glanced significantly at Richard's shrunken limbs.

"You are the best of friends, Balfour—indeed, the only man that ever *was* my friend." He stopped, as if overcome by an emotion that was so strange to him. "At midnight, then, to-morrow, I shall begin my work; and in an hour from that time, if all goes well, I shall be at the spot appointed. If I fail, you will remember Wheal Danes?"

"Yes, yes; but you will not fail. Keep a good heart," whispered the old man, as he hurried away at an approaching footstep.

But, in reality, Balfour had no hope. His experience of such attempts, and his knowledge of the difficulties to be surmounted in the present instance, forbade any expectation of Richard's success, even in the matter of getting outside the prison walls; and, supposing that was done, and the wood reached, what was to be looked for further but slow starvation or death from the sharp-tipped arrows of the wintry wind? Still, Balfour's help was promised, and would be given; the old cracksman had many faults and vices, but he was not one to desert a friend at a pinch, and Richard Yorke was really dear to him.

As for Richard, notwithstanding the seasonableness of the other's offer, and although he was himself almost convinced that without such aid he could never effect his object, no sooner was he left alone than he regretted that he had passed his word to put off the attempt another day. Suppose he should transgress some prison regulation between this and then, or be reported by his hostile attendant without having committed a transgression! There were thirty-six hours of such perilous delay before him, and his impatience was already at fever-heat. By standing on his metal wash-stand, and peering through his bars, he could see that the coil of rope still lay in its accustomed place that afternoon, but would it remain there till to-morrow night? The very act of thus climbing to his window, which he could not resist, was a serious offense; and if by any chance he should be found in possession of the file—then all was over. He was fully determined only to part with it with life itself. For once, the picture of Trevethick and his son-in-law (for he had heard before he left Cross Key of Harry's marriage with his rival), unsuspecting, complacent, and exposed to the full force of his revenge, failed to occupy his gloating thoughts; they were fixed as ever there, but on the means and not upon the end—his whole being was engrossed in the coming enterprise. He feared the warder should read that forbidden word "Escape" in his eager eyes, or on his restless lips. A change of cell or a sudden examination of his bed-furniture—no uncommon occurrence—would prove his ruin. He took the file out of his mattress, and placed it in his breast: let that man beware who found it there!

At last the long night, which should have found him free, passed by, and the next weary day. The appointed time had come.

It was past midnight, and not a sound was heard in the vast prison; there was no moon, but a few stars shone on him as he worked at the iron bars; the noise of his file was muffled —he had rubbed it well with soap—but every now and then he paused and listened. He half fancied he could hear the distant tramp of the patrols, who, musket in hand, watched the walls of Lingmoor from the roofs of its four stone towers; but it was only fancy, and, at all events, no one else but they was stirring. Years ago he had gauged those bars, and calculated that not less than three must be sawn through to give his body room to pass; but that was when he was young and plump and vigorous. He was vigorous now—the fever within him seemed to give him the strength of ten—but he was an old man to look at, and the flesh had left his bones. So much the better; there were only two bars to file instead of three. Finding the space sufficient, he twisted his blanket into a rope, fastened it to the broken bars, and so, by its aid, slipped noiselessly into the yard.

That portion of the prison was low, and consisted but of two stories; another cell window was immediately beneath his own, but, as he knew, it was not used for prisoners. Still, he trembled as he slipped past it. Suppose a hand had been pushed through to clasp his limbs, or a voice had given the alarm, and warned the watchful guards! But his feet touched ground in safety. His eyes, accustomed for long years to cleave the darkness, guided him straight to the shed and to the coil of rope. He seized it as the shipwrecked mariner clutches that which is thrown him from the shore to drag him through the roaring breakers, and then, winding it about his waist, he retraced his steps. To return to his cell window was comparatively easy; but to stand upon its narrow ledge, and, clutching the parapet with his fingers, to draw himself up thereby, was a task that few, without the hope of liberty to spur them, could have accomplished. Three times he failed; without something more of purchase for his hold, he felt the thing was beyond his powers. The question was, how broad was the stone coping? If, by a sudden spring, he could catch the other side of it, he might succeed; but if he missed, his hands would slide from the smooth surface, his feet could not regain their stand-point, and he would fall backward twenty feet or so upon the stone courtyard.

There was nothing for it but to run the risk. He gathered his strength together, shut his eyes, and made a vigorous spring: one hand caught a firm gripe, and, after a sharp struggle, the other gained it; then he drew himself slowly up, and lay down in the gutter of the roof to gather breath and look about him. The prison was built like the four spokes of a wheel; and, indeed, with the high wall circling round it, did closely resemble that image. Nearly the whole of the building could have been seen, had it been light enough, from his present position; but, as it was, only the west wing was dimly visible, with its guardian tower standing blackly up against its dark back-ground of wintry night sky. He could not make out the sentry on its top; but now and then, when his circuit brought him nearest to his hiding-place, he could hear his measured foot-fall.

Like a creeping thing, for he scarce used hand or foot at all, Richard slowly crawled and slid along the sloping roof, then swiftly over the vertex, while the patrol was at the most distant portion of his round, and then once more, motionless and almost breathless, he lay down behind the western parapet. The exercising-yard, into which it was his object to drop, was just below him; but it was necessary to find some object to which to fasten his rope; and here he perceived how futile would have been his plan of escape without assistance from without; for here, having slid down it, he must needs leave his rope tied to a neighboring chimney. There was not length enough to cut off, and be of any service afterward for the descent of the external wall, nigh sixty feet in height. If Balfour failed him, it was now, indeed, clear to him that his whole design must fail. Yonder towering wall, higher even than his own present elevated position, could never be scaled by foot and hand, with only the help of a spout—nay, he doubted whether, even if he found the promised rope in position, he could even make use of that; for, though agile, he had none of the sailor's cunning.

He made fast the coil which he had with him, however, and watching his opportunity, slid off the parapet into space. Such a feat seems easy enough to read of; but to slide without noise down a loose and swinging rope for so great a distance is no slight task to one unused to such gymnastics; and, besides, he had to check himself at intervals (which took the skin off from his hands, although at the time he did not feel it), lest he should suddenly reach the ground with a dull thud. He accomplished this in safety, and once more paused, his back pushed hard to the prison wall, while the warder passed, whose form he could now even make out, it was so immediately above him; then he crossed the yard with a swift but anxious step to its north corner, and peered about in the gloom for the promised rope; the spout was there, smooth and ineffectual enough as a means of exit, but no rope.

His heart died within him, and his hands trembled with anxiety and trepidation as they felt in vain for it along the smooth and lofty wall. Richard's brain began to reel. He leaned his trembling brow against the cold iron of the spout, and endeavored to think the matter out. He was sure of Balfour; he felt certain that nothing but sudden and dangerous illness would have prevented him from keeping his word. But perhaps he had not been able to obtain a rope; such things were watchfully looked after in the neighborhood of Lingmoor Prison, and might even not be procurable. Yet had such been the case, Balfour would not have volunteered that form of assistance. He was of opinion that the rope was there, then, and if so, it must have been thrown over by means of a stone, or weight of some kind. In that case, if the stone had rolled after reaching the ground, the rope might not be hanging like a plumb-line from the wall, but at an angle from it, and at some distance. He began to move, then, in a parallel line from the wall, still feeling right and left; and on the third trial he caught in his stretched-out hand a string—a string-line such as a boy uses for his kite; and for an instant, the sense of the inefficacy of such means to effect his purpose froze him with despair. But presently pulling on the string, he found it gather in his hand, and pulling softly on, more string, and then an end of thin but wire-strong rope, and then more rope. What was best of all was, that this rope was knotted at intervals of every foot, so as to afford a strong, firm hold.

After many yards of this had been hauled in he found resistance; the end of it was evidently fast on the other side. Richard passed the rope round the bottom of the iron spout, and beneath an iron clasp, that prevented its slipping upward, and then made it taut. It was a perilous bridge even then, and supposing the watcher with his musket had not been, as he was, within easy gunshot of him; but it led from prison walls to liberty, and Richard did not hesitate for a moment to commit himself to it. Hand over hand, foot after foot, he dragged himself with infinite effort slowly upward; but it was not now in his power to watch the patrol, and secure the most favorable moment for crossing the wall top, as he had done in the case of the roof. As ill luck would have it, just as the sentry came to the northward portion of his beat, Richard's form was vaguely visible against the sky, upon the very summit of the wall. The next instant he had crossed it, and at the hoarse cry, "Who's there?" had glided rapidly down upon the other side. The sentry's gun was at his shoulder, and its sharp report rang through the silent night just as the convict reached the ground. The starlight was just sufficient, as the warder subsequently swore (and truly), to see the man was hit; he staggered and fell, but crawled away directly, and was lost in the surrounding gloom.

At the same moment all the prison seemed to wake to light and life, and the alarm-bell clashed out its hoarse notes of warning on the wintry air.

CHAPTER XXXIX.

NEWS FROM LINGMOOR.

Mrs. Basil kept her word with her lodger, and (thanks to the chaplain) gave into his hand a catalogue of the great Crompton sale some hours at least before the details of it were made public; on the receipt of which Solomon at once left town. His absence was felt to be a relief by all parties. The work of ingratiating herself with his hard, coarse nature, independently of the personal loathing with which Mrs. Basil regarded him, on Richard's account, was very hard, and rest was grateful to her. Mrs. Coe was always more at ease when business took her husband from his home. Charley hailed his departure, since he could now enjoy the society of his Agnes without stint.

He was, as usual, at Soho one morning, when Harry, sitting alone in the drawing-room, engaged in needle-work, was alarmed by a shrill shriek, followed by a heavy fall on the floor beneath, in Mrs. Basil's parlor. She had heard the front-door closed but a minute before, and the thought that was never wholly absent from her mind now flashed upon it with terrible distinctness—the Avenger had come at last! Her next hurried reflection was one of thankfulness that neither Charley nor Solomon was at home. Then, pale and trembling, she stole out on the landing of the stairs, and listened intently. Not a sound was to be heard save the throbs of her own fluttering breast. The cook and the waiting-maid, who alone composed the domestic staff, had apparently not heard the noise; for the former was singing loudly in the kitchen, as was her wont when she had been "put out," as happened some half dozen times per diem. It was frightful to think that in yonder parlor her once-loved Richard might even then be closeted with his mother, deaf to her appeals for mercy, resolute for revenge, and only demanding where his enemies might be found: it was better to face him than to picture him thus. That his sudden appearance had terrified Mrs. Basil into a fit she had little doubt from that shriek and fall; and, indeed, all was now so still within there that she might be dead. The fear for her offspring, however, made Harry almost bold. Indeed, as has been said, she did not entertain any apprehension of personal violence at Richard's hands; and, perhaps, in spite of Mrs. Basil's assurance to the contrary, she had some hope of moving him from his set purpose by her prayers and tears. Step by step, and clinging to the hand-rail for support, for her limbs scarcely obeyed her will, she descended the stairs, stood a moment in the passage, listening like a frightened hare, and then opened the parlor door. There was no one within it: yes, upon the hearth-rug lay the motionless form of Mrs. Basil; she was lying on her face; and, rushing forward, Harry knelt down beside her, and strove to lift her in her arms. Some instinct seemed to forbid her to call for assistance.

"What is it? what is it?" gasped the old woman, looking vacantly up in the other's face.

"You have been unwell, dear madam. I am afraid you have had a fainting fit; but, thank Heaven, you are better now."

Harry was truly grateful; first, that her original suspicion had proved to be unfounded; secondly, that Mrs. Basil was alive. She had contrived to place her in a sitting posture, with her back against the heavy arm-chair; and now she brought a carafe of water from the side-board, and sprinkled her face and hands.

"Let me call Mary, and we will get you up to your own room as soon as you feel equal to the effort."

Mrs. Basil's eyes had closed again. Her face was white and stiff as that of a corpse; but she shook her head with vehemence. "The door—lock the door!" she murmured.

Not without some hesitation, for she began to fear that her companion was wandering in her mind, Harry obeyed her. "Get me into my chair. Oh, why did I ever wake to weary life again!"

"What has troubled you? Can any new misfortune have happened to us?" inquired Harry, woefully.

"To *you*—no," answered the old woman, with sudden fierceness; "to me—yes. Do you see that letter?" She pointed to one lying beneath the table. "Twenty years ago that would have been my death-warrant; but now I am so used to suffer that, like the man who lived on poisons, nothing kills. Read it—read it."

The letter was an official one; the envelope immense, with "On her Majesty's Service" stamped upon it, and out of all proportion to the scanty contents, which ran as follows:

"Lingmoor Prison, *December* 22.

"Madam,—I am instructed by the Governor of this Jail to acquaint you with the sad news that your son, Richard Yorke, is no more. Four weeks ago he escaped from prison by night, and took refuge in an adjoining wood. His body was discovered only four days ago, and an inquest held upon it, when a verdict was returned in accordance with the facts. I am, Madam, yours obediently,

"Thomas Sparkes (*for the Governor*).

"I am instructed to inclose a locket with miniature, which was found upon your son on his arrival here. The rest of his property will be forwarded by rail."

This locket contained the little picture of Harry painted by Richard himself, and which, though he had contrived to secrete while at Cross Key, had been taken from him at Lingmoor.

Harry's breast was agitated by conflicting emotions. To know that her boy was safe—that there could be no murder done—gave her a sense of intense relief, which could scarcely be called selfish. But that reflection was but transient, and a passionate burst of sorrow succeeded it. The only man she had ever loved—around whom centred her most precious memories—had died, then, thus miserably, after miserable years of bondage endured on her account. She saw him with her mind's eye once more as when he had clasped her in his arms for the first time upon the ruined tower—as when he had rained his kisses on her lips beside the Wishing Well—in his youth and beauty and passion. Her nineteen years of loveless wedlock were swept away, and left her as she saw herself in the little portrait he himself had painted, and which was now his legacy. His menaces and vows of vengeance against her and hers were all forgotten; her woman's heart was loyal to him whom she had owned its lord, and once more did him fealty.

"Oh, Richard, Richard, my dear love," cried she; "God knows I would have died to save you!"

"Come here, Harry—come here," whispered Mrs. Basil, "and let me kiss you. I would that I could weep like you; but the fountain of my tears has long been dry. I thought you would have been glad to feel that you and yours were safe—that retribution was averted from the man, your husband; but I now see I did you wrong. Your heart is touched—you remember him as he was before the taint of crime was on him."

"It never was!" cried Harry, passionately. "He never meant to wrong my father of a shilling."

"Well said, dear Harry; well said. He was himself a wronged—a murdered man. Imprisoned for nineteen years, and then to perish thus! And yet men talk of Heaven's justice! My boy! my boy!"

The two women were silent for a while—the one gazing with dry eyes but tender yearning face upon the other, as she rocked herself to and fro, and shook with stifled sobs.

"Dear Harry, you must not desert me now," pleaded the former, pitifully; "I am very old, and this has broken me. He was my all—my only one on earth—and he is dead. I shall not trouble you long. We two, child, were the only ones that loved him, and we love him still. Let me cling to you, Harry, since it is but for a little while; and let us talk of him together, when we are alone, and think of what he was. So bright, so gay, so— Oh, my boy! my boy!"

The tears rushed to the mother's eyes at last. Hard Fate was softened for a while toward its life-long victim; and side by side sat the two bereaved women, each striving to comfort the other, after woman's fashion, by painting in its brightest colors that dead Past which both deplored. Begotten of their common sorrow, Love sprang up between them, and on one side confidence; and into Mrs. Basil's hungry ears Harry, for the first time, poured the story of her courtship. Richard's death had cemented between them the bond which it would seem to have destroyed. The fatal letter lay open on Harry's lap, but the envelope had fallen on the floor. Stooping to pick it up, she found something still within it—some folded slips from a local newspaper, with an account of the inquest, the details of which the governor's clerk had, perhaps humanely, preferred to communicate in that form, to be read or not as the mother's feelings might dictate to her. The two women read it together, not aloud, for neither had the voice for that. With most of the evidence there recounted we are already familiar. It was proved that No. 421 had long been in a desponding, brooding state; but, as only a year intervened between the expiration of his term of punishment, his attempt to escape was almost unaccountable, and certainly unparalleled. No punishment was impending over him. The opinion of the authorities was expressed that the convict's reason was unhinged. The method of obtaining his freedom showed indeed considerable cunning, but also an audacity that was scarcely consistent with sanity. The height of the prisoner was known, and his proportionate reach of arm; and it seemed incredible how he could have succeeded in reaching the parapet above his cell window; in that attempt he must have risked certain death. His descent from the roof was explained by the presence of the rope. The immediate means by which he surmounted the external wall were, of course, evident enough, since the rope was there also; but the question was, how did it come there? The prisoner must have been assisted by some one outside the wall. The warder who fired the shot which subsequently proved fatal had seen but one man; but the night was dark, and the whole affair had passed very rapidly. Indeed, the convict had only fully shown himself when at the top of the wall, and the musket had been fired almost at a venture. On the alarm being given, pursuit was at once attempted; but, under cover of the night, the fugitive had gained Bergen Wood. The next morning his footsteps were traced so far, and it was proved that he was unaccompanied. A cordon was placed round the wood, and the place itself thoroughly searched for many days. It was deemed certain, from the report of the scouts who were made use of on such occasions, that the convict had not left that covert to seek shelter in any hamlet in the neighborhood; the quest was therefore still continued. Not, however, until three weeks afterward was No. 421 discovered. It was supposed that the unhappy fugitive had died of his wounds upon the very night of his escape, for the body was so decomposed that it could never have been identified but for its convict clothes; the nights had been wet and tempestuous, and it lay in an unsheltered part of the wood, a mere sodden heap of what had been once humanity. The bullet that had been the cause of death was, however, detected in the remains.

What an end to the high-spirited, handsome lad that had been the pride of his mother, the joy of his betrothed! What wonder that they sat over the bald record of it with bowed-down faces, and filled up the gaps with only too easily imagined horrors! Each kept hold of the other's hand, as though in sign of the dread bond between them, and sat close to one another in silence. Presently Harry started up, at the sound of a latch-key in the house door.

"That is Solomon," cried she.

"Impossible," said Mrs. Basil. "He told me himself that he should stop for the last day's sale, and to-day is but the fifth."

"Hush! it is."

Yes, it was certainly Solomon's voice in the passage; and apparently, by the answering tone, he had a male companion with him.

Harry seized the letter, with its inclosures, and thrust them into her bosom, which, full of grief for his victim, seemed to spurn her husband's approach. Then she heard him calling her impatiently, as was his wont, from the foot of the stairs.

"Harry, come down; I have brought a gentleman home with me. Let's have something to eat at once, will you?"

"Answer him—answer him!" gasped Harry. She could not speak; her tongue seemed paralyzed.

Mrs. Basil rose at once, walked with steady step to the door, and opened it. "Your wife is here, Mr. Coe. I am glad you are come home, for she is far from well, and I was getting quite nervous about her."

"She *must* be ill," grumbled Solomon, "not to be able to say 'Here,' when I am breaking a blood-vessel with holloing to her in the attics. Come in here, Sir." This to his companion—a man considerably his senior, thin and spare, who stood peering curiously at the landlady. "I am sorry to see you unwell, wife. I have brought a friend to stay with us for a day or two. Mr. Robert Balfour—Mrs. Coe."

CHAPTER XL.

A PROJECTED PARTNERSHIP.

THOUGH by no means in either the mental or physical condition in which a lady should be who is called upon to play the part of hostess, Harry was not displeased that Solomon had not returned alone. The presence of this stranger, whom she greeted mechanically, and almost without a glance at his features, was welcome to her, because it was likely to distract from herself her husband's regards. What she would like to have done would have been to shut herself up alone in her chamber, to weep and pray. As it was, she had to be cheerful, to affect an interest in her husband's late expedition, and pleasure at his unexpected return. Mrs. Basil was here invaluable; you would never have imagined that it was the same woman—so stricken and full of anguish but a few minutes before, and now so self-possessed and cheerful. But she had been used to playing parts throughout her life, and acting was easy to her. She dreaded silence, lest with it should come observation and remark upon the agitation and distress only too visible in Harry's countenance; and yet it was difficult, even for her, to keep up the ball of small-talk, for Solomon was always slow and scant of speech, and the new-comer rarely opened his mouth, and then only to utter a monosyllable. His manner, too, was embarrassing; he turned his white and stony face from one woman to the other, like an automaton, but with a weird and searching gaze.

They had never so much as heard his name before, for Richard had been cautious never to mention Balfour in his letters, since they were, of course, perused by the authorities, and friendships were not encouraged at Lingmoor; but, on the other hand, it was evident that these ladies had an interest for the visitor. Presently, while they were yet all below stairs, arrived Charles and Agnes, which effected, indeed, diversion enough, but also a great disturbance and alteration for the worse in Mr. Coe's temper. No sooner, as it seemed to him, had his back been turned, then, than the intimacy between this girl and his son, which he had strictly forbidden, had been recommenced, and with the connivance and encouragement of his wife too, or else how should the lad dare thus to bring her home? For the first time Solomon was openly rude to Agnes; and the latter, being a girl of spirit, resented it by quietly rising to depart. Charley, rash and impetuous, rose to accompany her. Solomon stormed displeasure; and it seemed that the presence of the visitor would have been wholly inadequate to prevent a family scene, when Agnes herself interposed with dignity. "No, Charles; I would rather go alone. If your father objects to my presence here, it shall not be intruded; and if he considers your company a condescension, I can not accept it upon such terms."

Charles would have taken her arm, in defiance of all consequences, and led her off under Solomon's nose; but this opposition on her part offended him. He was almost as angry with her for thwarting him as he was with his father. It was a triangular duel, the combatants in which were narrowly watched by the disregarded stranger. When Agnes got her way and departed, "That's a girl of character," observed he, with a cynical smile.

"She is a girl without a penny," answered Solomon, gloomily, with a scowl at his son, "upon whom this young fool wishes to throw himself away."

"What! so early?" observed Mr. Balfour, good-humoredly addressing Charles. "When I was your age, I thought of enjoying life, and not of marriage. I don't wonder, however, that any girl should strive to enslave so handsome a young fellow as your son, Sir. It is quite natural, and there is no need to blame her, and far less *him*."

Ashamed, perhaps, of having exhibited such violence of temper before his guest, Solomon was very willing to be mollified, and grimly smiled approval of these sentiments; Charles, too, though fully resolved to set himself right with Agnes on the morrow, was not displeased with the visitor's remark; but the two women justly resented it as an impertinent freedom. If Charles's thoughts had not been so preoccupied with his own wrongs—the deprivation of his Agnes's society, which he had promised himself for the rest of the day, and the snub which he conceived she had administered to him—he would have noticed too, for he was by no means wanting in observation, that the new-comer's manner to his hostess and Mrs. Basil was not what it should have been. It was not absolutely rude, but it was studiously careless of their presence. He no longer stared at them as at first, but, on the contrary, seemed to ignore the fact of their existence—never addressed them; and if either spoke to him, replied as briefly as possible, and then turned at once to Solomon or his son. Mrs. Basil concluded that he was a vulgar fellow, who, having penetration enough to discover that the males had the upper hand in the establishment, did not give himself the trouble to conciliate the less important members of it; but Harry, always timid and suspicious, was alarmed at him; his air had, in her eyes, something hostile in it as well as contemptuous. She could not understand, and therefore mistrusted, the influence he had evidently obtained over her husband, and which already had superseded that of Mrs. Basil.

That Solomon should no longer take pains to make himself agreeable to the latter, now that he had obtained from her his object, was, to any one who knew his character, explicable enough; but why should this stranger have taken her place as his counselor and friend? The idea of some personal advantage was, of course, at the bottom of it; but it was clear, not only to sage Mrs. Basil, but even to Harry—since even a moderately skillful looker-on sees more of the game than the best player—that in any contest of wits Solomon would have small chance with his new friend. The opinion of Mrs. Basil was, that some new speculation, in some manner connected with the Crompton sale, had been entered into by the two men, and that Mr. Balfour would in the end secure the oyster, while Mr. Coe was left with the shell. But Harry had darker forebodings still; she was instinctively confident that there was enmity at work in the new-comer, as well as the readiness common to all speculators to overreach a friend. There was a look in his pallid face, when it glanced, as he thought unheeded, on either Charles or Solomon, which, to her mind, boded ill. If it did so, it was certainly unsuspected by those on whom it fell. Mr. Coe had apparently never found a companion so agreeable to him; and, curiously enough, this idea seemed to be shared by Charles. According to his own account, Mr. Balfour had been abroad in Western America for many years, and had there retrieved a fortune which, originally inherited, had been speedily dissipated in the pleasures of the town. His long absence from such scenes had by no means dulled his taste for them, and his conversation ran on little else. He had a light rattling way with him—that, to Harry's view, resembled youthful spirit no more than galvanism in a corpse resembles life, and which was certainly not in harmony with his age and appearance—and very graphic powers of description; he expressed himself curious about the changes in public amusements since he left town, near twenty years ago, and seriously placed himself under Charles's guidance on the expeditions of pleasure for which the latter was always ready. To this, strangely enough, Solomon made no objection, notwithstanding that his own purse-strings had to be drawn pretty wide to supply these extravagances. His new friend had only to suggest that he should give the lad a five-pound note to enjoy himself with, and the thing was done at once.

As for himself, Mr. Balfour seemed to be made of money, so freely did he spend it; and if he did not offer the use of his purse to his young companion, it was only, as he told him, because he feared to offend his pride. "Besides," said he, when they were alone together on one of these expeditions of amusement, from which Solomon, whose notions of enjoyment were mainly confined to money-making, always excused himself upon pretense of having business to do, "it is only right your father should be made to fork out; he is as rich as Crœsus. It is quite unreasonable that he should stint you in enjoyment when, one day or another, you will have all the pleasures of life to pick and choose from."

It would have tested Solomon's new-born friendship severely if he could have heard Mr. Balfour dilate upon this topic, which he did with such earnestness and fervor that the lad was soon convinced of those great expectations which the cautious reticence of his parents had so long concealed from him. On the other hand, Charley's companion deduced an argument from this fair prospect which was not so welcome to the lad; he maintained that, under the circumstances, it would be madness to risk his father's displeasure by uniting himself irretrievably to Agnes, or to any other young woman. "My good offices will be always at your disposal, my lad," urged he, gravely, "and I don't deny that, at present, I have considerable influence with Mr. Coe; but it would not be proof against so flagrant an act of disobedience as that which you contemplate. The great bulk of his property is at his own disposal; and his nature, if I may speak plainly to you in so important a matter, is obstinate and implacable. At all events, there is no hurry, since you and this charming young lady are but boy and girl at present. Life is uncertain, and you may be your own master any day; wait till you are so, or wait for a little, at all events, to see what may turn up; and in the mean time, lad, enjoy yourself." The last part of Mr. Balfour's advice, at all events, was palatable enough, and that much of it Charles accepted; in doing which, as was anticipated, the whole intention of his Mentor became fulfilled. Plunged in dissipation, the young man thought less and less of his love; gave himself little trouble, though he still avowed his unalterable attachment, to set himself right with her; grew more and more dissatisfied with his own home, at the same time that that of Agnes became less and less attractive; and, in short, he drifted away daily farther and farther from the safe moorings of love and duty.

Harry perceived all this with a dread so deep that it even drove her to invoke her husband's aid against this man, who, inexplicable as his hostility might be, was bent, she firmly believed, upon the ruin of her darling boy. With Solomon, as she well knew, the fact of his son's dissipation was not likely to move him to interfere; he saw that the companionship of Balfour was gradually producing an estrangement between Charles and the portionless artist's daughter, and so far he cordially approved of it, nor cared to question by what means this new friend made himself agreeable. She had no argument available except that of expense, and, to her astonishment and dismay, this failed to affect her prudent spouse.

"Just let things be a while," was Solomon's reply, "and mind your own business. It is quite true the lad's throwing my money in the gutter at a fine rate; but in the end I shall get it all back again, and more with it. This Balfour takes me for a foolish doting father, but he shall pay for all himself before I've done with him. I throw a sprat to catch a whale; and neither you nor any other fool shall interfere with my fishing."

Harry dared not say more; her husband had been in the worst of humors ever since he had returned from Crompton, and was all the more brutal and tyrannical to her that he had to be civil and conciliatory to his new friend, and involuntarily indulgent, upon his account, to Charles. The unhappy mother was powerless to check the evil the growth of which was so patent to her loving instinct, and there was none to whom she could look for help. Mrs. Basil had no longer any influence with Solomon, and, besides, she was seriously ill, and had now been confined to her own room for weeks. In her extremity, Harry had even resolved to make a personal appeal to this man Balfour; to ask him in what her husband had injured him, to adjure him to forgive the wrong, or at least not to visit it upon her Charley's innocent head. But she shrank with an inexplicable terror from putting this design into effect; she felt she should humiliate herself to no purpose; he would deny, in his cold, cynical way, that he entertained any thing but friendship for her astute husband and affection for her bright and impulsive son. Besides, to say truth, she was afraid to speak with the man; and she had a suspicion that this weird and shadowy fear was in some degree shared by Mrs. Basil; at times she even imagined that it was not so much indisposition as a desire to avoid his presence that caused the landlady to absent herself from the family circle.

Mr. Coe, at all events, entertained no such prejudice against his guest; day by day he grew more communicative with him, and more solicitous to hear his opinions, with which he seldom failed to agree. The two men were in reality, as it was easy to see, as opposite in character as the poles. Mr. Balfour was, and apparently always had been, a man of pleasure; but he had seen men and cities, and his remarks were shrewd, and selfish, and worldly-wise enough. It was rarely that his talk ever strayed to matters of business, so that Solomon was perforce a listener; but that unambitious part he played to admiration.

Upon one occasion, however, their after-dinner converse happened to turn upon partnerships; Solomon urged their great convenience, how one man brought money and the other brains, and how pleasant it must be for the former to live at ease while the latter gathered honey for him, both for present use and for the wintry store. He rose with the familiar subject to quite a flight of poetry.

Mr. Balfour, with half-shut eyes and a mocking smile, dilated upon the sentiment involved in such communities of enterprise, the sympathy engendered by them, and the happy social effects that were produced by them. His host either did not, or would not, perceive that these remarks were ironical, and pursued the subject to its details, proportions of profits, balance-sheets, etc., until Charles rose with a yawn, and left his two elders together.

"Well, Balfour," said Solomon, frankly, as soon as they were alone, "this talk reminds me of the matter that first introduced us to one another—your purchase of that outlying bit of the Crompton property, Wheal Danes."

"I WILL GIVE YOU A THOUSAND POUNDS DOWN FOR THAT CROMPTON LOT."

"Ay," replied the other, carelessly lighting another cigar. It was quite wonderful to see how many cigars Mr. Balfour got through daily; you might have almost thought that he had been denied tobacco for years by his physician, and had only just been permitted to resume the habit.

"Yes; you disappointed me there immensely, I must confess. I went down to the sale on purpose to secure it."

"So you told me, or, at least, so I guessed from your manner; and yet I don't know why you should have been so sweet upon it. It's only a bare bit of ground with a round hole in it, close by the sea."

"That's all," said Solomon, puffing at his clay pipe. "What on earth could have made you buy it?"

"Well, I told you once. I lost my yacht off Turlock, when coming to England last autumn, and very nearly my life with it. When one escapes with a whole skin from such a storm as wrecked me there, the first piece of dry land one comes to seems very attractive. I happened to be cast ashore beneath that very spot, and so I took a fancy to it. If I had been a good Papist I should have built a chapel there to my patron saint in gratitude for my preservation; as it was, I resolved to erect a villa for myself there. It will have an excellent view, and the situation is healthy. If you seek for any other reason for the purchase, I have none to give you; it was a whim, if you like, but then I can afford to indulge my whims."

"This one cost you a good deal, however; you gave five hundred pounds for it, did you not?"

Balfour nodded assent.

"A great sum for a few barren acres," said Solomon, thoughtfully.

"Yes; and so the trustees of the estate thought, Mr. Coe. They closed with my offer sharp enough, and withdrew the lot from public competition; else, perhaps, I should have got it cheaper."

"Not if I had been bidding against you," observed the host, significantly.

"You don't say so! You were never shipwrecked thereabouts, were you? Oh, I remember: you were brought up in the neighborhood. You had some tender recollection of the spot, perhaps, with relation to madame up stairs. What creatures of sentiment you men of business sometimes are—dear me!"

"I did live near the spot," said Solomon, slowly, "though I should deceive you if I pretended that that had any thing to do with my wish to possess it."

"You would not deceive me, my good friend," answered Balfour, coolly; "but, as you were about to say, it would not be frank. Let us be frank and open, above all things."

"I wish to be so, I assure you," was Solomon's meek reply. "When I offered you a hundred pounds for your bargain, I think I showed you that deception was no part of my nature. In all matters of business I always go straight to the point at once."

"As in the present instance, for example," remarked the guest, with an imperturbable smile.

"I am coming to the point, Mr. Balfour—once for all. I will give you a thousand pounds down for that Crompton lot—twice the money that you gave for it within a month; that's twelve hundred per cent. per annum."

Balfour shook his head. "I am not a religious man, my dear Sir—far from it. But I believe, like Miss Joanna yonder, in inspirations: all my whims are inspirations, and therefore sacred. It was an inspiration that made me buy Wheal Danes, and I mean to keep it. If you offered me ten thousand pounds, I'd keep it."

Solomon was silent for a while, his heavy brows knit in thought; then once again he advanced to the attack. "You may keep it, and yet share the profit, Mr. Balfour."

"The profit?"

"Ay, the profit. I told you I was going to be frank with you, but you would never guess *how* frank. I am about to put thousands a year into your pocket, on condition that you will let me fill my own at the same rate. We were talking of partnerships just now; let us be partners in Wheal Danes."

"Balfour and Coe sounds natural enough," returned the other, coolly. "But I must hear your plan."

"My plan is a secret—invaluable, indeed, as such—but which, once told, will be worth nothing—that is, to *me*."

"You may do as you like, my friend, about revealing it," yawned Mr. Balfour. "I care nothing for your plan; only, until I hear it I stick to my plot, my lot, my acreage. Tell me the whole story without reservation—don't attempt to deceive me on the slightest point—and then you shall have your way. We will divide this land of gold between us, or, as seems to me much more likely, browse like twin donkeys on its crop of thistles."

"I have nothing but your bare word to trust to," said Solomon, doubtfully; "but still, I must risk it. Come, it's a bargain. Then, here's my hand upon it."

"Never mind my hand, my good friend," returned the other, coolly. "In the part of the world from which I hailed last, folks didn't shake hands, and I've fallen out of the habit. Come, give us this story of Wheal Danes."

"It's a very old one, Mr. Balfour. The plot of ground you purchased gets its strange name from an ancient tin mine that is comprised in it, once worked by the Romans, but disused since their time. There are many such in Cornwall."

"So I've heard," said Balfour, while the other sipped his glass. It was curious to contrast the grave and earnest manner of the host with the careless and uninterested air of his guest, who presently, as the narrative proceeded, leaned his face upon his hand and gazed into the fire, an occasional glance sideways at his companion through his fingers alone testifying that his attention was still preserved. He never stirred a limb nor winked an eyelid when Solomon came out with his great secret.

"This mine that is said to be worked out, Mr. Balfour, and which you have purchased by mere accident, as being in the same lot with your proposed building-ground, will, I have reason to believe, turn out a gold mine."

"You don't say so! I did not know that there *was* gold in Cornwall."

"There is as good, or at least there are metals that bring gold—tin and copper; and Wheal Danes is full of the latter. The old Romans worked it for tin only, and left their prize just as it was getting to be worth having. There's a copper vein in the lowest level of that mine that may be worth all the old Carew estate."

"And you have seen this vein?"

"No; but my wife's father, John Trevethick, as good a judge as any man on earth, or under it, saw it, and told me of its existence on his death-bed—"

"When did he die, and how? Was it a lingering, painful death, or was he struck down suddenly?" interposed Balfour. "I ask," added he, hastily, for Solomon looked up in wonder at his companion's vehemence, "because the credibility of such a story as you tell me would depend upon the state of the man's brain."

"He did die a painful and a lingering death, but his wits were clear enough," answered Solomon. "It was ten years ago, and more, but I mind it as well as though it was but yesterday—indeed, I've thought of little else since. 'The best legacy I have to leave you, Sol, lies in these last words of mine,' said he; 'so do you listen, and lay them to heart.' Then he told me how, as a boy, he had once explored Wheal Danes in play with other boys, and found the copper lode in a certain spot. He was not so young even then but that he knew the value of such a find, and he had held his tongue; and though he visited the place pretty often—for he couldn't help that—he kept the secret close from that time until his death."

"He had never told any other person but yourself, you think?" inquired Balfour, curiously.

"No one to speak of. There was one fellow who had an inkling of the thing, it seems, but he is dead now. I read of it in the newspaper quite lately. He died in jail, or rather in escaping from it, and had never been in a position to profit by his suspicion. You may say, in fact, that not a living soul besides John Trevethick ever knew this secret. For fifty years he strove to possess himself of this mine; he even offered for it, valueless as it was thought to be, four times the money you did; only Carew was mad and obstinate; and now, for ten years, I have had my own eyes fixed upon it, and got the earliest news of when it was in the market, as I thought, when, here, without a hint to guide you, a whiff of fortune blows it to your hand. It's a hard case *I* call it—devilish hard."

"Well, it *is* hard," said Balfour; "that is, supposing all you say is true. But frankly, my good Sir, I don't believe you. I mean no offense; but, since you have not seen the lode with your own eyes, you must pardon me for doubting its existence."

"Well, then, Sir, I *have* seen it, and that's the long and short of it. I would not take such a thing on trust from an angel."

"So I suspected," observed Balfour, coolly. "But as you have told me one lie you may tell me another. What am I to believe now?"

"The mine is yours, Sir," answered Solomon, gruffly. "Let us go down together and look at it. If Trevethick and I were mistaken—and I'll bet you a thousand pounds that we were not—it is but coming back again, and—"

"And being made the laughing-stock of all the folks among whom I mean to spend my days," interrupted Balfour. "No, no. If we go, I'll not have a soul to know of it. And mind you, if this turns out to be a mare's nest, I sha'n't be pleased, my friend."

"It will not do that, Sir, you may take my word for it," answered Solomon, earnestly; "and as for going *incog.*, that matter's easy. I can start for Gethin, which is my home, and but a stone's-throw from the very place, on pretense of business; and you, a day or two after, may come down to the inn at Turlock, just to see your purchase. We need not be so much as seen together, if you so prefer it."

"I would much prefer it," observed Balfour, sententiously.

"Very good. Then here's my plan: my father-in-law used to visit Wheal Danes at night; from his doing so, instead of its drawing dangerous attention to the place, as one would think, the rumor arose that the old mine was haunted; corpse-candles, with no hand to carry them, were seen there going up and down the levels, and so the poor fools shunned it after dark. Well, let *us* take torch and ladder, and play at corpse-candle. What say you?"

"Well, I'll come," said Balfour, reluctantly, "though I don't much like the chance of being made a fool of. What day will suit you best to start? All's one to me."

"I'll start to-morrow," said Solomon, with excitement. "Do you come down, as if into Midlandshire, on Friday: that's an unlucky day with Turlock folk, but not with you, I reckon?"

"You're right there, man," answered Balfour, slowly. "Well?"

"On Saturday, at midnight, I will meet you at the old pit's mouth. Come, there's my hand upon it."

This time Balfour took his companion's hand, and griped it firmly.

"Then, that's a bargain, partner," cried Solomon, gayly. "Fill up your glass. Here's luck to the old mine!"

"Here's luck," echoed Balfour, looking steadily at his host, "and to our next merry midnight meeting!"

"Ay, good! Here's luck!" quoth Solomon.

CHAPTER XLI.

IN THE TOILS.

SOLOMON started for Gethin on the ensuing morning; but his wife did not, as usual, find his departure a relief, since Balfour remained behind. Her last instructions from her husband were to treat this unwelcome guest with marked consideration, and to let him have his way in every thing. He also hinted, though it was scarcely necessary to insure her obedience, at certain brilliant prospects which were about to present themselves, through Balfour's means, if he were only kept in good-humor. Harry would have much preferred to relinquish his favor at the price of his absence; but not so her son. Notwithstanding the disparity in their ages, he and this new acquaintance were already fast friends. The latter had laid himself out to please the lad, and had succeeded; partly, perhaps, from the very novelty of companionship, for Charley knew no one in town, and was tired of taking his pleasure therein alone, but chiefly through his store of agreeable anecdotes, all illustrative of the enjoyments which wealth conferred, with which Balfour tickled his ears.

"In a few years—perhaps sooner, who knows?—all these things of which I speak will be within your own means. You will be rich; and he who is so can please himself in almost every thing. You can then marry your Agnes, if you will, without fear of being disinherited; or, what is better and more likely, you may choose from a score of Agneses, or even take them all."

He had a light amusing way with him, this Balfour, that hid the cynicism which would otherwise have jarred upon his young companion; for Charles, though selfish and fond of pleasure, was good-natured, and had not reached that period of life when our sherry must needs not only be dry, but have bitters in it. He was genuinely fond of his mother; yet even in this short time Balfour, as she well knew, had taught him to disobey her; not setting her at open defiance, indeed, but regarding her advice and remonstrances with a sort of tender contempt. She meant all for his good, his Mentor admitted, but women had not much knowledge of the world; and if a young man was not to be his own master at eighteen, he must look to be in leading-strings all his life. Harry perceived her darling's plastic nature changing daily for the worse in the hands of this crafty potter; and though it was an admission humiliating to her, as a mother, to make, she made it to Mrs. Basil in her sick-room.

"Mr. Balfour is doing my Charley harm," she said. "He is an altered boy already, and yet my husband talks as though we are never to be rid of the man. What money, what gain, can ever compensate for the demoralization of our child?"

"Nothing, indeed," said Mrs. Basil, quietly. "But have a little patience. Is not this gentleman going on Friday?"

"Yes; but he will come back again. It is only some business that calls him into Midlandshire. He does not even take all his luggage away. I have a great mind to tell him point-blank that his presence in this house—at all events in Mr. Coe's absence—is unwelcome; but I dare not do it; I am afraid."

"Yes, your husband would be very angry, without doubt," said Mrs. Basil, thoughtfully.

"That is not it. I am afraid of the man himself. He reminds me of that hateful creature—what is he?—in the opera, for which Mr. Aird gave us the tickets, and which Agnes went with us to see—Mephistopheles."

"What a strange fancy! He is only a sour, pleasure-jaded man. If I was not so ill I would speak to him myself; but you are right not to do so; that is your husband's place, who has brought him here. Let things be as they are till Friday."

Harry sighed, but perforce assented. Friday came, and Mr. Balfour went as he had designed, but not without stating at breakfast his intention of returning on the ensuing Monday or Tuesday at latest, and even making an engagement with Charley to spend the latter evening with him at the theatre.

"Do you happen to know when my husband will be home?" inquired Harry, timidly.

"No, madam. He was good enough to say, however, that his absence was to make no difference as to my remaining here as his guest."

This reply, which might easily have been made offensive, was delivered with the most studied courtesy: it cut the hostess's ground from under her; for it had answered the very objection which she had intended to imply. She felt herself not only defeated, but reproved.

"Let us hope you will both return together," said she.

"I do not think that very probable," answered Mr. Balfour, slowly.

An hour later and he had departed, his hostess, under pretense of being engaged with her sick friend up stairs, not having so much as shaken his hand. Charles, indignant at this slight, would have accompanied him to the railway station, but Balfour would not hear of it. For this he had two reasons: in the first place, he was anxious to keep his route secret; and secondly, it was a part of his system to give the young man no sort of trouble or inconvenience on his account. He wished every association that linked them together to be one of pleasure.

Mrs. Basil, as we have said, had not made her appearance that morning below stairs; she was, in fact, no better, but rather worse: that news from Lingmoor, outwardly borne so well, had shaken her to the core. Still, no sooner had Balfour left than she made shift to rise, and even came down to dinner. She discussed with Charley, who had a considerable regard for her, the character of their late guest—not with hostility, as his mother was wont to do, but with the air of one who asks for information, and has confidence in the verdict which she seeks. The lad, flattered by this implied compliment to his sagacity, answered her questions readily enough. He praised his friend, of course, and thought he praised him even when he spoke ill of him. He repeated his pungent sayings, and served up his anecdotes—such of them as were adapted, at least, for the ears of the ladies—anew. By this means he hoped to bring his hearers to a better opinion of so capital a fellow; and in Mrs. Basil's case he apparently succeeded. His mother still reiterated her opinion that Mr. Balfour was a dangerous personage, and not a fit companion for any young man. Charles smiled at this, for it was the almost literal fulfillment of a prophecy which Balfour had made to him, and believed in that gentleman's sagacity, accordingly, more than ever. Women were so ludicrously prejudiced; the fact of Mrs. Basil's—"the white witch"—not being so was an exception that proved the rule. She had been evidently interested in his anecdotes, of one of which she had even requested to hear the particulars twice over; not that, in his own judgment, it was the best, but, being of a weird sort, it had probably struck her fancy. It had lost in the telling, too—for he did not pretend to have the gift of narrative, as Mr. Balfour had—and his mother had seen in the story in question nothing at all.

Mrs. Basil came down stairs no more after that evening. She grew worse and worse, and was not only confined to her room, but to her bed. Harry was not much with her; she seized with avidity this opportunity of being alone with Charley to undo, as far as she could, Mr. Balfour's work with him. This was not hard, for the boy was a creature of impulse, and swayed for good or ill with equal ease. But she discovered that it would be useless to attempt henceforth to conceal from him the nature of his future prospects. He was now firmly convinced that he was the heir to a large fortune, and she regretted too late that she had left the disclosure to a stranger. What grieved her much more, and with reason, was that an attempt which she now made to bring the influence of Agnes to bear upon him proved unsuccessful; the girl resolutely refused to come to the house in the absence of its master, and contrary, as she knew, to his express commandment. Charley himself, too, whose visits to Mr. Aird's studio had been intermitted for some time, was received in Soho with coldness. It was not in Harry's nature to understand this independence of spirit, and she deeply deplored it on her son's account. She had looked to this young girl to be his guardian angel, and had never anticipated that she could possibly decline to watch over a charge so precious. She would not allow, even to herself, that her son's own conduct was as much the cause of this as her husband's ill favor; but she saw in it, clearly enough, the mark of the cloven hoof, the work of Balfour.

Sick Mrs. Basil could give her small comfort, though she did not attempt to defend their late visitor, as she had so unwarrantably appeared to do when discussing him with Charley.

"The man is gone, my dear," said she, wearily; "perhaps he may never come back: let us not meet troubles half-way. Charley has a kind, good heart"—for "the white witch" showed great favor to the lad at all times—"and all will come right at last."

She seemed too ill and weary to argue the matter, and Harry left her, as she thought, to repose. No sooner was she gone, however, than the closed lids of Mrs. Basil were opened wide, and revealed a sleepless and unutterable woe. Her sharp, pinched face showed pain and fear. Her parched lips muttered unceasingly words like these, which were, perhaps, the ravings of her fevered brain: "I am sure of it now, quite sure; those stags, those stags! There is no room for hope. His heart has become a stone, which no power can soften. It is no use to speak, or rather I am like one in a dream who watches murder done, and can not cry out."

CHAPTER XLII.

THE MINE AT MIDNIGHT.

Mr. Balfour—for so we must call him now, since he is attired respectably, travels first-class, and, moreover, even looks like a gentleman—did not go to the Midlands, as he had given out was his purpose, but took his ticket to Plymouth, to which place the railway had just extended in those days. He bought neither book nor newspaper, but sat in the corner, with his hat drawn over his eyes, for the whole nine hours, thinking. From Plymouth he posted to Turlock, where he arrived late at night, and without having broken fast since morning. He took no pains either to divulge or conceal his name; he asked no questions, nor was asked any except "whether he preferred to sleep between sheets or blankets"—for Turlock was still an out-of-the-way region, and the little inn about three-quarters of a century behind our modern caravansaries, with their "daily fly-bills" and "electric bells."

After dinner, which he scarcely touched, he wandered out—it was his habit to do so, as he told the hostler, who was also the night-chamberlain—and did not return till long after midnight. He observed, as he gave the man half a crown for sitting up for him to so late an hour, that the moon looked very fine upon the sea.

"You must be a painter, I guess, Sir," said the hostler, with a grin of intelligence.

"Why?" asked Balfour, sharply. "What makes you think that?"

"Well, Sir," returned the man, apologetically, "I mean no offense; but it is always the gentlemen-painters—or, at least, so they say at Gethin, and I wish more of 'em came here—as is so free with their money, and so fond of the moon."

"Lunatics, eh?" said the new arrival, with a loud, quick laugh. "Well, I'm no painter, my friend."

Then he took his candle and retired to his room, but not to bed. He disarranged the bedclothes and rumpled the pillow; then walked softly to and fro in his slippers until morning. On the following day he made no attempt to visit his newly acquired property, but strolled about the harbor, or stood in sheltered and, therefore, secluded places in the rocks, watching the winter sea. His meals at the inn were sent down almost as they were served up, yet he showed no sign of weakness or fatigue, but in the evening sallied forth as before. The night was very cloudy, with driving showers, and the landlady good-naturedly warned him of the danger of venturing on the cliff-path, which was narrow, and had been broken in places by a late storm.

"I will take care," said he, mechanically.

"Perhaps you would like supper—some cold meat, or something—since you have eaten so little, placed in your sitting-room against your return?"

"Yes, yes," said he, approvingly; "you are right; I shall doubtless be hungry to-night." Then he went out into the bleak, black night.

He hung about the harbor as before until near eleven, when all the lights of the little town had faded away, save that at the inn, which was burning for him alone; then he climbed the cliff, and pushed southward along the very path against the dangers of which he had been cautioned. He walked fast, too, with his gaze fixed before him, like one who has an appointment of importance for which there is a fear of being late. Presently he struck inland over the down, when he began to move less quickly, and to peer cautiously before him. All was dark: the grass on which he trod seemed to be black, until he suddenly arrived at a large circular patch of it which *was* black, and made the surrounding soil less sombre by contrast. This was the mouth of a great pit; and he sat on the brink of it, with his face to seaward, and his ear in his hollowed hand, listening. Nothing was to be heard, however, but the occasional scud of the rain, and the ceaseless roar of the now distant waves. Far out to sea there was a round red light, which fell upon him at regular intervals, its absence making the place which it had filled more dark than elsewhere. It had a weird effect, as though some evil spirit was keeping watch upon him, but he knew it for what it was—the revolving lamp of a light-house. Presently, in the same direction as the red light, he perceived a white one, which, though moving slowly, was certainly advancing toward him; nor did it, like the other, become obscure.

"He is coming," said Balfour to himself, with a great sigh. He had begun to have doubts of the other's keeping his appointment; though, indeed, it was not yet the time that he had himself fixed for it. The light came on, quite close to the ground, and with two motions—across as well as along. It was that of a lantern, which guided thus the footsteps of a tall, stout man, who bore upon his shoulders a ladder so long that it both projected above his head and trailed behind him. Balfour rose up, and stood motionless in the path of the new-comer till this light fell full upon him. "Hollo!" cried the man, a little startled by the white, worn face that so suddenly confronted him, although he had been looking for it. "Is that you, Mr. Balfour?"

"Yes. Hush! There is no need to mention names."

"Quite true, Sir; but you gave me quite a turn," remonstrated the other, "coming out of the darkness like a ghost. This Wheal Danes, at midnight, puts queer thoughts into one's head."

"John Trevethick was not afraid of coming here," observed Balfour.

"Well, so he always said. He told me at the last that he only pretended to believe in any of the foolish stories that folks talk about, and in favor of which he used to argue. But he's dead and gone, and *that* don't make this place less uncanny. Nobody since his time has been a-near it; they think he haunts the pit, it seems, so every body gives it a wide berth, both night and day. We shall see, however, and pretty soon, I hope, whether that notion can not be got over. Why, in six months' time we ought to have a hundred men at work here."

"Let us hope so. But in the mean time you say nobody comes here even in the daytime, eh?"

"Never. The place lies out of the way, you see: about midway between the cliff-path and the road."

"That's well," said Balfour, mechanically. "And you have not been babbling to any one of our prospects, Mr. Coe—nor of me, I hope?"

"Certainly not, Sir; that was the first article of our partnership, as I understood. Not a soul at Gethin has heard a whisper of Wheal Danes, or of your coming; they think I'm fast asleep at my own house, this instant. But it's been hard work lugging this cursed ladder up here in such a breakneck night as this, *I* can tell you, and I am glad enough to rest a bit."

"Well, it's all over now, Mr. Coe."

"Except that I have got to take it back again," grumbled Solomon.

"True, I had forgotten that. We must not leave it here, must we?"

"Of course not. I do not complain of the trouble, however, only you must admit I've kept my tryst under some little difficulties, eh, partner?" and Solomon chuckled self-approval.

"You will be paid in full for all, my good Sir," answered Balfour, gravely; "that is," he added, hastily, "if the mine should turn out as you predict. How deep is it? That ladder of yours will surely never reach the bottom."

"No, indeed. Did I not tell you that there are three levels, each about the same depth? The copper lode lies at the bottom of the last, in the northeastern corner. You will find I have concealed nothing from you. Well, I have got my breath again now. Are you ready, Mr. Balfour?"

"Quite; but walk slowly, I beg, for your lantern is very dim."

"Yes, yes. But wait a minute; I came here yesterday and hid something." Solomon seated himself upon the edge of the pit, with his legs hanging over, and began to peer and feel about him.

"Take care what you are at," cried Balfour, eagerly; "you may slip down and kill yourself, sliding along like that."

Solomon laughed contemptuously. "Never fear, Sir; I have had too many mischances with mines to fear them. I have fallen down worse places, and been shut up in others far deeper and darker than Wheal Danes, without food or candle, for a week, and yet lived through it. The shaft has not yet been dug, I reckon, as will prove— Oh, here's the torch."

He dragged from under the overhanging rim of the pit a piece of wood like a bludgeon, one end of which was smeared with pitch; and placing the lantern with its back to the wind, pushed the stick inside, which came out a torch, flaming and dropping flame.

"There's our corpse-candle!" cried Coe, triumphantly; "that would keep us without witnesses, even if any one were so bold as, in a night like this, to venture near Wheal Danes, to trespass on Tom Tiddler's ground, where we shall pick up the gold and the silver." There was a wild excitement, quite foreign to his habit, about this man, and he whirled the torch about his head in flaring circles.

"Keep your wits steady, if you please," observed Balfour, sternly.

"It is over now, Sir, and I am in the counting-house again," answered Solomon, submissively. "I felt a little exhilarated at the prospect of plucking a fruit that has been ripening for fifty years, that's all. This Wheal Danes is the very aloe of mines, and it is about to blossom for us only. You had better take the torch yourself; the lantern will serve for me; but just show a light here while I place the ladder."

Balfour held the blazing pine aloft, and disclosed the gaping mouth of the old pit, its margin wet with the rain, and its sheer sides slippery with the damps of ages.

"It would be easy enough to get down without this contrivance," observed Solomon, grimly, as he carefully adjusted the ladder, the foot of which was lost in gloom; "but it would take us some trouble to find our way back again without wings."

"In daylight, however, I dare say it looks easier," said Balfour, carelessly.

"It may look so, but it ain't. Nothing but a sea-gull ever goes in and out of Wheal Danes; even the bats keep there, where indeed they are snug and warm enough."

"It doesn't feel very warm at present," replied the other, who did not seem to be in a hurry to explore this unpromising territory.

"Ay, but you wait till we get to the lower level; you might live there, if the rats would let you, for a whole winter, and never need a fire."

"Oh, there are rats, are there? Why, what do *they* live upon?"

"Well, that's *their* look-out," laughed Solomon; "they would be very glad to have *us*, no doubt. It would be only just in my case, for I have lived on them before now; with rats and water a man may do very well for a week or two."

"What! there is water laid on in this establishment, is there?"

"No; the low levels are quite dry. But come, let us see for ourselves. We are losing time. I will start first, and do you follow close upon me, but without treading on my fingers;" and Solomon placed his heavy foot upon the first rung.

"No, no," said Balfour, drawing back; "I will not trust myself on the same ladder with a man of your weight. When you are at the bottom give me a call, and then I'll join you."

"As you like, Sir," responded Solomon, civilly; but his thick lips curled contemptuously, and he muttered, "So this man is lily-livered after all; so much the better: it is well to have a coward for a partner."

The next moment his descending form was lost in the gloom.

Balfour waited, torch in hand, until an "All right," that sounded like a voice from the tomb, assured him that his companion had reached terra firma. Then he descended very carefully, and joined him.

"Stand close to the wall, Sir, while I move the ladder," said Coe; "your head don't seem made for these deep places. Ah, here's the spot. This is a drop of twenty feet."

"And what is the depth of the last level?"

"Five-and-twenty. But don't you be afraid; the ladder will just reach it, only you won't have so much to hold on by at the top. It's only the getting down that's unpleasant; you'll find going back quite easy work. And then, just think of the lode!"

Solomon began to be anxious lest his companion's fears should induce him to give up the expedition altogether. It had never entered into his mind that what was so easy to himself could prove so formidable to another; and, besides, he had somehow concluded that Balfour was a man of strong nerves.

"Make haste," said the latter, in the tone of one who has achieved some mental victory: "let us go through with it."

In the second level it was perceptibly warmer. Dark, noiseless objects began to flit about the torch, and once something soft struck against Balfour's foot, and then scampered away.

He looked behind him, and not a trace of light was to be discerned, while before him was impenetrable gloom, except for the feeble gleam of his companion's lantern. Above him the roof was just discernible, from which long strings of fungi, white and clammy, hung down and brushed against his face as he moved slowly forward.

"Come on!" said Solomon, impatiently, whose spirits seemed to rise in this familiar scene. "We are only a few score yards from Golconda."

Balfour stopped short. "I thought you said there was another level?" There was a strange look of disappointment in his face, and even of rage.

"Yes, yes, and here it is," cried the other, putting down the ladder, which he had carried from place to place. "It is only depth that separates us from it. They dug well, those Romans, but left off, as you shall see, upon the very threshold of fortune. You have only to be a little careful, because the ladder does not quite reach."

He descended, as before, in advance, while Balfour followed slowly and cautiously. "How steep and smooth the rock is!" observed he, examining its surface.

"Yes, indeed; it is like a wall of marble. But what matters that? It baffles the rats, but not us. Here is the land of gold, here is— What the devil are you at?"

Solomon, in his impatience, had stridden on to the object of his desires; and Balfour, halting midway in his descent, suddenly retraced his footsteps, and having reached the top, was dragging the ladder up after him.

Solomon heard this noise, with which his ear was familiar, and his tone had some alarm in it as he cried out, "I say, no tricks, Mr. Balfour."

There was no reply. He hastened back to the spot he had just left, and from thence could dimly perceive his late companion sitting on the verge of the steep wall, peering down upon him.

"Come, come, a joke is a joke," remonstrated Coe. "What a fellow you are to be at such games when an important matter is at stake! Why, here is the lode, man."

"It is very valuable, I dare say, Mr. Coe, but it is worth more to one man than to two."

"Great Heaven! what do you mean?" cried Solomon, while a sudden sweat bedewed his forehead. "You would not murder a man to dissolve a partnership?"

"Certainly not. I shall leave him to die, that's all. He and the rats will have to settle it together. Six months hence, perhaps, we may have a picnic here, and explore the place. Then we shall find, where you are now standing, some well-picked bones and the metal part of your lantern. That will cause quite an excitement; and we shall search further, and in the northeast corner there will be found a copper lode. I will take your word for that."

"Mr. Balfour, I am sure you will not do this," pleaded the wretched man. "It is not in man's nature to treat a fellow-creature with such barbarity. You are trying to frighten me, I know, and I own you have succeeded. I know what it is to be shut up in desolate, dark places alone, out of reach of succor; and even for eight-and-forty hours or so it is terrible."

"*What must it be, then, to suffer so for twenty years?*"

It was a third voice that seemed to wake the echoes of that lonesome cavern. Solomon looked up in terror, and beheld a third face, that of Robert Balfour, but transfigured. He held the glowing brand above him, so that his deep-lined features could be distinctly seen, and they were all instinct with a deadly rage and malice. There was a fire in his eyes that might well have been taken for that of madness, and Solomon's heart sank within him as he looked.

"Mr. Balfour," said he, in a coaxing voice, "come and look at your treasure. It sparkles in the light of my lantern like gold, and you shall have it all if you please; I do not wish to share it with you."

"So you take me for a madman, do you? Look again; look fixedly upon me, Solomon Coe. You do not recognize me even yet? I do not wonder. It is not you that are dull, but I that am so changed by wrong and misery. My own mother does not know me, nor the woman of whom you robbed me nineteen years ago. Yes, you know me now. I am Richard Yorke!"

"Mercy, mercy!" gasped Solomon, dropping on his knees.

Richard laughed long and loud. The echoes of his ghastly mirth died slowly away, and when his voice was heard again it was stern and solemn. "It is my turn at last, man; I am the judge to-day, as you were the witness nineteen years ago who doomed me wrongfully to shame and misery. Night and day I have had this hour in my mind; the thought of it has been my only joy—in chains and darkness, in toil and torment, fasting and wakeful on my prison pillow, I have thought of nothing else. I did not know how it would come about, but I was sure that it would come. You swore falsely once that I was a thief; I am now about to be a murderer, and your whitening bones will not be able to witness against me."

"I never swore it, Mr. Yorke," pleaded Solomon, passionately.

"Your memory is defective," answered Richard, gloomily; "you forget that I was in court myself on that occasion. You did your very worst to blacken me before judge and jury, and you succeeded."

"But it was Trevethick—it was father-in-law who urged me to do it; it was indeed."

"I know it," replied the other, coldly; "he was a greater villain than yourself, but unhappily an older one. Death has robbed me of him, and made my vengeance incomplete. Still there is something left for me. While you die slowly here— But no; I shall wait at Turlock for that to happen. A strong man like you, who have rats to live upon, may last ten days, perhaps. Well, when you are dead, I shall return to your London house, and lead your son to ruin. You permitted me to begin the work in hopes of getting half this mine; I shall finish it while you are in sole possession of the whole of it."

"Devil!" cried Solomon, furiously.

"The appellation is a true one, my good Sir; but I was a man once. Evil is now my good, thanks to your teaching. Look at me—look at me, and see what you have brought me to at eight-and-thirty! You almost drove me mad, and it was easy, for I had the Carew blood in my veins; but I contrived to keep my wits for the enjoyment of this hour. I feel very old, and have few pleasures left, you see. It is impossible, unfortunately, to return here and see you rot; there would be danger in it; just the least risk in the world of somebody coming here to look for us. I must be off now, too, for there is a worthy man sitting up for me at the inn, and I have got to take this ladder back to Gethin."

A cry of mingled rage and despair burst forth from Richard's foe.

"What! you had calculated upon the absence of that ladder producing suspicion? It is curious how great wits jump together: that had also struck me. I shall take it back, for I well know where it ought to be; I am quite familiar with your house at Gethin, as you may remember, perhaps. You may keep the lantern, which will not be missed; but, if you will take my advice, you will put out the light, to preserve the candle—as an article of food. Put it somewhere where the rats can not eat it, and it may prolong your torments half a day. You can also eat the horn of the lantern, but you will doubtless preserve that for a *bonne bouche.* You are not superstitious, else I would suggest that your father-in-law's spirit is exceedingly likely to haunt that northeastern corner down yonder."

Here there was a dull scrambling noise, a violent struggle as of feet and hands against a wall, and then a heavy thud.

"Now that is very foolish of you, Solomon, to attempt to get out of a place which you yourself informed me could never be escaped from without wings. I sincerely hope you have not hurt yourself much. I hear you moving slowly about again, so I may leave you without anxiety. Good-by, Solomon." Richard waited a moment, a frightful figure of hate and triumph, peering down into the pit beneath, where all was now dark. "You are too proud to speak to a convict, perhaps. Well, well, that is but natural in so honest a man. I take my leave, then. You have no message, I conclude, for home?"

An inarticulate cry, like that of a wild animal caught in a snare, was the only reply.

"That is the worst of letting his candle go out," mused Richard, aloud; "some rat has got hold of him already." Then, with a steady foot and smiling face, which showed how all his previous fears had been assumed, he retraced his steps, and mounted to the upper air. The sky was clearer now; and, casting the torch, for which he had no further need, far into the mine, and shouldering the ladder, he started for Gethin at good speed. It was past two o'clock before he reached his inn at Turlock; but before he retired to rest he sat down to the supper that had been prepared for him, but without the appetite which he had anticipated.

CHAPTER XLIII.

THE SMOKING-ROOM OF THE GEORGE AND VULTURE.

Robert Balfour did not remain at Turlock, as he had originally intended. Perhaps the vicinity to Wheal Danes was not so attractive to him as he had promised himself that it would be, although not for a single instant did his purpose of revenge relax. Other considerations, had he needed them, were powerful, now that he had taken the first step, to keep him on that terrible path which he had so long marked out for himself. To disclose the position of his victim now would have been not only to make void his future plans, but to place his own fate at Solomon's mercy. Yet he found his heart less hard than the petrifaction it had undergone, the constant droppings of wrong and hardship for twenty years, should have rendered it. He did not wake until late, and the first sound that broke upon his ear was the tinkling of the bell of the little church, for it was Sunday morning. He compared it for a moment with something that he had been dreaming of: a man in a well chipping footsteps for himself in the brick wall, up which he climbed a few feet, and then fell down again. Then a pitiful, unceasing cry of "Help, help!—help, help!" rang in his ears, instead of the voice that called people to prayers. Even when that ceased, the wind and rain—for the weather was wild and wet—beating against the window-pane, brought with them doleful shrieks. Sometimes a sudden gust seemed to bear upon it confused voices and the tramp of hurrying feet; and then he would knit his brow and clench his hand, with the apprehension that they had found his enemy, and were bringing him to the door. Not the slightest fear of the consequences to himself in such a case agitated his mind; he had quite resolved what to do, and that no prison walls should ever hem him in again; but the bare idea that Solomon should escape his vengeance drove him to the brink of frenzy. He would have left the place at once, but that he thought the coincidence of his departure with the disappearance of his foe might possibly awaken suspicion; so he staid on through the day, waiting for the news which he knew must arrive sooner or later. At noon he thought the landlady wore an unusually grave air, and he felt impelled to ask her what was the matter. But then, if there was nothing—if she only looked sour, as folks often did, just because it was Sunday—she might think him too curious.

From his window, a little later, he saw a knot of people in the rain talking eagerly together, and one of them pointing with his hand toward Gethin. But they were too far off to be overheard, and he did not dare go down and interrogate them. It was his object to appear utterly indifferent to local affairs, and as a total stranger. He felt half stifled within doors, and yet, if he should go out, he knew that he would be incontrollably impelled to take the cliff path that he had followed the preceding night, to watch that nobody came near the place that held his prey, and thereby, like the bird who shows her nest by keeping guard too near, attract attention. The tidings for which he waited came at six o'clock, just as he was sitting down to his dinner. The parlor-maid who served him had that happy and excited look which the possession of news, whether it be good or bad, but especially the latter, always imparts to persons of her class.

"There's strange news come from Gethin, Sir," said she, as she arranged the dishes.

"Indeed," said Balfour, carelessly, though he felt his brain spin round and his heart stop at the same moment. "What is it?"

"Mr. Coe, Sir, a very rich man—he as owns all Dunloppel—has disappeared."

"How's that?"

"Well, Sir, he went to his room last night, they say, at his usual hour, but never slept in his bed, and the front-door was found unlocked in the morning, so that he must have gone away of himself. That would not be so odd, for he is a secret sort of man, as is always coming and going; but he has taken nothing with him; only the clothes he stood in."

"Well, I dare say he has come back again by this time, my good girl. What's this? Is there no fish?"

"No, Sir; the weather was too bad yesterday for catching them, and all last night there was a dreadful sea: that's what they fear about Mr. Coe—that he has fell into the sea. His footsteps have been tracked to the cliff edge, and there they stop."

"Poor fellow! Has he any relatives?"

"Oh yes, Sir; a wife and son—a very handsome, nice young gentleman."

"Then his widow will be rich, I suppose?"

"Oh, pray, don't call her a widow yet, Sir; let us hope her husband may be found. It's a dreadful thing to be drowned like that on a Sunday morning; and for one who knows the cliff path so well as he did, too. He was a hard man, and no favorite, but one forgets that now, of course."

"You have also forgotten the Harvey Sauce, my good girl; oblige me by bringing it, will you?" said Mr. Balfour, beginning to whistle something which did not sound like a psalm tune. "You must excuse my hard-heartedness, but I had not the pleasure of knowing this gentleman."

An hour afterward the solitary guest had left the inn, and was on his road to Plymouth. His departure caused little surprise, for the weather was such as to induce no visitor to prolong his stay.

Whether from his long enforced abstinence from society, or from the unwelcome nature of his thoughts, Robert Balfour was always disinclined to be alone. His expeditions with Charley in search of pleasure had been, though he did not find pleasure, more agreeable to him than the being left to his own resources; and now this was more the case than ever. He preferred even such company as that which the smoking-room of an hotel afforded to none at all. The voices of his fellow-creatures could not shape themselves, as every inarticulate sound did to his straining ear, into groans and feeble cries for aid. Not twenty-four hours had elapsed since his prisoner was placed in hold, so that such sounds of weakness and agony must have been in every sense chimerical; and yet he heard them. What, then, if these echoes from the tomb should always be heard? A terrible idea indeed, but one which bred no repentance. It was not likely that remorse should seize him in the very place where his hated foe had clutched and consigned him to *his* living grave.

The hotel at which he now put up was the same at which he had then lodged; this public room was the same in which he had smoked his last cigar upon his fatal visit to the Miners' Bank. He had had only one companion then, but now it was full of people. By their talk it was evident that they were townsfolk, and all known to one another; in fact, it was a tradesmen's club, which met at the *George and Vulture* on Sunday nights through the winter months. In spite of his willingness to be won from his thoughts, he could not fix his attention on the small local gossip that was going on about him. Men came in and out without his observing them; and indeed it was not easy to take note of faces through the cloud of smoke that filled the room; he was fast relapsing into his own reflections, wondering what Solomon was doing in the dark, and if he slept much, when an event occurred which roused him as thoroughly as the prick of a lance or a sudden douche of cold water.

"Let us have no misunderstanding and no obligation—that is my motto."

The speaker was a thin, gray man, whose entrance into the apartment Balfour had not perceived, and who was seated in an elevated chair, which had apparently been reserved for him as president of the assembly. The face was unfamiliar, for twenty years had made an old man of the astute and lively detective; but his phrase, and the manner of delivering it, identified him at once as his old friend Mr. Dodge.

"It was in this very room," continued the latter, "that I sat and talked with him as sociable as could be, not a quarter of an hour before I put the darbies on him; and it's a thing that has been upon my mind ever since. I was only doing my duty, of course, but still it seemed hard to take advantage of such a frank young fellow. As for stealing them notes, it's my belief he had no more intention of doing it than I had."

"And yet he got it hot at the 'sizes, Mr. Dodge, didn't he?" inquired one of the company.

"Got it hot, Sir?" replied Mr. Dodge, with dignity; "he got an infamous and most unjustly severe sentence, if you mean that, Sir. Of course what he did was contrary to law, but it's my opinion as the law was strained agin him. There was some as swore hard and fast to get him punished as knew he deserved no such treatment. Why, the girl as he loved, and whose picture I found upon him myself when I searched him, and gave it him back, too—ay, that I did—even she took a false oath, as Weasel himself told me, who was his lawyer, and had built up his case with that same hussy for its corner-stone. Ah!" said Mr. Dodge, with a gesture of abhorrence, "if there ever was a murdered man, it was that poor young fellow, Richard Yorke."

"But I thought he got twenty years' penal servitude," observed the same individual who had interposed before, and whose thankless office it seemed to be to draw the old gentleman out for the benefit of society.

"I say he was murdered, Sir. He was shut up for nigh twenty years, and then shot in the back in trying to get away from Lingmoor. It was the hardest case I ever knew in all my professional experience. Lord, if you had seen him —the handsomest, brightest, gayest young chap! And he was what some folks call well-born, too; he was the son—that is, though, in a left-handed sort of way, it's true—of mad Carew of Crompton, about whose death the papers were so full a month ago or so; and that, in my judgment, was the secret of all his misfortune: it was the Carew blood as did it. To take his own way in the world; to seek nobody's advice, nor use it if 'twas given; to be spoiled and petted by all the women and half the men as came nigh him; to own no master nor authority; to act without thought, and to scorn consequences—well, all that was bred in the bone with him."

"Then he had never any one to look after him at home, I reckon, Mr. Dodge?"

"Well, yes; he had a mother; and though she was a queer one too, she loved him dearly. She was the cleverest woman, Weasel used to say, as ever he had to do with; and a perfect lady too, mind you. She worked to get the poor lad off like a slave; and when all was over, instead of breaking down, as most would, she swallowed her pride, and went down on her bended knees to that old miserly devil, Trevethick, the prosecutor, and to his son-in-law, Coe, likewise: they lived down Cross Key way—where was it?—at Gethin—and begged and prayed him to join in petitioning in her son's favor. She got down there the very day after his lying daughter was married to Solomon Coe, he as has got Dunloppel, and is a big man now. But he'll never be any thing but a scurvy lot, if he was to be king o' Cornwall. I shall never forget the way he insulted that poor young fellow when he was took up. Damme, I would have given a ten-pound note to have had *him* charged with something, and I'd ha' seen that the handcuffs weren't none too big for his wrists neither."

"And this Trevethick refused to help the lady, did he?"

"Why, of course he did. He broke her heart, poor soul. I saw her when she passed through Plymouth afterward, and she looked twenty years older than before that trial. Even then she didn't give the matter up, but laid it before the crown. But poor Yorke had offended government—helped some fool or another through one of them public examinations; he had wits enough for any thing, had that young fellow. But there—I can't a-bear to talk about him; and yet somehow I can't help doing on it when I get into this room. He sat just where that gentleman sits yonder. I think I see him now, smoking the best of cigars, one of which he offered to me—for he was free as free; but I was necessitated to restore it, for I couldn't take a gift from one as I was just a-going to nab. 'Thank you kindly,' says I, 'but let us have no misunderstanding and no obligation.' Poor fellow! poor fellow!"

No more was said about the case of Richard Yorke; but it was evidently a standing topic with the chairman of the *George and Vulture* club. A yearning to behold and embrace that mother who had done and suffered so much for his sake took possession of Richard's soul. His heart had been steeled against her when he found harbored under her roof the objects of his rage and loathing; but he felt now that that must have come to pass with some intention of benefit to himself. The very truth, indeed, flashed upon him that she entertained some plan of frustrating his revenge against them, with the idea of protecting him from the consequences that were likely to ensue from it; and he forgave her, while he hated his foes the more. He would carry out his design to the uttermost, but very cautiously, and with a prudence that he would certainly not have used had his own safety been alone concerned; and then, when he had avenged himself and her, he would disclose himself to her. The statement he had just heard affected him deeply, but in opposite ways. The justification of himself in no way moved him—he did not need that; it was also far too late for his heart to be touched by the expression of the old detective's good-will, though the time had been when he would have thanked him for its utterance with honest tears; but the revelation of his mother's toil and suffering in his behalf reawakened all his dormant love for her, while it made his purpose firmer than ever to be the Nemesis of her enemies and his own.

As he went to bed that night the clock struck twelve. It was just four-and-twenty hours since he had left his victim in the bowels of Wheal Danes. If a free pardon could have been offered to him for the crime, and the mine been filled with gold for him to its mouth, he would not have stretched out his hand to save him.

CHAPTER XLIV.

STILL HUMAN.

Mr. Balfour atoned for his previous indifference to the wares of the news-boy by sending him next morning to the station for all the local papers. In each, as he expected, there was a paragraph headed *Mysterious Disappearance*, and as lengthened an account as professional ingenuity could devise of the unaccountable departure of Mr. Solomon Coe from his house at Gethin. The missing man was "much respected;" and, "as the prosperous owner of the Dunloppel mine, which had yielded so largely for so many years, he could certainly not have been pressed by pecuniary embarrassments, and therefore the idea of suicide was out of the question." Unlikely as it seemed in the case of one who knew the country so well, the most probable explanation of the affair was that the unfortunate gentleman, in taking a walk by night along the cliff top, must have slipped into the sea. The weather had been very rough of late and the wind blowing from off the land, which would have accounted—if this supposition was correct—for the body not having been washed ashore. "In the mean time an active search was going on."

Balfour had resolved not to return to London for at least ten days. Mrs. Coe and her son would, without doubt, be telegraphed for, and he could not repair to their house in their absence. The idea of being under the same roof alone with his mother was now repugnant to him. He felt that he could not trust himself in such a position. It had been hard and grievous, notwithstanding his resentment against her, to see her in company with others, and her absence of late from table had been a great relief to him. With his present feeling toward her it would be impossible to maintain his incognito; and, if that was lost, his future plans—to which he well knew she would oppose herself—would be rendered futile. He had seen with rage and bitter jealousy that both Harry and her boy, and especially the latter, were dear to her; and it was certain she would interfere to protect them, for their sake as well as for his own. He had other reasons also for not returning immediately to town. It might hereafter be expedient to show that he *had* really been to Midlandshire, where he had given out he had designed to go; and, moreover, though his purpose was relentless as respected Solomon, he did not perhaps care to be in a house where hourly suggestions would be dropped as to the whereabouts of his victim, or the fate that had happened to him. Harry and her son might even not have gone to Gethin, and in that case their apprehensions and surmises would have been insupportable.

Richard was more human than he would fain believe himself to be. Though he had gone to bed so inexorable of purpose, it had been somewhat shaken through the long hours of a night in which he had slept but little, and waked to think on what his feverish dreams had dwelt upon—the fate of his unhappy foe, perishing slowly beside his useless treasure. More than once, indeed, the impulse had been strong upon him that very morning to send word anonymously where Solomon was to be found to the police at Plymouth. Remorse had not as yet become chronic with him, but it seized him by fits and starts. There had been a time when he had looked (through his prison bars) on all men with rage and hatred; but now he caught himself, as it were, at attempts at self-justification with respect to the retribution he had exacted even from his enemy. Had he not been rendered miserable, he argued, supremely wretched, for more than half his lifetime, through this man's agency? for it was certain that Solomon had sworn falsely, in the spirit if not in the letter, and caused him to be convicted of a crime which his rival was well aware he had not in intention committed. His conduct toward him on the occasion of his arrest had also been most brutal and insulting; while, after conviction had been obtained, this wretch's malice, as Mr. Dodge had stated, had known no cessation. In the arms of his young bride he had been deaf to the piteous cry of a mother beseeching for her only son.

But, on the other hand, had not he (Richard) deeply wronged this man in the first instance? Had he not robbed him—for so much at least must Solomon have known—of the love of his promised wife? If happiness from such an ill-assorted union was not to have been anticipated, still, had he not rendered it impossible? If their positions had been reversed, would not he have exacted expiation from such an offender to the uttermost? He would doubtless have scorned to twist the law as Solomon had done, and make it, as it were, the crooked instrument of his revenge. He would not, of course, have evoked its aid at all. But was that to be placed to his credit? He had put himself above the law throughout his life; he had never acknowledged any authority save that of his own selfish will; nay, he owned to himself that his bitterness against his unhappy victim had been caused not so much by the wrong he had suffered at his hands as by the contempt which he (Richard) had entertained for him. Without materials such as his father had possessed to back his pretensions he had imagined himself a sort of irresponsible and sovereign being. (Such infatuation is by no means rare, nor confined to despots and brigands, and when it exists in a poor man it is always fatal to himself.) His education, if it could be called such, had doubtless fostered this delusion; but Mr. Dodge was right; the Carew blood had been as poison in his veins, and had destroyed him.

All this might be true; but such philosophy could scarcely now obtain a hearing, while his enemy was dying of starvation in his living tomb. It was in vain for him to repeat mechanically that he had also suffered a sort of lingering death for twenty years. The present picture of his rival's torments presented itself in colors so lively and terrible that it blotted out the reminiscence of his own. The recollection of his wrongs was no longer sufficient for his vindication. He therefore strove to behold his victim in another light than as his private foe—as the murderer of his friend Balfour, the history of whose end may here be told.

On the night that Richard escaped from Lingmoor, it was Balfour, of course, who assisted him, and who was awaiting him in person at the foot of the prison wall. The old man's arms had received him as he slipped down the rope; and the object at which the sentry had fired had been two men, though in the misty night they had seemed but one. Balfour had been mortally wounded, and it was with the utmost difficulty that, laden with the burden of his dying friend, Richard had contrived to reach Bergen Wood. As his own footsteps were alone to be traced along the moor, the idea of another having accompanied his flight—though they knew there was complicity—had not occurred to the authorities. Balfour had hardly reached that wretched asylum when he expired, pressing Richard's hand, and bidding him remember Earl Street, Spitalfields. "What you find there is all yours, lad," was his dying testament and last words of farewell. And over his dead body Richard swore anew his vow of vengeance against the man that had thus, though indirectly, deprived him of his only friend. He had watched by the dead body, on its bed of rotten leaves, through that night and the whole of the next day; then, changing clothes with it, he had fled under cover of the ensuing darkness, and got away eventually to town.

He had found the house in Earl Street a wretched hovel, tenanted by a few abjects, whom the money found on Balfour—which he had received on leaving prison—was amply sufficient to buy out. Once alone in this tenement, he had easily possessed himself of the spoil so long secreted, and, furnished with it, he had hastened down to Crompton—the news of Carew's death having reached London on the very day that he found himself in a position to profit by it. The very plan which he had suggested to Balfour, whose name he also assumed, he himself put into execution. He made a private offer for the disused mine, which was gladly accepted by those who had the disposal of the property, acting under the advice of Parson Whymper. Trevethick, the only man that had attached any importance to the possession of it, was dead; and it was not likely that any one at the sale should bid one-half of the sum which this stranger was prepared to give for the mere gratification of his whim. The mine itself, indeed, had scarcely been mentioned in the transaction; it merely formed a portion in the lot comprising the few barren acres on which this capricious purchaser had expressed his fancy to build a home. "Disposed of by private contract" was the marginal note written in the auctioneer's catalogue which dashed Solomon's long-cherished hopes to the ground.

Richard staid on in the neighborhood to attend the sale. It attracted an immense concourse; and no less than a guinea a head was the price of admission to those who explored the splendid halls of Crompton, discussing the character of its late owner, and retailing wild stories of his eccentricities. Poor Parson Whymper, who had not a shilling left to him—for Carew had died intestate, though, thanks to him, not absolutely a beggar—was perhaps the only person present who felt a touch of regret. He had asked for his patron's signet-ring, as a keepsake, and this request had been refused on the part of the creditors; he wandered among the gay and jeering crowd like a ghost, little thinking that the one man who looked at him with a glance of pity was he whom he had once regarded as the heir of Crompton. It was the general opinion now that the unhappy chaplain had been Carew's evil genius, and had "led him on." Even Richard bestowed but that single glance upon him; he was looking in vain for the face that had so terrible an interest for himself. He had not heard that Trevethick was dead, but he knew it was so the instant that his eyes fell upon Solomon Coe, and all his hate was at once transferred to his younger enemy. The business upon which this man had come was as clear to him as though it had been written on his forehead. The first gleam of pleasure which had visited his dark soul for twenty years was the sight of Solomon's countenance when, on the sixth day's sale, the auctioneer gave out that lot 970 had been withdrawn. Solomon might have received the intimation long before but for the cautious prudence which had prevented him from making any inquiries upon the subject. For a minute or two he stood stunned and silent, then hurriedly made his way to the rostrum. Richard, who was sitting at the long table with the catalogue before him, kept his eyes fixed upon its pages while the auctioneer pointed him out as the purchaser of the lot in question. He knew the inquiry that was being asked, and its reply; he knew whose burly form it was that thrust itself the next minute in between him and his neighbor; every drop of blood in his body, every hair on his head, seemed to be cognizant that the man he hated most on earth was seated cheek by jowl with him—that the first step in the road of retribution had been taken voluntarily by his victim himself. The rest is soon told. Solomon at once commenced his clumsy efforts at conciliation; and his endeavors to recommend himself to the stranger's friendship were suffered quickly to bear fruit. He invited him to his house in London, which, to Richard's astonishment and indignation, he found to be his mother's home; and, in short, fell of his own accord into the very snare which the other, had he had the fixing of it, would himself have laid for him.

And now, as we have said, when all had gone exactly as Richard would have had it go, and Solomon was being punished to the uttermost, the executor of his doom was beginning to feel, if not compunction, at all events remorse. No adequate retribution had indeed overtaken Harry. To have made her a widow was, in fact, to have freed her from the yoke of a harsh and unloved master; but the fact was, notwithstanding the perjury of which he believed her to have been guilty, he had never hated her as he had hated the other authors of his wrongs. She had once on the rock-bound coast at Gethin preserved his life; she had accorded to his passion all that woman can grant, and had reciprocated it; not even in his fiercest hour of despair had he harbored the thought of raising his hand against her; he had hated her, indeed, as his betrayer, and as Solomon's wife, but never regarded her with that burning detestation which he felt toward her husband. There was another motive also, though he did not even admit it to himself, which, now that his chief foe was expiating his offense, had no inconsiderable weight in the scale of mercy as regarded the others.

His endeavors to win Charley's favor had had a reflex action. In spite of himself, a certain good-will had grown up in him toward this boy, whom his mission it was to ruin. If there had been less of his mother in the lad's appearance, or any thing of his father in his character, his heart might have been steeled against his youth and innocence of transgression. As a mere son of Solomon Coe's he would have beheld in him the whelp of a wolf, and treated him accordingly; but between the wolf and his offspring there was evidently as little of affection as there was of likeness. The very weaknesses of Charley's character—his love of pleasure, his credulity, his wayward impulsiveness, of all which Balfour had made use for his own purposes—were foreign to the nature of the elder Coe; while the lad's high spirit, demonstrativeness, and geniality were all his own. If he had one to guide as well as love him—a woman with sound heart and brain, such as this Agnes Aird was represented to be, what a happy future might be before this youth! Without such a wise counselor, how easy it would be, and how likely, for him to drift on the tide of self-will and self-indulgence to the devil! The decision rested in Richard's own hands, he knew. Should he blast this young life in the bud, in revenge for acts for which he was in no way accountable, and which were already being so bitterly expiated? The apprehension that Solomon might even yet be found alive perhaps alone prevented Richard from resolving finally to molest Harry and her son no further. If his victim should have been rescued, his enmity would have doubtless blazed forth afresh against them as inextinguishable as ever, but in the mean time it smouldered, and was dying out for want of fuel. If he had no penitence with respect to the terrible retribution he had already wrought, the idea of it disturbed him. If he had no scruples, he had pangs: when all was over—in a day or two, for even so strong a man as Solomon could scarcely hold out longer—he would doubtless cease to be troubled with them; when he was once dead Richard did not fear his ghost; but the thought of this perishing wretch at present haunted him. He was still not far from Gethin, and its neighborhood was likely to encourage such unpleasant feelings. He had only executed a righteous judgment, since there was no law to right him; but even a judge would avoid the vicinity of a gallows on which hangs a man on whom he had passed sentence.

He would go into Midlandshire—where he was now supposed to be—until the affair had blown over. That watching and waiting for the Thing to be discovered would, he foresaw, be disagreeable, nervous work. And when it happened, how full the newspapers would be of it! How Solomon got to the place where he would be found would be as much a matter of marvel as the object of his going there. If the copper lode—the existence of which Richard did not doubt—were discovered, as it most likely would be when the mine became the haunt of the curious and the morbid, it was only too probable that public attention would be drawn to the owner. The identification of Robert Balfour with the visitor who had visited Turlock might then be established, whence would rise suspicion, and perhaps discovery. Richard had no terrors upon his own account, but he was solicitous to spare his mother this new shame. He had been hitherto guiltless in her eyes, or, when blameworthy, the victim of circumstances; but could her love for him survive the knowledge that he was a murderer? But why encourage these morbid apprehensions? Was it not just as likely that the Thing would never be discovered at all? Once set upon a wrong scent, as folks already were, since the papers had suggested the man was drowned, why should they ever hit upon the right one? Wheal Danes had not been explored for half a century. Why should not Solomon's bones lie there till the judgment-day?

At this point in his reflections the door opened—he was taking his breakfast in a private sitting-room—and admitted, as he thought, the waiter. Richard stood in such profound thought that it was almost stupor, with his arms upon the mantel-piece, and his head resting on his hands. He did not change his posture; but when the door closed, and there was silence in place of the expected clatter of the breakfast things, he turned about, and beheld Harry standing before him—in deep black, and, as it seemed to him, in widow's weeds!

CHAPTER XLV.

FACE TO FACE.

If Solomon himself, half starved and imbecile with despair, had suddenly presented himself from his living tomb, Richard could not have been more astonished than at the appearance of his present visitor. He had left her but three days ago for Midlandshire. How was it possible she had tracked him hither? With what purpose she had done so he did not ask himself, for he had already read it in her haggard face and hopeless eyes.

"Have I come too late?" moaned she in a piteous, terror-stricken voice.

"For breakfast?—yes, madam," returned Richard, coldly; "but that can easily be remedied;" and he feigned to touch the bell. His heart was steel again; this woman's fear and care he felt were for his enemy, and for him alone. It was plain she had no longer fear of himself.

"Where is my husband?" she gasped out. "Is he still alive?"

"I am not your husband's keeper, madam."

"But you are his murderer!" She held out her arm, and pointed at him with a terrible significance. There was something clasped in her trembling fingers which he could not discern.

"You speak in riddles, madam; and it seems to me your humor is somewhat grim."

"I ask you once more, is my husband dead, and have I come too late?"

"I have not seen him for some days; I left him alive and well. What makes you think him otherwise, or that I have harmed him?"

"This"—she advanced toward him, keeping her eyes steadily fixed upon his own—"this was found among your things after you left my house!"

It was a ticket-of-leave—the one that had been given to Balfour on his discharge from Lingmoor. It seemed impossible that Richard's colorless face could have become still whiter, but it did so.

"Yes, that is mine," said he. "It was an imprudence in me to leave such a token among curious people. You took an interest in my effects, it seems."

"It was poor Mrs. Basil who found it, and who gave it to me." Her voice was calm, and even cold; but the phrase "poor Mrs. Basil" alarmed him.

"The good lady is still unwell, then, is she?"

"She is dead."

"Dead!" Richard staggered to a chair, and pressed his hands to his forehead. The only creature in the world on whom his slender hopes were built had, then, departed from it! "When did she die?" inquired he in a hollow voice, "and how?"

"On the evening of the day you left, and, as I believe, of a disease which one like you will scarcely credit—of a broken heart."

Her manner and tone were hostile; but that moved not Richard one whit; the cold and measured tones in which she had alluded to his mother's death angered him, on the other hand, exceedingly. If his mother had died of a broken heart, it was this woman's falsehood that had broken it; and yet she could speak with calmness and unconcern of the loss which had left him utterly forlorn! He forgot all his late remorse; and in his eyes glittered malice and cruel rage.

"I do not fear you," cried she, in answer to this look; "for the wretched have no fear. The hen will do battle with the fox, the rabbit with the stoat, to save her young. If I can not save my husband, I will save my son. I have come down here to do it. You are known to me now for what you are—a jail-bird. If you dare to meet my Charley's honest face again, I will tell him who and what you are."

"Did Mrs. Basil tell you that, then?"

"Thus far she did," cried Harry, pointing to the ticket which Richard had taken from her hand. "Is not that enough? She warned me with her latest breath against you. 'Beware of him,' said she; 'and yet pursue him, if you would save your husband and your son. Where Solomon is, there will this man also be. Pursue, pursue!' I did but stay to close her eyes."

"And so she knew me, did she?"

"She knew enough, as I do. Of course she could not guess—who could?—your shameful past, the fruit of which is there!" and again she pointed to the ticket.

"*My* shameful past!" cried Richard, rising and drawing himself to his full height. "Who are you, that dare to say so? Do you, then, need one to rise from the dead to remind you of *your* past! Look at me, Harry Trevethick—look at *me!*"

"Richard!" It was but one word; but in the tone which she pronounced it a thousand memories seemed to mingle. An inexpressible awe pervaded her; she stood spell-bound, staring at his white hair and withered face.

"Yes, it *is* Richard," answered the other, mockingly, "though it is hard to think so. Twenty years of wretchedness have worked the change. It is you he has to thank for it, you perjured traitress!"

"No, no; as Heaven is my judge, Richard, I tell you No!" She threw herself on her knees before him; and as she did so her bonnet fell, and the rippling hair that he had once stroked so tenderly escaped from its bands; the color came into her cheeks, and the light into her eyes, with the passionate excitement of her appeal; and for the moment she looked almost as he had known her in the far-back spring-tide of her youth.

"Fair and false as ever!" cried Richard, bitterly.

"Listen, listen!" pleaded she; "then call me what you will."

He sat in silence while she poured forth all the story of the trial, and of the means by which her evidence had been obtained, listening at first with a cold, cynical smile, like one who is prepared for falsehood, and beyond its power; but presently he drooped his head and hid his features. She knew that she had persuaded him of her fidelity, but feared that behind those wrinkled hands there still lay a ruthless purpose. She had exculpated herself, but only (of necessity) by showing in blacker colors the malice of his enemies. She knew that he had sworn to destroy them root and branch; and there was one green bough which he had already done his worst to bend to evil ways. "Richard, Richard!" said she, softly.

He withdrew his chair with a movement which she mistook for one of loathing.

"He hates me for their sake," thought she, "although he knows me to be innocent. How much more must he hate those who made me seem so guilty!" But, in truth, his withdrawal from her touch had a very different explanation. He would have kissed her, and held out both his hands, but for the blood which he dreaded might be even now upon them. He saw that she loved him still, and had ever done so, even when she seemed his foe: all the old affection that he thought had been dead within him awoke to life, and yet he dared not give it voice.

"You have said my husband was alive and well, Richard?"

"I said I had left him so," answered he, hoarsely.

"Then you have spared him thus far; spare him still, even for my sake; and, for Heaven's sake, spare my son! Harden not your heart against one more dear to me by far than life itself. He has done you no wrong."

Richard shook his head; he yearned to clasp her to his breast; he could have cried, "I forgive them all," but he could not trust himself to speak, lest he should say, "I love you."

"You have seen my boy, Richard, many times. The friendship you have simulated for him must have made you know how warm-hearted and kind and unsuspicious his nature is. You have listened to his merry laugh, and felt the sunshine of his gayety. Oh! can you have the heart to harm him?"

Still he did not speak; he scarcely heard her words. The murdered man was standing between her and him; and he would always stand there, seen by him, though not by her. From the grave itself he had come forth to triumph over him to the end.

"Richard"—her voice had sunk to a tremulous whisper—"I must save my son, and save you from yourself, no matter what it costs me. You little know on the brink of what a crime you stand."

He laughed a bitter laugh; for was he not already steeped in crime? She thought him pitiless and malignant when he was only hopeless and self-condemned.

"Do you remember Gethin, Richard, and all that happened there? Can you not guess why I was made to marry—within—what was it?—a month, a week, a day—it seemed but the next hour—after I lost you? You have had twenty years of misery for my sake; but so have I for yours. Did my husband love me, think you? Did he love my child? He had good cause, if he had only known, to hate us both. Can you not guess it?"

He looked at her with eager hope—a trembling joy pervaded him. But hope and joy had been strangers to him so long that he could scarce recognize them for what they were.

"My Charley is yours also, Richard—your own son."

Richard burst into tears. There was somebody still to love him in the world—his own flesh and blood—somebody to live for! The thought intoxicated him with delight; a vision of happiness floated before him for an instant; then was swallowed up in darkness, as a single star by the gloom of night. His own flesh and blood; ay, perhaps inheriting the same nature as his father. It was only too likely, from what he had seen of the lad; and he had himself done his best to develop the evil in him, and to crush the good.

"Don't weep, dear Richard: kiss me."

He shrank from her proffered lips with a cold shudder. "Nay, I can not kiss you. Do not ask me why, Harry. Never ask me; but I never can."

She looked at him with wonder, for she saw that his wrath had vanished. His tone was tender, though woeful, and his touch as he put her aside was as gentle as a child's.

"As you please, Richard," said she, humbly, and with a deep blush. "I only wished for it as a token of your forgiveness. It is not necessary; those tears have told me we are reconciled. But you will kiss Charley."

"Nay; he must never know," answered Richard gloomily.

"I had forgotten," said Harry, simply. "You can guess by that the loyalty of my heart toward you, Richard. I forgot that to reveal it would be to tell my darling of his mother's shame. But you will be kind and good to him; you will undo what you have done of harm; you will lead him back to Agnes, and then he will be safe."

"Yes, yes," muttered Richard, mechanically; "I will undo so far as I can what I have done of harm. I will do my best, as I have done my worst."

He rose hastily, and rang the bell. Harry eyed him like some attached creature that sympathizes with but can not comprehend its master.

The waiter entered.

"I shall not go by the train," said Richard; "let a carriage and pair be brought round instantly, without a moment's delay."

The waiter hurried out to execute the order.

"But you will surely return home, Richard, after what has happened?" said Harry, thinking of his mother's funeral.

"The dead can wait," returned he, solemnly. "Go you back to town. In three days' time, if you do not hear from me, come down to Gethin with Charles and Agnes."

"But I dare not, unless my husband send for me."

"He *will* send for you," said Richard, solemnly; "or others will in his behalf."

Without one word or sign of farewell he suddenly rushed by her, and was gone. A carriage stood at the front-door of the hotel, which had just returned from taking a bride and bridegroom to the railway station, and she saw him hurry into it.

"Fast! fast!" she heard him cry, through the open window; and then he was whirled away.

CHAPTER XLVI.

CURTIUS.

Richard had many subjects for thought to beguile his lonely way to Gethin, but one was paramount, and absorbed the rest, though he strove to dismiss it all he could.

He endeavored to think of his dead mother. His heart was full of her patient love and weary, childless life; but her portrait faded from his mind like a dissolving view, and in its place stood that of Solomon Coe, haggard, emaciated, hideous. Still less could he think of Harry and her son, between whom and himself this spectre of the unhappy man rose up at once, summoned by the thought of them, as by a spell. It did not occur to Richard even now that he had had no right to kill him; but he shuddered to think, if he had really done so, how this late opening flower of love which he had just discovered would blossom into fear and loathing. In that case his heart would have been softened only to be pierced. His mother's death, the knowledge of Harry's fidelity, and of the existence of his son, to whom his affection had been already drawn, unknowingly and in spite of himself, had dissolved his cruel purpose. He was eager to spare his mother's memory the shame of the foul crime he had contemplated, and passionately anxious that in the veins of his new-found son there should at least run no murderer's blood.

"Faster! faster!" was still his cry, though the horses galloped whenever it was practicable, and the wheels cast the winter's mire into his eager face. This haste was made, as he well knew, upon the road to his own ruin. To find Solomon alive was to be accused of having compassed his death. There was no hope in the magnanimity of such a foe. But yesterday Richard had cared little or nothing for his own safety, and was only bent upon the prosecution of his scheme against his foe; now life had mysteriously become dear to him, and he was about to risk it in saving the man he had hated most on earth from the doom to which he had himself consigned him. He had calculated the possibilities which were in his own favor, and they had resolved themselves into this single chance—that Solomon might be induced, by the unconditional offer of Wheal Danes and its golden treasure, to forego his revenge. His greed was great; but his malice, as Richard had good cause to know, was also not easily satisfied. Moreover, even if his victim should decline to be his prosecutor, he would still stand in great peril. It was only too probable that he would be recognized at Gethin for the stranger that had so lately been staying at Turlock; he had not, indeed, mentioned his assumed name at the latter place; but his lack of interest in the fate of Solomon—whose disappearance had been narrated to him by the waitress—and his departure from the town under such circumstances, would (in case of his identification) be doubtless contrasted with this post-haste journey of his to deliver this same man. He had made up his mind, however, to neglect no precautions to avoid this contingency. It would be dark when he got to Gethin; and his purpose once accomplished he might easily escape recognition, unless he should be denounced by Solomon himself. In that case Richard was fully determined that he would glut no more the curiosity of the crowd. He would never stand in the prisoner's dock, or be consigned again to stone walls. The gossips should have a dead man's face to gaze at, and welcome; they might make what sport they pleased of that, but not again of his living agony. Then, instead of his being Solomon's murderer, he would be his victim. To judge by his present feeling, thought Richard, bitterly, this man would not enjoy his triumph even then. Revenge, as his mother had once told him, was like a game of battle-door—it is never certain who gets the last stroke. If Solomon was now dead, starved skeleton or rat-eaten corpse as he might be, Richard felt that he would still have had the advantage over him.

"What is it? Why are we stopping?" cried he, frantically, as the man pulled up on the top of a hill.

"Let me breathe the horses for an instant," pleaded the driver; "we shall gain time in the end."

"How far are we still from Gethin?" inquired Richard, impatiently.

"In time, two hours, Sir, for the road is bad, though me and the horses will do our best; but the distance is scarce twelve miles. Do you see that black thing out to seaward yonder? That's the castled rock. He stands out fine against the sunset, don't he?"

"Yes, yes; make haste;" and on they sped again at a gallop.

Within a mile or two of this spot Richard had first caught sight of that same object twenty years ago. The occasion flashed upon him with every minutest circumstance, even to the fact of how hungry he had been at the moment. The world was all before him then, and life was young. Now, prematurely aged, his interest centred in three human beings, and one of those was his bitter enemy.

The dusk thickened into dark; and the tired horses—for the stage had been a very long one—made but slow way.

"Faster! faster!" was Richard's constant cry, till the brow of the last hill was gained, and the scanty lights of Gethin showed themselves. Then it suddenly struck him for the first time what unnecessary speed had been made. Why, this man, Solomon, strong and inured to privation, had, after all, been but eight-and-forty hours in the mine, and would surely be alive, unless the rats had killed him. Where had he somewhere read of a strong man overpowered in a single night by a legion of rats, and discovered a heap of clean-picked bones by morning?

The inn, as usual at that season, showed few signs of life; but there were some half dozen miners drinking at the bar.

"Keep those men," said Richard to the innkeeper; for Solomon had long delegated that office to another, though his own name was still over the door, and the *Gethin Castle* was still his home. "I shall want their help to-night."

"Their help, Sir?" said the astonished landlord.

"Yes; but say nothing for the present. Bring me a bottle of brandy and some meat—cold chicken, if you have it; then let me have a word with you."

Richard did not order the food for himself. While it was being brought he sat down in the very chair that he had used so often—for he had been ushered into his old parlor—and gazed about him. There were the same tawdry ornaments on the mantel-piece, and the same books on the dusty shelf. Nothing was altered except the tenant of that room; but how great a change had taken place in *him!* What a face the dingy mirror offered him in place of that which it had shown him last! When the inn-keeper returned his mind involuntarily conjured up old Trevethick, as he had received from him the key of the ruin, and doggedly taken his compliments upon its workmanship. Truly, "there is no such thing as forgetting;" and to recall our past to its minutest details at the judgment-day will not be so impracticable as some of us would desire.

Richard had made up his mind exactly as to what he would say to this man, but a question suddenly presented itself, which had been absent from his thoughts from the moment that he had resolved to rescue his enemy. It was a very simple one, too, and would have occurred to any one else, as it had done already many times to himself.

"Has Mr. Coe been found yet?"

He listened for the answer eagerly, for if such was the case, not only was his journey useless, but had brought him into the very jaws of destruction. He would have thrown away his life for nothing.

"No, Sir, indeed—and he never will be," replied the inn-keeper. "When the sea don't give a man up in four-and-twenty hours, it keeps him for good—at least we always find it so at Gethin."

"Well, listen to me. My name is Balfour. I knew Mr. Coe, and have had dealings with him. We had arranged a partnership together in a certain mine; and it is my opinion that he came down here upon that business."

"Very like, Sir. He was much engaged that way, and made, they say, a pretty penny at it."

"I was at Plymouth, on my way to join him, when I heard this sad news. I came to-day post-haste in consequence of it. The search for him must be renewed to-night."

"Lor, Sir, it is easy to see you are a stranger in these parts! I wouldn't like to go myself where poor Mr. Coe met his end, on so dark a night as this. It's a bad path even in daylight along Turlock cliff."

"He did not take that way, at least I think not. Have you a ladder about the premises?"

"Yes, sure."

"And a lantern?"

"Now that's strange enough, Sir, that you should have inquired for a lantern; for we wanted one just now to see to your horses, and, though they're looking for it high and low, it can't be found nowhere."

"It doesn't strike you, then, that Mr. Coe might have taken it with him?"

"Lor, Sir," cried the inn-keeper, with admiration, "and so he must ha' done! Of course it strikes one when the thing has been put into one's head. Well, 'twas a good lantern, and now 'tis lost. Dear me, dear me!"

Golden visions of succeeding to the management of the inn, and of taking to the furniture and fixings in the gross, had flitted across this honest gentleman's brain, and the disappearance of the lantern affected him with the acute sense of pecuniary damage. The general valuation would probably be no less because of the absence of this article.

"Send out and borrow another, as many, in fact, as you can get," said Richard, impatiently; "and get ready a torch or two besides. Pick out four of the strongest men yonder, and bid them come with me, and search Wheal Danes."

"What! that old pit, Sir? You'll not find a man to do it—no, not if they knowed as master was at the bottom of it. You wait till morning."

"Your master *is* at the bottom of it. I feel sure he took the lantern with him to search that mine. I will give them a pound apiece to start at once. Pack up this food, and lend them a mattress to bring him home upon. Be quick! be quick!"

Richard's energy fairly overpowered the phlegmatic inn-keeper, whose conscience, perhaps, also smote him with respect to his missing master; and he set about the execution of these orders promptly. Wheal Danes, he had truly hinted, was a very unpopular spot with its neighbors after nightfall; but, on the other hand, sovereigns were rare in Gethin, and greatly prized. In less than half an hour the necessaries which Richard had indicated were procured, and a party, consisting of himself, four stalwart miners, and the inn-keeper, started for the pit. These were followed by half the inhabitants of the little village, attracted by the rumor of their purpose, which had oozed out from the bar of the *Gethin Castle*. The windy down had probably never known so strange a concourse as that which presently streamed over it, with torch and lantern, and stood around the mouth of the disused mine. The night was dark, and nothing could be seen save what the flare of the lights they carried showed them—a jagged rim of pit without a bottom. Notwithstanding their numbers there was but little talk among them; they had a native dread of this dismal place, and, besides, there might now be a ghastly secret hidden within it. A muffled exclamation, half of admiration, half of awe, broke from the circling crowd as, the ladder planted, Richard was seen descending it torch in hand. No other man followed; none had volunteered, and he had asked for no companion. They watched him, as the countrymen of those who had formerly worked Wheal Danes might have watched Curtius when he leaped into the gulf; and as in *his* case, when they saw the ladder removed, and the light grow dim, and finally die out before their eyes, it seemed that the pit had closed on Richard—that he was swallowed up alive. No one, unless the strange story about their missing neighbor which this man had brought was true, had ventured into Wheal Danes for these fifty years! They kept an awe-struck silence, straining eye and ear. Some thought they could still see a far-off glimmer, others that they could hear a stifled cry, when the less fortunate or the less imaginative could hear or see nothing. But after a little darkness and silence reigned supreme beneath them; they seemed standing on the threshold of a tomb.

CHAPTER XLVII.

WHAT WAS FOUND IN WHEAL DANES.

A FULL half hour—which to the watchers above seemed a much longer interval—had elapsed since Richard had disappeared in the depths of Wheal Danes, and not a sign of his return had reached the attentive throng.

"I thought he'd come to harm," muttered a fisherman to his neighbor; "it was a sin and a shame to let him venture."

"Ay, you may say that," returned the other, aloud. "I call it downright murder in them as sent him."

"It was not I as sent him," observed the inn-keeper, with the honest indignation of a man that has not right habitually on his own side. "What *I* said to the gentleman was, 'Wait till morning.' Why should *I* send him?" Here he stopped, though his reasons for not wishing to hurry matters would have been quite conclusive.

"Why was he let to go down at all, being a stranger?" resumed the first speaker. "Why didn't somebody show him the way?"

"Because nobody knowed it," answered one of the four miners whose services Richard had retained, and who justly imagined that the fisherman's remark had been a reflection on his own profession. "I'd ha' gone down Dunloppel with him at midnight, or any other mine as can be called such; but this is different."

"Ay, ay, that's so," said a second miner. "We know no more of this place than you fishermen. There may be as much water in it as in the sea, for aught we can tell."

"It's my belief they're more afraid of the Dead Hand than the water," observed a voice from the crowd, the great majority of which was composed of fisher folk.

No reply was given to this; perhaps because the speaker, an old cripple, the Thersites of the village, was beneath notice, perhaps because the remark was unanswerable. The miners were bold enough against material enemies, but they were superstitious to a man.

"If Solomon Coe were alive," continued the same voice, "he wouldn't ha' feared nothin'."

"That's the first word, old man, as ever I heard you speak in his favor," said a miner, contemptuously; "and you've waited for that till he's dead."

"Still, he would ha' gone, and you durstn't," observed the old fellow, cunningly, "and that's the p'int."

These allusions to the Dead Hand and to the missing Solomon were not of a nature to inspire courage in those to whom it was already lacking, and a silence again ensued. There was less light, for a torch or two had gone out, and the mine looked blacker than ever.

"Well, who's a-going down?" croaked the old cripple. "The gentleman came from your inn, Jonathan, and it's your place, I should think, to look after him."

"Certainly not," answered the inn-keeper,

hastily. "These men here were hired for this very service."

"That's true," said the first miner. "But what's the use of talking when the gentleman has got the ladder with him?"

"There's more ladders in the world than one," observed the cripple. "Here's my grandson, John; he and half a dozen of these young fellows would fetch Farmer Gray's in less than no time. Come, lads—be off with ye."

This suggestion was highly applauded, except by the miner who had so injudiciously compromised himself, and was carried out at once.

When the ladder arrived the three other miners, ashamed of deserting their comrade, volunteered to descend with him. The excitement among the spectators was great, indeed, when these four men disappeared in the levels of Wheal Danes, as Richard had done before them. The light of their combined torches lingered a little in their rear; the sound of their voices, as they halloed to one another or to the missing man, was heard for several minutes. But darkness and silence swallowed *them* up also, and the watchers gazed on one another aghast.

It is not an easy thing, even for those accustomed to underground labor, to search an unfamiliar spot by torch-light; the fitful gleam makes the objects on which it falls difficult of identification. It is doubtful whether one has seen this or that before or not—whether we are not retracing old ground. Even to practiced eyes these objects, too, are not so salient as the tree or the stone which marks a locality above-ground; add to this, in the present case, that the searchers were momently in expectation of coming upon something which they sought and yet feared to find, and it will be seen that their progress was of necessity but slow. They kept together, too, as close as sheep, which narrowed the compass of their researches, and caused their combined torches to distribute only as much light as one man would have done provided with a chandelier. They knew, however, that their predecessor had descended into the second level, so that they did not need to explore the first at all. The ground was hard, and gave forth echoes to their cautious but heavy tread; their cries of "Hollo!" "Are you there?" which they reiterated, like nervous children playing hide-and-seek, reverberated from roof to wall.

Presently, when they stopped to listen for these voices of the rock to cease, there was heard a human moan. It seemed to come up from a great depth out of the darkness before them. They listened earnestly, and the sound was repeated—the faint cry of a man in grievous pain.

"There must be another level," observed the miner who had volunteered the search. "This man has fallen down it."

They had therefore to go back for the ladder. Pushing this before them, the end began presently to run freely, and then stopped; it had adjusted itself by the side of the shorter ladder which Richard had brought down with him.

"He could not have fallen, then," observed a miner, answering his comrade's remark—as is the custom with this class of great doers and small talkers—at a considerable interval.

"Yes, he could," replied the one who had first spoken. "See, his ladder was short, and he may have pitched over."

They stood and listened, peering down into the darkness beneath them; but there was no repetition of the cries. The wounded man had apparently spent his last strength, perhaps his last breath, in uttering them.

"He must be down here somewhere. Come on."

The situation was sufficiently appalling; but these men had lost half their terrors, now that they knew there was a fellow-creature needing help. They descended slowly; and he who was foremost presently cried out, "I see him; here he is."

The man was lying on his face quite still; and when they lifted him, each looked at the other with a grave significance—they had carried too many from the bowels of the earth to the pit's mouth not to know when a man was dead. Even a senseless body is not the same to an experienced bearer as a dead weight. The corpse was still warm, but the head fell back with a movement not of life.

"You were right, mate. His neck is broke; the poor gentleman pitched over on his head."

"Stop a bit," exclaimed the man addressed; "see here. Why, it ain't him at all—it's Solomon Coe."

An exclamation of astonishment burst involuntarily from the other three.

"Then where's the other?" cried they all together.

"I am here," answered a ghastly whisper.

Within but a few feet of Solomon, so that they could hardly have overlooked him had not the former monopolized their attention, lay Richard, grievously hurt. Some ribs were broken, and one of them was pressed in upon the lungs. Still he was alive, and the men turned their attention first to him, since Solomon was beyond their aid. By help of the two ladders, side by side, they bore him up the wall of rock; and so from level to level—a tedious and painful journey to the wounded man—to the upper air.

He was carried to the inn upon the mattress which his own care had provided for another; while the four miners, to the amazement of the throng, once more descended into the pit for a still more ghastly burden.

Richard could speak a little, though with pain. By his orders a messenger was dispatched that night to Plymouth to telegraph the news of the discovery of her husband's body to Mrs. Coe. His next anxiety was to hear the surgeon's report, not on his own condition, but on that of Solomon. This gentleman did not arrive for some hours, and Richard was secretly well pleased at his delay. It was his hope, for a certain reason, that he would not arrive until the body was stiff and cold.

He saw Richard first, of course. The case was very serious; so much so that he thought it right to mention the fact, in order that his patient might settle his worldly affairs if they needed settlement.

"There is no immediate danger, my good Sir; but it is always well in such cases to have the mind free from anxiety."

"I understand; it is quite right," said Richard, gravely. "Moreover, since the opportunity may not occur again, let me now state how it all happened."

"Nay, you must not talk. We know it all, or at least enough of it for the present."

"What do you know?" asked Richard, with his eyes half shut, but with eager ears.

"That in your benevolent attempt to seek after Mr. Coe you met with the same accident—though I trust it will not have the same ending—as that unfortunate gentleman himself. He pitched upon his head and broke his neck, while you fell upon your side."

"That is so," murmured Richard. "He and I were partners, you see—"

"There, there; not a word more," insisted the doctor; "your deposition can wait."

And having done what he could for his patient, he left him, in order to examine the unfortunate Solomon. His investigation corroborated all that he had already heard of the circumstances of his death, with which also Richard's evidence accorded. An observation made by one of the miners who had found the body, to the effect that it was yet warm when they had come upon it, excited the surgeon's ridicule. "It is now Tuesday morning, my friend," said he, "and this poor fellow met with his death on Saturday night for certain. He could not, therefore, have been much warmer when you found him than he is now."

"Well, me and my mate here we both fancied—"

"I dare say you did, my man," interrupted the doctor; "and fancy is a very proper word to apply to such an impression. If you take my advice, however, you will not repeat such a piece of evidence when put upon your oath, for the thing is simply impossible."

"Then I suppose we be in the wrong," said Dick to Jack; and on that supposition they acted.

In this way too self-reliant Science, whose mission it is to explode fallacies, occasionally assists in the explosion or suffocation of a fact, for Solomon Coe had not been dead half an hour when his body was found.

When Richard, alone on his errand of mercy, was approaching the brink of the third level, he could hear Solomon calling lustily for help. Nay, it was not only "Help!" but "Murder!" that he cried out; and notwithstanding the menace that that word implied toward himself, Richard hurried on, well pleased to hear it; the vigor of the cry assured him that his enemy was not only living, but unhurt. As the light he carried grew more distinct to him, indeed, these shouts redoubled; but when it came quite near, and disclosed the features of its bearer, there was a dead silence. The two men stood confronting one another—the one in light, distinctly seen, looking down upon the other in shade, just as they had parted only eight-and-forty hours ago. To one of them, as we know, this space had been eventful; but to the other it had seemed a lifetime—an age of hopes and fears, and latterly of cold despair, which had now been warmed once more to hope only to freeze again. For was not this man, to whom he had looked for aid, his cruel foe come back to taunt him—to behold him already half-way toward death, and to make its slow approach more bitter? But great as was his agony Solomon held his peace, nor offered to this monarch of his fate the tribute of a groan.

"I am come to rescue you," said Richard, in low but distinct tones; "to undo the evil that I have already done, although it was no less than you deserved, nor an overpayment of the debt I owed you. In return you will doubtless denounce me as having meant to murder you."

No answer. If Richard had not heard his cries, it would have seemed that this poor wretch had lost the power of speech. His huge head drooped upon his shoulder, and he leaned against the rocky wall as though his limbs could not have otherwise supported themselves; they shook, indeed—but was it with weakness or with hate?—as though he had the palsy.

"Well, you will have reason to do so," continued Richard, calmly, "for I did mean to murder you. In ten minutes hence you will find yourself among your neighbors, free to act as you please. I shall make no appeal to your mercy; it would, I know, be as fruitless as was yours to mine the other day; but if you abstain from molesting me, this mine, with all its hidden treasure, shall be your own. I have nothing more to say."

Solomon answered nothing. "Perhaps," thought Richard, "he still doubts me.—Well, here is the ladder;" and he suited the action to the word. Solomon's great hand flew out from his side, and clutched a rung as a dog's teeth close upon a bone; a dog's growl, too, half triumph and half threat, came from his deep chest; then he began slowly to ascend, keeping his eyes fixed on Richard. The latter drew back a little to give him space, and watched him with folded arms.

"Now," said Solomon, stepping off the ladder with the prolonged "Ha!" of one who breathes freely after long oppression, "it is *my* turn!"

"What are you about to do?" asked Richard, calmly.

"What! you think we are quits, Richard Yorke, do you? or at least that when I had seen you hung it would seem so to me? You don't know what it is to die here slowly in the dark; you are about to learn that."

"Indeed."

"Yes. You complained the other day of my having used the law against you. Well, you shall not have to reproach me with that a second time. We are about to change places, you and I, that's all. You shall keep sentry down yonder till Death comes to relieve *you*. It was indiscreet in you to venture here alone to dictate terms, my friend."

Solomon's voice was grating and terrible; it had grown hoarse with calling. His form was gaunt and pinched with hunger; his eyes flashed like those of some starving beast of prey.

"I swear to you I came here to rescue you, and with no other purpose," said Richard, earnestly. "I was not afraid of you when you were hale and strong, and much less now when you are weakened with privation; but I do not wish to have your blood upon my hands. I came here to-night—"

"Is it night?" interrupted the other, eagerly. "I did not know that it was night; how should I, in this place, where there is no day? Well, that was still more indiscreet of you, for I shall get away unseen, while you lie here unsought."

"Your scheme is futile. There are fifty men about the pit's mouth now. I have told them—"

"Liar!" Solomon darted forward; and Richard, throwing away the torch, as though disdaining to use any advantage in the way of weapon, grappled with him at once. At the touch of his foe his scruples vanished, and his hate returned with tenfold fury. But he was in the grasp of a giant. Privation had doubtless weakened Solomon, but he had still the strength of a powerful man, and his rage supplied him for the time with all that he had lost. They clung to one another like snakes, and whirled about with frantic violence. Whichever fell undermost was a dead man for certain. For a few moments the expiring torch still showed them each other's hot, vindictive faces; then they battled in the dark, with laboring breath and eager strain, swaying they knew not whither. At last the huge weight of Solomon overbore his lesser antagonist. Richard's limbs gave way beneath him, and he fell, but fell through space; for in their gyrations they had, without knowing it, returned to the top of the ladder. His foe, fast clutched, fell with him, but, pitching on his head, was killed, as we have seen, upon the instant.

This was the true history of what had occurred in the mine, as Richard, on his bed of pain, recalled it step by step, and strove to shape it to his ends.

CHAPTER XLVIII.

MAKING PEACE.

Whether Richard's own injuries proved fatal or not was with him a matter of secondary importance. His anxiety was to prove that they were received by misadventure; upon the whole, matters promised favorably for this, and were in other respects as satisfactory as could reasonably be expected. The blood of Solomon Coe was upon his own head. Richard had no need even to reproach himself with having struck in self-defense the blow that killed his enemy; and he did not reflect that he was still to blame for having, in the first instance, placed him in the mine. He had at least done his best to extricate him, and his conscience was (perhaps naturally) not very tender respecting the man who had repaid his attempt at atonement with such implacable animosity. At all events, Richard's mind was too much engaged in calculating the consequences of what had happened to entertain remorse. The question that now monopolized it was, what conclusion was likely to be arrived at by the coroner's inquest that would, of course, be held upon the body. The verdict was of the most paramount importance to him, not because upon it depended his own safety (for he valued his life but lightly, and, besides, his inward pain convinced him that it was already forfeited), but all that now made life worth having—the good regards of Harry and her son. He had no longer any scruple on his own part with respect to accepting or returning their affection. His fear was, lest, having been compelled to take so active a part in the rescue of the unhappy Solomon, something should arise to implicate him in his incarceration.

Fortunately he was far too ill to be summoned as a witness. His deposition alone could be taken, and that he framed with the utmost caution, and as briefly as was possible. His wounded lung defended him from protracted inquiries. Solomon himself had proposed the idea of a partnership in Wheal Danes, and his interest in the mine, the knowledge of which had suggested to Richard the place of his concealment, had evidently proved fatal to him. That he should have broken his neck just as Richard had broken his ribs on such a quest was by no means extraordinary; but how he ever reached the spot where he was found at all, without the aid of a ladder, was inexplicable. The line of evidence was smooth enough but for this ugly knot, and it troubled Richard much, though, as it happened, unnecessarily. Had the place of the calamity been a gravel-pit at Highgate, it would have been guarded by constabulary, and all things preserved as they were until after the official investigation. But Wheal Danes, from having been a deserted mine, had suddenly become the haunt of the curious and the morbid. There was nothing more likely than that Solomon's ladder had been carried off, and perhaps disposed of at a high price per foot as an interesting relic. The presence of the half-extinguished torch that Richard had flung away in the second level (and which should by rights have been found in the third) was still more easily explained: there were a score of such things now lying about the mine, which had been left there by visitors. In short, an "active" coroner and an "intelligent" jury could have come to no other conclusion than that of "accidental death;" and they came to it accordingly.

Other comforters had arrived to the wounded man, before the receipt of that good news, in the persons of Harry and her son and Agnes. There was a reason why all three should be now warmly attracted toward him, which, while it effectually worked his will in that way, gave him many a twinge. They looked upon him, as did the rest of the world, as the man who had lost his life (for his wound was by this time pronounced to be fatal) to save his friend. He told them that it was not so, and they did not believe him. He had not the heart to tell them how matters really stood; but their praise pained him more than the agony of his wound, and he peremptorily forbade the subject to be alluded to. This command was not difficult to obey. Solomon's death, although the awful character of it shocked them much, was, in reality, regretted neither by wife nor son: such must be the case with every husband and father who has been a domestic tyrant, no matter how dutifully wife and son may strive to mourn: his loss was a release, and his memory a burden that they very willingly put aside; and, in particular, his name was never mentioned before Agnes without strong necessity.

Mrs. Coe, always at her best and wisest in matters wherein her son was concerned, had never told this girl of the part which Robert Balfour had taken against her. It would have wounded her self-love to have learned that the influence of a comparative stranger had been used, and with some effect, to estrange her Charley. She would scarcely have made sufficient allowance for a man of the world's insidious arts, notwithstanding the circumstances that had so favored them. Thus Harry had justly reasoned, and kept silence concerning him. Agnes had therefore set down the gradual cessation of her lover's visits to Soho, and his growing coldness, solely to the hostility of Solomon. They had pained her deeply, though she had been too proud to evince aught but indignation; still she strove to persuade herself it was but natural that this lad, entirely dependent upon his father for the means of livelihood, and daily exposed to his menaces or arguments, should endeavor to steel himself against her; that he really loved her less she did not in her own faithful heart believe. It was, however, with no thought of regaining his affection that she had obeyed the widow's hasty summons on the news of the catastrophe at Wheal Danes, but solely from sympathy and affection. She had always loved and pitied her, for Harry had shown her kindness and great good-will; and, notwithstanding the girl's high spirit, she did not now forget, as many would have done, all other debts in that obligation so easy of discharge, namely, "what she owed to herself."

Her presence, notwithstanding the sad occasion of it, at once reawakened Charley's slumbering passion, and the coldness with which she received its advances only made it burn more brightly, like fire in frost. He felt that he had not even deserved the friendship she now offered him in place of her former love, and was patient and submissive under his just punishment. He hoped in time to re-establish himself in her affections; but at present, somewhat to Mrs. Coe's indignation, she had showed no sign of yielding. He did in reality occupy the same position in her heart as of old; but now that he was rich, and his own master (for his mother was his slave), she was not inclined to confess it. Had he been poor and dependent, she would have forgiven him readily enough; nor are such natures unparalleled in her sex, notwithstanding the pictures which are nowadays presented to us as types of girlhood.

Such, then, was the mutual relation in which these two young people stood, who ministered by turns (for Harry was always with him) to the wants of the dying Balfour. The feelings with which he was regarded by all three were in curious contrast with their former ones. What those of Harry were now toward him we can easily guess; her hate and fear had vanished to make room for love—not the love of old times, indeed, but a deeper and a purer passion; it could never bear fruit, she knew—it was but a prolonged farewell. To-morrow, or the next day, Death would interpose between them; but in the mean time they were together, and she clung to him.

Charley, on the other hand, with whom Balfour had once been such a favorite, felt, though attentive to his needs, by no means cordially toward him. Gratitude for the fancied service he had done to his late father compelled him to give Richard his company; but it was not accorded willingly, as heretofore. He could not but set down to the account of his companionship the present frigidity of Agnes, and at first he had even seen him a material obstacle to his hopes. This audacious man of the world, who had at one time so excited his admiration, had suddenly become in his eyes an impudent *roué*, who even on his sick-bed was only too likely to make their past adventures together the subject of his talk. True, his mother had told him that Mr. Balfour was now an altered man; but the young gentleman had entertained some reasonable doubts of this conversion. His manner to the sick man was so reserved and cool, indeed, that it seemed to all but Richard (who guessed the cause of it, and yet felt its effect more bitterly than all) unkind. This behavior on the part of his former ally did not injure Balfour in the regards of Agnes; she resented Charley's conduct, and did her best to redress it by manifesting her own good-will; she had herself had experience of his shifting moods and causeless changes of demeanor, and perhaps she was willing to show what small importance she attached to his capricious humors. Thus it happened that Richard and herself "got on" together much better (as well, of course, as much more speedily) than the former could have hoped for; for indeed he had, with reason, expected to find a bitter enemy in Agnes. He improved this advantage to the utmost by taking occasion, in Charley's absence, to praise the lad, under whose displeasure he manifestly lay. She answered that he had not, at least from Mr. Balfour's lips, deserved such praise.

"Nay, nay," said Richard, gently; "it is I who have not deserved the lad's good-will; and you, my dear young lady, ought to be the last to pity me, as I see you do."

"How so?" asked she, in surprise.

"Because," answered he, gravely, "I once strove to keep him from you."

She looked annoyed, and cast a hurried glance toward the place where Mrs. Coe had been sitting; but there was now only an empty chair there. The widow had purposely withdrawn herself, in accordance with Richard's wish. Agnes could scarcely leave the sick man without attendance.

"When I say, 'keep him from you,'" continued Richard, "I mean that, being lonely and friendless (as you see I am but for you three), the society of this bright boy was very dear to me, and I selfishly strove to secure it when he would fain have been elsewhere. I needed, as you may well imagine, authority to back me in such efforts, but, unhappily for him, I possessed its aid. He now resents, and very naturally, the restraint which my companionship once imposed upon him, and sets down to my account the estrangement which he so bitterly rues. An old man's friendship is of no great worth at any time; but weighed in the balance against a woman's love—"

"Sir!" interrupted Agnes, with indignation.

"Pardon me," continued Richard, gently; "I see you do not love him. I am deeply grieved, for the sake of this poor lad, who is as devoted to you as ever, to find it so, and to feel that it was in part my fault. I will ask him to forgive me if he can."

"Nay, Mr. Balfour, I beseech you, don't do that," cried Agnes, with crimson cheeks.

"As you please," murmured he, gravely. "But, remember, a few days hence, or perhaps a few hours, and I may be beyond his forgiveness. It will then rest with you, young lady, to clear my memory. You are not angry with me—you can not be vexed with a dying man."

"No, no." She was sobbing violently; her heart was touched, not only by his own condition, as she would have had him believe, but by these confidences respecting Charley. There is nothing more dear to a young girl than the testimony of another man to her lover's fealty; the witness himself is even guerdoned with some payment of the rich store he bears; and from that moment Balfour was not only forgiven by Agnes, but even beloved by her.

CHAPTER XLIX.

REST AT LAST.

THAT the termination of Richard's malady would be fatal did not from the first admit of doubt, but he lingered on beyond all expectation. The spring came on and found him yet alive at Gethin. He was never moved from the room to which he had been carried after his mischance—the same which had been his bedroom in the old times, when he was full of strength and vigor—wherein he had so often lain awake, revolving schemes to win his Harry, or slept and dreamed of her. The comparison of his "now" and "then" was melancholy enough, but it was not bitter. His pain was great, but not out of proportion to his comfort. He had still Harry's love, and he had even that of two other hearts besides, which he had reconciled and drawn together. In him Charles had had an unwearying advocate with Agnes, and at last he had won his cause. She had been driven to take refuge in her last intrenchment—her poverty—and Richard had made that untenable.

"You will not be an heiress, perhaps, my dear," he had said to her, "though you deserve to be one; but neither will you be undowered. I have left you all I have. Nay, it is not much—a few score acres by the sea—but they will soon be yours."

She had accepted them unwillingly, and under protest; but a day came when it became necessary for her to remonstrate with the sick man once again concerning this matter, sorry as she was to thwart or vex him; she therefore requested to have a few minutes' talk alone with him.

"Dear Mr. Balfour," said she, gently, "I am going to disobey you in once more reopening the matter of your kind bequest. Something has happened which has given the affair a wholly different aspect. Among the visitors yesterday to that dreadful mine, to which people still flock, there was a Mr. Stratum—a young engineer, it seems, of some reputation; and in his researches in Wheal Danes they say he has hit upon a great treasure, or what may turn out to be such."

"Ay," said Richard, with a smile; "what's that?"

"A copper lode. It is curious that so many folks should have come and gone there and never found it before; but there it is, for certain. Mr. Stratum has seen Charles, and tells him that he can hardly trust himself to speak of its probable value."

"Well, I congratulate you, my dear, on being an heiress."

"Nay, my dear Mr. Balfour, but this must not be. Overborne by your kind pressure I consented to receive this bequest—a considerable one in itself, indeed—for what it was. I could not now take advantage of your ignorance of its real value; it distresses me deeply to give you trouble in your present sad condition, but you must see yourself that circumstances compel me."

"Give me the will, my dear; it is in yonder drawer. Here is a letter folded in it in my handwriting. What does the superscription say?"

"*To Agnes Aird.*"

"Just so. You were to have opened it after my death, but you may read it now. Please to do so aloud."

"MY DEAR YOUNG LADY,—When I am gone, it is my earnest desire that your marriage with Charles Coe shall take place as early as may be found convenient. He will make a good husband to you, I think; I am sure you will make him a good wife. He loves you for your own sake, which is the only love worth having. But, as it happens, you are very rich. In the mine which I have left you—in the northeastern corner of the bottom level—there is a copper lode, the existence of which is known to me, and to me only. I have every reason to believe that it will be found in the highest degree productive, and for your dear sake I trust it may be so. True, you will have money enough and to spare for your own needs, but wealth will not spoil you—in your hands it will be a great good. To the two injunctions which here follow I have no means to give effect, and must trust solely to your loyal heart to carry them out. I do so with the most perfect confidence. (1.) I wish that this bequest of mine, be the value of it ever so great, be strictly settled, upon your marriage, on yourself and your children, so that it can not be alienated by any act of your husband; and this I do not from any preference to yourself over him, or from any prejudice against him, God knows. (2.) In case the estate of Crompton, of which Wheal Danes formed a fragment, should again be in the market, and the mine turn out so valuable that its proceeds should enable you to purchase such estate (without inconvenience or damage to your interests), I do enjoin that you do so purchase it, and make Crompton your future home. This is a 'sick man's fancy,' some will tell you; and yet you will not neglect it."

"And you *will* not, Agnes dear?" whispered Richard, eagerly, when she had thus finished. "This is the last favor I shall ever ask of you. Promise me! promise me!"

"Oh, Sir, I promise you," cried Agnes, earnestly, and scared by his anxious feebleness; "your wishes shall be obeyed in all points."

"Good girl, good girl," sighed he; and though the effort pained him sharply, his face exhibited a great content. "Send Charley to me," said he, presently, in a faint voice.

"But you are tired already," remonstrated Agnes. "You have talked enough for to-day; see him to-morrow."

"To-morrow!" repeated Richard, with a smile that chilled her heart. "There will be no to-morrow, dear, for me. Reflect hereafter that you made my last day a happy one. Kiss me, daughter." This term, which was uttered very fondly, did not surprise her, for she little guessed its full significance. She bent down, and kissed his forehead. "Send me Charley."

Those were the last words she ever heard him speak.

Agnes had told the young fellow how much feebler Mr. Balfour seemed that day, and warned him to make his interview as brief as possible; but Charley was of a sanguine temperament, and to his view the sick man looked better. The recent excitement had heightened his color, and, besides, he always strove to look his best and cheerfulest with Charley.

Balfour told him all that he had already said to Agnes respecting the provision he had made for her; he thought it better to relieve her from that task. But, to do Charley justice, he was neither grasping nor jealous. Nothing seemed more natural to him, or even more reasonable, than that Agnes should be made sole heiress.

"As for me, I should only make a mess of so much money," said he, laughing. "*She* understands how to manage"—meaning that she had a talent for administration of affairs—"five thousand times better than I do. Her father has taught her all sorts of good things, and that among them. You see the poor governor and I—we never pulled together. Perhaps if I had had a father a little less unlike myself, I might have been a better son, and a wiser one. It was unfortunate, as Mrs. Basil used to say. You remember her, of course?"

"Yes, indeed."

The sick man's tone was so full of interest that Charley, with great cheerfulness, proceeded to pursue this subject.

"She was an excellent old soul; and, for her age, how sprightly and appreciative! I remember—the very last time she came down to dinner—telling her that story of yours about the stags in harness, and it so interested her that she made me repeat it. It seemed to remind her of something that she had heard before; and yet the incident was original, and happened within your own experience, did it not?"

"It did," said Balfour, hoarsely.

"I am tiring you, my dear Sir," said Charley, anxiously. "What a fool I have been to chatter on so, when Agnes particularly told me to be brief! I shall leave you now, Sir; I shall indeed. Is there any thing I can do for you before I leave?"

"Nothing, nothing. If I strove to take Agnes from you, lad, I did my best to make her yours again. You don't dislike me now, dear boy, do you?"

"Dislike you, Sir!" cried the young man. "That would indeed be base ingratitude; you were always most kind to me, and you have loaded my Agnes with benefits. I can not say, Sir, how unhappy it makes me to see you lying here in pain, and—"

"And dying, Charley. Yes, you are sorry for me, good lad."

"Indeed, indeed I am, Sir."

"When your Agnes left me last she kissed me on the forehead—here. I would not ask it else—but—kiss me, Charley."

The sick man's voice was very weak and faint, but its tones were full of pathos. In some surprise, but without the least hesitation, the young man stooped down and kissed him. "I shall leave you now, dear Mr. Balfour, and only hope my thoughtless chatter may not have done you mischief. I will send my mother to you, who is so quiet, and so good a nurse, as an antidote. Good-by for the present, Sir."

"Good-by, dear lad—good-by."

Richard well knew it was good-by, not for the present, but forever.

When Mrs. Coe came into the sick man's room she perceived in him a change for the worse, so marked that it alarmed her greatly, and she was about to softly pull the bell, when Richard stopped her with a look.

"Don't ring," whispered he, faintly. "Sit down by me, Harry; put your little hand in mine. I am quite happy. Our boy has kissed me."

"You did not tell him? He does not know?" inquired Harry, anxiously.

"Nay, dear, nay; I am not quite so selfish as that," answered he, gently.

There was a long pause.

"Do you think my mother knew about him?" asked Richard, presently.

"Oh yes—though I strove to deceive her—from the first moment she saw him, Richard, she knew it well. We never spoke of it, but it was a secret we had in common. She loved him as though he had been your very self; I am sure of that."

"And she knew *me* too, Harry."

"Impossible! She could never have concealed that knowledge—with you before her; for you were her idol, Richard."

"It was afterward," murmured the dying man. "When I had left the house Charley told her something I had related to him, which convinced her of my identity. I see it all now. She felt that I was bent on vengeance, and sent you after me to use that weapon of which she knew you were possessed. If we once came face to face, and you reproached me, my secret was certain to come out—just as it did, Harry—and then you had but to say, 'Charley is your son.'"

"But why did she not tell me who you were?"

"Because, if you were too late—if the mischief had been done on which she deemed me bent—if your—if Solomon had come to harm, she would not have had you know that Richard Yorke—the father of your child—had blood upon his hands. Oh, mother, mother, your last thought was to keep my memory free from stain!"

He spoke no more for full a minute; no sound was heard except the distant murmur of the sea, for the day was fine and windless. The April sun shone brightly in upon the pair, as if to bless their parting.

"Where is Charley?" murmured he.

"He is gone with Agnes for a walk; they will not be long; they talked of going to the Watch Tower. You remember the old Watch Tower, Richard?"

"Well, ah, well!" answered he, smiling. "It is just twenty years ago. How often have I thought of it!"

For a moment—before they separated forever—these two seemed to themselves to relive the youth to which another generation had succeeded.

"Agnes is a far better girl than I was, Richard; but she can not love our boy more than *I* loved *you.*"

Richard answered with a smile that glorified each ghastly feature, and brought out in them a likeness to himself of old.

"She will be his good angel, Harry," whispered Richard, gravely, "and will guard him from himself. He will need her aid, but it will be sufficient. I trust, I believe, that evil is not Bred in the Bone with him, as it was with me."

There was a long, long silence, broken by a silvery laugh, which came through the half-opened window like a strain of cheerful music, then was suddenly cut short.

"Hush, Charley; you forget," said the soft voice of Agnes; "he may be sleeping."

Through the calm spring air the reproof was borne into the sick man's room as clearly as the sound which had called it forth.

"He is so happy," whispered Harry, gently; "you must forgive him; remember he does not know."

"Yes, yes; it is better so. Dear Charley—happy, happy Charley!"

And a smile once more came over the sick man's face, which did not pass away, for Death had frozen it there.

L'ENVOI.

YEARS have passed since Richard Yorke was laid in the church-yard on the hill at Gethin, close beside his mother, whose bones Harry's pious care had caused to be transported thither.

> If aught of things that here befall
> Touch a spirit among things divine—
> If love has force to move us there at all,

her ghost was glad. "In time," thought Harry, "I too shall lie by his side, at last, once more."

Old Trevethick's prophecy was accomplished in the almost fabulous success that attended the working of Wheal Danes. If its shares are not quoted in the market, that is because the family have retained it in their own hands, in spite of the most dazzling offers.

Mr. Dodge has a codicil to his story at *The George and Vulture* now, and expresses his infinite satisfaction at the fact that "that 'ere Coe" came to grief in the end, as he had so richly deserved to do. "I don't doubt," says he, "that while he was underground with the bats and rats he thought of that poor lad as he had treated so spiteful. Things mostly does work round all right" (he would add) "under Providence, whose motto (if I may say so without disrespect) is summat like mine: 'Let us have no misunderstandings and no obligation.'" On the other hand, what "sticks in Mr. Dodge's throat," as he expresses it, and is "a'most enough to make a man an infidel," is, that "the widow of that 'ere Coe—she as was young Yorke's ruin—is living at Crompton (in the very house his father had) with all her brood."

Mr. Dodge is right in his facts, if not in his deductions. Out of the proceeds of the mine the whole home-estate of Crompton has been purchased by Charles Coe, or rather by his wife; and they both dwell there quite unconscious that he is the lineal descendant of the mad Carew, with whose wild exploits the country side still teems. If the old blood shows itself, it is but in quick starts of temper, and occasional "cursory remarks," which sound quite harmless in halls that have echoed to the Squire's thunderous tones; and even at such times Agnes can calm him with a word. If the open hand which is Bred in the Bone with him scatters its *largesse* somewhat broadcast, the revenues of Crompton, thanks to her, are in the main directed to good ends. In that stately mansion, whose hospitality is as proverbial though less promiscuous than of old, not only is there room for Mrs. Coe the elder to dwell with her young folks, without jar, but in a certain ground-floor chamber, the same he used to inhabit in old times, there dwells an ancient divine, once Carew's chaplain. He is still hale and stout, and has a quiet air that becomes his age and calling. Life's fitful fever is past, and he lives on in calm. The children—for there is small chance of Crompton being heirless in time to come—are very fond of him; and grandmamma spends so much time in the old gentleman's apartments, that Charley declares it is quite scandalous. What *can* Parson Whymper and she have to talk about in common? In spite of the attractions of her beautiful home, and the infirmities of advancing years, not a summer passes without Mrs. Coe the elder revisiting Gethin. The castled rock, up which she used to run so lightly, is beyond her powers; she is content to gaze on that with dewy eyes; but she never fails to seek the church-yard on the hill.

"He was what one would call a hardish husband to her, was old Solomon," say the neighbors; "and yet you see, when a man is dead, how a wife will keep his memory green!"

THE END.

www.ingramcontent.com/pod-product-compliance
Lightning Source LLC
LaVergne TN
LVHW021413110826
845150LV00007B/1901
9781425510374